William Hobson
(1820–1891)

William Hobson (1820–1891)

Pioneer, Minister, and Founder of the Evangelical Friends Church (Quakers) in the Pacific Northwest

JULIE M. ANDERSON

WIPF & STOCK · Eugene, Oregon

WILLIAM HOBSON (1820–1891)
Pioneer, Minister, and Founder of the Evangelical Friends Church (Quakers) in the Pacific Northwest

Copyright © 2021 Julie M. Anderson. All rights reserved. Except for brief quotations in critical publications or reviews, no part of this book may be reproduced in any manner without prior written permission from the publisher. Write: Permissions, Wipf and Stock Publishers, 199 W. 8th Ave., Suite 3, Eugene, OR 97401.

Wipf & Stock
An Imprint of Wipf and Stock Publishers
199 W. 8th Ave., Suite 3
Eugene, OR 97401

www.wipfandstock.com

PAPERBACK ISBN: 978-1-6667-1363-3
HARDCOVER ISBN: 978-1-6667-1364-0
EBOOK ISBN: 978-1-6667-1365-7

11/16/21

Scripture quotations are taken from the *Holy Bible,* King James Version.

Photographs are included courtesy of the George Fox University Archives.

To my Newberg Friends Church family past, present, and future.

MANY THANKS TO . . .

Judy Woolsey, Volunteer Copy Editor

Charles Kamilos, Senior Librarian Emeritus, George Fox University

Rachel Thomas, University Archivist, George Fox University

Gwen Gosney Erickson, Quaker Librarian and College Archivist, Guilford College

Contents

Introduction ix

Prologue xiii

1 | Quaker History, Testimonies, Culture, and Traditions in a Nutshell 1

2 | Early Years in North Carolina 59

3 | Pioneering on the Iowa Frontier 92

4 | To the Pacific Northwest and Back Twice, Then to Stay 143

5 | Planted in a Garden of the Lord 190

Bibliography 259

Introduction

I first became interested in William Hobson in the late 1990s when I worked at George Fox University in the Murdock Library. My supervisor, Charlie Kamilos, asked me to organize a shelf of old materials that had been sitting for awhile because they were time consuming to catalog. Among those materials I found a plain, antique notebook, not unlike a modern composition book. When I flipped open the cover the following handwritten words jumped off the page and grabbed my attention:

> Wm Hobsons [sic] memorandom [sic] 14 day of 9 mo. 1870. just [sic] home from Iowa Yearly Meeting. And having had a prospect of Religious service near the Pacific Coast And being now liberated and encouraged to atten[d] thereto. I am now seeking opportunities to bid the people Farewell in these parts and every way get ready to leave home for perhaps nearly a year. And on the 21 of 11 mo. Took the Cars at Union Station in Hardin Co. Iowa for California and arrived at Sanjose the 30th. Returned the forepart of seventh month 1871. On the 11 of 5 mo. 1875 Started again for a visit to the same countries and arrived at Sanjose the 14. visited [sic] in Cal[ifornia] ...Oregon & Washington Ter[ritory] ... Returned in 9 mo. 1876 and Moved [sic] to Oregon Chehalem Valley reached our new home the 27 of 11 mo. 1876.[1]

At the time, I was not well acquainted with William Hobson. I knew he was considered the founder of Quakerism in Newberg, Oregon and by extension the Northwest Yearly Meeting of Friends, but that's about all, so I was curious about this piece of history I held in my hands. However, there was no time to do much more than leaf through the pages, note the manuscript's significance to Charlie, and continue on with organizing the shelf. A few years later, I learned more about Hobson from Gregg Koskela, the lead pastor of Newberg Friends Church at the time. He used to mention

---

1. Hobson, "Memorandum," 1.

Hobson in sermons periodically, mainly focusing on his obedience in following God's direction to come out to the Pacific Northwest and form a Quaker community. I learned from Gregg that Hobson and a man named John Henry Douglas disagreed about how to conduct meetings in the early days of the congregation. It seemed that Hobson preferred the old, unprogrammed way of worship and Douglas was convinced that a pastoral or evangelistic system, as Hobson called it, with programed worship was the way to go. I also learned Hobson wore an impressive full beard, from a photo Gregg projected on the large screen at the front of the sanctuary. During the next several years, curiosity about Hobson's notebook never left the back of my mind, surfacing periodically, just to be submerged again under the demands of everyday life.

In early 2011 a desire to work with the manuscript bubbled up yet again and this time I felt led by God to transcribe William Hobson's "Memorandum," the notebook I had unearthed so many years ago. Charlie graciously gave me a digital file of the scanned manuscript and I started in. As I transcribed, I read Myron Dee Goldsmith's doctoral dissertation "William Hobson and the Founding of Quakerism in the Pacific Northwest," in order to get some perspective. He submitted his dissertation to Boston University in 1962 as part of the requirement for a doctorate in philosophy. Dr. Goldsmith's scrupulous research and unsurpassable scholarship as Hobson's first biographer continue to inspire me. I have relied heavily on his work for further research ideas and for certain information that can no longer be gathered. He interviewed members of Hobson's family now deceased and looked at a few source materials that have since been lost. I have also relied on his integrity in researching various meeting minutes back east that I have not been able to look at myself. Dr. Goldsmith was a member of Newberg Friends Church and a professor of Religious Studies at George Fox College from 1962 to 1994.

It took me a few years of off-and-on again work to transcribe Hobson's "Memorandum," and by the time I finished I felt the way was clear to write a biography of Hobson. Dr. Goldsmith's dissertation put me on to Hobson's "Diaries," multiple notebooks similar to Hobson's "Memorandum," which were microfilmed by Edward P. Thatcher in the 1960s. Fortunately, the George Fox University Archives owns a copy of the two microfilm reels containing Hobson's "Diaries." It took me two years to transcribe them in preparation for writing this book. William Hobson had a distinctive and neat hand, except when traveling on the train or by boat, and though certain sections were worn and hard to decipher, the work was very rewarding. I have quoted his "Diaries" throughout and used them as my main source for understanding Hobson's lifestyle, personality, and motivations. They cover the following stretches of his life: 1859 to 1865, 1870 to 1878, and 1885 to 1891. They truly are more diaries than journals, giving abundant information about his daily life, tasks, and the weather and rather less information about his internal life, though there are certain passages that clearly illustrate his thoughts, feelings, and spiritual views. He wrote one autobiographical section covering his early years. It is unclear which years Hobson's "Memorandum" span, though it seems fairly certain he began it on Ninth Month 14, 1870, and finished sometime after moving to Newberg. I rely on the "Memorandum" less heavily.

In addition, I have read Quaker history extensively from various eras and authors, read many biographies and autobiographies of Friends contemporary with Hobson, and looked at newspaper and journal articles pertinent to the topic. I researched enough information to fill several books, so the task at hand has been to present what would be of most interest to the reader. I hope I have succeeded.

I must admit that my bias, as a member of Newberg Friends Church, leans towards describing Hobson's life and work as it pertains to his move to and ministry in Newberg. However, I have attempted to portray Hobson's life as a child and young adult in North Carolina, his migration to the Old Northwest, and his time at Honey Creek, Iowa with as much detail as possible. His early and midlife experiences had Kingdom value in and of themselves, as well as giving him the necessary experience to make the most of his time in the Chehalem Valley.

The importance of William Hobson to Pacific Northwest Friends is not to be underestimated. He organized Friends living in the Newberg area into Chehalem Monthly Meeting, the precursor to today's Newberg Friends Church and Northwest Yearly Meeting of Friends. He encouraged Friends from back east to emigrate to Newberg swelling the ranks of the Quaker community in the Chehalem Valley and in the Pacific Northwest as a whole. He introduced many different varieties of fruit trees to the Chehalem Valley and was an accomplished horticulturist. He supported education and visited Friends Pacific Academy often, as well as the local public school. He was a recorded Friends minister and often spoke or prayed in meeting. He preferred to worship in the traditional unprogrammed Friends way and conducted the meetings of Chehalem Monthly meeting in silence, punctuated by vocal service from whomever felt led by the Spirit to speak, pray, and/or (later on) sing. Newberg Friends Church's practice of open worship is a continuation of that tradition. I often think of Hobson's influence on Newberg Friends in particular and on the city of Newberg in general, wondering if he once walked where I'm walking or if he enjoyed the same view of Chehalem Mountain or Hess Creek. After reading his "Diaries," I have come to think of William Hobson with great respect and fondness as "Uncle William," as Friends in Newberg addressed him when he was alive. It is my hope that by tracing the movement and direction of the Holy Spirit in Hobson's life, we will all be encouraged by his example to step out in obedience to God when he calls.

Prologue

William Hobson died in Newberg, Oregon on Sixth Month 25, 1891, at the age of seventy-one, about seven months after his beloved wife Sarah. He was laid to rest next to her in the Friends Cemetery, not far from where the original Chehalem Monthly Meeting house stood. His life came to an end just as money was being raised for a new brick meeting house meant to replace their outgrown original meeting house and less than a month before Northwest Friends received permission from Iowa Yearly Meeting to become their own independent yearly meeting, in Ninth Month 1891. It wasn't until two years later that the first session of Oregon Yearly Meeting was held on Sixth Month 3, 1893, as the opening paragraph of the very first Oregon Yearly Meeting Minutes states.

> A request was presented from the Friends residing in Oregon, comprising the two Quarterly meetings of Newberg and Salem, asking that a Yearly Meeting be established at Newberg in Oregon, in 6th month, 1893, and to be known as Oregon Yearly Meeting. This meeting without a dissenting voice, unites in granting the request, and with the approbation of other Yearly Meetings, the meeting will be opened at the time suggested in the request. Minute number 23 of Iowa Yearly Meeting of Friends, held from the 8th to the 15th of 9th month, 1891. Stephen M. Hadley, Clerk[1]

The first Oregon Yearly Meeting Sessions took place in the nearly completed new church building located in the 300 block west of College Street. This is where Friends Pacific Academy, now George Fox University, stood before moving to its present location east of Meridian Street and north of Highway 99W. Veldon J. Diment states in *First Fifty Years: A Record of the First Fifty Years in the Life of Pacific College*, that the Friends Pacific

---

1. Oregon Yearly Meeting, *Minutes of Oregon Yearly Meeting of Friends Church, 1893*, 3.

Academy buildings, Pacific College since Fifth Month 1891, were moved to their new site by the opening of school in 1892.² The *Newberg Graphic* reported on Seventh Month 22, 1892, that "the moving of the college buildings from the old grounds to the new site is now an accomplished fact" and that "the work of excavating for the basement for the new church is done and brick lying will begin on the foundation next week."³ Therefore, work on the new church started about the time they were finishing up with moving the college buildings. Amos Stanbrough, in his thesis, "History of Pacific College," asserts that the meeting house was not quite finished, but finished enough to meet in, by the first yearly meeting sessions in 1893.⁴ At any rate, while William Hobson may have been aware of the school's name change he passed away before the first opening of Friends Pacific Academy as Pacific College in Ninth Month 1891, and he never set foot in the new meeting house, though he was certainly aware of the plan to build one. According to Chehalem Monthly Meeting Minutes, building a new meeting house was proposed at a congregational business meeting as early as Eighth Month 1886, the same time Chehalem Monthly Meeting became Newberg Monthly Meeting.⁵

Hobson also just missed Newberg Monthly Meeting's transition from unprogrammed worship to pastor led programmed worship, a change he resisted, but was resigned to, out of a desire to remain in unity with the meeting. He wrote about his views on the evangelistic system, as he called it, in his journal as follows:

> I united with Friends in movement under the Evangelistic System. It being now some of the approved Order of Iowa Y[early]. M[eeting]. Yet in one of my Speeches on this Occasion I stated that I had boldly told friends here, some considerable time ago. And would now tell JH Douglas that Mo[nthly]. M[eeting] ... in connexion [sic] with Quar[terly Meeting] ... & Yearly [Meeting] Can do all this Evangelistic & Pastoral work; just as well, & better too, without, this thing [the evangelistic system] than with; when once we are sufficiently stirred up to Action. Because the more the work is brought down to all of us & before us the better. And it is due to all the members of the M[onthly]. M[eeting]. to know how the work is going on and to have a part in it. It is due to M[onthly] M[eeting] ... acting body to know

2. Diment, *First Fifty Years*, 6.

3. "College Buildings" and "Local News," *Newberg Graphic* (Newberg, OR), July 22, 1892, https://oregonnews.uoregon.edu/lccn/sn96088233/1892-07-22/ed-1/seq-3/.

4. Stanbrough, "History of Pacific College," 15.

5. "Chehalem Monthly Meeting Minutes," 161.

how the work of the Church is going on. And work should come before it. How good when a Minister brings to view a work & obtains a minute therefor from his M[onthly] Meeting and again reports to it the work done. I further Stated that I had said before friends lately that this Evangelistic & Pastoral System had done some good & would yet do some more if we keep within careful bounds & don't run wild on it or with it. But when once we become sufficiently stirred up to action And come to know well what M[onthly] Meetings are for we need to study much to know We will scarcely need the Evangelistic System.[6]

Connor Edmonds suggests, in his dissertation "William Hobson and William Keil: Religion and Polity in Nineteenth Century Oregon," as have others, that Chehalem Monthly Meeting waited until Hobson's last illness played out to install a pastor out of respect for his views and leadership. He writes that Douglas and his party "were gracious enough to wait for Hobson to die a physical death before fully implementing the evangelical system."[7] However, Hobson's above view on the matter seems to indicate he was not set against the pastoral system enough to block the hiring of a pastor. Also, the Newberg Monthly Meeting Minutes indicate a natural progression towards implementing the pastoral system in the traditional Friends manner, slowly, with due diligence exercised, while striving to listen to and obey the Holy Spirit. At any rate, there does not seem to have been a conscious effort on the part of the congregation to wait for Hobson's death before adopting the pastoral system, for it was not until almost a year after Hobson died that John Henry Douglas was called as the first pastor of Chehalem Monthly Meeting. He occupied a type of transitional role operating more like a resident minister until Thomas Brown was hired as the first official pastor in Tenth Month 1892.[8] Whatever the motivations and process, the fact remains that Hobson passed away before the pastoral system was adopted by Newberg Monthly Meeting.

The *Newberg Graphic* reported that "the funeral of Uncle Wm. Hobson was attended by a large number of people" and that "Jesse Hobson and family, were here last week during the last sickness and death of Wm. Hobson."[9] So, at least one of his sons, Jesse, was with him at the end. Most likely, his son Samuel who was living in Newberg at the time, was also in attendance,

6. Hobson, "Diaries," reel 1 of 2, 5/30/1890.

7. Edmonds, "William Hobson and William Keil: Religion and Polity in Nineteenth Century Oregon," 75.

8. "Chehalem Monthly Meeting Minutes," 93, 95, 100, 106–7.

9. "Local Events," *Newberg Graphic* (Newberg, OR), July 3, 1891, https://oregonnews.uoregon.edu/lccn/sn96088233/1891-07-03/ed-1/seq-3/.

as well as his daughter Anna who lived nearby and helped to take care of Hobson while he was sick. Two other daughters and a son preceded him and Sarah in death.

During the first Oregon Yearly Meeting Sessions as noted in the *Newberg Graphic*, "... the committee on memorials made a report. No written memorials were presented but Rev. J.H. Douglas spoke very feelingly on the lives of Wm. Hobson, Benjamin Miles, Rebecca Clawson and Mary Pinkham. Jane B. Votaw, Mary E.K. Edwards, John Edwards and others spoke much in the same way. Nathan H. Clark said he and his wife and R. J. Mendenhall were the only ones present who knew Wm. Hobson when He was boy. His whole life was proof of the fact that it was not necessary for a young man to sow wild oats."[10]

So, who was William Hobson? What does a life deeply dedicated to God from a young age look like? And what is his legacy? It is the aim of this book to explore these questions and offer some answers. Hobson was a farmer and a minister of the Gospel. He was a son, brother, husband, father, and a staunch Friend. He was a pioneer with a strong work ethic. He was passionate about growing fruit, especially peaches. At age fifty, about twenty years after building a home and farm from scratch in the wilderness and starting a Friends meeting in remote Honey Creek, Iowa, he had a distinct calling from God to pull up stakes and organize a Quaker community somewhere on the West Coast.[11] After a lengthy and diligent search for the proper place, he and his wife Sarah settled in the Chehalem Valley. He quickly organized Friends already living in the area and wrote many letters encouraging Friends from back east to move out to Newberg. Under his leadership, Chehalem Monthly Meeting was started in 1878 and a small meeting house was built by 1880.[12] He was active in Chehalem Monthly Meeting worship and pastoral care as one of several recorded ministers. He also supported beginning a Friends school and visited it often as it grew. In many ways, he was an ordinary man, but in others he was an extraordinary servant of God, willing to grow and change in the Spirit.

William Hobson lived his life in obedience to God, moment by moment, day by day, and year by year, which resulted in a great sowing of saplings for the Kingdom of God. He was faithful to set in roots without knowing fully what the outcome might be. Twice he planted healthy rootstock in frontier places that grew into thriving Quaker communities, dedicated to God and

10. "Oregon Yearly Meeting of Friends Church," *Newberg Graphic* (Newberg, OR), July, 7, 1893, https://oregonnews.uoregon.edu/lccn/sn96088233/1893-07-07/ed-1/seq-2/#words=man+oats+sow+wild+young.

11. Hobson, "Diaries," reel 1 of 2, 2/2/1873.

12. "Chehalem Monthly Meeting Minutes," 1, 54.

the spreading of the Gospel. Often, he followed through on concerns to visit his neighbors or travel long distances in order to spread the love of God. His willingness to follow God's call to organize a Friends settlement in the Far West set the stage for today's Evangelical Friends Church, also known as the Northwest Yearly Meeting of Friends. He opened the door to the formation of a Friends college, now called George Fox University, that has become a nationally known evangelical Christian university. And while he did not live to see the full harvest of fruit that sprang up from his spiritual orchard, he saw enough to know, without a doubt, that his costly obedience to God had been blessed.

1

Quaker History, Testimonies, Culture, and Traditions in a Nutshell

Ye are my friends, if ye do whatsoever I command you. Henceforth I call you not servants; for the servant knoweth not what his lord doeth: but I have called you friends; for all things that I have heard of my Father I have made known unto you.

JOHN 15:14–15

IMPORTANCE OF QUAKER HISTORY

In order to accurately consider William Hobson in his time and place, a brief look at Quaker history and practices is in order. Doing so will help to shed light on the environment Hobson both grew up in and chose to live in as an adult. It will also help us to see just how much the Quaker way changed in the span of Hobson's lifetime. Elbert Russell offers a useful framework for the study of Friends history in his book *History of Quakerism*. He divides the story of Quakerism into three main sections as follows: "Rise of the Society (1647–1691) from George Fox's great experience to his death, [the] Age of Quietism (1691–1827), from George Fox's death until the separation of 1827 in America, and The Revival and Reorganization of Quakerism (1827–1941), from the separation of 1827 until the present time."[1] For Russell, the present time was 1941. The history pertinent to a study of William Hobson falls within the scope of Russell's first and second historical categories and part of the third. Therefore, the following quick look at Quaker history and practices will begin with the birth of George Fox and end with the decade in which Hobson's life on earth ended, the 1890s, sticking with broad trends as much as possible. Also, since Hobson was an American Friend, the main emphasis will be on American Quakers.

It is important to note that starting with the founder of the Society of Friends, George Fox, many prominent Quakers kept journals and diaries. These Friends records are recognized by scholars as a distinct body of literature. Friends were also prolific letter, book, and tract writers, giving us a look into their public lives, as well as their personal lives. Contemporary accounts of Friends in journals, diaries, letters, and other writings are often the best glimpse of time, place, and thought we could have, so a few short biographical illustrations of unique individuals from a variety of time periods will be included as appropriate. William Hobson followed in this Friendly literary tradition with the diaries he kept and the many letters he wrote, the bulk of which, unfortunately, have been lost in antiquity.

RISE OF THE SOCIETY OF FRIENDS (1624 TO 1691)

George Fox was born in Leicestershire, England, in 1624, one year before King Charles I ascended the throne, as John Punshon notes in *Portrait in Grey*,[2] and just under 200 years before William Hobson was born halfway around the world in the United States of America. Hobson's time and environment were significantly different from that of Fox, but growing up Quaker he was infused with many of the religious and social beliefs Fox had come to be convinced of in the mid–seventeenth century and which had resulted in the formation of the Society of Friends. Hobson read the *Journal of George Fox* as a boy, several more times throughout his life, and quoted Fox several times in his diary,[3] so it's good to study Fox a bit in light of his influence on Hobson, as well as to get a sense of what the start of the Society of Friends was like. George Fox's journal, edited by Rufus Jones at the turn of the twentieth century, reveals much about Fox's life and beliefs.

1. Russell, *History of Quakerism*, xxi.
2. Punshon, *Portrait in Grey*, 41.
3. Hobson, "Diaries," reel 1 of 2, 1/20/1890; reel 2 of 2, 1/21/1868, 2 entries uncertain dates [1870s?], 11/21/1873, 4/25/1874, 7/7/1874, 1/20/1875, 1 entry [1886] just before 11/8/1886.

As a young man, George Fox became disenchanted with the established church. He sought a deeper more meaningful connection with God than either the Church of England or the Puritan Church he grew up in could provide. He consulted with a number of priests and pastors in his quest for spiritual understanding, from whom he received very little or no help at all. He continued to relentlessly pursue God in spite of these failings of the clergy and experienced a series of "openings" from God that met his spiritual needs beautifully, beginning with the following famous revelation recorded in his journal:

> When all my hopes in them [the clergy] and in men were gone, so that I had nothing outwardly to help me, nor could I tell what to do, oh, then, I heard a voice which said, 'there is one, even Christ Jesus, that can speak to thy condition;' and when I heard it, my heart did leap for joy. Then the Lord let me see why there was none upon the earth that could speak to my condition, namely that I might give him all the glory.[4]

This direct revelation from God was pivotal in Fox's spiritual life and marked the beginning of his ministry.

George Fox was primarily an evangelist. He felt a strong call to tell the world about the life changing experience of Jesus speaking to his condition, so that all people everywhere might also put their trust in the Lord. He wrote in his journal that he was

> sent to turn people from darkness to the Light, that they might receive Christ Jesus; for to as many as should receive Him in His Light, I saw He would give power to become the sons of God; which power I had obtained by receiving Christ. I was to direct people to the Spirit that gave forth the Scriptures, by which they might be led into all truth, and up to Christ and God, as those had been who gave them [the Scriptures] forth.[5]

Fox traveled all around England preaching anywhere and everywhere including, but not limited to, churchyards, town squares, and in prisons. As well as the preaching of the gospel, his message consisted of several compelling new ways of interacting with God that attracted others who also felt disenfranchised from the established church.

Fox did not set out to create a new denomination. His intention was merely to share with everyone he met the wonderful, deep intimacy with God he had found through trust in Jesus Christ. He wanted everyone to

---

4. Fox, *Journal*, 82.
5. Fox, *Journal*, 102–3.

experience a real, authentic relationship with God, free from all the trappings of formal religion. At first, he worked within the framework of established denominations. But eventually, this began to change. Punshon notes that the turning point in Fox's ministry came while traveling through Lancashire, when he was led to climb Pendle Hill in late spring of 1652.[6] It was from this point on that Fox began a more organized mission to bring people to the Light of Christ. Fox stated that "as we travelled we came near a very great hill, called Pendle Hill, and I was moved of the Lord to go up to the top of it . . . From the top of this hill the Lord let me see in what places he had a great people to be gathered."[7] Shortly after this opening on Pendle Hill, George Fox gathered around him "a band of preachers only slightly less gifted than himself . . . [and won] the support of the Fells of Swarthmore Hall."[8]

For the most part, members of the Church of England did not understand where he was coming from. It was mainly other dissenters that joyfully embraced his message and joined the swelling ranks of the Society of Friends, though there were a few Anglican ex-clergy and other exceptions. Margaret Fell, who later became Fox's wife, was a notable convert for she was a woman of means and high standing in the community. She and her first husband, a judge who did not completely embrace Quakerism, were willing to open their Lancashire home, Swarthmore Hall, to traveling Friends as a place to stay. They also hosted meetings and helped Friends financially. In fact, Margaret served as a kind of ministry coordinator for Friends, keeping a wide correspondence with traveling ministers and managing the Kendal fund--a fund set up to help Friends with their financial needs.[9]

So, what was Fox's message and why was it so attractive to so many people? First and foremost, he preached salvation through Jesus Christ. He also emphasized that salvation was available to anyone who paid attention to the Light of Christ shed abroad in their heart and who chose to put their trust in him. Fox desired that all people everywhere might experience a vibrant, intimate relationship with God, being therefore equipped to live in the same power and Spirit that the apostles lived in. Union with a personal God was desirable and possible, for the same power that raised Jesus from the dead was alive and active in believers. Fox also believed that the Holy Spirit inspired the Scriptures and was, therefore, the guide to understanding them.

In addition to salvation through trust in Jesus, Fox preached that the Kingdom of God was a spiritual reality in the process of being accomplished

---

6. Punshon, *Portrait in Grey*, 54.
7. Fox, *Journal*, 150.
8. Fox, *Journal*, 151.
9. Punshon, *Portrait in Grey*, 63.

in the now. People did not need to wait for the Kingdom of God to come later with Jesus's return at the end of time, but rather could live in victory in the present moment through the power of the Holy Spirit. He also believed that the Apostolic Church was being restored after a great, dark epoch of apostasy. This was not necessarily a new idea, but he embraced it with a certain vital urgency well communicated to others. Jesus had come to teach his people himself, as the end days were likely quite near, and all believers needed to take up their standard in the Lamb's War, which was not a physical battle, but rather a battle for souls.

Fox's experiences and beliefs gave rise to certain actions that created conflict with authority and resulted in persecution. Since the Spirit was equally available to all people who chose to trust Jesus, regardless of rank, ethnicity, or gender, all people were equal in God's eyes, wiping out the need for class and other distinctions. Therefore, as Thomas Hamm explains on the *Quaker Speak* YouTube channel, Friends used the familiar "thee" and "thou" as opposed to the formal "you" even when speaking to those in authority or those of higher social standing. This was viewed as disrespectful in society at large and as contempt of court when up before a magistrate. Likewise, when Friends refused to bow, curtsey, or tip their hats as a sign of respect to those of higher social standing, perceived disrespect was often met with hostility and sometimes violence. The aristocracy did not like to see their power or prestige challenged and neither did the Church of England.[10]

Another stand that got Friends in trouble was their stubborn refusal to swear oaths. They followed implicitly Jesus's command in Matt 5:34–37 to "let your communication be, Yea, yea; Nay, nay: for whatsoever is more than these cometh of evil." Complete and consistent honesty was integral to the Friendly lifestyle and Friends believed that swearing an oath was tantamount to admitting there might be times when they weren't being entirely truthful. It was also important to Friends that they swear allegiance to God alone. Both the Long Parliament and Restoration governments considered the refusal to swear an oath a sign of sedition. They were very much afraid of people engaging in plots to overthrow their regimes and mistakenly placed Friends in the category of conspirators. More than once Fox could have been released from jail sooner if he would have sworn an oath of allegiance to the government or monarchy, but he adamantly refused to swear.

Since Jesus was the Present Teacher, sacraments and outward ordinances such as water baptism, communion with the elements, and ordination were considered no longer necessary or helpful. Instead there was baptism by the Holy Spirit and communion with Jesus in the attentive awareness of

---

10. Hamm, "History of Quaker Plain Speech."

his Presence. Outward signs got in the way of Inward Truth and the liturgy was abandoned. Early meetings for worship consisted of large amounts of preaching interspersed with silence, not the other way around as it was in Hobson's time. According to Pink Dandelion in *Quakers: A Very Short Introduction*, those who agreed with what the minister offered would often moan and groan in agreement. Those engaging in vocal ministry would stand to deliver their message and those offering prayer knelt while others stood, men with their hats off. Anyone was allowed to speak and pray, even women. Meetings were often loud and enthusiastic.[11]

It is interesting to note that later on an integral part of the new church order was, as Punshon points out, "the creation of a structure of women's meetings with considerable pastoral responsibility at each level of the organisation [sic], for Fox took the view that women have an integral place in the Church and this was the best way to encourage them to take it."[12] Meeting houses were often divided by moveable screens into men's and women's meetings and they conducted business separately, though messengers could be sent between. This is very strange to modern sensibilities, but at the time it was quite progressive. The idea being that women were better able to minister to their own sex than were men, and that by meeting separately women wouldn't be held back (by men) from expressing themselves fully. Officially, Friends have encouraged women to live into callings as ministers and believed that they were equal in God's eyes, though action has not always followed belief.

The Church of England considered Quaker views on the sacraments blasphemous and their worship chaotic and overly emotional. Also, Friends angered leaders in the Church of England by maintaining that since Christ had come to teach his people himself, hired priests and pastors (many of whom being paid by the aristocracy obtained a living out of financial greed and were not suited to the ministry) were unnecessary. Friends did not see the need for a "hireling minister" to conduct a worship service, marriage service, or funeral. Since all had equal access to the Holy Spirit anyone could preach, pray, or sing during meeting, as the Holy Spirit led. Also, it was enough to make a marriage commitment by standing up and declaring intent in gathered worship (with the prior approval of the meeting) and it was enough to gather as a community with worshipful silent respect at the graveside of a loved one, without the services of a priest. Therefore, Friends refused to pay tithes to the Church of England meant for the upkeep of priests and church

---

11. Dandelion, *Quakers*, 11.
12. Punshon, *Portrait in Grey*, 85.

buildings, breaking the law and paying for it dearly. For this stand, many Friends suffered confiscation of property, fines, and imprisonment.

Early Friends were also prosecuted under laws prohibiting vagrancy, as they traveled about the countryside preaching and exhorting. These laws were used as an excuse to imprison Friends who, as travelers with homes to return to, were not true vagrants. Friends were also charged with blasphemy. At the time space was often left at the end of a church service for anyone who wished to speak to do so. Friends took advantage of this to try to win people to Christ, but their views were regarded with such suspicion they were often shouted down or prosecuted for sacrilege. Between refusing to pay tithes, the vagrancy laws, allegations of blasphemy, and various other charges designed to punish or shut Friends up, they suffered imprisonment in large numbers. At one point during the Restoration, so many adult Friends were in jail, children, with a few women continued to hold weekly meetings for worship on their own.[13] Also, as Ralph Beebe reports in *Garden of the Lord*, "during the first 25 years of Quakerism about 15,000 Friends were jailed, of whom about 450 died. George Fox was imprisoned eight times for a combined total of about six years."[14] Persecutions under the Long Parliament and during the Restoration came in waves. Without times of respite, it seems that the Quaker movement may have died out, the suffering was so great.[15] Thankfully, Friends were quite resilient and determined to live out their convictions come what may.

The derogatory nickname "Quakers" was bestowed upon Fox and his followers by one frustrated justice "Bennet, of Derby, who was the first that called us Quakers because I [Fox] bade them [the officials of the court] tremble at the word of the Lord."[16] Punshon points out that the name stuck because it accurately described how Friends often quaked or trembled when praying and worshiping in the Spirit. Early on, Friends called themselves Children of Light from John 12:36[17] along with several other names used interchangeably, such as Friends of Jesus, Publishers of Truth, and Primitive Christianity Restored or Revived, as described by Max Carter on the *Quaker Speak* YouTube channel.[18] Interestingly enough, Punshon reports that the earliest usage of the name "Society of Friends" occurred in 1793, long after

---

13. Russell, *History of Quakerism*, 102.
14. Beebe, *Garden of the Lord*, 8–9.
15. Russell, *History of Quakerism*, 106.
16. Fox, *Journal*, 125.
17. Punshon, *Portrait in Grey*, 71.
18. Carter, "How Quakers Got Their Name."

Fox's death.[19] Friends and Quakers are used interchangeably today. At any rate, Fox and many other early Friends were not deterred from sticking to their convictions by taunts, violence done to their persons, or wrongful imprisonment springing from speaking truth to power or from faithfulness to deliver their message.

They were also not deterred from continuing to go out and preach the gospel in spite of the numerous difficulties and persecutions they encountered in their local communities and throughout the nation. In 1654 "a large company of Quaker evangelists, not quite seventy in number, spread out through the Kingdom in pairs like the seventy sent forth in Luke 10. Known as the 'Valiant Sixty' by modern Friends they began to take their message into all parts of the country."[20] They traveled two by two all throughout England spreading the Good News. The Valiant Sixty suffered public ridicule, the embarrassment of the stocks, whippings, beatings, and other violence done to their persons, including incarceration in filthy, stinking jails, but even in the face of this mistreatment many people became convinced Friends and joined the movement. Also, not surprisingly, many of the valiant traveling ministers became leaders in the Society. Sadly, many also died in prison.

Unfortunately, persecutions persisted under King Charles II. But according to William Braithwaite's *Second Period of Quakerism*, William Penn and George Whitehead, two notable men who helped bridge the gap between the first and second generation of Friends, worked hard not only to aid Friends in prison, but also to work for religious liberty. Penn became a convinced Quaker in 1667 at twenty-three years of age. His father, Admiral Sir William Penn, enjoyed King Charles II's favor at court and opposed his son's religious views.[21] Others did too, and young Penn was imprisoned several times. In 1681 Penn "accepted an enormous tract of land on the west bank of the Delaware River" in America from King Charles II as payment for a debt owed his father.[22] Charles II named the colony Pennsylvania. Penn took the opportunity to organize the Pennsylvanian government based on Friends principles and the colony flourished for a time, being as close to a Quaker Utopia as one could get. However, Penn was required to spend a great deal of time at court in England to maintain his "Holy Experiment." This meant he was unable, regrettably, to spend much time physically in Pennsylvania.

---

19. Punshon, *Portrait in Grey*, 71.
20. Punshon, *Portrait in Grey*, 63.
21. Braithwaite, *Second Period of Quakerism*, 55.
22. Punshon, *Portrait in Grey*, 97.

George Whitehead was instrumental in acquiring a pardon for imprisoned Friends from King Charles II, which freed almost 500 people, mostly Friends but also some other dissenters, from jail.[23] Later, he stood with Fox and Penn in defense of the organization of Friends into local and quarterly men's and women's meetings, a system Fox had devised and implemented throughout the nation. After George Fox's death in 1691 Whitehead and Stephen Crisp became co-leaders of the Society, but "Crisp soon died leaving Whitehead as the main guide of the Society, down to his death in 1723."[24]

Besides Quaker core beliefs and the civil disobedience that sprang from them, Friends engaged in certain actions that simply made them downright peculiar, actions that almost invited prejudice if not persecution from their neighbors. They refused to use the common names for days and months, a practice adopted from other dissenting sects, considering them to be of pagan origin. Instead they numbered the days starting with First Day for Sunday and on through the week ending on Seventh Day, otherwise known as Saturday. They followed a similar procedure with months, numbering them in the same fashion First through Twelfth instead of using the conventional names.[25] They called churches "steeple houses" and their own places of worship "meeting houses." Friends were committed to living simple lives, dressing plainly and modestly, speaking the truth at all times, conducting their business in complete honesty, and living at peace with all people. When Fox was asked if he would take up arms for the Commonwealth against Charles Stuart he told Lord Protector Oliver Cromwell's men, "I knew whence all wars arose, even from the lusts, according to James's doctrine; and that I lived in the virtue of that life and power that took away the occasion of all wars."[26] Early Friends not only believed there was no place for physical violence in the Kingdom of God, they lived it out in the face of dangerous consequences.

As more and more people were convinced of the Truth, they began meeting together in private homes. Slowly the meetings grew, and Fox saw the need for organization, since these small independent churches were hard pressed to make it on their own. It is true, that they were unified in the movement of the Holy Spirit and encouraged by traveling ministers who taught and coordinated the individual churches, but centralization was still necessary for the health of the Society. Also, persecution had disrupted the

---

23. Braithwaite, *Second Period of Quakerism*, 83–84, 148.

24. Punshon, *Portrait in Grey*, 101.

25. I have chosen to use the old-fashioned Quaker terms for days and months throughout this book.

26. Fox, *Journal*, 128.

traveling ministry. In 1667 five monthly meetings were set up in London and over the next year Fox traveled throughout Great Britain reorganizing Friends meetings.[27] According to Thomas Hamm in *Quakers in America*, Fox implemented a system of meetings in which the local meeting met weekly for worship, then monthly for business, and then quarterly with other monthly meetings in the general vicinity.[28] Eventually, London Yearly Meeting, an assembly of representatives from all the monthly meetings in Great Britain, was added as the capstone gathering.[29] Also as the Society grew and Friends emigrated across the water, yearly meetings slowly spread throughout America. This system of church organization is still in place today, though many yearly meetings have dropped quarterly meetings.

As Dean Freiday editor of *Barclay's Apology in Modern English* notes, just a year before George Fox rode round the country coalescing the Society into meetings and William Penn joined Friends, a young man named Robert Barclay was convinced in Scotland, in 1666, at the age of 18.[30] A decade later, in 1676, Barclay completed one of the most influential Quaker books in the history of Quakerism, *An Apology for the True Christian Divinity*.[31] His *Apology* is considered the most systematic theology of the Quaker faith ever written, and current Faith and Practice documents might be considered a modern extension of his work. Freiday tells us that the *Apology* "is also uniquely personal in being a 'thinking through' of his [Barclay's] own religious journey from the strict Calvinism of his youth, to the Roman Catholicism of his schooling, and finally to his Quaker convincement."[32] Hobson mentions both *Barclay's Apology* and *Barclay's Catechism* in his diary. He states that he read the *Catechism* as a young boy and mentions giving away several copies when an adult.[33] "Barclays Apol[ogy]" is written in his journal on a list of books he most likely gave away or loaned out to others, and toward the end of his life he writes, "I notice that B's [Barclay's] Apology was written about 25 years after the rise of Friends."[34] It is safe to say that Hobson read each work at least once and likely re-read them at various times throughout his life.

27. Punshon, *Portrait in Grey*, 72, 85.
28. Hamm, *Quakers in America*, 26.
29. Punshon, *Portrait in Grey*, 90.
30. Barclay, *Barclay's Apology in Modern English*, xv.
31. Punshon, *Portrait in Grey*, 122.
32. Barclay, *Barclay's Apology in Modern English*, ix.
33. Hobson, "Diaries," reel 2 of 2, 1/21/1868, 22 (Hobson's numbering), 1/23/1874, reel 1 of 2, 5/15/1875.
34. Hobson, "Diaries," reel 2 of 2, 12/8/1863, 11/27/1876?, reel 1 of 2, 7/31/1866.

Overall, Barclay is orthodox in his doctrine, but he introduces several theological concepts unique to Quakers. Here are a few of the more significant ones pulled from his *Apology*. His doctrine of the Inward and Unmediated Revelation can be distilled into the belief that the only way to know God and see God at work is through the Holy Spirit. Therefore, the Scriptures were inspired by the Holy Spirit, cannot be understood without the Holy Spirit, and are a secondary rule, subordinate to the Holy Spirit. However, he is emphatic in his statement that openings from God must be confirmed by Scripture.

Also according to Barclay, Jesus's redemption of humanity is universal. This is one of the core beliefs Friends hold: that Jesus died for every person who has ever lived and all are capable of accepting his free gift of rescue from sin and death, or conversely rejecting it.[35] Barclay also affirmed the centrality of the Atonement and the need to choose to trust in Jesus as Lord, declaring that "a divine supernatural seed or light is in all men (vehiculum Dei) either received in the heart so that Christ takes form and is brought forth or denied and wickedness ensues."[36] So Barclay considered the Inner Light or Inner Guide to not be part of the natural person, but rather a Seed planted by God in each human heart drawing them towards salvation and trust in Christ. Related to this, Barclay's Doctrine of Perfection was not a claim that humans can be perfectly righteous like God, but rather a conviction that those who embrace Jesus are strengthened by him to avoid sin and live into their calling as Children of Light. Barclay contended that as people grow in spiritual maturity it is possible, though easier said than done, to achieve a state of sinlessness, with God's help.

True worship, said Barclay, consists of either an individual or the assembled community of believers waiting on God in silence, until the Spirit moves either with silent power or by inspiring people to preach, sing, pray, or praise out loud. Also, the outward practices of baptism and communion are unnecessary symbols of the inward workings of the Holy Spirit. Baptism and the Lord's Supper were to be practiced for a while by the apostles, but were meant to be discontinued when the New Covenant came into full effect. Washing the body does not make the heart clean. That requires a Baptism of the Holy Spirit and Fire. The flesh and blood of Jesus are spiritual food not physical food. According to Barclay true communion is partaking of the Bread of Life, at anytime, in the inward self.[37]

---

35. Barclay, *Barclay's Apology in Modern English*, 20, 40, 60, 82.
36. Barclay, *Barclay's Apology in Modern English*, 88–89.
37. Barclay, *Barclay's Apology in Modern English*, 156, 248, 304, 329, 356.

William Hobson (1820-1891)

William Hobson, like Fox, Penn, Whitehead, Fell, Barclay, and many other Friends in later decades, experienced God in a personal way, early in life, as a child, teen, and young adult. As a small child, Hobson felt the call to preach, and he remained close to God the whole of his life. He trusted in Jesus Christ as Lord and Savior. He exercised his calling as a recorded minister, often preaching or praying out of the settled silence of worship, as well as going on pastoral visits and some longer ministerial journeys. He was active in the business of the monthly, quarterly, and yearly meeting. Like Fox he desired to help build people up in the faith with the assistance of the Holy Spirit. He believed in the basic Testimonies of Friends as Fox, Barclay, and other early Friends had put them forth, as the Quakers of his time understood them. He was for peace. He would choose to affirm rather than swear an oath. He never partook in water baptism or communion. He opposed singing or music of any type in meeting, though he seemingly changed his mind about this a little as he got older. He spoke and dressed plainly his entire life and used the plain numbering system for dates. He embraced simplicity and was never paid for his work as a minister. He opposed slavery. He believed women had as much right to preach as men and he believed that Scripture was inspired by the Holy Spirit. However, church practices and discipline, as well as Quaker culture, looked significantly different in Hobson's time from that of Fox's. This meant that the way Hobson lived out the Quaker Testimonies and experienced church life was somewhat different from early Friends, though the basic tenants were there. Also, he did not experience the same level or kind of persecution as early Friends. But let's not get ahead of ourselves.

So far, we have looked at the beginnings of Quakerism in England. However, it didn't take long for Friends to reach the shores of America. The first Quakers who traveled to America were almost without exception missionaries and they encountered severe persecution from both Puritan and Anglican colonists. In 1656 Mary Fisher and Ann Austin were the very first Friends to arrive in America. They were promptly arrested, imprisoned, and deported to Barbados by the Massachusetts colonial government.[38] However, according to Allen and Richard Thomas in their book *History of the Friends in America*, Friends were not deterred and by 1661 New England Yearly Meeting was organized. It became the first yearly meeting in America.[39] Rufus Jones describes in *Quakers in the American Colonies*, how Friends then spread south and east into Virginia, Maryland, and New Jersey. They continued to experience persecution throughout the Colonies,

---

38. Russell, *History of Quakerism*, 40.
39. Thomas and Thomas, *History of the Friends in America*, 4th ed., 69.

with the exception of Carolina, though to a lesser degree than they had in England. At this time, harassment consisted mainly of fines for missing First Day worship at Church of England services, unlawful assembly when they met for their own services, refusing to baptize their children, and the like.[40] Notably, Quakers were the first organized religious body in Carolina, part of which became Hobson's home state, North Carolina. When William Edmondson, a traveling minister from Ireland, visited the region in 1672, the original Friend in Carolina, Henry Phillips, hadn't set eyes on another Friend for seven years.[41] However, as time passed many more Friends settled in Carolina. In fact, enough Friends came that Quakers were in political control of Carolina until about 1700 and even were blessed with a Quaker governor for a time, John Archdale, who served in 1695 and 1696.[42] But Friends in general, throughout the Colonies, began to withdraw from government at this time due to their testimony against oaths and a growing conviction, right or wrong, that political life was not especially helpful in growing the Kingdom of God.

As the Society in America increased in numbers due to convincements (conversions), growing families, and immigration from England, Friends began to migrate west and south. Eventually they enjoyed a presence in all the original Colonies, including, of course, Pennsylvania, the only colony that started out with a government based on Quaker principles. Traveling ministers made a big impact on the Society in the Colonies by providing continuity in the way they worshiped and conducted public life, and by stressing unity in purpose, conformity to the Testimonies, and spiritual instruction and support. They helped to strengthen and build up meetings in rough frontier settlements where just staying alive was a chore. Friends in America not only survived, but also thrived due to the support of British ministers who made long, dangerous journeys across the Atlantic to encourage and uphold them.

AGE OF QUIETISM (1691 TO 1827)

With the passing of William Penn and George Whitehead, the Society of Friends began to center down into what turned out to be a long age of Quietism. Friends became less interested in evangelism and focused more intensely on internal systems, church organization, living out the Testimonies, morality, philanthropy, and building up the Society as a kind of hedge

---

40. Jones, et al., *Quakers in the American Colonies*, 271–72.
41. Russell, *History of Quakerism*, 110.
42. Thomas and Thomas, *History of the Friends in America*, 4th ed., 88.

against the evils of the world. Quaker historians of the orthodox ilk are generally critical of this descent into introspection, blaming generations of Friends until the revival in the mid-nineteenth century for a certain loss of spiritual zeal and a wandering away from Christian orthodoxy, including in their critique a severe decline in the reading of Scripture. It is undeniable that the emphasis did change significantly from the fiery compulsion of Fox and other early Friends to share the gospel with everybody everywhere, through anointed preaching and the testimony of the Bible. During the Age of Quietism evangelism unintentionally took a back seat to building up the Society of Friends internally. And Bible reading and study were sorely neglected. Many people did become convinced Friends during this period of Quietism, but it was not easy to embrace Quakerism at the time, as it required conforming to peculiar ways and giving up all the outside world had to offer. Also, as a general rule, Friends were not actively seeking converts. If they did preach, they did so spontaneously, rather reluctantly, and mostly only in their own meetings.

However, Fox's conviction that those who were in Christ could live triumphantly in the power of the resurrection, just like the apostles, remained as a subtle flame burning brightly in the hearts of many Friends who desired to sink down into the presence of God and dwell with him in the quiet, yet powerful center of his saving love. This deep yearning to seek God and live a life dedicated to obeying Jesus, the Present Teacher, profoundly changed not only the way Friends lived, but also the way they interacted with people in the world at large, speaking truth to power and caring lovingly for those whom others regarded as inferior or who were mistreated by mainstream society.

Though Scripture was not read consistently during meetings, ministers did sometimes recite it from memory or read it as the Spirit led. During this period, many Friends continued to read the Bible individually or during times of family worship, though for the majority of Friends Bible reading was not a priority. A significant number of Friends didn't even own or have access to a Bible. This began to change, however, towards the beginning of the nineteenth century when First Day Schools (Sunday Schools) were started in America and Bible societies began distributing Bibles to Friends families.

Leading Friends of this period wanted to get themselves and worldly distractions out of the way so they could narrow their focus on God. The rules, spoken and unspoken, and the systems they developed were put in place as a means to mortify the flesh and keep their eyes fixed on the Lord. As a result of this, a distinctive Quaker culture formed, a culture that kept the world at bay, fencing Friends in and closing them off, not only from what was "creaturely" in the world, but also from the worldwide church. Unfortunately, this Quaker culture slowly accomplished the opposite of what leaders intended in the beginning and for many the forms and customs became overly important in and of themselves, rather than useful as a means to know God better. However, it would seem that Quietism and all it entailed was not a detour in the upward movement of the Society, but more of a traffic jam, in and through which God worked to bring about the unique Quaker Christian witness that, among many others, William Hobson typified as an orthodox, evangelical Christian Friend.

Some Quaker historians contend that the Quietism of Friends was organic within the Society and merely confirmed by the Quietist movement that developed outside the Society. There definitely were tendencies towards Quietism in the Quaker view of life with God. For example, the belief that Jesus is our Present Teacher and with us in the midst of the worshiping congregation, or indeed anywhere we recognize him, and the belief that if one is focused on God any moment or activity can be sacred, lend themselves easily to the concept of getting the self completely out of the picture. But early Friends were not especially quiet in their worship practices and were much more focused on sharing Truth with their unbelieving neighbors. The advent of Quietism in Quakerism seems more like a "which came first, the chicken or the egg?" question. It's also important to remember that all of Christendom was influenced by Quietism to some degree. Friends were not as alone in these changes as they may have thought.

As Friends began to adopt the ways of Quietism, their worship became considerably more subdued and fewer people participated in verbal ministry. Instrumental music, which had never been a part of Friends worship, was frowned upon as a distraction in the pursuit of God, as was corporate singing, since everyone might not be able to agree in their souls with the words that were sung. Therefore, for Quaker Quietists, music was not an approved part of corporate worship. This did not change until the evangelistic innovations in the mid–nineteenth century became widespread. Also, Bible reading and especially study was greeted with suspicion as "creaturely activity" that detracted from the immediate ministry of the Holy Spirit. There were still many brightly shinning stars, especially among the traveling ministers, but the rank and file of the Society of Friends had lost their sparkle.

In its purest intention, the Society was not after some kind of universalist supernatural or religious experience. Most leading Friends were not trying to make God in their own image or indulging in self-worship. They were attempting to get themselves out of the way in order to experience God more authentically. They thought this was the best way to lean into God's resurrection power. And often they did. In many meetings, there was nothing mysterious about God's leadings or the worshipers' willingness to obey his direct commands. The movement of his Spirit with spontaneous, silent power or through the audible words of his ministers truly occurred. The Society that had traditionally been more of a prophetic movement than a contemplative one, retained its prophetic voice through the faithfulness of ministers who responded, at great personal cost, in obedience to the call of God to engage in verbal ministry, often traveling far from home to minister to other Quaker congregations or to serve as missionaries. God wasn't hiding from Friends and many truly experienced his deep love and provision.

However, for many this Quietist movement, especially due to the neglect of Scripture reading, was a descent into spiritual stagnation, legalism, and Universalism. Some meetings met for years without anyone engaging in verbal ministry. With very little preaching from the Bible, let alone Bible reading and study, to temper the emphasis on centering down in the Spirit, the spiritual life of the Society became unbalanced. Friends became much too focused on silent waiting before the Lord and completely paralyzed by the fear of running before the Spirit. It became a difficult and awful thing to be "forced" by God to speak in worship and verbal ministry took more courage and conviction than some people had. It is easy to see in hindsight that their overemphasis on absolute passivity before God let Friends down in the end, as our later exploration of the 1827–1828 division will prove.

Another result of embracing Quietism was that the nature of the phrase the "Light of Christ" became ambiguous. Russell asserts that "early Friends never gave exact theological definition to the Inner Light."[43] The best scholars can tell, this was their way of speaking about the work of the Holy Spirit in their lives. But as time went by, the original understanding was lost or muddied and Friends began to talk about the "Light," the "Inner Light," or the "Inward Guide," which may or may not have referred to the work of the Holy Spirit, depending on who you were talking to. Russell goes on to explain that for early Friends the "Inner Light" was a way to describe three understandings of how the Holy Spirit works in people's lives. First, God can be known to and within the human heart, implying that God can be worshiped anywhere and at any time, dissolving the wall between sacred and profane. Friends took this seriously, believing any thought or activity can be sacred if one is focused on God. Second, all human beings have the ability to recognize and respond to God, making all people equal in his eyes. Ideally, this did away with class and ethnic distinctions and made way for women and children, as well as men, from all walks of life and nationalities, to hear from God and act in unity with his Spirit. Third, "Inner Light"

---

43. Russell, *History of Quakerism*, 48.

was a designation for the reality of knowing God inwardly, or recognizing the work of the Holy Spirit in the human heart.[44] By the mid-to-late eighteenth century, while many still considered the above phrases to accurately describe the "Light of Christ" at work in their hearts, without explicit teaching or Bible study, for many the "Inner Light" lost its connection with the work of the Holy Spirit and become a kind of nebulous, universal bond with a distant Deist version of God or devolved into a synonym for a person's conscience. The designation "Inner Light" became shorthand for a type of self-reliance on "that of God in every man" rather than on God himself.

Quietism also changed the way Friends viewed salvation. Thomas Hamm notes that most Friends of this era embraced an interpretation of the "Inward Light," as a Seed planted in each human soul by God, a Seed drawing individuals to Christ. They believed further that if Friends continued to be obedient to the Seed it would grow and produce good fruit in their lives. Thus, the states of sanctification and justification were thought to be entwined in a life-long dance, through which believers were reconciled with God over time and slowly made fit for heaven as they allowed the Seed to grow. God initiated salvation and sanctification through grace, but Friends could work with him in the process.[45] Barclay had introduced the idea of the Seed in his *Apology*, but this new way of looking at justification and sanctification added a layer to Barclay's theology that he probably did not intend. For Barclay, the line between justification and sanctification was drawn much more clearly. He believed that the moment an individual responded to the Seed and accepted Jesus they were rescued from their sins.[46] Hamm says Friends came to believe that part of cultivating the Seed involved undergoing "seasons of divine visitation that often took the form of suffering or depression." These spiritual baptisms were considered part of the process of salvation and purification and came to be known collectively as "bearing the cross."[47] Such ordeals were celebrated as a means of growing in holiness and maturing spiritually and as a result, Barclay's view of the Seed faded into the background.

Obviously, this understanding of salvation made it difficult for Friends to engage with other Christian denominations who believed that justification and sanctification were two separate experiences. Many Quietist Friends also placed undue emphasis on Barclay's belief that the Holy Spirit inspired Scripture, elevating the Spirit over Scripture, instead of treating the

---

44. Russell, *History of Quakerism*, 49–52.
45. Hamm, *Quakers in America*, 30.
46. Barclay, *Barclay's Apology in Modern English*, 265.
47. Hamm, *Quakers in America*, 30.

Spirit and Scripture as two indivisible divine agents, working together to reveal God to the world. Contention over just what the "Seed" meant, the "Inner Light" meant, and how the relationship between the Holy Spirit and Scripture worked, helped to bring about the division among Friends in the early nineteenth century.

The practice of birthright membership also contributed to the isolation of Friends from the world at large. London Yearly Meeting initiated birthright membership in 1737 with the following minute as reported by the Thomas brothers, "'All Friends shall be deemed members of the Quarterly, Monthly, and Two-Weeks Meeting within the compass of which they inhabited or dwelt the 1st day of the Fourth Month, 1737'; and 'the wife and children to be deemed members of the Monthly Meeting of which the husband or father is a member, not only during his life but after his decease.'" The intent was to keep accurate records of membership in order to better help the poor. However, there were some unintended consequences. The Allen brothers go on to say that "the vast importance of this step was not appreciated for some time. It changed the Society of Friends from a church of believers, at least in theory, to a corporation or association of persons some of whom always would be of those who were not spiritually minded."[48] Over time, being born into a Quaker family and following the outward practices was enough for one to be considered a Friend, and many did not pay any attention to the spiritual reasons behind Quaker customs or even to any spiritual matters at all.

To complicate matters, Friends, at this time, did not engage in formal teaching of what they believed, but expected those from the outside who were convinced, as well as their own children who were growing up in the Society, to absorb their beliefs by participating in First Day worship, business meetings, and the life of the community. Therefore, the reasoning behind certain beliefs and practices was not always communicated directly, contributing to the sense that following Quaker traditions was what made one a Quaker, rather than placing trust in Jesus Christ or agreeing with a set of spiritual beliefs.

Friends had always been suspicious of creeds, though Barclay, in the *Apology*, had for all intents and purposes set one out. They did, however, develop a Discipline and sets of questions, called the Queries, that were designed to encourage both individuals and whole congregations to periodically examine the state of their souls. Punshon, states that the "'Discipline' was a generic name for the rules of Quaker church order and the religious principles to which Friends were expected to conform." He goes on to say

---

48. Thomas and Thomas, *History of the Friends in America*, 5th ed., 108–9.

that the "idea behind it was discipleship and in seeking to understand the institution one should lay aside any unpleasant connotation the word may have now." As a covenantal church, Friends most certainly held beliefs in common that governed both worship and community life.

Punshon also explains that the "Queries" began as a means of gathering information from subordinate meetings, but later were "used to obtain information about the spiritual condition of the Society also, and meetings were expected to deliberate and return written answers to a superior meeting."[49] The "Queries" became a way to exert influence over and control meetings because the "right" answer was implied and as such revealed Quaker values of the day. So while Friends beliefs and expectations for community living were not always communicated directly, they were most definitely communicated in practice, and adherence to them was required for good standing as a member in the Society.

Friends continued to uphold the beliefs and practices of the earlier era, while adding to and subtracting from them with the changing times. They remained firm in their practice of the Peace Testimony and were often still persecuted for their stand against violence in any form. Many Friends in America suffered for refusing to fight in the French and Indian War (1756 to 63) or declining to pay military taxes. Some were in the path of the two warring armies and were killed or lost their land. Later on they were fined for not helping financially with the Revolutionary War (1775 to 83) effort and for, yet again, refusing to fight. They were looked at with suspicion by their neighbors from both sides, since they chose not to engage in the conflict at all. Friends experienced similar distrust and persecution during the Civil War (1861 to 65) in spite of humanitarian aid to soldiers and civilian victims on both sides. To be sure, some Friends did fight and contribute money during war times, but officially the Society retained their commitment to the Peace Testimony and men who chose to fight were usually disowned by their meetings.

Friends continued to refuse to financially support the Church of England, which ceased to be an issue in England after parliament passed the Toleration Act of 1869 and in America after the Revolutionary War. They continued to refuse to pay their ministers, participate in water baptism, or partake of the "supper" as they called communion with the elements. Women continued to serve as ministers, though business meetings were still split by gender. Friends in this period also continued to hold very simple wedding and funeral services, use numbers for the days of the weeks and

---

49. Punshon, *Portrait in Grey*, 136.

months, speak plainly, eschew oaths, and embrace simplicity in their daily lives. Their reputation for honest business dealings remained unparalleled.

From the very beginning slavery sat heavily on George Fox's heart. He encouraged masters to treat their slaves kindly and to free them after a period of service.[50] London Yearly Meeting condemned slavery in an epistle for the first time in 1754.[51] During the Quietist era, many Friends were active in the abolitionist movement in both England and America. They encouraged members of the Society and all others to emancipate their slaves. Friends like Levi Coffin, helped to conduct escaped slaves to freedom on the Underground Railroad and emancipated their own slaves, decades before Abraham Lincoln's Emancipation Proclamation took effect in 1863 and the 13th Amendment to the Constitution was ratified in 1865. Hamm states that "by 1784 all of the American yearly meetings had ruled that members who owned slaves must make arrangements to free them or lose their membership."[52] Many Friends also refused to buy or trade goods produced by slaves. Native Americans were treated with similar respect.

One individual that many consider to be the quintessential Friend of this time period was John Woolman. He was born one hundred years before Hobson and died about fifty years before the division of 1827–1828. Woolman was a recorded Friends minister and he traveled in the ministry through many of the Colonies, always under a religious concern and with the approval of his home monthly meeting in New Jersey. He gave up a successful retail business and supported himself with tailoring and crops from his orchard, in order to live out his belief in the Quaker testimony of simplicity. He also had some training as a lawyer. As part of his conviction that slavery was an unnecessary evil for both slave and master, he refused to treat slaves as property when writing wills and would not write a bill of sale for a slave. After Philadelphia Yearly Meeting adopted a minute encouraging Quakers to free their slaves, Woolman visited many Quaker slave owners with a view to gently encourage them to emancipate their slaves. In several cases he was successful. He also visited the Wyalusing Native Americans in Pennsylvania under a concern for their spiritual well-being. Towards the end of his life he developed a concern about the oppressive conditions that workers who dyed cloth were forced to toil in, so he took to wearing undyed clothes. He also expressed remorse that at one time he had sold in his shop sugar, rum, and molasses produced by slave labor. He died

---

50. Fox, *Journal*, 491 (footnote).
51. Smith "American Anti-Slavery and Civil Rights Timeline."
52. Hamm, *Quakers in America*, 35.

of smallpox while on a religious journey in England.[53] Punshon writes that Woolman's "personal courage, purity of life and perceptive social criticism have attracted admirers and disciples far beyond the Society of Friends."[54] Woolman's dedication to simplicity, purity, and his gentle, yet unbending moral witness are qualities that place him squarely in his time. Also, his concerns to travel in the ministry, to work against slavery, and to live out social justice as best he was able, typify the Quaker Quietist life.

While many customs and beliefs remained similar to those of early Friends, at least in theory, Quietism changed worship practices and theology in ways that brought a tightening up of church organization, a change in the way that the Testimonies were lived out, and the development of an even more distinctive Quaker culture. Quaker peculiarities became more exaggerated as a means of keeping outside worldly influences at bay. Before, simple, modest clothing without specific guidelines had been embraced by Friends. Now there were very specific guidelines for materials, colors, and styles that qualified as proper Quaker dress. Grays and blacks dominated, though there were regional differences. Some well-off Friends also wore expensive material, while keeping to the Quaker colors and patterns, which other Friends saw as a breach in the simplicity testimony. Plain speech was not really necessary anymore for pointing out the equality of all people. It was strange to non-Quakers, antiquated, and it set Friends apart from others in a kind of spiritual superiority, the opposite of its original equalizing purpose. However, Friends clung to it, as well as to the plain way of numbering days and months.

At this time in Friends' history, all individuals and families in the Society were encouraged to refrain from reading novels, attending or acting in plays, playing instruments, singing, dancing, card playing, drinking alcohol to excess, gambling, smoking or chewing tobacco, and any other such frivolous activities. Many of these things were objected to, not so much in and of themselves, but rather because they took time away from worship of and focus on God and were, therefore a detriment to spiritual life. Engaging in such activities might solicit a visit from the overseers, with a view to bringing a member back into the straight and narrow path that leads to God. If they refused to change their behavior "disownment" (removal from Quaker fellowship) might ensue. A Friend could also be "disowned" for marrying-out of the Society, fist-fighting, going to war, using bad language, arguing with a neighbor, choosing not to speak or dress plainly, or seemingly by

---

53. Woolman, *Journal and Major Essays of John Woolman*, summary of book, but see especially timeline pages 17–20.
54. Punshon, *Portrait in Grey*, 115.

looking crosswise at an elder. Of course, deeper moral breaches were also dealt with in the same manner: premarital sex, adultery, theft, murder, and the like. William Hobson's own father was disowned for a time, though reinstated later, because of a dispute with a neighbor.

It was fairly easy to avoid disownment or to be reinstated to membership. All one had to do was repent in person or in writing. But it needed to be genuine repentance, for the elders and the overseers, bodies responsible for the moral purity of the church, took their job seriously. The intent was to help people stay right with God, though there is evidence that at times such correction became purely political or legalistic, and sometimes petty personal differences came into play. However, it is interesting to note that disowned Friends were not always banned from attending services or participating in the life of the community. They just couldn't be members or hold leadership roles.

This strict and seemingly repressive existence was simply the Quaker way of life. Friends were very serious in their pursuit of holiness. Thomas Hamm writes in *Transformation of American Quakerism*, "Friends summed up that whole lifestyle—the baptisms, the tribulations, the repudiation of the world, and the plain life—in the phrase 'bearing the cross.' 'No cross, no crown,' William Penn had written in the 1680s, and Friends saw the 'personal cross as the way of salvation.'"[55] Friends believed it was necessary to take up their cross daily to follow Jesus and work out their own salvation with fear and trembling. Their serious demeanors and plain lives were a testimony to a fallen world that they were set apart for God. This was the Quaker church culture that Hobson grew up in.

It is important to take a minute to describe the rather complex church organization in place at this stage in Quaker history, relying on the descriptions in Rufus Jones's *Later Periods of Quakerism*, so we can better understand Hobson's role as a Friends minister, traveling minister, and church planter. London Yearly Meeting, set up by George Fox and early Friends over a number of years in the late 1660s and early 1670s, was still considered the "mother" yearly meeting during the Quietist period, and as such had the most influence on other yearly meetings of any other. Though technically each yearly meeting stood on its own authority, there was much communication between yearly meetings in the form of official letters called epistles. Traveling ministers also brought news back and forth. But what does the term yearly meeting actually mean? It's used to refer to both a particular regional area in which certain monthly meetings were established, as well as to an annual gathering of those meetings at a central location. Of course,

---

55. Hamm, *Transformation of American Quakerism*, 6.

entire churches couldn't participate in the annual yearly meeting sessions, so each meeting sent representatives, who then reported back to their local congregations.

New meetings, similar to what we would call church plants today, sprang up under the authority of established yearly meetings. In their infant state, new churches were called preparative meetings. These congregations worshipped and held business meetings on their own. But when several preparative meetings became large enough, they could apply to the nearest yearly meeting for monthly meeting status, which would then include several preparative meetings doing business together. So, like with yearly meetings, monthly meetings referred not only to when they were held, but also referred to the geographical area they covered (eg., Honey Creek Monthly Meeting). Each Preparative Meeting would do some local or initial business, which they would later report to the Monthly Meeting. The separate congregations would also do other pertinent business together. Sometimes, a monthly meeting might consist of only one meeting, if there were no other meetings near enough to join with easily. This was common on the American frontier. Jones reports that the "Monthly Meeting held the power to admit new members, to disown members, to give and receive certificates of removal, to build meeting–houses, to arrange for the marriage of its members, to take care of all meeting property in its possession, to have charge of all its records, to nominate all persons believed suitable for official stations, and to appoint representatives to Quarterly Meeting."[56]

When there were enough monthly meetings within easy traveling distance, the representatives would get together four times a year for quarterly worship and business meetings, at which representatives to yearly meeting sessions would be appointed, among other business. And when there were several quarterly meetings in a larger region, they could apply for their own yearly meeting status. This is why Newberg Friends Church, first called Chehalem Monthly Meeting, was for many years considered a part of Iowa Yearly Meeting. Iowa Yearly Meeting members had issued the "minute" (a term for documenting congregational discernment) granting Hobson their approval to travel to the West Coast with the intention of establishing a Friends community in a favorable location. When Hobson accomplished the goal and started a meeting at Newberg, Oregon, in the Chehalem Valley he did so with the backing of Iowa Friends. Eventually, Iowa Yearly Meeting approved another "minute" granting monthly meeting status to the congregation at Newberg. Chehalem Monthly Meeting remained under Iowa Yearly Meeting's jurisdiction until approval was

---

56. Jones, *Later Periods of Quakerism, Vol. 1*, 110–11.

given for Pacific Northwest Friends to become their own yearly meeting several years later.

Jones tells us that yearly meetings were made up of "all the members living in a defined area of country, and [were] the highest source of legislative authority in the Society for the membership within its boundary." Yearly meetings heard reports from quarterly meetings and dealt with business having to do with all the meetings under its auspices. Yearly meetings also issued epistles detailing the "substance of its spiritual deliberations during the sittings."[57] Independent Friends churches were unheard of at the time. If individual Friends moved or chose to attend a different meeting, their certificate of membership would be presented to their intended new monthly meeting, upon approval of their previous monthly meeting.

Generally speaking, meeting houses were built simply, but well, with little or no adornment, reflecting both the early Friends repudiation of symbols and the quietist conviction to cut themselves loose from the "creature." Plain wooden benches or chairs were arranged in rows and a raised set of benches at the front of the house, called facing benches, were reserved for the ministers and elders, who faced the congregation. Meetings were conducted mostly in silence, punctuated with prayer or preaching from ministers as they felt led. Meetings were open to all, and theoretically anyone could speak, even children, but it was unusual for anyone but ministers to break the silence. Relying on the Holy Spirit for direction in what to say in meeting was taken very seriously. Though music was not a part of Friends worship, some ministers spoke in a kind of sing–song chant, a practice that later lost popularity. To signal the end of the meeting everyone shook hands with their neighbors. In most areas, one weekday meeting was also held in the afternoon. Friends of this period rarely met at night. Business meetings were also held with a worshipful reverence, beginning with open worship, but they were a little more lively. The Queries were read and answered and meeting business, such as finances, helping the poor, changes to the Discipline, membership issues, disownments, engagements, and other community concerns were discussed. Decisions were made when the presiding clerk arrived at a "sense of the meeting" by discerning the movement of the Holy Spirit amongst the congregation. A minute would then be formed, and the congregation would either approve or disapprove the presiding clerk's conclusions. Meeting houses often had dividers that could be moved into place for separate men's and women's business and then be stored away for First Day worship. At this time, there was no First Day School and no corporate Bible reading or study.

---

57. Jones, *Later Periods of Quakerism*, Vol. 1, 111.

Meeting leadership was composed of three groups: elders, ministers, and overseers. At first, elders and ministers were terms used interchangeably. Later the duties of elders and ministers were separated, and they became distinctly different roles in the congregation. Elders were generally individuals who arose out of the meeting by proving themselves over time to be august, seasoned, and spiritually mature persons, either male or female. They were persons who displayed a strong adherence to the Quaker Testimonies and way of life. Elders were charged with the spiritual and moral care of the ministers and congregation. They met with ministers in "Select Meetings" to lend them spiritual support and guidance. They also presided over meetings for worship, from the facing bench. According to Jones, most elders had an unusual ability to settle deeply into the silence, yet still notice who fell asleep or was distracted and amazingly enough, without a watch, determine the exact proper moment to end a meeting.[58] Russell describes elders of the Quietist period as "'solid, weighty and experienced Friends appointed by the monthly meetings to sit with the ministers in the ministers meeting to consider the state of the ministry, to aid young ministers and finally to have oversight of spiritual conditions in the church."[59] They ended up becoming the "guardians of custom" as Jones describes it. The elders guarded Quaker culture and practices by exerting a wordless force over their ministers and congregations. They were quick to correct ministers they felt had overstepped their bounds and kept tight control over the meeting; doing little, however, to effectively help ministers to mature in their calling or strengthen their public speaking skills, as any preparation for preaching was considered running ahead of God.

Elders were responsible for writing the Discipline and Queries, and in hindsight, were considered to be the strongest old-school force in the Society. They added much to the "weight, dignity and moral power" of the Society, but were in many ways repressive and authoritarian.[60] Russell puts it this way, "[elders] became the guardians of tradition and as such were a conservative force. They became the repositories of sound doctrine, the interpreters of the Quaker literature and the ruling class in the Society."[61] In general, orthodox Quaker historians blame the elders of this period for stunting the spiritual growth of the Society and for an abuse of power. At the very least, their emphasis on tradition, duty, and rigorous observance of Quaker culture cast an oppressive pall over the Society. It was partly in

---

58. Jones, *Later Periods of Quakerism*, Vol. 1, 121–22, 126.
59. Russell, *History of Quakerism*, 220.
60. Jones, *Later Periods of Quakerism*, Vol. 1, 127–28.
61. Russell, *History of Quakerism*, 222.

response to this perceived spiritual stagnation, brought about by the elders' strict adherence to Quaker culture and practice, that revival Friends embraced new worship innovations after the separation of 1827–1828. Many who broke from the old ways felt they were getting out from under the "dead hand of the past."

Overseers evolved as a kind of subset of the elders and were established as a part of meeting leadership beginning around the mid 1770s.[62] Their duties as described by the Allan brothers were as follows: to serve as a membership committee, to watch for any in spiritual or physical need in the congregation, to speak with people who have sinned and/or fallen away from the Friends lifestyle and try to restore them to the church, to report to the elders any who choose not to be restored, to manage church property, in some cases, and to prepare congregational answers to the Queries.[63] While the elders focused more on ministerial support and spiritual care of the congregation, the overseers became, in a sense, their enforcers. To be sure, there most likely were grievous sins that needed to be addressed within congregations. But there were also things like dropping the plain speech or plain dress, marrying-out, frivolous purchases, and the like, that were just lapses from conformity to Quaker culture. The overseers are primarily remembered as a moral watchdog group that contributed to the oppressive spiritual climate the elders presided over.

Jones tells how ministers were individuals called by God to speak or pray in worship and to perform pastoral visits among the congregation. We can discover in many journals written by Friends ministers, also known as "Public Friends," that the calling to verbal ministry often followed a certain pattern. Most ministers knew from a very young age that they were called to a deep relationship with God and sometimes even that they would be required to preach in later life. They often experienced a season of rebellion against God as a young adult, which resulted in returning to him during a time of intense personal revival. Jones points out that most ministers experienced spiritual refining after "deep trials, often marked by illness or terrible tension,"[64] which may or may not have included a time of turning away from God. The struggle to obey the call to speak in meeting was intense and painful. There was such a fear of running ahead of the Spirit that it was excruciatingly difficult to break the silence of worship, but most accounts of Friends ministers describe a specific time when they could no longer hold

---

62. Jones, *Later Periods of Quakerism*, Vol. 1, 124–25.

63. Thomas and Thomas, *History of the Friends in America*, 5th ed., 19, 108 (footnote).

64. Jones, *Later Periods of Quakerism*, Vol. 1, 201

out against the command to speak and were compelled to break the quiet with a spontaneous word from God.

It seems that speaking in meeting became easier as time passed, but not for everyone and not all the time. Ministers did not prepare notes, though it's likely that they prayed and studied during the week and that perhaps God used that prayer and study, at times, to inspire verbal ministry. Other times verbal ministry was completely spontaneous. They took obedience to the leading of the Holy Spirit very, very seriously and ministers also described times when they were held back from speaking. They referred to such an experience as "travailing with the suffering seed." This was a time of centering down to the point where they could "discover 'the state and condition' of the meeting, through which they could travail in birth pains for the suffering seed" of repentance to grow in the congregation.[65] The minister suffered vicariously with a congregation as the Spirit worked in their broken places, in order to bring God's healing work to fruition. The hope was that silently identifying with the congregation's sin, pain, grief, and/or lack of forgiveness would open up space for the Holy Spirit to soften hearts and bring the congregation into a state of reconciliation with God and their fellow human beings. Jones also writes that ministers sometimes "felt themselves moved to remain mute so as to 'starve the people from words,' and to turn them from any trust in the creature."[66] The idea was to allow for a direct word from God to form in the souls of those meeting, so the minister would keep quiet in order not to get in the way of the Spirit.

Over time, as an individual consistently spoke in meeting in an edifying way, their gift would be recognized by the elders and they would be recorded as a minister. Essentially, this meant nothing more than noticing that the minister had a special gift or calling and supporting them in that calling. No special education or training was required to become a minister, only a God-given gift for verbal ministry, exercised over time, and conformity to the Friends lifestyle. Also, the ministers of this period were not paid for preaching or pastoral care, in keeping with longstanding Quaker tradition. Friends believed that the gospel and spiritual support ought to be offered free of charge. Being a minister was not a profession among Friends, but rather a calling.

Often, ministers would develop a concern for visiting other Friends congregations. They would bring their concern before the monthly meeting and, if approved, the monthly meeting would issue a traveling minute. This traveling minute was presented to each congregation a minister visited and

---

65. Jones, *Later Periods of Quakerism, Vol.1*, 86–87
66. Jones, *Later Periods of Quakerism, Vol. 1*, 63.

used like a letter of introduction. Traveling ministers helped to keep the beliefs and practices of Friends uniform. They promoted unity in the Spirit and strengthened ties with Friends in the different regions of the United States as well as with Great Britain. There was a general concern among ministers at the time for what they considered the low state of Quakerism. They felt called to build up the spiritual life of the Society as well as strengthen people's commitment to the Quaker way of life. Traveling ministers sacrificed much in order to follow through on their concerns. These adventurous ministers were often away from home and family for months on end and more often than not, traveling conditions during their journeys were terrible. However, there are numerous stories of the direct intervention of God in the lives of these obedient men and women as they tramped difficult roads following his will and way. The Society owes much to the obedience of traveling ministers who were willing to follow God's direction at great cost to themselves and their families.

One such traditional Quietist Quaker minister was Joseph Hoag. He lived in New York and Vermont and made numerous religious journeys. He traveled throughout New England, up into Canada and as far south as North Carolina and Virginia. Hoag and his wife Huldah, also a minister, had ten children, several of whom also became Friends ministers. In fact, their son, Lindley Hoag, was influential in Hobson's life. Joseph Hoag is probably most famous for his 1803 vision in which he predicted the Civil War,[67] but he had his first vision around ten years of age. He describes in his journal that he envisioned his father becoming a Public Friend in their local meeting. Then, very soon after this, his father encountered much opposition from church leadership and even from members of his own family, because he preached the Gospel Truth. Everything in this vision came to pass just as it was revealed to Hoag, not long after.[68] As an adolescent he went through a period of rebellion against God, mostly due to the weightiness of God's hand upon him, but he eventually broke out triumphant, put mutiny behind him, and decided to follow wholeheartedly the calling on his life to follow God as a minister.

Hoag did not take sides leading up to, during, or after the division of 1827–1828, but stood firm in the Lord Jesus Christ and traditional Quaker spiritual life. At one point, he wrote in his journal, "I desire you may be so warned and instructed that you may take care and never be drawn away, or prejudiced against any one, without first knowing both sides; then let truth and justice be your standard, lest you fare like those poor men, who were

---

67. "Hoag, Joseph, 1762–1846."
68. Hoag, *Journal*, 13–16.

all three favored ministers [now apostate], while they kept to the Master's leadings, and only judged as He gave them judgement."[69] He did not agree with Elias Hicks's theology or Joseph John Gurney's evangelical leanings. Because of this he was worried that his journal would be destroyed, by one side or the other, and he placed it in the safe keeping of a friend to protect it. Sadly, when it was published five years after his death, it caused a division in Scipio Monthly Meeting (New York).[70] Hoag continued to have visions and God inspired openings throughout his life. Out of these revelations and openings he often spoke prophetic words in meeting and during pastoral visits. Because of this he inspired awe in others, and either fierce devotion or fierce opposition.

Hoag spoke with many of Elias Hicks's supporters, and even Hicks himself, in the hopes he could lead them to salvation in Jesus and back into traditional Quakerism. He wrote in his journal concerning the Hicksite principles as follows: "I had opposed those principles in every part of the Quarterly meeting, where ever I found them, showing that is was rotten infidelity, wrapped up under the plausible pretext of a more profound, religious knowledge, than Friends had ever attained to before."[71] He did not tell much about pursuing social justice in his journal, unlike Woolman, but wrote a lot about visions, openings, prophetic opportunities, standing firm against the Adversary, lessons learned through sicknesses, spiritual baptisms, and being faithful to speak the word of the Lord as it came to him. He exemplified the Quaker idea of "bearing the cross." He was faithful to listen to and obey God regardless of the personal cost, and at times the cost was great. In his lifetime he met with persecution, opposition, hardship on the road, and serious illness. Joseph Hoag was the epitome of a faithful Quaker traveling minister in the Quietist period.

It is important to note that Friends of this period were not immune to the fever of Manifest Destiny which infected the entire nation in the eighteenth and first half of the nineteenth centuries. Scores of Friends moved west into unsettled territory. When the Ordinance of 1787 created a slavery free Northwest Territory, the area that later became the states of Ohio, Indiana, Illinois, Wisconsin, and Michigan became a prime destination for southern Friends who wanted to escape the degradation of living in slave states. To be sure there were also those who sought cheap land, a fresh start in less crowded areas, adventure, or various combinations thereof. Even William Hobson caught the fever. He and his young family left North

69. Hoag, *Journal*, 57–58.
70. "Hoag, Joseph, 1762–1846."
71. Hoag, *Journal*, 301.

Carolina for the untamed wilderness of northwestern Iowa in 1847, where they built up a farm and orchard from scratch. Just under thirty years later they left this prosperous spread behind and transplanted to Oregon in 1876. It was not unusual for families who moved west to move even further west at a later date.

Russell points out that towards the beginning of the Friends migration the majority of southern Quakers emigrated to Ohio and Indiana. Quite a few Friends also emigrated west from Pennsylvania, New Jersey, New England, and other eastern states. Later, like the Hobsons, Friends moved further west into Iowa, as well as Kansas, Nebraska, and later still, like the Hobsons again, as far as the West Coast. Russell states that "it has been estimated that from 1800 to 1860 not less than 6000 Friends emigrated from the southern states."[72] Some meetings migrated en masse. Some meetings lost so many members they barely survived. This was especially true in North Carolina. Yearly meetings in South Carolina, Georgia, and Virginia were laid down because so many Friends moved from those states, though a few Virginian monthly meetings joined with Baltimore Yearly Meeting. Friends who remained in North Carolina and Baltimore felt bereft, but also sensed that they had a special calling to witness to the unbelieving communities around them and to help support the African American population there. They suffered much hardship during the Civil War. Difficult as it was for those left behind, the resettlement of Friends greatly expanded the influence of Quakerism across America. Jones reports that the following yearly meetings came into existence due to emigration and growth in membership: "Ohio in 1813, Indiana in 1821, Western (in Western Indiana) in 1858, Iowa in 1863, Canada in 1867, Kansas in 1872, Wilmington (in Western Ohio) in 1892, Oregon in 1893, California in 1895 and Nebraska in 1908."[73] While many changes have taken place since then, this accurately describes the spread of the Society across America during Hobson's lifetime plus a little before and beyond.

The Age of Quietism spanned just over a century, during which Friends developed a distinct culture and church organization that hedged them in from the rest of the world. This included observing the Quaker Testimonies and codifying rules surrounding dress, speech, ways of doing business, who they married, and how they spent their free time, among other things; a collection of mores known simply as the Discipline. This along with the institution of birthright Quakerism resulted in widespread spiritual stagnation, due to an overemphasis on legalism, performance, and entitlement which

---

72. Russell, *History of Quakerism*, 274.
73. Jones, *Later Periods of Quakerism*, Vol. 1, 433–34.

ushered the Society into a kind of religious stupor. Keeping the Discipline and Testimonies became more important than anything else. And the lack of Scripture reading helped to perpetuate this sorry state of affairs.

However, some were able to keep a profound commitment to following Jesus, by centering deeply down into his Spirit, reading Scripture, and by giving prophetic utterance and testimony to his saving grace through his death on the cross. This was most prevalent in, though not limited to, ministers and other leaders in Quaker communities. Journals kept by traveling ministers and other prominent Friends testify to the deep spiritual maturity of many Quakers in this period and to their conviction that, just as the Bible teaches, Jesus is the Messiah. Some were profound intercessors, accomplished preachers, and prophets. Many had visions or experienced direct words from God, as well as divine guidance from the Holy Spirit in the daily circumstances of their lives. Also, some individuals and families did study the Bible, which did much to grow them in the Lord. Sadly though, the enthusiastic evangelism exhibited by George Fox and other early Friends was much subdued in this period of Quaker history.

As American Friends moved into the nineteenth century, the old Quaker habits and beliefs were questioned by some who desired spiritual renewal and rejuvenation, causing disagreement about how to move the Society forward. Some Friends wanted a return to the evangelistic enthusiasm of George Fox and the early Quakers, with an emphasis on bringing lost sheep into the fold. They were not yet interested in sweeping away unprogrammed worship, they still upheld the Quaker Testimonies, and believed it best not to participate in outward sacraments, but they were beginning to chafe under the constraints of silent worship with limited verbal ministry. Also, they were no longer content to live under what seemed to them the restrictive, anachronistic Discipline and Quaker culture. Among other things, they were done especially with disownments for marrying–out. They felt spiritually constricted and suffocated. Because of this, they engaged in push back against what they saw as the stifling, tyrannical control of the elders and overseers, which predictably caused those in authority to clamp down harder. This made things even more intolerable for those who felt a stirring towards change. The influence of Methodism and the Evangelical Church of England began to be felt as new ways of understanding sanctification, justification, and the Atonement crept into the Society. A desire for the formation of sound doctrine and theology was beginning to stir. Influence from other denominations also brought about an increased interest in Scripture reading. Furthermore, many were beginning to crave a clearer definition of the "Inner Light" as the "Light of Christ" or the Holy Spirit. Significant spiritual renewal and awakening occurred as evangelical Friends sought to shake off the fog of a long spiritual nap. Friends who thought this way came to be known as Orthodox Friends.

Other Friends were quite content with the Discipline and silent worship. They saw no reason to change Quaker traditions or culture. They believed that by maintaining the old ways they were following the original intention of George Fox. They viewed outside influences from other denominations with suspicion and hostility. For them Quakerism was still a hedge against the world. These Friends persisted in the belief that Bible study and preparation for verbal ministry was "creaturely activity" and "running ahead of God." In their estimation, the Spirit could inform them of everything they needed to know about God and how he works, if they could just center down properly. Some read and knew the Bible well, but saw it as a secondary rule to direct revelation from God. These Friends continued to define the "Inner Light" as a "Seed" drawing people to Jesus, who was the best example of a true human, because he obeyed God perfectly in every way. Salvation was still considered to be a long journey marked with "baptisms" and suffering. But for many the "Inner Light" had ceased to be about the Holy Spirit inspiring individuals to trust in the historical Jesus as the Messiah and became more about growing that of God in every person and surrendering to the Inner Christ. Creeds and systematic theology were abhorrent to these Friends. They were not trying to force their beliefs on anyone and only wanted freedom to hold them without condemnation. Friends who thought this way came to be known as Hicksite Friends, named after Elias Hicks, a traveling minister who held the above beliefs and made them public. Not everyone who sided with Hicks and his followers agreed wholeheartedly with his theology, rather they wanted to be free to believe as they liked. At any rate, it is obvious that these two groups of Friends, the Orthodox and the Hicksites, as they came to be called, were moving in very different directions. Something had to give and by the end of the 1820s, regrettably, something did.

REVIVAL AND REORGANIZATION OF QUAKERISM IN AMERICA (1827 TO 1860)

When William Hobson was just seven years old, in Fourth Month 1827, Philadelphia Yearly Meeting met for the last time as a unified body. The prelude to separation was not without contention as disagreements flared on the floor of the meeting, but was for the most part peaceable. Even though Hicks's supporters had stacked the meeting with extra representatives, Orthodox Friends maintained control of the Select Meeting and the Meeting for Sufferings. Also, the presiding clerk, Samuel Bettle, who was on the Orthodox side, kept his seat due to a technicality and not through unity of the meeting.[74] Friends in opposition cried foul. They believed, not without cause, that their concerns were not given enough weight by those in authority and felt especially disrespected by Bettle. Those who sympathized with Hicks had hoped to install John Comly as presiding clerk, but he reluctantly acquiesced to his former seat as assistant clerk. According to Jones, Comly believed strongly that separation was inevitable and was only concerned that it occur "in the peaceable spirit of the non-resisting Lamb." Under the leadership of Comly, Hicksite Friends met at Green Street Meeting house in the evenings during yearly meeting sessions. They began making plans for a "quiet retreat from the scenes of confusion." During the last session of yearly meeting the news that a large group of Hicks sympathizers had been organizing with the intent to form their own separate yearly meeting was reported from the floor. Jones states that the news about Comly's party meeting elsewhere "electrified the yearly meeting and produced a profound stir throughout the house." After this bombshell, Philadelphia Yearly Meeting approved a concern from the women's meeting to form a committee to visit all the quarterly and monthly meetings in order to promote unity and harmony between Friends. The meeting then closed quietly with a reading of the minutes, Orthodox Friends having retained control of the meeting the entire time.[75] Thus, Orthodox and Hicksite Friends were quietly torn asunder.

Differences between Hicksite Friends and Orthodox Friends in Philadelphia Yearly Meeting were too sharp, by now, for unity and harmony to be restored. There was very little desire for reconciliation on either side. In fact, the inflexibility of the Orthodox branch encouraged Hicks's sympathizers to separate out and the adamant stand the Orthodox took against Comly's group caused many on the fence to side with the Hicksites. Orthodox Friends believed they were defending the church against heresy, while the Hicksites could no longer stand the Orthodox insistence on creed and doctrine or their seeming condemnation of the Hicksite desire for religious freedom. Two months later in Sixth Month 1827, Hicksite Friends had organized further and later that year they determined to meet annually in Fourth Month, as a separate yearly meeting, shadowing the Orthodox meeting they had seceded from.[76] About two thirds of Philadelphia Yearly Meeting left to form their own parallel yearly meeting.[77] Unfortunately, this

---

74. Russell, *History of Quakerism*, 314.
75. Jones, *Later Periods of Quakerism, Vol. 1*, 465–67.
76. Russell, *History of Quakerism*, 315–16.
77. Hamm, *Quakers in America*, 42.

separation led to several unkind scenes between former friends and family members and contentious tussles over congregational property that caused grief and bitterness for years to come.

The quiet shattering of Philadelphia Yearly Meeting was a watershed moment in American Quakerism, leading to divisions in five out of seven American yearly meetings, to lesser or greater degrees, and affecting Friends everywhere, including William Hobson, for decades after. London Yearly Meeting recognized and supported the smaller Orthodox Philadelphia Yearly Meeting as legitimate, lending their superlative support to the Orthodox cause. As news spread that Philadelphia had split, American Quakers were severely shaken. Representatives from both sides of the rift visited at yearly meetings around the country precipitating significant divisions in New York and Ohio, as well as smaller divisions in other yearly meetings. Punshon lists out the different separations. He reports than New York and Baltimore Yearly Meetings were made up predominantly of Hicksite Friends, so the Orthodox seceded from those meetings. Ohio Yearly Meeting was closer to half and half, causing a devastating division and weakening effective ministry on both sides. Indiana Yearly Meeting was mostly Orthodox with only about a fifth of Friends there leaning towards the Hicksites, who seceded fairly peacefully. Seceding Hicksites in New England were even fewer, while Virginia and North Carolina, Hobson's home state, did not split significantly. They remained almost entirely Orthodox.[78] Hamm states that "the Hicksite Separation probably left about 60 percent of American Friends with the Orthodox and 40 percent with the Hicksites."[79] Whatever the statistics, by 1830 American Quakerism was irreparably divided.

Many complex factors contributed to the separation of American Quakerism into Hicksite and Orthodox branches. Some of the most obvious causes were as follows: serious theological disagreements, new philosophies that shaped American culture in the aftermath of the American and French Revolutions, the influence of evangelical British traveling ministers, and class differences between rural and urban Friends. American Friends in all regions were forced to grapple with these issues to some extent. Even the yearly meetings that remained mostly Orthodox were affected by the separations in their sister meetings, though in a limited way, when they interacted in matters of membership transfers, correspondence, and the endorsement of traveling ministers.

---

78. Punshon, *Portrait in Grey*, 175–76.
79. Hamm, *Quakers in America*, 43.

As far back as 1808, Stephen Grellet had labored with Elias Hicks over what he believed was unsound doctrine.[80] Grellet, an effective traveling minister, was a convinced Friend of aristocratic French heritage, according to Marie Haines in *Brave Rebels*, and a strong evangelical, though he had grown up a Roman Catholic.[81] Hicks was a farmer and minister from upstate New York, a birthright Quaker, who "received an irregular education, much like any other farm boy, though he had a logical mind and an eloquence that was able to draw thousands to hear him preach."[82] He was one of the greatest and most esteemed traveling ministers of his time, though he never felt a call to preach overseas. It wasn't until later in his ministry, as larger numbers of Friends began to look for greater clarity as to just exactly what the term "Inner Light" meant, that his beliefs were questioned by more leading Friends than Grellet.

As a staunch Quietist Friend, Hicks believed he was defending traditional Quakerism against the corrupting influences of other denominations, such as Methodism or the evangelical branch of the Church of England. He also believed in religious freedom and chafed under the authority of Friends with evangelical leanings who used positions of power to spread and defend their theology. Hicks defined the "Inward Light" or "Inward Guide" as a little bit of God in everyone that could be encouraged to grow into an acceptance of the "Inward Christ," through prayer and continuing revelation from God alone. Therefore, all outward forms or helps were unnecessary hindrances to God's direct communion with the centered human soul. He considered education to be useless to the spiritual life, since the Spirit could communicate with and through any willing soul; and he considered prepared sermons to be worse than useless, for he believed that anything besides spontaneous, Spirit inspired preaching was a distraction from the present revelation of God. Apparently, the physical world had very little attraction for Hicks, though he denied charges of dualism that were thrown his way.

Hicks's prejudice against anything external that might get in the way of the movement of the Spirt extended to the Bible. He was well read in the Bible and considered it a worthy book, but he denied that the Bible was authoritative, once again strongly emphasizing the superiority of continuing revelation. Hicks also denied there was any such thing as original sin, believing instead that all people are born innocent and sin comes later as the moral sense is developed. Hicks denied the divinity of Jesus and considered him to be a man prone to sin like any other. But Hicks believed Jesus did not

---

80. Russell, *History of Quakerism*, 304.
81. Haines, *Brave Rebels*, 63–72.
82. Punshon, *Portrait in Grey*, 172.

sin, even once, because he was more obedient to the "Inward Guide" than any other man before or since.[83] In the same vein, he believed that the death of Jesus on the cross had no personal value for the individual. It was just an outward sign of Jesus being especially obedient to God. He also thought that the main significance of the crucifixion was for the Jews, in that God was fulfilling his promise to his Chosen People. The most important thing was to let the "Inward Christ" develop free from all "creaturely" distractions. The Thomas brothers sum up Hicks's theology by pointing out that he "held that the coming and work of Christ Jesus in the flesh, the Scriptures, and all outward teaching were to be classed among the outward things and therefore in no sense essential."[84] Also, according to Hicks, heaven and hell did not exist and neither did Satan. Therefore, placing trust in the historical Jesus for the forgiveness of sins through his blood shed on the cross was not important to Hicks. This meant it was also not especially important to him to make converts to his beliefs. He just wanted to be left alone to believe as he saw fit and thought others ought to have the same freedom. This, he contended, was how Friends had operated since the beginning of Quakerism. It must have been a great blow when his home meeting in New York disowned him.

It is important to note that Hicks's theology was never officially adopted by any group of Friends. Most likely, this is because not everyone grouped under the Hicksite umbrella fully agreed with Hicks. While many of the Friends called Hicksites did agree with his beliefs, several others supported Hicks because they saw him as one of them, a farmer, a plain Friend, and a traditional Quietist Quaker. Others simply eschewed the dogma and creeds of the Orthodox. Some were pulled towards the Hicksite side by family and intimate friends they could not bear to part with. Others gravitated towards the Hicksites because of personality clashes with Orthodox leaders, what they perceived to be abuse of power on the Orthodox side, or because of disillusionment with internal church politics. Many Friends who didn't agree with the Orthodox and were, therefore, only loosely affiliated with the Hicks's party, did not appreciate being called Hicksites, but it was too late. The broad category stuck even if it wasn't entirely accurate. It is uncertain how many members left the Society entirely, forsaking both branches of Friends, as a consequence of the separation.

Orthodox Friends presented a somewhat more united front, though undoubtedly some remained in their home meetings because of familial ties, long-time friendships, and other reasons mirroring the motivations of many who joined the Hicksite camp. Staunch Orthodox Friends believed

---

83. Punshon, *Portrait in Grey*, 306.
84. Thomas and Thomas, *History of the Friends in America*, 5th ed., 124.

they were continuing in the tradition of Friends since the time of George Fox, just like their Hicksite counterparts. These Friends defined the "Inner Light" as the Holy Spirit, one part of the Trinity, the other parts being Jesus and the Father. They continued to stipulate that all humans are created in the image of God and therefore can respond to "that of God in them" when inspired by the Holy Spirit. This would then lead an individual into a salvation experience through trust in the person of Jesus the Messiah. Central to Orthodox theology were the main evangelical beliefs that descendants of the Orthodox branch of Quakers still embrace today. The Orthodox believed in original sin, the existence of heaven and hell, and Satan. They also believed in the virgin birth, that Jesus is both man and God, in his death on the cross for the forgiveness of sins, his resurrection from the dead, and his ascension. They were certain that he was coming again to judge the living and the dead. The Atonement was especially important to the Orthodox, so when Hicks and his followers dismissed the importance of the crucifixion, the Orthodox considered them dangerous and heretical. Not only that, but it felt like a personal attack on the most important thing in their lives, their relationship with the Present Teacher, Jesus, who had saved them out of sin, reconciled them with the Father, and was transforming them into holy people through the ministry of the Holy Spirit.

Another point of difference included Orthodox views on justification and sanctification. Quietist Friends, as previously discussed, considered justification and sanctification to be inseparable, a long process of salvation that included many "baptisms" in the Spirit in which believers suffered and were required to bear their crosses stoically in order to prove their devotion to God. Orthodox Friends saw justification as separate from sanctification. It was possible, they contended, for justification to take place instantaneously. It was as simple as trusting in Jesus's death on the cross and asking him to forgive your sins. This was all that was needed to be reconciled with the Father. Sanctification was the long process of spiritual growth that came after justification, after you had already been set apart for God. It might include crosses to bear and suffering, but weathering those things well was a matter of leaning on Jesus and the power of the Holy Spirit, not proving yourself able to bear up under suffering in your own strength. Sanctification was growing in holiness. It bears mentioning again that this was not just an idea Orthodox Friends held or borrowed from other faith traditions, but a deeply personal and emotional experience. Orthodox Friends truly believed that they were saved by the grace of God from sin, made right with God the Father through Jesus's sacrifice on the cross, able to grow in holiness by the working of the Holy Spirit in their souls, and given eternal life. Because of this, they wanted everyone to know the saving grace of God through the blood of Jesus and were not satisfied with anything less. Hicksite Friends could not embrace their view of the Atonement, justification, and sanctification and didn't understand the emotional significance these things held for the Orthodox, which obviously caused significant tension within the Society.

Orthodox Friends also harked back to Barclay's assertion that continuing revelation had to be balanced with Scripture: the Holy Spirit could not contradict the Bible and vice versa. They considered Scripture to be inspired by God, true, and authoritative. This resulted in an increase in Bible reading among Orthodox Friends. They could not understand why Hicksites dismissed the Bible and made it a secondary rule. And Hicksite Friends could not understand why Orthodox Friends would rely on anything but the "Inner Guide" to teach them the truth about God.

Many have blamed, or praised, depending on their point of view, evangelical traveling ministers from England for helping to exacerbate the divide between Hicksite and Orthodox Friends. Punshon reports that "between 1810 and 1840 a group of strong British evangelical Friends visited America--William Forster, Anna Braithwaite, Thomas Shillitoe, and Joseph John Gurney. They carried the prestige of the parent body with them and are considered by some to have contributed materially to the separations of 1827–1828 in the United states."[85] Several of these British Quaker ministers had collaborated with individuals from other denominations in their efforts to eradicate slavery in Great Britain and America, as well as in other social justice causes like school and prison reform, picking up some of their theology along the way. Many who had grown up Friends, were significantly influenced by the low church evangelical movement in the Church of England and the Methodist revival movement. Still other British ministers were converts to Quakerism from Anglicanism, Methodism, and other denominations. These British ministers traveled around the United States preaching evangelical doctrine, converting many, and fostering renewal in many others. As fervent converts to evangelicalism themselves, they defended and spread their views because they genuinely believed in the necessity of salvation through the blood of Jesus in order for the human heart to be made right with God. According to Russell, some of the British ministers even "followed Elias Hicks about during his last two preaching tours in Philadelphia Yearly Meeting, denouncing his doctrines in public."[86] This must have been intolerable for Hicks and his supporters, and it likely contributed significantly to bad feelings between the two sides. Even after the splits in Ohio and New York, Thomas Shillitoe shadowed Hicks around

---

85. Punshon, *Portrait in Grey*, 167.
86. Russell, *History of Quakerism*, 305.

to various monthly meetings trying to undo his teaching.[87] Also, there were a considerable number of pointed letters and pamphlets circulated by prominent individuals on both sides, which did very little to improve relations between the two groups.

Some of the more devastating results of the separation were long lasting and deeply distressing. In places, entire monthly meetings separated from yearly meetings, taking their stand, whether Hicksite or Orthodox, in unity. In other regions, heart wrenching scenes played out as individual monthly meetings experienced separation within their congregations. In those fractured meetings, many life-long friendships suddenly ended, just like that. Friends and family members who had worshiped in the same congregation since birth were simply gone, leaving only pain and heartache behind. In some cases parents separated from children, brothers and sisters stopped talking to each other, and extended family took sides against each other. Some meetings were so severely depleted that they were barely able to continue. Hamm notes that for about a decade after the split Orthodox congregations used the Discipline to disown anyone who even thought about adopting Hicks's theology, such was their zeal to defend the unity and purity of Quakerism.[88] Their fear of "unsoundness" made them ruthless. Obviously, this did not help matters, but rather widened the gulf between Hicksites and Orthodox. In many regions lawsuits continued to churn up bad feelings between the two sides as parties fought over the ownership of meeting houses, church funds, schools, cemeteries, and other property. Also, some chose not to forgive personal slights and hurts, allowing resentment to fester, all the while weakening the witness of Friends in the larger world. After all, Friends styled themselves as peacemakers. Where was peace now?

Slowly, over time, Friends began to heal and each group moved forward in their own manner. Hicksites continued to worship in the traditional way and were especially active in matters of social justice, including emancipation for both slaves and women, among other good causes. Orthodox Friends continued to make social justice a priority, but also concentrated on forming a statement of belief emphasizing "more strongly than ever the deity and sacrifice of Jesus Christ, and ... the authenticity of the Scriptures."[89] They had been recognized by London as keeping the true faith, therefore they believed that "guarding the heritage" was their duty.[90] Ralph Beebe points out one good thing that came out of this terrible divide--it opened the door for the

---

87. Russell, *History of Quakerism*, 290.
88. Hamm, *Transformation of American Quakerism*, 19–20.
89. Thomas and Thomas, *History of the Friends in America*, 5th ed., 143.
90. Jones, *Later Periods of Quakerism, Vol. 1*, 485.

revival that sprang up mid-century among Orthodox Friends.[91] Obviously, the Hicksites didn't see it that way then or later. They never did form a statement of belief and as aforementioned never officially adopted Hicks's beliefs. The emotionalism of the revival would have appalled Hicksite Friends. And the innovations the revival gave birth to would have been strongly opposed by Hicksites as unnecessary, unhealthy, and un-Quakerly. Many Quaker historians point out that both sides needed each other, that they could have tempered each other and modified the extreme elements in each camp, and that each branch was the poorer for the split. While there may be an element of truth in this, the fact is that the majority of those involved at the time absolutely did not see it that way. The Orthodox considered the Hicksites heretical and the Hicksites considered the Orthodox to be authoritarian in an extremely un-Quakerly way. Unfortunately, though many attempts have been made to unite the two streams back into one rushing river, these two branches of the Society remain unreconciled to this day. And since William Hobson not only grew up in Orthodox North Carolina Yearly Meeting, but also clearly adhered to Orthodox theology his whole life long, we will now leave the Hicksite stream behind and focus solely on the Orthodox.

In the decades after the separation of 1827-1828 Orthodox Friends felt a great need to solidify not only what they believed, but also how to live out what they believed. Unfortunately, this led to further separation within the Orthodox branch, due to disunity about how to move forward as a Society. Historically, the second large division among Friends, confined to the Orthodox this time, has been called the Wilburite separation, named after an American Friend, John Wilbur. It's probably more correct to name it the Gurneyite-Wilburite separation because British Friend Joseph John Gurney had just as big a hand in the conflict. In the mid-to-late nineteenth century, several yearly meetings, beginning with New England Yearly Meeting in 1845 and ending about a decade later with Ohio Yearly Meeting, experienced significant separations. These fissures between Friends previously united against the Hicksites were precipitated by an inability to agree with each other about how to express their Orthodox faith, mainly having to do with changes brought to the Society by evangelicalism. Several Orthodox yearly meetings did not separate but, as a unified whole took sides against other Orthodox yearly meetings with which they could not see eye to eye. Disagreement centered mainly around issues of theology, the role of the Bible in Christian life, and modes of worship. Also, as with the Hicksite split the influence of British Friends, influences from other denominations, and clashes between personalities, as well as local issues contributed to divergent

---

91. Beebe, *Garden of the Lord*, 22.

ways of doing Orthodox Quakerism. The events that took place in this turbulent half century among Orthodox Friends are difficult to describe, as everything was in flux. Some meetings took years to split while others split swiftly, and some meetings that remained Gurneyite for a time, split later when revival swept through the Gurneyite yearly meetings.

Punshon tells how in the 1830s British minister Joseph John Gurney developed a concern to make a religious journey to America. However, while his local meeting willingly endorsed a traveling minute, London Yearly Meeting did so reluctantly and after much discussion. Within London Yearly Meeting there was significant opposition to his concern from a number of individuals who did not agree with Gurney's strong evangelistic tendencies. And though the details of the meeting were meant to be confidential, Gurney's adversaries widely publicized London Yearly Meeting's lack of unity over his fitness to travel in the ministry. In particular, a minister from New England, John Wilbur, actively spread the news of London's disharmony over Gurney's concern, with the intent to poison American Friends against him. Wilbur and his supporters were trying to discredit Gurney in America before he even arrived. However, Gurney did not let the opposition deter him, though he felt it keenly as a personal attack. During his journey to America in 1837 he preached to thousands of ordinary citizens and to Congress, and also visited with President Van Buren.[92] Russell notes that Gurney was a revitalizing force in the Society, replacing the apathy of the old system with a "vision of new possibilities."[93] For many he was a breath of fresh air.

Obviously, the wind coming off Gurney was not so fresh in John Wilbur's estimation. Wilbur did not approve of Gurney's "'overactive and restless spirit.'"[94] As a staunch Quietist New England Friend from Rhode Island, he took exception to many of Gurney's new ideas. Growing up Wilbur received a fairly good education and later, as an adult, taught school. He became an elder in his home meeting at twenty-eight, and was recorded as a minister in 1812, ten years later. He believed George Fox had received a special anointing from God to usher in a "revival of apostolic Christianity,"[95] and was very much a traditionalist in the Quietist mode, especially when it came to silent worship, as was Gurney. According to Errol T. Elliot in *Quakers on the American Frontier*, Wilbur was also dedicated to the plain life, as was Gurney. Wilbur saw this as continuing in the work of George Fox, as did Gurney. However, their similarities stop there. Wilbur never deviated from

92. Punshon, *Portrait in Grey*, 197.
93. Russell, *History of Quakerism*, 349.
94. Hamm, *Quakers in America*, 49.
95. Jones, *Later Periods of Quakerism, Vol. 1*, 510.

the conviction that the guidance of the Inner Light and the inner experience of God was paramount in the Christian life. He participated in the old-time prophetic preaching style and was distrustful of Bible reading or spiritual instruction. Wilbur was undeniably orthodox in theology, but he practiced his orthodoxy differently from Gurney. Theirs was, Elliot emphasizes, "mainly a disagreement of emphasis between inwardness and outwardness [sic] in faith and practice."[96] Jones agrees that the two men approached orthodoxy from completely different viewpoints. Wilbur insisted that the supernatural "Inner Light" was granted to humans by God to assist toward salvation, while Gurney was all about doctrine, the authority of Scripture, and imputed justification. Wilbur absolutely did not agree with Hicks's beliefs and considered the 1827–1828 separation to have been the work of Satan.[97] But he was deeply invested in the Quietist Quaker way. Wilbur sincerely believed that "Gurneyites were slighting the work of Christ within us [while] the Hicksites denied the work of Christ with out [sic] us."[98] It is clear that he believed in the Atonement, but he also believed in the ministry of the "Inner Light" and he felt strong enough disagreement with Gurney's take on Quakerism to oppose him, not only in writing, but to his face.

Wilbur was highly suspicious of anything that smacked of "creaturely activity." He was strongly opposed to Bible societies, Bible study, and even the appearance of preparation for worship. Wilbur was also vehemently against participation with other denominations in philanthropic causes. And since Gurney participated in and championed both these things, it's easy to see why Wilbur stood against him. Wilbur also mistakenly thought that Gurney believed Scripture had more authority than the Spirit that inspired it. And adding insult to injury, Gurney's conviction that justification and sanctification can be two separate experiences led Wilbur to believe that Gurney was turning his back on the traditional Quaker viewpoint in this matter. Wilbur continued to believe that justification and sanctification are entwined with each other in a long harrowing road to salvation and that Gurney "offered a way 'to avoid the painful endurance of the baptism of fire and the Holy Ghost.'"[99] Wilbur considered it necessary to call Gurney to account. Russell reports that Wilbur "felt it his duty to oppose Gurney and expose his errors by letters and in public and private talks."[100] Regrettably,

---

96. Elliot, *Quakers on the American Frontier*, 73–74.
97. Jones, *Later Periods of Quakerism, Vol. 1*, 513, 539–40.
98. Elliot, *Quakers on the American Frontier*, 72.
99. Hamm, *Quakers in America*, 49.
100. Russell, *History of Quakerism*, 351.

the two men never reconciled over their differences and remained opposed to each other until Gurney's death.

Gurneyite Friends assigned a large share of the blame for the Hicksite split to decades long neglect of Bible reading and study, which they believed had deposited the Society in an unprecedented low state. Historically, Friends did not organize First Day Schools and engaged in very little religious instruction at home or in meeting. Neither adults nor children heard much, if any, Scripture read during worship, though ministers sometimes preached on biblical themes or texts. Most Friends did not read or study the Bible at home either, though there were exceptions, and therefore did not encourage their children to either. Parents were either concerned about interfering with the "Inner Light" in their children's hearts or didn't know how to teach kids about spiritual things, or both. A significant number of Quaker families did not even own Bibles. Also, many were Friends by tradition rather than conviction.[101] Myron Dee Goldsmith points out in his dissertation "William Hobson and the Founding of Quakerism in the Pacific Northwest," that after the Hicksite division, large numbers of Friends embraced with great enthusiasm Gurney's emphasis on learning and interacting with Scripture. Gurney's cousin, Hannah Backhouse, visited America in the years 1830 through 1835 promoting Bible literacy and starting First Day Schools in countless meetings around the country.[102] Gurney's own visit in the late 1830s reinforced Hannah's work.

In the beginning, First Day Schools were little more than opportunities to read or recite memorized scripture as a whole congregation. Over time, as study and teaching became more prevalent, congregations were split up into classes by age. Also, Bible reading groups and societies that met during the week sprang up all throughout American Quakerism, contributing to the increasing gulf between Gurneyite and Wilburite Friends. The rise of Bible reading and study among Gurneyite Friends in the mid-nineteenth century was a major factor in preparing the way for renewal and revival within their ranks later in the century.

The majority of Friends in New England Yearly Meeting were Gurneyites and they wanted to push Wilbur out. Sadly, they accomplished their goal through nefarious means. In 1843 Wilbur's home meeting refused to disown him, so the quarterly meeting dissolved the monthly meeting and assigned his membership to a neighboring monthly meeting, which then swiftly disowned him. His supporters were understandably outraged and

---

101. Thomas and Thomas, *History of the Friends in America*, 5th ed., 121–22.
102. Goldsmith, "William Hobson and the Founding of Quakerism in the Pacific Northwest," 139.

a separation occurred within the yearly meeting two years later in 1845.[103] About 500 Wilburites pulled out of the approximately 7000 Friends who made up New England Yearly Meeting. As with the 1827–1828 division there were high feelings on both sides and legal battles over property ensued. The Wilburites considered their yearly meeting to be the true yearly meeting, but the courts sided with the Gurneyites.[104] More importantly London, Dublin, North Carolina, Indiana, and Baltimore all decided to remain in correspondence with the Gurneyite New England Yearly Meeting, continuing the practice of exchanging yearly meeting epistles and recognizing each other's ministers. The need to decide which yearly meetings to correspond with also precipitated, over time, secessions of Wilburite Friends in New York, Baltimore, Ohio, and Iowa. Philadelphia Yearly Meeting refused to read epistles from either side and continued to receive membership transfers from both bodies, effectively isolating themselves from the larger body of American Friends.[105] Philadelphia, quite understandably, did not want to encourage a repeat of the 1827–1828 schism. Whether burying their head in the sand was an appropriate way to cope, is up for debate. Ohio Yearly Meeting, on the other hand, struggled for nine years with what to do and finally split in 1854. Sharp disagreement over who should be approved as yearly meeting clerk was apparently the last straw for Ohio Friends. Wilburites were the larger body in Ohio and when they separated from Gurneyite Friends, as the Thomas brothers note, they took an important steadying influence with them.[106] It is true that Gurneyite Friends in Ohio were some of the more extreme in terms of embracing mainstream evangelical practices, relative to other yearly meetings. Louis Thomas Jones notes in *Quakers of Iowa*, that Iowa Friends held on in tension together until 1877 when differences in Bear Creek, Madison County became so sharp due to revival breaking out, that Wilburite Friends could no longer worship with Gurneyite Friends. Events in Bear Creek precipitated separations is several other monthly meetings resulting in two separate Iowa Yearly Meetings by 1884, about a decade after the Hobsons settled in Oregon.[107] Pacific Northwest Friends were not immediately affected by the split in Iowa, even though they were still a part of Iowa Yearly Meeting at the time. They did not officially join the Wilburites, however, they also did not begin to change their Quietist mode of worship until the late 1880s.

103. Punshon, *Portrait in Grey*, 199.
104. Thomas and Thomas, *History of the Friends in America*, 5th ed., 149.
105. Punshon, *Portrait in Grey*, 198.
106. Thomas and Thomas, *History of the Friends in America*, 5th ed., 150.
107. Jones, *Quakers of Iowa*, 163–74.

Adding to the complexity of the times, it is clear that Gurneyite Friends had their differences, too. Hamm makes a very insightful distinction between what he calls Renewal Friends and Revival Friends within the Gurneyite camp. Renewal Friends were excited about change. They believed the Society needed revitalization and a return to the spiritual fervor of George Fox and early Friends like William Penn. But they believed it could be done within the framework of traditional worship and the traditional mode of Quaker life. Revival Friends also hoped for revitalization and an increase in spiritual enthusiasm, but they felt that the old practices stifled the movement of the Spirit and they rebelled against them. Both Revival Friends and Renewal Friends dived into Bible reading, Bible study, and First Day Schools with gusto. Both were hopeful that new spiritual life could be breathed into Quakerism. Also, education became increasingly important to both Renewal and Revival Friends. As a result, they began to see that they could live in the world without being corrupted by the world. However, Renewal Friends much preferred to worship in the old, Quietist manner and could not be persuaded to give up plain speech or dress. They also continued to emphasize that God's Kingdom could be realized on earth, since Jesus our Present Teacher is with us at all times and in any situation.

The trouble was that Revival Friends were no longer content with the traditional Friends worship style and mode of life. In fact, they were desperate to throw off the weight of the "dead hand of the past." They believed that the Holy Spirit was doing a new work among Friends. Because of this, they were willing to adopt elements of worship from their Methodist and Baptist neighbors such as hymn singing, the mourner's bench, altar calls, and prayers for the conversion of individuals. Some even went so far as to engage in the sacraments of baptism and the Lord's Supper. And to a certain extent, they lost the emphasis on God's Kingdom realized in the now, that Friends had embraced for decades. Renewal Friends appreciated the fact that revivals got results: new believers in Jesus Christ were exactly what Renewal Friends hoped a revitalized Society of Friends would bring about. However, they believed that the conversion tactics of Revival Friends went too far. The emotion and noise of it all was especially distasteful to Renewal Friends. Renewal Friends were reformers, but they wanted to preserve the dignity and distinctiveness of Friends. Revival Friends wanted to bust it all up and begin something entirely new,[108] though many claimed that they were simply bringing back the evangelistic zeal of George Fox. The conflict between Renewal and Revival Friends was not so much over theological matters, but rather a disagreement over how to worship and evangelize.

---

108. Hamm, *Transformation of American Quakerism*, 42, 92–96.

Revival Friends, who were in the majority, were also mostly from the younger generation and in their zeal, they tended to run roughshod over "dear old Friends" who resisted the revival movement. In their defense, they did not intend to hurt Renewal Friends. Revival Friends truly believed that God was showing up in a new way and bringing a much needed infusion of new life into the Society. They sincerely thought that anyone who stood in the way of this outpouring of God's Spirit was standing in the way of God. Right or wrong, this made for several distressing scenes in meeting houses across America as Renewal Friends were ignored or forced out of meetings they had attended for decades. Renewal Friends who could not abide the new innovations in worship either joined older Wilburite congregations or formed their own Conservative meetings. In some cases, they may have also moved further west to avoid uncomfortable changes. Some continued on in their home meetings, watching helplessly as the revival wave swept away Quakerism as they knew it. William Hobson was not firmly planted in either camp, though he tended to lean more towards renewal than revival.

One famous Revival Friend, Allen Jay, expressed regret for pressing so hard and forcing conservative renewal Friends out during the 1873 revival in Indiana. Later in life he believed that both sides would have been better off without the separation. He writes, "I was a member of the [Western] yearly meeting at that time, enjoyed the revival movement and remember how determined we were to save souls, not thinking of those we might injure in the attempt or how we might cripple the church and mar the harmony by pressing our views too fast."[109] Jay was, however, an unusual human being and unusual in his moderate views. He was born a Friend in Ohio, though as an adult he made his home in Indiana. His family was one that chose to read the Bible, pray, and worship at home, though they were considered strange for doing so. He reports that at age thirteen, after hearing a sermon in meeting about yielding to God's love, he knelt down and prayed out loud in the family orchard, contrary to his Friends training, and after confessing his sins "sweet peace" filled his heart.[110] This he names as the moment of his conversion. In spite of a cleft palate, which sometimes made him difficult to understand, Jay became a Public Friend in 1859 and a recorded minister in 1864.[111] He experienced visions and had a gift of speaking to individuals to point them to God in specific circumstances and in particular ways, as God directed. Jay believed that "all the later Wilburite, or 'Conservative,'

---

109. Jay, *Autobiography of Allen Jay*, 119.
110. Jay, *Autobiography of Allen Jay*, 23.
111. Jay, *Autobiography of Allen Jay*, 82-89.

separations were caused by the breaking out of the revival spirit."[112] He was himself involved in several revivals as a leader. And though he felt sympathy for Hicksites and Wilburites, he remained thoroughly Orthodox and evangelical. His preaching was most often focused on themes that would reach lost souls. Jones characterizes him as "one of the wisest and steadiest of all these young [revival] leaders."[113] Jay lived the rest of his life as a consistent, sturdy leader among Gurneyite Friends in America and abroad, including service for six years as superintendent and treasurer at Earlham College. He served as superintendent of the Baltimore Association, and was instrumental in building up several Friends schools besides Earlham, including Guilford and Whittier Colleges.[114] Mark Minear, in *Richmond 1887*, explains how he was also an indispensable contributor to the Richmond Conference and Declaration, as well as the Five Years Meeting that followed, helping to unify Gurneyite Friends in both doctrine and practice.[115] Allen Jay's legacy to Friends is not to be underestimated.

But let's back up for a minute. What was the impetus for revival? We've already noted that Bible reading and study helped to open the way for revival. Another important opening consisted of socioeconomic changes that were occurring during the nineteenth century. Early pioneers had carved settlements out of raw wilderness. It took all they had just to survive. There was no time to spare on changing the way they worshiped and lived. But by the time their children grew up life was considerably easier on the frontier. Farm equipment became mechanized and many farmers were able to specialize in specific crops. Towns sprang up, public schools were organized, churches were established, and municipal offices were founded. The telegraph was installed all across America. With completion of the transcontinental railroad in 1869 America was connected from sea to shining sea. The train made traveling long distances much easier, as well as increasing the exchange of goods between regions. Labor saving devices like cook stoves, laundry mangles, and sewing machines made everyday life a little easier for families. There was a little more leisure time, time to read the Bible, *Friend's Review*, and the newspaper. There was time to think and dream. There was time to consider spiritual matters and the state of the Society. People got together to sew, to pray, to read, to listen to lectures, and to talk or debate. The frontier was no longer raw and wild. It was becoming civilized.

112. Jay, *Autobiography of Allen Jay*, 110.
113. Jones, *Later Periods of Quakerism, Vol. 2*, 898.
114. Jay, *Autobiography of Allen Jay*, 344, 393.
115. Minear, *Richmond 1887*, 44–45.

However, as Hamm puts it "economic and social factors cannot explain everything that was happening among Orthodox Friends during the mid-nineteenth century."[116] He comes to the conclusion that the separations had more to do with the way people thought and believed than changes in frontier life. Historians from earlier generations see it differently, but it's clear that doctrinal issues precipitated the initial Gurneyite-Hicksite separation, because at that point nobody was advocating a change in worship mode or lifestyle. Later separations among Gurneyites may have also occurred for doctrinal reasons, but they also came about not so much because of differences in belief, but rather because of differences in worship and spiritual life practices as a result of participation in spontaneous evangelical revivals. And while most accounts of this period in Quaker history point out how the desire for spiritual renewal among Gurneyite Friends, the increase in Bible reading and study, and the changing frontier all helped to create a climate in which revival could flourish, none of them, not even Hamm gives more than a glance at the obvious. Revival is not dependent on any human, belief, action, or socioeconomic state. Such things may foster an opening for revival, but true revival is a gift from God, pure grace, and cannot be forced. For reasons known only to God, he decided to pour out his Holy Spirit on certain Friends congregations in the mid-to-late nineteenth century and favor them with his presence in such a way that they could not help but respond with confession, repentance, and exuberant praise for his saving work in their lives. Jones reports that revival among evangelical Gurneyite Friends "swept on from meeting to meeting and from state to state until every section of the country was touched by it and it finally transformed the fundamental character of Quakerism in America." He goes on to remark that "it closed one epoch and inaugurated another, and it began at the same time a new type of Quakerism."[117] Friends in America would never be the same.

General meetings and Friends publications also had a role to play in making space for revival. As part of the renewal movement, Friends had gotten in the habit of holding general meetings which were meant for Bible reading and religious instruction. These general meetings were taken over in the 1870s for the promotion of evangelical revival teachings, Bible study and prayer, by leaders such as David B. Updegraff and John Henry Douglas in Ohio, and Rhoda and Charles Coffin, Esther and Nathan Frame, Dougan Clark Jr., and Luke Woodard in Indiana.[118] Gatherings that began as teaching meetings slowly morphed into evangelical worship services and often

---

116. Hamm, *Transformation of American Quakerism*, 42.
117. Jones, *Later Periods of Quakerism, Vol. II*, 868.
118. Hamm, *Quakers in America*, 51.

resembled Methodist camp meetings.[119] Revival spread, says Minear, from meeting to meeting through the preaching of the Coffins, Douglas, Updegraff, Woodward, the Frames, and others like, John S. Bond, Allen Jay, Eli and Sybil Jones, and Lindley Hoag, to name a few. Furthermore, everybody who felt a call was encouraged to speak, pray, or sing in general meetings, not just ministers. Often general meetings were led by lay people, prompting participants to think of the current revival movement as similar to the fervent activity of early Friends. Minear tells how Benjamin Trueblood, a Friend instrumental in bringing peacemaking among Friends up to date and also a proponent of the pastoral system, considered the revival and its results to be a departure from formalism akin to that of the first Friends breaking away from the Anglican and Puritan churches in seventeenth century England. He believed that Quakers were now free from a dark possibly apostate century of Quietism.

Also according to Minear, widely read Friends journals like *Friends Review* and *Christian Worker* also played a role in the spread of revival. *Friends Review* published accounts of revivals back east and promoted evangelical theology in its articles. But for some *Friends Review* was not evangelical enough and in 1871 *Christian Worker* became a strong supporter and obvious promoter of revival by networking leaders and yearly meetings and keeping them apprised of revival progress.[120] These publications helped create a climate in which revival thrived.

All the revival leaders are worth getting to know, but in the interest of brevity Allen Jay, who we have already met, and Rhoda Coffin will serve as good examples of revival leaders. In her autobiography, *Rhoda M. Coffin: Reminiscences*, Coffin describes how she was born Rhoda Johnson in 1826 in rural Ohio. At a young age, she prayed out loud to God behind the barn next to a hay rick asking him to make her his child and a Methodist like her cousins, so she could pray out loud all the time. She considered this to be the moment of her conversion, but did not feel free to share the event with her parents, as they instructed their children to pray silently. Even though Rhoda's parents brought her up in the traditional Quietist Friends way, they did value and teach their children the Bible. She married Charles Coffin, a "stiff Quaker" in 1847, at twenty-one years of age, in the traditional Friends way. They settled in Richmond, Indiana, near Charles's parents. Even though Charles was dedicated to the Quietest Quaker way, from the start they determined together to hold family worship every day. As time passed Rhoda and Charles came to the conclusion that Friends were following man

119. Hamm, *Transformation of American Quakerism*, 72–74.
120. Minear, *Richmond 1887*, 18, 68.

and not God by keeping to the old Friends traditions and practices. Constraint against praying out loud continued to be a sticking point for Rhoda. She taught a children's First Day School and longed to pray audibly, but felt restricted. Over time, with the encouragement of her father-in-law, she learned to obey the Spirit and pray out loud when nudged. Charles and his father were life-long members of the American Bible Society and Rhoda helped with the work of passing out Bibles house to house while praying for conversions, as she believed that the Society had lost much of its vitality. She wrote that "after many, many years of vitalizing active service, in which [Friends] bore a strong testimony for spiritual worship and against formalism, [they] had, through this protesting against formalism in other churches, become very formal."[121]

Rhoda felt spiritually repressed and inhibited, as did Charles, and with the support of Charles's parents they began to lead Bible study groups. This opened the way for revival at Indiana Yearly Meeting Sessions in 1860 and resulted in a prayer meeting at the Coffin home that met weekly for four years afterward. Rhoda was recorded as a minister in 1867. Both Rhoda and Charles were instrumental in setting up First Day Schools, Bible classes, reading circles, tract readings, cottage prayer meetings, and the like. They were also very busy in a number of humanitarian causes including among other things prison reform and the improvement of insane asylum conditions. The Coffins traveled abroad some and were very interested in promoting foreign missions. Rhoda died in 1909 at age 83 after a prolonged illness. Allen Jay spoke at her funeral giving testimony to her life and work.[122] All agreed she ran the race well.

Just like Friends ministers had similar experiences that led them to vocal and pastoral ministry, revival leaders underwent similar experiences as well, that prepared them for their unique style of ministry. Most revival leaders recalled specific moments of conversion. This usually involved praying out loud to God asking for forgiveness and salvation, with a corresponding distinct impression that God had accepted them as his children. Many revival leaders grew up in homes where family worship and Bible reading was a priority. Also, several were influenced by Methodist friends or relatives. Rhoda Coffin had extended family who were Methodists and Charles Finney, the great Methodist revival leader, was a close friend of the Updegraff family. In fact, David Updegraff's mother, Rebecca, was one of the group that asked for a special youth meeting at Indiana Yearly Meeting in 1860

---

121. Coffin, *Rhoda M. Coffin*, 79.

122. Coffin, *Rhoda M. Coffin*, the details of Rhoda Coffin's life are summarized from this volume.

that sparked revival there. Her influence on her son was likely instrumental in his revival work. Likewise, he was a great influence on his friend Dougan Clark who he met at Haverford when they were at college in the early 1850s. Several other leaders, like Esther and Nathan Frame had switched from Methodism to Quakerism. In the Frames' case, Esther had a call to preach that Methodists refused to recognize because she was a woman, so she and her husband became Friends.[123] Most, though not Methodist to begin with, were very sympathetic to Methodist worship practices and beliefs.

Regardless, all the revival leaders expressed a longing for renewal and rejuvenation. They felt stultified by the weight of Quaker tradition and practice. They wanted to burst through "the old crust of habit."[124] Because of this, revival ministers, even those who had received stiff Quaker upbringings, were willing to embrace certain unconventional, as far as Friends were concerned, methods of bringing people to Christ. Innovations like singing hymns, altar calls, vocal prayer, and testimonies from any and all congregants, and in extreme cases partaking in the Lord's Supper and water baptism, were introduced because revival Friends wanted to wake up the Society to the life and resurrection power that was available to anyone who put their trust in Jesus. Revival Friends continued to fervently believe that the Holy Spirit was sweeping through Quakerism and that the Lord was doing a new work among Friends.

According to Punshon, the revival at Indiana Yearly Meeting in 1860 is one of the earliest instances of revival among Friends. A concern was brought forward by John Henry Douglas, Murray Shipley, Rebecca Updegraff, Charles and Rhoda Coffin, and others, to hold an evening worship meeting for young Friends at which older Friends would be required to remain silent. Accounts differ, but it seems reasonable to state that over one thousand individuals attended the meeting and over one hundred gave their testimony or prayed out loud "and for the first time in Friends recorded history for a hundred and fifty years, somebody sang a hymn" during worship.[125] Jones tells how following this meeting Sybil Jones, a charismatic and beloved minister, expressed a concern to meet with all who had attended the evening meeting. She hosted an appointed prayer meeting at the Coffin home which was attended by about one hundred fifty people. It continued on a regular basis, helping to promote the spread of revival.[126] Rhoda Coffin reported that "for six months the Church was the recipient of

---

123. Minear, *Richmond 1887*, 38–39, 60.
124. Jones, *Later Periods of Quakerism, Vol. II*, 904.
125. Punshon, *Portrait in Grey*, 199.
126. Jones, *Later Periods of Quakerism, Vol. II*, 896–97.

great grace, hundreds were brought to a full acceptance of new life. Three hundred and seventy-five were added to the Church. The revival spread all over the city."[127] This experience in Indiana Yearly Meeting was not unique. Jones notes that "wherever there was a prepared leader who gathered a Bible class about him, as Allen Jay did, or who succeeded, as a number of young Friends did, in forming a reading circle for prayer and study, there came a sudden increase of interest and life and enthusiasm."[128] Revival was springing up everywhere.

One other instance of revival that will serve to illustrate the effects it had on Friends took place in 1867 at Bear Creek, near Bangor, in southwest Iowa. Traveling ministers John S. Bond and Stacy E. Bevan, two men that William Hobson had previously ministered with, held an appointment at Bear Creek on their way to religious service in Kansas. Darius B. Cook in his book, *History of Quaker Divide* quotes from a letter written by Bevan that gives us a glimpse of the proceedings:

> We made a brief stay at Bear Creek and held one public meeting at least, where the power of the Lord was wonderfully manifested. Many hearts were reached and all broken up, which was followed by sighs and sobs and prayers, confessions and great joy for sins pardoned and burdens rolled off, and precious[sic] fellowship of the redeemed. But alas, some of the dear old Friends mistook this outbreak of the power of God for excitement and wild fire and tried to close the meeting, but we kept cool and held the strings, and closed the meeting orderly. But after meeting they administered a large dose of "elder tea," with a request to make tracks for home. But we informed them that we had minutes from our Monthly Meetings showing that we were members in good standing, and preferred to pursue our journey and accomplish our important mission. After faithfully commending the tender plants and young lambs of the fold to God and the word of his grace, we went on our way rejoicing that we were counted worthy to be used of God in the salvation of souls, even if it was blended with a little bitter "elder tea."[129]

A decade later, at the close of Bear Creek Quarterly Meeting Benjamin B. Hiatt and Isom P. Wooten opened a revival meeting during which an altar call was made. About twenty individuals walked down the aisles immediately, but others who followed felt so compelled that they climbed over seats

---

127. Coffin, *Rhoda M. Coffin*, 87.
128. Jones, *Later Periods of Quakerism, Vol. II*, 899–900.
129. Cook, *History of Quaker Divide*, 66.

to get to the front. Some who remained seated became the center of praying groups, some people were crying, others were singing. Several Friends who were not on board with revival innovations, got up and walked out. One old woman "before departing, standing in front of the 'mourners bench' declared that the Society of Friends was now dead, that this action had killed it."[130] Obviously, as revival spread, some just did not feel clear to join in.

Revival slowed or came to a stop during the Civil War (1861 to 1865). Many Friends experienced persecution and financial difficulties for refusing to fight or join the war effort. Relationships were strained in some families and between friends when individuals decided to disregard the Peace Testimony and engage in the conflict. Most meetings disowned any Friend who chose to fight in the war.

William Hobson does not mention the Civil War in his diary at all, but towards the end of Fourth Month 1860, Hobson wrote in the margin of his diary "Started to N.C." and entries on that page are picked up in different handwriting. Later at the beginning of Seventh Month 1860, entries are resumed in Hobson's handwriting, indicating that he had likely returned from a journey to "N.C.," well before the war began about ten months later in Fourth Month 1861. He also records later in his diary that he went on a journey to North Carolina in 1860.[131] Presumably he went to visit friends and relatives still living in North Carolina, including his father, but the diary yields no further information than that the trip took place. We can surmise that a journey at that time to the south was a little risky. His father, Stephen Hobson, continued to live in North Carolina during the war. He owned a foundry at which he manufactured iron for the confederacy. Quaker conscientious objectors did not have to fight in the war if they were employed by Stephen Hobson at his foundry. When the war was over he was paid off in worthless Confederate script.[132] One of Hobson's brothers, Caleb, fought and died in the War Between the States.

Shortly after the Civil War revival picked up again, and in two decades had spread as far as the Pacific Northwest. Revival brought with it several changes among Gurneyite Friends. Slowly, in fits and starts, the formal trappings of Quakerism began to fall away from Gurneyite meetings. Many older Friends, including William Hobson, retained plain speech until their last breath, but they did not expect their children to continue with "thee" and "thou." The rigid dress code was relaxed and secular names for days and

130. Cook, *History of Quaker Divide*, 165–66.

131. Hobson, "Diaries," reel 2 of 2, 4/20/1860, 7/2/1860, "Notes of William Hobson, Religious personal notes from 1872–1875," 68.

132. Goldsmith, "William Hobson and the Founding of Quakerism in the Pacific Northwest," 163–64.

months came into wider use. Also, the old ways of performing marriages and funerals slowly faded away, to be replaced by more mainstream Christian practices. Instead of sticking strictly with the old traditions Friends embraced what came to be called "Simplicity." So while they did abandon plain speech, they did not abandon truth telling, keeping their word, or honesty in business dealings. They no longer dressed peculiarly, but they did dress simply and modestly. They began to use some of the world's vernacular, but did not embrace the world's values. They continued to cling to the Peace Testimony and the Oaths Testimony and to have confidence that the Kingdom of God was realized among them through Jesus, the Present Teacher. Gurneyites continued to be active in social concerns, philanthropy, and education. Quaker community was still highly prized, as was the ministry of women. Programmed worship continued to make room for God-centered silence, commonly called communion after the manner of Friends, nestled in amongst the music, Scripture reading, public prayer, and sermon, though many of the unspoken traditions of worship were dropped. Men no longer removed their hats and stood for prayer, the sing-song recital of ministers was dropped, and the friendly handshake signaling the end of meeting became obsolete. Men and women no longer held separate meetings for business. Also, eventually meeting houses became known as Friends Churches.

Some of the other results of revival among Friends have already been hinted at. Obviously, Friends separated into different expressions of Quakersim: Gurneyite, and Conservative. And even within fired up Gurneyite Friends there was disunity. Some, led by David Updegraff in Ohio, were convinced that water baptism and communion must be practiced in order to be true to Scripture. However, the majority of Gurneyites saw no need for outward signs of invisible grace and they also supported their views with Scripture. Other points of contention had to do with the nature of justification, sanctification, and defining the "inner light." These issues made for very hot debate.

Another concern arose due to the large number of converts to orthodox Gurneyite Quakerism in the latter half of the nineteenth century. Russell reports that "between 1870 and 1890 the growth of the membership in some yearly meetings was marvelous, [but] exact figures are difficult to obtain."[133] He includes a Gurneyite yearly meeting membership table in his *History of Quakerism*. Just as an example Western and Iowa Yearly Meetings were up to 15,091 and 11,124 members respectively in 1896, an increase of 3,091 members in Western and 2,124 in Iowa over a span of twenty-three years. Even Ohio and Indiana, yearly meetings which lost about half their

---

133. Russell, *History of Quakerism*, 432.

memberships during the Gurneyite–Wilburite separation added a little over one thousand members in the same twenty-three year period.[134] This exciting influx of new converts created an increased need for discipleship and instruction in Friends ways. Most new members were saved in revival meetings and had no understanding of Friends history, culture, or practice and were especially bemused by silent worship. They also, understandably, formed attachments to the individual ministers who had helped them to meet Jesus and come to trust in his lordship. This led many Friends to consider releasing ministers to full time, paid ministry positions. Others, naturally, continued to be opposed to "hireling ministers," so yet another point of disunity arose among Gurneyite Friends.

Four years before William Hobson's death a partial answer to the concern to unify Gurneyite Friends was realized by the Richmond Conference, hosted by Indiana Yearly Meeting in 1887. Hamm notes that this push to gather all the Gurneyite yearly meetings together was led by "more moderate Gurneyites, many of [whom had been] the renewal movement reformers of the 1860s, [who] seeing good in many of the innovations, chose to remain and try to blunt the radicalism of the revivalists."[135] According to Minear, ninety-five delegates attended the conference, including Friends from twelve yearly meetings. A few unofficial representatives from Philadelphia Yearly Meeting also attended. Some of the weightier Friends who participated were Joseph Bevan Braithwaite (London), James Carey Thomas (Baltimore), John Henry Douglas (Iowa), David B. Updegraff (Ohio), Esther Frame (Indiana), and Allan Jay (Indiana). During the five-day conference many of the differences Friends had with each other were discussed with respect and consideration. Also, a declaration of faith was approved by the gathered body.

The first order of business was to address the following query: "'Is it desirable that all the Yearly Meetings of Friends in the world should adopt one declaration of Christian doctrine?'"[136] In fairly short order, Friends decided that it was desirable, as long as the declaration was not a creed, but rather a statement of faith. A committee was appointed to write a declaration of faith which would then be presented for approval or rejection to the larger group. Interestingly enough, James Carey Thomas had already asked Joseph Bevan Braithwaite and James E. Rhoads, president of Bryn Mawr College, to begin work on a declaration of faith.[137] They started writing, se-

---

134. Russell, *History of Quakerism*, 434.
135. Hamm, *Quakers in America*, 53.
136. Minear, *Richmond 1887*, 108, 112.
137. Hamm, *Transformation of American Quakerism*, 137.

questered away in Allan Jay's study, even before the committee was formed. It was written mainly by Braithwaite with Rhoads serving as secretary. Braithwaite did not come up with new material, but rather compiled previously approved Friends writings which he had brought with him for the purpose.[138] Hamm notes that the Richmond Declaration of Faith, despite coming from a committee "heavily weighted with moderate Friends" was "a monument to the impact of evangelical thought on the society." He goes on to write that its treatment of "God, the Holy Spirit, the Fall, the Bible, and conversion would have satisfied almost any evangelical denomination [and] it gave little attention to the Inner Light." However, the issues of sanctification, worship, and ministry were more in the moderate mode and the rejection of the ordinances entirely was unacceptable to more extreme revivalists like Updegraff.[139] Minear notes that the declaration was approved by the conference, but it carried no real authority, playing merely an advisory role to yearly meetings. Nonetheless, ten of the participating yearly meetings approved the Richmond Declaration of Faith, including Iowa Yearly Meeting under which Hobson's Chehalem Monthly Meeting resided. London and Ohio reported on the conference and published the Declaration in their minutes, but did not approve it. This was the closest thing to a creed Friends had produced since Barclay's *Apology*.

As Braithwaite and Rhoads worked on the declaration, Friends at the conference discussed several topics of interest. The "woman question" sprang up organically during discussion about the mission of Friends in the world. General approval and support was given to the ministry of women among Friends as being equal to that of men. Though there was concern that if the pastoral system was adopted by the Society the ministry of women would suffer, which, to a certain extent was realized. The conference did agree that consolidating foreign missions efforts would be desirable and recommended that all the yearly meetings work together in this endeavor. But the "woman question" was brought up again during this conversation, because men had almost entirely turned over mission work to women. Female Friends were making sure that their voices were heard and that their equality before the Lord was recognized.

The conference decided that a discussion on the ordinances was unnecessary, because the majority of yearly meetings were against practicing water baptism and the Lord's Supper; the matter was already settled.[140] Predictably, Updegraff was not happy about this. He had spoken out against

---

138. Minear, *Richmond 1887*, 122.
139. Hamm, *Transformation of American Quakerism*, 137–38.
140. Minear, *Richmond 1887*, 68, 116–18, 132, 138–41.

creating a creed, seemingly not because he was worried about quenching the Spirit, but because he wanted to practice the ordinances. Updegraff disagreed with the outcomes of the conference because they weren't tolerant enough for him.[141] There was much discussion, but no agreement over how worship should be conducted. Some favored completely silent worship, others full-on programming with music, prayer, Scripture reading, and a sermon with an invitation to come up to the mourner's bench. Still others believed in varying degrees of these practices, landing somewhere in between the extremes. The longest discussion took place around the question of whether or not to call and pay pastors. No consensus was reached.[142]

The Richmond Conference, for the most part, achieved the purpose of its organizers. Gurneyite Friends came out of the experience more united and with a resolve to meet together again periodically.[143] And while the Richmond Declaration was in no way meant to be authoritative or prescriptive, it did serve as a strong statement of faith that yearly meetings could unite behind. It also communicated in a clear way, with the larger Christian community and the world, just what evangelical, Gurneyite Friends believed.

As the nineteenth century drew to a close, American Quakerism looked substantially different than it had at the time of George Fox or even at the end of the eighteenth century. For one thing, Friends had significantly increased and migrated north and south, establishing meetings all across the country including meetings in California and the Pacific Northwest. Also, they became less secluded from the world as the frontier became more civilized. One thing that did not change was the Quaker commitment to social justice in several areas, such as abolition, prison reform, improved care for the mentally disabled, relief for the poor, and the promotion of peace.

A significant number of Friends coming out of the turbulent nineteenth century had completely left behind the plain life and unprogrammed worship for a new way of being Quaker. Friends had suffered through the 1827–1828 separation, with some, who came to be known as Hicksites, retaining the old traditions, choosing to emphasize continuing revelation over Scripture, and deemphasizing the Atonement. Others, who came to be known as the Orthodox, chose to embrace evangelicalism, began to seriously study the Bible, and emphasized the need to trust in and follow the crucified Christ. Sadly, the Orthodox experienced further widespread separations mid-century, as some who followed Joseph John Gurney continued to push the envelope with changes like Bible study, First Day Schools, and

141. Hamm, *Transformation of American Quakerism*, 130.
142. Minear, *Richmond 1887*, 119–29.
143. Thomas and Thomas, *History of the Friends in America*, 5th ed., 198.

prayer groups. They felt stifled by what they called the "dead hand of the past." Wilburites disapproved of embracing "creaturely activity," like Bible study and did not approve of evangelical innovations in worship. They were happy with things just as they were. Mixed up with this difference of religious expression were widespread and significant revivals all across the country in mid–to–late century, with a brief interruption during the Civil War. Where there was revival there was also significant change in worship including practices such as hymn singing, instrumental music, verbal prayer, testimonials, sermons, and altar calls. These worship services were unrecognizable from seventeenth and early eighteenth century unprogrammed Quietist Friends meetings. Some Friends who could not abide such alterations in worship joined older Wilburite meetings or started their own Conservative meetings. Even among Gurneyite yearly meetings there were differences, but the Richmond Conference and Declaration helped to bring some degree of unity to these Friends. Through the creation of a statement of faith they achieved some common ground and also gave witness to their beliefs. By the turn of the twentieth century, programmed worship led by paid pastors was the norm in evangelical yearly meetings. It is now time to end this brief look at Quaker history and focus on getting to know the main subject of this book, William Hobson, both a product and an agent of the tumultuous transformation of Quakerism in the nineteenth century.

2

Early Years in North Carolina

Train up a child in the way he should go:
and when he is old, he will not depart from it.

PROV 22:6

CHILDHOOD

William Hobson was born Second Month 4, 1820, in southern Surry County, North Carolina, a region that was later absorbed by Yadkin County. His family home was located near Deep Creek Monthly Meeting and was within sight of the Blue Ridge Mountains rising up about twenty miles to the northwest. In the 1960s Myron Dee Goldsmith visited the Hobson family "two-room log house . . . located near a branch of Forbush Creek, a tributary of Deep Creek . . . one [room] above the other connected by a stairway . . . [where] an ancient fireplace still rises at one end of each room."[1] The Hobson home was plain, but comfortable and perhaps larger than most in the neighborhood.

According to Goldsmith and Seth B. Hinshaw in *Carolina Quaker Experience 1665-1985*, Deep Creek Monthly Meeting was a well-established

---

1. Goldsmith, "William Hobson and the Founding of Quakerism in the Pacific Northwest," 75-76.

congregation, having been approved as a monthly meeting by Deep River Quarterly Meeting in 1793. Hobson grew up close to present day Yadkinville, about fifty miles west of the larger New Garden settlement.[2] According to the North Carolina Yearly Meeting tercentenary publication *Carolina Quakers: Our Heritage Our Hope*, the first members at Deep Creek were made up of "families from Ireland, Nantucket, Pennsylvania, Virginia, New Jersey, and from Cane Creek, Centre, Deep River, and other meetings in North Carolina. Many of these members were pioneers, and after getting meetings firmly established, some two-thirds of them moved farther west."[3] Both New Garden and Deep Creek were established in the northern Piedmont region of North Carolina.

Hinshaw notes that "from the standpoint of church history, the most amazing fact about early Carolina is the measure of religious freedom expressed in the Charter granted by King Charles II in 1663 . . . " This charter, mostly formulated by John Locke with the help of Lord Shaftsbury, provided for unprecedented freedom of religion. It reads, as quoted by Hinshaw, "'no person . . . shall be in any ways molested, punished, disquieted, or called into question for any differences in opinion or practice in matters of religious concernment, but every person shall have and enjoy his conscience in matters of religion throughout all the province.'"[4] Largely due to this atmosphere of religious tolerance Friends, for all practical purposes, ran the colony during the last fourth of the seventeenth century.[5] North Carolina Yearly Meeting was established in 1698 in the eastern part of the colony. Starting in 1787 yearly meeting sessions alternated between the eastern and western parts of the state, until yearly meeting was fixed at New Garden in 1813. North Carolina Yearly Meeting included meetings from what would later become South Carolina.[6] Friends retained political control over Carolina until about 1700 when the Church of England began a serious push to take charge of the colonial government, according to Francis Anscombe, in *I Have Called You Friends*.[7] Rufus Jones agreed, noting that the Church of England deliberately began a campaign of oppression against Quakers and

---

2. Goldsmith, "William Hobson and the Founding of Quakerism in the Pacific Northwest," 65; Hinshaw, *Carolina Quaker Experience*, 181. Hinshaw reports that North Carolina Yearly Meeting was held at New Garden from 1813–1882 except for 1880 when it was held in Friendsville, Tennessee.

3. Hinshaw and Hinshaw, *Carolina Quakers: Our Heritage*, 145.

4. Hinshaw, *Carolina Quaker Experience*, 1–2.

5. Hinshaw, *Carolina Quaker Experience*, 8–9.

6. White, "History of North Carolina Yearly Meeting," 6–7. Carolina was split into two colonies North and South Carolina in 1712.

7. Anscombe, *I Have Called You Friends*, 65–66.

other dissenters in Carolina, passing laws that made it difficult for Quakers to continue to participate in the government through political appointments or other positions of authority in their communities. Friends refused to take oaths of office or to swear allegiance to the king and so they were forced out of public life by the Anglican influenced colonial government. As in other Colonies, Carolina Friends were oppressed in other ways by the Church of England, such as being fined for refusing to attend Anglican church services, for gathering unlawfully in their own worship services, for refusing to baptize their babies, and for other similar transgressions.[8] These persecutions were not unlike the suffering early Friends had experienced in England at the beginning of the Friends movement, though not nearly as severe.

Later North Carolina Friends also suffered considerably during the Revolutionary War. Their position of neutrality and flat out refusal to bear arms did not sit well with either the Royalists, on one hand, or the Patriots on the other. The Colonial government considering them to be treasonous to king and country imposed steep taxes on Friends. Many Friends also endured the seizure of property and goods by the colonial government. To be sure some North Carolina Friends gave in and enlisted, but they were disowned by their home meetings for refusing to lean into the Friends Peace Testimony. Most Friends endured harassment during the Revolutionary War with silent strength. They stood firmly in their conviction that any and all violence is against the commands of Jesus and, as a result, they paid a great financial cost, endured personal humiliation, and suffered the loss of valued members of the Society who chose to fight. Some North Carolina Friends lived where the fighting was heavy and even though the majority did not take up arms, the conflict adversely affected Friends residing in combat zones. Several battles were fought in the Piedmont and Friends helped the wounded from either army equally. According to Hinshaw after the battle of Guilford Courthouse in 1781, members of New Garden Meeting buried a number of the dead, laying Royalists and Patriots to rest side by side in the meeting graveyard.[9] Joseph Crosfield writing to his father from New Garden in 1845, reported that the "Friends' meeting house [New Garden] was the British hospital [during the battle of Guilford Courthouse] & there are stains of blood upon the oak boards forming the ceiling many feet square these being the floor of the old meeting house."[10] That was a strange economy!

8. Jones, et al., *Quakers in the American Colonies*, 270–72.
9. Hinshaw, *Carolina Quaker Experience*, 49–51.
10. Crosfield, "North Carolina Yearly Meeting of 1845," 115–116.

Another issue that separated North Carolina Friends from their neighbors was the stand they took against slavery. By 1784 all American yearly meetings including North Carolina agreed that Friends must free their slaves or be disowned. Hinshaw reports that the refusal of North Carolina Yearly Meeting's members to own, buy, or sell slaves was at best met with disbelief and at worst met with outright hostility from their neighbors. They also ran into difficulties when manumitting their slaves. Some Friends had inherited their slaves and "setting them free would have meant possible recapture by slave traders who would have sold them to plantation owners in the deep South."[11] In order to make sure this didn't happen, Hinshaw says, Friends gave their freed slaves to the yearly meeting who then owned them in the eyes of the law, but in practice treated them as free people. Many slaves in the yearly meeting's care, were encouraged to travel west with migrating Quaker families, pretending to be owned by them until they reached free territory. Some in a similar manner also journeyed west with visiting Friends who were going home. These slaves were then officially manumitted once out of the South and helped by Friends to begin their own farms or trades as free people. Also, some North Carolinian slaves were conducted to freedom on the Underground Railroad. Interestingly, the Underground Railroad was run by concerned individuals and never officially endorsed by North Carolina Yearly Meeting or any other, possibly because conductors on the Underground Railroad might be required to lie or engage in violence while moving their "cargo" north.[12]

Friends were looked on with suspicion and contempt by their slave holding neighbors, who did not understand the Quaker conviction against slavery and were afraid of losing their way of life. These difficulties were intensified leading up to and during the Civil War and were complicated by a strict official adherence to the Peace Testimony, both at the yearly meeting level and among Friends leadership in local meetings throughout North Carolina. In most cases any Friend who joined the army, on either side, was summarily disowned by their home meeting, just like during the Revolutionary War. Friends who were clearly against slavery and who also refused to join their Confederate neighbors in violence against Union troops, were severely persecuted as Unionist sympathizers. Many families were financially, emotionally, and mentally devastated in a kind of horrible repeat of the Revolutionary War tribulation. Again, some gave in to the pressure and chose to fight like William Hobson's brother Caleb. Others supported the Confederacy, under duress, in a non-violent way with money or goods, as

---

11. Hinshaw, *Carolina Quaker Experience*, 131.
12. Hinshaw, *Carolina Quaker Experience*, 132–35.

did Hobson's father. William, his wife Sarah, and their children were not affected directly by abolitionist influences or the Civil War. They never owned slaves and they had long since removed to Iowa, a free territory, by the beginning of the fighting.

While at New Garden Boarding School Hobson signed a petition protesting the use of goods manufactured through slave labor, giving us the only documented indication of his personal views on slavery. Goldsmith reports that William and "a group of other students apparently felt that the school was inconsistent in its testimony against slavery, for in the term of school beginning Eleventh Month, 26th, 1838, they addressed a petition to the committee managing New Garden Boarding School. In the petition, they castigated slavery in strong terms and called for the school to cease using products, such as sugar, which were produced by the labor of slaves."[13] Hobson was not formally an abolitionist, but he clearly believed that slavery was wrong, consistent with Quaker convictions. He gave monetary aid to "Blacks" or "freedmen" at least five times as recorded in his diary.[14] It seems to have been a pattern with him to donate money at quarterly meeting with the intention of helping African Americans who were in need. He also mentions taking part in an "African Meeting" one time during quarterly meeting. This was likely a committee formed to help African Americans in various ways. The best indication of his acceptance of African Americans as fellow human beings who deserved to be treated with dignity and respect, is revealed in a diary entry in the spring of 1865 when a preacher who had formerly been a slave gave a sermon at Honey Creek. Hobson tells how there was a "meeting in afternoon at Honey Creek a Colored man a Baptist preach-er had an appointed meeting. He preached well was near 60 years old had been a slave until about 16 [months] ago."[15] The stain of slavery upon the south was one of the many reasons large numbers of southern Friends relocated to the north and west in the decades leading up to the Civil War and was very likely one of the reasons the Hobsons left North Carolina in 1847.

While Quaker settlements in North Carolina were fairly well established at the beginning of the nineteenth century, life was still pretty rustic. Goldsmith points out that families who settled near Deep Creek, in southern Surry County, were isolated from their neighbors by the lay of the land or more accurately the flow of a river. The Yadkin River rushed east along the northern border of the region and then took a sharp turn to the south,

---

13. Goldsmith, "William Hobson and the Founding of Quakerism in the Pacific Northwest," 104–05.

14. Hobson, "Diaries," reel 2 of 2, 2/8/1864, 2/31/1864, 2/5/1865, reel 1 of 2, 10/4/1872, undated entry just after 7/25/1875.

15. Hobson, "Diaries," reel 2 of 2, 2/8/1864, 2/31/1864, 2/26/1864, 6/4/1865.

effectively cutting Deep Creek Monthly Meeting off from the larger Friends settlement at New Garden to the east and from some smaller settlements, not necessarily Quakers, to the north. This river was not easy to cross, especially after heavy rain. To the south was mainly unsettled wilderness or what Goldsmith describes as "brushy mountains." Goldsmith goes on to report that in the early nineteenth century North Carolina earned the unflattering nickname the "Rip Van Winkle State." This was a reference to Washington Irving's *Rip Van Winkle*, a short story first published in 1819 about a man who took a twenty-year nap and slept through the American Revolution. North Carolina economy did lag significantly behind the rest of the nation. Crops were poor, manufactured goods were inferior, and more importantly, it was difficult to get the meagre goods that were produced to market. Even though the moderate climate was good for growing both fruit and grain, most farmers barely eked out an existence on subsistence farms because the soil had been depleted after decades of farming in the area. In 1820, William Hobson's birth year, 98 percent of the population was marked rural on the United States census. The census also indicated that North Carolina per capita income was the lowest of any state in America. Surry County and specifically the remote settlements in the Yadkin Valley were especially poor and undeveloped with terrible roads which made traveling and the distribution of goods extremely difficult. However, Goldsmith adds that settlers had other options open to them besides farming and small rural industries sprang up here and there, including a small industrial center established by William Hobson's dad.[16]

According to Earl H. Davis and Marie Davis Wiles in their genealogical compilation *Hobson: Descendants of George and Elizabeth Hobson*, William Hobson's great-great-great grandparents George and Elizabeth (Lindley) Hobson immigrated to America from Great Britain arriving in Pennsylvania in 1697. Most likely they were not Quakers, as the marriage records concerning their son, George Jr. and Hannah Kinnison reveal. We know Hannah was a Quaker because she was disowned by her monthly meeting for marrying-out. However, she was welcomed back into membership after writing a letter of repentance. George and Hannah eventually moved to Orange County, North Carolina, settling near Cane Creek Monthly Meeting. Hannah was received into membership there by certificate from Goshen Monthly Meeting, Chester County, Pennsylvania.[17] It is unclear as to whether or not George Jr. became a Quaker.

---

16. Goldsmith, "William Hobson and the Founding of Quakerism in the Pacific Northwest," 71-74.

17. Davis and Wiles, *Hobson*, 6-7, 11-16, 168-69.

Stephen Hobson Sr., one of the sons of George Jr. and Hannah, and the great-grandfather of William Hobson, was born in 1742 in Frederick County, Virginia. He was about two years old when his parents moved to the Cane Creek area in North Carolina. His first wife Anne was the mother of Stephen Jr., William's grandfather. Stephen Sr. outlived three wives and died in 1825 when his great-grandson William was five years old. Stephen and Anne were Quakers.

William's grandfather Stephen Jr. was born to Stephen Sr. and Anne (Barnes) Hobson in 1763. Stephen Jr. married Rachel Vestal in 1785 in Orange County, North Carolina, when he was twenty-two and she was twenty-seven.[18] Goldsmith notes that in 1787 Stephen Jr. and Rachel were approved for certificates of removal from Cane Creek to Deep River and that "they [Stephen Jr. and Rachel] were found as active and respected members of Deep Creek Monthly Meeting soon after it was set up on Fourth Month, 6th, 1793."[19] So, we see that Stephen Jr. and Rachel were raised as Quakers. They continued to embrace the Quaker faith all their adult lives.

According to Goldsmith, Stephen Jr. and Rachel had eight children. The son they named Stephen later became William's father. When Stephen Jr. died young, at only forty years of age in 1803 he left his son Stephen III, a large inheritance including land and money.[20] This gave Stephen III a leg up financially in poor, rural Surry County. He worked hard to develop his inheritance. The land was good for farming and orchards, but he also branched out into light industry, including iron mines, a forge, and a grist mill.

Stephen III and Mary (Bond) Hobson, William's parents, were born not quite a month apart in the winter of 1800.[21] They grew up near Deep Creek Monthly Meeting in Quaker families. They cleared both the men's and the women's meeting marriage committees and were married the traditional Friends way in meeting at Deep Creek in 1817. Goldsmith asserts that both the Hobson and Bond families were active in Deep Creek Monthly Meeting since the beginning of that congregation in 1793. Mary was Stephen III's first wife of four and they had six children together, the first of whom was William. His brother David was born in 1822, sister Anna in 1824, brother Jesse in 1826, brother Stephen in 1828, and brother Caleb in 1831.[22] Hobson

18. Davis and Wiles, *Hobson*, 168–69.

19. Goldsmith, "William Hobson and the Founding of Quakerism in the Pacific Northwest," 66.

20. Goldsmith, "William Hobson and the Founding of Quakerism in the Pacific Northwest," 66–67.

21. Davis and Wiles, *Hobson*, 154, 290–91.

22. Goldsmith, "William Hobson and the Founding of Quakerism in the Pacific Northwest," 68, 76 (footnote 2).

reports that "Mother deceased when I was about 10 years old, leaving 6 children behind her the youngest about 8 months old,"[23] though if Caleb was born in 1831 William must have been eleven years old when Mary died.

Goldsmith searched North Carolina Yearly Meeting records and William Wade Hinshaw's famous *Encyclopedia of American Quaker Genealogy* for more information on Mary Bond's family. He was able to find Quaker records of the family as far back as William's great-grandparents and no further. Goldsmith notes that Edward Bond, William's great-grandfather on the maternal side was accepted into membership at New Garden Monthly Meeting by request Fourth Month 28, 1759. He married Ann Mills in 1764 and they became founding members of Deep River Monthly Meeting when it began in 1778. Their sixth son of nine, John, who would later become Mary's father and William's grandfather was born in 1769. He married Mary Huff in 1791 and their daughter, also named Mary, became William's mother. So, we see that William Hobson's Quaker heritage went back at least two generations and probably three on both sides of the family.

Goldsmith goes on to add that Hobson's grandfather John Bond served Deep Creek as an overseer, elder, and minister during different seasons of his life. He traveled in the ministry, with the approval of Deep Creek, in North Carolina, Ohio, Indiana, Virginia, and Tennessee and he continued to minister actively even in his old age. Apparently, he was a well-loved minister in good standing, and he must have had a wholesome influence on his grandson William, who mentions in his diary that he took to heart his grandfather's preaching on the wisdom that leads to peace. William also praised his grandfather for his teaching and example which was a blessing to him.[24] In many ways William followed in his grandfather John Bond's footsteps.

Beginning First Month 28, 1868, shortly before his forty-eighth birthday, Hobson wrote a brief account of his early days growing up in the family home near Deep Creek Monthly Meeting. This is where the bulk of information about his early life comes from. He wrote forty-six short notebook pages describing his family life, spiritual life, and schooling because he felt it was "a duty which [he] owe[d] to my children and others for the Truths sake to write some account of my life and the gracious dealings of the Lord to my soul; from early childhood." He reports that both his parents were "well concerned members of the Society of Friends Who took much care to

---

23. Hobson, "Diaries," reel 2 of 2, notebook beginning 1/21/1868, 4 (Hobson's numbering).

24. Goldsmith, "William Hobson and the Founding of Quakerism in the Pacific Northwest," 68–70.

train their children 'in the way they should go.'"[25] Goldsmith notes that for children raised in the Hobson home "a steady moral walk was the objective, in which by heeding the Inward Guide, one was kept in the narrow way that leads to life."[26] Hobson remembers his mother, Mary, as "a remarkably plain woman in her attire"[27] and both his parents were concerned not to make, recommend, or sell clothing that was not plain. Likely they also applied plain living standards to other areas of their family life. Much later William expressed gratefulness for his mother's dedication to plain dress in his diary:

> yesterday and to day [I] have much execised [sic] praying mourning for our children for our children [sic] and some of our neighbors children who are friends. Because so going after the fashions. Oh, how thankful I am that my mother nipped the first blossom of pride in me and laid the gospel axe to that root in me which brought it forth. How different is it now with many mothers who even start [illegible crossed out] [work] in the fashions to a considerable extent. And being thus started they are sure to go on or else have a much harder conflict to overcome.[28]

It was a sad day when Mary died at age thirty-one leaving six children for William's father, Stephen, to raise on his own.

William recalls his mother as a contented woman who led a righteous life and who, he was certain, went straight to heaven when she died. She often read to her children from the New Testament and taught them the alphabet using the same as a textbook. According to William, Mary was an energetic housewife and had nimble hands and fingers. Young William grew up believing it was "wrong for anyone to get mad; for I never saw my mother in an ill humor, at any time. She was tender and merciful towards her children."[29] However, this did not make her soft or lax with discipline. Hobson said of his mother

> when we did wrong she took care to instruct us, And to tell us of the suffering that would be ours for wrong doing, after telling

---

25. Hobson, "Diaries," reel 2 of 2, notebook beginning 1/21/1868, 1 (Hobson's numbering).

26. Goldsmith, "William Hobson and the Founding of Quakerism in the Pacific Northwest," 94.

27. Hobson, "Diaries," reel 2 of 2, notebook beginning 1/21/1868, 4 (Hobson's numbering).

28. Hobson, "Diaries," reel 1 of 2, 2/22/1873.

29. Hobson, "Diaries," reel 2 of 2, notebook beginning 1/21/1868, 2 (Hobson's numbering).

us we were in danger by doing a little wrong of being led on and on into more and perhaps bring much misery upon ourselves in this life; and that being at worst, almost as nothing to what the portion of the wicked is in next world. After saying something of this sort, if father was not present, She frequently reminded us of our faults for a good while by saying she thought best to tell our father of it when he came home. Whom she taught us was head of the family and must be obeyed, and who would know well how much punishment to give us, that we might be warned and mend our ways and [shun] the punishment which is the portion of the wicked in the next world."[30]

Goldsmith adds a detail about Mary that William does not. Mary served as an overseer at Deep Creek Monthly Meeting.[31] This shows that she was well respected by her peers as a leader and an exemplary member of Deep Creek. As an overseer, she was charged with helping to maintain the moral and spiritual purity of the community in concert with the elders.

William credits his dad with helping him to remain strong in the Lord: "I am very thankful still for the guardian care of my father which was watchfully exercised toward me for my good, whilst I was young. For as much as I desired to do right; And as much as I knew of the joy of the christians [sic] path; and of being led by the voice of the heavenly Shepperd [sic]. I can Testify that his care toward me was an additional help to keep me in the way I should go for many years."[32] After Mary's death Stephen was understandably grief stricken and very lonely, though his faith never wavered, as William tells it. Much of the care of the younger children fell to William after his mother's passing. Stephen remarried when William was twelve years old to a young woman named Mary Vestal, known to be an exemplary Friend who William "loved and did highly esteem for her virtues."[33] However, she died about a year later leaving behind an infant son. William continued to help care for his six siblings, several of whom were colicky, and to help run the household.[34] As the eldest, this was expected of him.

---

30. Hobson, "Diaries," reel 2 of 2, notebook beginning 1/21, 1868, 2–3 (Hobson's numbering).

31. Goldsmith, "William Hobson and the Founding of Quakerism in the Pacific Northwest," 79.

32. Hobson, "Diaries," reel 2 of 2, notebook beginning 1/21/1868, 17–18 (Hobson's numbering).

33. Davis and Wiles, *Hobson*, 290.

34. Hobson, "Diaries," reel 2 of 2, notebook beginning 1/21/1868, 18–19 (Hobson's numbering).

Three years later his father married again, to a woman named Ariadne Moore,³⁵ and some of the burden of caring for his siblings was lifted from William, though he doesn't seem to have thought it much of a burden. William noted that his

> mothers [sic] children, (except the youngest, then a little boy; and who showed some more wrong traits of Character than the rest ever did) though not a very bad boy at that time) I think it might be said were mainly walking with God. To me that was one of the happiest times that I have ever passed through. We rose early. Wasted no time Was temperate in all things. Brother David was a strength to me many ways but especially by his great abstemiousness he would not litter his teeth with an apple between meals would say three times a day was often enough to eat and would eat apples &c as a part at meal time.³⁶

This is one of the first indications that William had a sweet tooth. Apparently, he liked to eat apples between meals as a treat, perhaps like we might eat a candy bar today.

The children spent two or three hours a day reading Friends books and the Bible, for they desired to be a good example of God's light in them. They also helped to keep their home and farm running smoothly. William as the older brother was the director of all their endeavors while their father was away on meeting business from time to time, but he felt like all the siblings were united in a sense of industriousness and duty. They kept up the garden, household, and farm in their Father's absence and continued to be helpful when he was home. William was a fledgling but able leader and he believed he did well by his younger siblings, as well as his father. His only regret as an adult was that the youngest of his mother Mary's children, Caleb, did not choose to follow Quaker ways. William says of his brother Caleb, that

> to our great sorrow [he] too little re-garded [sic] our love toward him and in a large measure trod under foot his own convictions of right as opened to his understanding by Christs [sic] teaching by his Spirit to the soul. He went more and more out into the broad road that leads to destruction; until he fully left Friends—Joined himself to the world, was lost in War in the Rebel army on the battlefield. This is a sorrowful picture to reflect upon; and looks like the fulfillment of that Scripture "He that being often reproved Hardeneth his neck shall suddenly be destroyed and

35. Davis and Wiles, *Hobson*, 290.
36. Hobson, "Diaries," reel 2 of 2, notebook beginning 1/21/1868, 31–32 (Hobson's numbering).

> that without remedy. I have no doubt but that for a long time
> he thought he would turn from the evil of his way and do better
> But how dangerous to put off the time; and go on sacrificing
> principle to be like other folks.[37]

William took the time to write in his diary transcripts of several letters sent to him by Caleb seeking to restore relationship with the older brother that he had looked up to as a child. Caleb reminded William of how they walked to school together happily as children and mourned the loss of their mother when he was an infant. He also mentioned the desire to return to God and so be able to see his mother in heaven.[38]

William mentioned that he wrote several letters to his brother Caleb, wondering if they were all received. A facsimile of the only one known to have been preserved resides in the George Fox University Archives. The letter is dated on William's thirty-seventh birthday, Second Month 4, 1857. He wrote in response to a request from Caleb in which Caleb asked William to buy some land for him with an eighty-acre military land warrant. Caleb had enclosed a bond given to him by the government as compensation for military service. William replied that he could not in good conscience buy the land being completely and utterly opposed to violence and war of any kind and the profit thereof. He returned the bond and wrote to his brother that "it becomes the duty of Christians to bear a faithful testimony against it [war]." He then goes on to implore Caleb to "sell all to obtain the one pearl of great price," appeals to Caleb and his wife to turn to Jesus, fondly remembers walking hand in hand with Caleb to school when they were kids, and tells him that he has the same earnest desire for Caleb's spiritual welfare as their mother did when she was alive.[39] It would seem that the two brothers reconciled as much as was possible over time and distance, but a great deal of sadness remained between them. William grieved over his brother's lack of faith and falling away from Friends and Caleb grieved their broken relationship.[40] William must have experienced significant heartache when Caleb was killed in battle.

William remembered his father as an industrious man, early to rise and involved in many different kinds of work including farming, milling,

---

37. Hobson, "Diaries," reel 2 of 2, notebook beginning 1/21/1868, 33–34 (Hobson's numbering).

38. Hobson, "Diaries," reel 2 of 2, notebook beginning 1/21/1868, 34–39 (Hobson's numbering).

39. William Hobson to Caleb Hobson, February 4, 1857.

40. Hobson, "Diaries," reel 2 of 2, notebook beginning 1/21/1868, 35–39 (Hobson's numbering).

retail, mining, and iron manufacturing. He was handy around the house and often made clothes or shoes at night.[41] In a short autobiographical document titled "Memories of Samuel Hobson," William's son, Samuel, confirms that his grandfather Stephen Hobson owned a large tract of land in North Carolina rich in coal and that he became very wealthy from the iron mines, factories, blacksmith shop, and mills that he developed, along with extensive farming and merchandising enterprises. Samuel claims that at one time Stephen employed 400 men.[42] This is likely an exaggeration, but Stephen probably did provide employment for many in the Deep Creek area.

Goldsmith points out that Stephen served Deep Creek as an elder and at various times attended quarterly and yearly meetings as a representative, indicating that he was well respected among his peers. He was often assigned work in the realm of education, among other duties. He also spent a fair amount of time away on meeting business.[43] Clearly, Stephen shared the general concern among North Carolina Quakers that quality, Friends influenced educational opportunities needed to be developed throughout the yearly meeting, since the state of education in North Carolina was shockingly low. William had a great deal of respect for his father. He followed in his father's footsteps, as far as a concern for education went, and was a life-long supporter of educational opportunities in each yearly meeting of which he was a part.

Hinshaw notes that at the beginning of the nineteenth century North Carolina Friends in general were very concerned with the universal lack of educational opportunities in the yearly meeting, as well as the reality that Quaker children were attending schools run by non–Friends, since there were so few Friends schools in operation. North Carolina Quakers were quite troubled that yearly meeting children were not receiving a "guarded" education. In fact, they believed quite the opposite was occurring as their children were exposed to all kinds of worldly evil in non–Friends schools, as well as being steeped in a culture in which slavery was accepted as normal. A "guarded" education in Friends schools was also highly sought after as a way to preserve Quaker values, train leaders for work within the yearly meeting, and make converts. Initially, North Carolina Yearly Meeting addressed this concern for proper Friends education with a proposal that each monthly meeting be given a certain number of Friends books, endorsed by the Society. These were to be added to libraries that had already been

41. Hobson, "Diaries," reel 2 of 2, notebook beginning 1/21/1868, 19–20 (Hobson's numbering).

42. Hobson, "Memories," 1.

43. Goldsmith, "William Hobson and the Founding of Quakerism in the Pacific Northwest," 81–82.

established towards the end of the last century by donations from monthly meeting members, though in some cases the new books may have been the beginning of entirely new libraries. Later, North Carolina Yearly Meeting established a Friends boarding school at New Garden with the intention of training teachers and leaders that could carry Friends ways into the next generation and keep North Carolina Yearly Meeting running.[44] Eventually, this goal was accomplished though at the time no one anticipated the unprecedented number of Quaker families that would migrate west.

Stephen Hobson was well educated and while he shared the general concern for educational improvement in North Carolina Yearly Meeting, he also more specifically had a concern for the education of his young children. When William was a small boy Stephen was appointed by the yearly meeting to act as curator of the Deep Creek Monthly Meeting library. The Deep Creek library was kept in the Hobson home and young William had free access to all the volumes, as did his siblings.[45] He and his brothers and sister never lacked for something wholesome to read. The Hobson children also attended school from time to time and as young adults benefitted from educational experiences at New Garden Boarding School.

We learn from William that when their children were young, Stephen and Mary Hobson took advantage of the educational opportunities that were available in their neighborhood at the time, some of which were not "guarded." However, they provided the best education they could in rural Surry County, North Carolina. Hobson writes that the first school he attended

> had a pious woman friend for teacher, [and] to–gether with the example and teaching of my grand–Parents; and other friends I regard as a great favor and blessing to me; being as a hedge about me to preserve me from evil, and to direct me to the voice of the Lord for further instruction and guidance I hope I will ever feel a weight of responsibility resting on me for the above training; and will not depart when I become old. I was about 7 years old when I first went to School and learned to read. and seemed for a while behind many others of my age in getting my lessons well: But my father and mother both took much time to assist us in getting our lessons well we bringing our books home at nights as regularly as our dinner basket. We were charged to mind our own lessons well at School. To obey the Teacher and

---

44. Hinshaw, *Carolina Quaker Experience*, 75–76.

45. Goldsmith, "William Hobson and the Founding of Quakerism in the Pacific Northwest," 80.

do right before all; endeavoring to set an example of Christian conduct before others.[46]

Thankfully, he had the support of his parents and grandparents in his early school days and the benefit of a "guarded" first school.

Later he attended a non-Quaker school, which was a trial, but also an opportunity to experience direction from God at a young age. It was while attending this school, around age eight or nine, that he first came to the realization that God was calling him to be a minister when he was grown, though he reported that he could

> hardly say when the the [sic] first impressions were made upon my mind that if I were faithful to my Maker he would some time require it of me to speak unto the people as a preacher: But believe I must have been very sensibly under that impression whilst attending the second School I well remember it was frequently my secret prayer that if the Lord required of me to be an example and a Teacher of his people. That he would give me wisdom to know his his holy ways and enable me to walk therein before the people. And qualify me with such know[l]edge & speech as the adversaries of Truth could not be able to gain say or resist which And I think I have much cause to thank the Lord for the measure of wisdom granted to me in heavenly mysteries; full as much and even more than I had expected; unless I had been more faithful in serving him. Whilst going to the second School which I think was a four months school and was not taught by a friend I fell under much obligation to my heavenly Father to live a righteous life before my schoolmates. I felt at this time the force of Christs [sic] words "Ye are the Salt of the earth." "Ye are the light of the world." "Let your light shine before men &c" Also "Blessed are ye when men shall revile you and persecute you &c." I was much established in the Truth and was willing to suffer persecution for righteousness sake. If I could only live so as to be accounted worthy by my Father in heaven. When the new school children sung lies in a play, I would not be in the ring for I never wilfully [sic] told a lie not even in fun. I thought "all liars were to have their part in the lake that burns with fire and brimstone" I cried when the Teacher taught the large scholars the worlds [sic] compliments. I believe we should be willing to suffer death rather than do wrong. They called me Stiff Quaker; Yet nearly every one seemed to love me. And one time I vividly recollect standing with others before the fire at

46. Hobson, "Diaries," reel 2 of 2, notebook beginning 1/21/1868, 4–5 (Hobson's numbering).

the Schoolhouse bearing reproach for Christs [sic] sake. And some said let Wm Hobson alone. He will be a preacher sometime. And it struck me with great fearfulness lest they would find it out on me for I knew it was my calling and many of my playmates, who who [sic] were not friends would use the plain language to me.[47]

So, it's clear that Hobson felt called to be a preacher at a tender age and that he believed he was asked by God to partner with him in order to set a good example to his classmates of a life dedicated to the Lord.

William was a keen reader and he and his siblings spent about three hours a day in study. He took full advantage of the library of Friends books maintained by his father in their home. William enjoyed reading "the Scriptures much; and many of Friends Books, as Fox's Journal Sewels [sic] History and many others. Barclay's Chatechism [sic] so suited my mind that I read it many times."[48] He also, as a young boy, studied a rather morbid little book popular in Friends circles at the time, called *Examples of Youthful Piety*, by Thomas Evans. The stated purpose of the author was to exhibit to "young persons the happy effects and peaceful termination of a religious life, in those of their own age."[49] This was a fancy way of saying that children often die, and they need to be prepared to meet their maker. The book goes on to tell the stories of ninety-nine good little children who were followers of Jesus and therefore lived useful though short lives for the Kingdom, after which they were welcomed into heaven (you might be the one lost sheep the Lord is looking for, see Matt 18:10–14). It is true, that in the early part of the nineteenth century infants and young children died at a much higher rate than today,[50] so this kind of child evangelism was perhaps not so melancholy as it seems to modern sensibilities. The book did contain an evangelistic appeal to accept Jesus as Lord and Savior at the back, after the short biographies. This little book had a significant impact on young William. He tells that shortly after his mother's death he read this "account of children who had passed away; Some of whom were younger than myself, who had been so good that they were not afraid to die: but had rather die if the Lord willed it and go to heaven; than stay longer in this world where temptations beset us. The account of their sinless condition, (for they felt

---

47. Hobson, "Diaries," reel 2 of 2, notebook beginning 1/21/1868, 6–9 (Hobson's numbering).

48. Hobson, "Diaries," reel 2 of 2, notebook beginning 1/21/1868, 22 (Hobson's numbering).

49. Evans, *Examples of Youthful Piety*, 3.

50. Roser, et al., "Child and Infant Mortality."

that their sins were all forgiven) served as a stimulus to greater vigilance in me."[51] Perhaps, reading it so soon after his mother's death increased its influence on young William.

He goes on, in his diary, to describe what sounds very much like a conversion experience similar to many told by Revival Friends like Rhoda Coffin and Allen Jay. He notes that there were stretches of days when he was not conscious of doing anything wrong, but that he lived

> in the sweetness of innocency [sic] . . . and could well appreciate the truth of the that Scripture which My grandfather (John Bond) preached so often, "That Wisdoms ways were ways of pleasant rest all her paths are paths of peace My meat & drink seemed to be to do the will of my Father who is in heaven. And I well knew the kingdom of heaven to be within; and that it was righteousness, and peace; and joy in the Holy Ghost. I hoped then to continue in this condition. And had the assurance if I did right with all my strength continually I should be kept in the narrow way that leads to life. My soul was full of thanks and praise unto my savior who had taken away my sins.[52]

Also, similar to Coffin, Jay, and other Friends who became leaders in the evangelical renewal and revival movements, young William sought out lonely places where he could "vocally pour out the feelings of [his] heart where none could hear [him]."[53] Remember, this was at a time when Friends generally did not pray out loud, except possibly in meeting and then infrequently. William continued to seek God and his ways and was tempted by Satan to withdraw from society, as a means of remaining in perfect communion with God. But he soon recognized that God required the opposite of him. He described reaching this understanding as follows:

> Oh what joy sprang in my soul for the brightness of that Light which then I saw in which a life of seclusion appeared very far from my Makers [sic] will concerning me. How then could I serve the Lord in this world as a preacher & Teacher of his people. And such such [sic] Scriptures as these now came before my view 'I pray not that thou shouldst take them out of the world but that thou shouldst keep them from the evil.' 'Ye are the Salt

---

51. Hobson, "Diaries," reel 2 of 2, notebook beginning 1/21/1868, 9–10 (Hobson's numbering).

52. Hobson, "Diaries," reel 2 of 2, notebook beginning 1/21/1868, 10–11 (Hobson's numbering).

53. Hobson, "Diaries," reel 2 of 2, notebook beginning 1/21/1868, 9–11 (Hobson's numbering).

of the earth' Ye are the light of the world' 'Let your light shine before men that they may see your good works; &c' Is a candle lighted to be put under a bushel or under a bed and not on a candlestick that it may give light unto all that are in the house. I was now ready to say Get thee behind me Satan I want none of thy Reasoning however fair for thou art a deceiver neither do I wish to have any will of my own, how long I shall stay among men, or what I shall do. But my life and joy is in Obedience to 'every word which proceedeth out of thy mouth.' O Lord my God, I now saw nothing in my way, but what I might go straight to heaven if it were the Lords [sic] will to take me and It looked so pleasant that way, that It was a joyous view. Nevertheless I continued to pray not my will but thine be done. Then the Lord made me understand that if I would be obedient to him he designed to continue my life amongst men until he should qualify me and use me as an instrument to do some considerable good in the world before his purpose in Creating me were fulfilled in this lower world This impression still lives with me; and if I do not fill the purpose I believe the fault will be found in me, by lack of being as constant with my whole soul and might devoted to Him and his cause in his own appointed way as he should from time to time manifest it to me. I now felt very strongly that I ought to walk as one whom the Lord had chosen out of the world; and therefore not of the world and ought not to sin any more but pray always that the Lords [sic] will be done in earth as it is in heaven. And ever since have felt that a material part of my duty consists in living so as to set an example of a righteous life before men.[54]

Undoubtedly, young William enjoyed an intimate bond with God as indicated by his devotion to prayer and Scripture reading. The godly teaching and example of his family and Deep Creek Friends also helped to deepen his relationship with God. During his first two decades the spiritual climate in the Hobson home, at Deep Creek, and in North Carolina Yearly Meeting in general, leaned towards orthodoxy and evangelicalism which probably influenced him significantly, even as a young child. It's also interesting to note that he followed the typical Quaker ministerial pattern in receiving an invitation from God to preach and live an exemplary Christian life at an early age. He heard the call young, he was tempted to turn away from it, he persevered through sin and adversity, and eventually embraced his vocation without reservation.

54. Hobson, "Diaries," reel 2 of 2, notebook beginning 1/21/1868, 12–14 (Hobson's numbering).

William went on to write that he continued to struggle to walk the straight and narrow path most days sinning a little and repenting except for one time when he forgot God for three days, the darkest three days of his life, and felt compelled to undergo a long and deep season of repentance. Conversely, one time when he was seriously ill and experiencing severe pain, he felt so perfectly at peace in the Lord that he believed he did not sin at all for four days and nights. As he put it, it "seemed to be a foretaste of heaven."[55] So, we see that several influences were at play in William's spiritual growth and general education which in those days were not so separated out as they are now. The example of his parents as well-concerned Friends, Bible reading, the perusal of Friends authors such as Fox, Barclay, and Sewel, author of *The History of the Rise, Increase, and Progress of the Christian People Called Quakers*, the primary schools he attended, and the spiritual climate of North Carolina Yearly Meeting, all contributed towards the spiritual growth and maturity of young William. And we mustn't forget the influence of *Youthful Piety*. This book probably ushered William into a more committed relationship with Jesus, as well as inspiring him to embark on the long road of sanctification.

YOUTH AND YOUNG ADULTHOOD

As hinted at previously William did receive some limited secondary education. In Eleventh Month 1837, his father paid for him to attend New Garden Boarding School (NGBS) a Friends school set up and run by North Carolina Yearly Meeting some fifty miles to the east of Deep Creek. The NGBS register shows that his brother David and sister Anna attended at the same time, with Stephen also footing the bill for them. William, David, and Jesse Hobson, another brother, appear in the register on Eleventh Month 2, 1838, and again on Eleventh Month 26, 1838, and William's name appears once more in Eleventh Month 1840.[56] The school records match William's recollections. He noted in his diary that he attended NGBS for a couple three-month terms starting when he was seventeen and a longer nine-month term when he was twenty-one, working for his father and teaching school in the interval. William paid for the 1840–1841 term, as he puts it, "on his own footing" and also paid for his sister Anna to attend for three months. Presumably, by age twenty-one William was on his own financially. He chose to attend NGBS as a young adult partly with the intention to be

---

55. Hobson, "Diaries," reel 2 of 2, notebook beginning 1/21/1868, 16–17 (Hobson's numbering).

56. "New Garden Boarding School Register: 1837–February 1842," 3, 22, 20, 38.

a good influence on the students and partly to be influenced by them. He wanted to participate in a genuine and wholesome Christian community. He was not disappointed in his expectations, and he believed in the NGBS experience so much he was willing to pay for his sister to attend, as well.[57]

NGBS was the forerunner of Guilford College. Dorothy Lloyd Gilbert, in her book *Guilford: A Quaker College*, notes that at NGBS the rules were extremely strict, though kindly enforced. She also points out that students could appeal to the administration for rule changes, which set NGBS apart from most schools at the time. While NGBS was technically coeducational, boys and girls were kept separate both by the regulations and by the construction of the building. Each sex was provided with separate sleeping quarters above separate classrooms, with guest rooms between the two dormitories. The office, sitting room, bookroom, and superintendents' living quarters were placed between the girls' and boys' classrooms on the first floor and even the dining hall was divided with a partition. This made it extremely difficult to communicate with any member of the opposite sex who was not a sibling or cousin.

According to Gilbert, in 1841 the decision was made to admit non-Friends students who were willing to abide by the rules and follow Friends ways. Non-Friends students were not required to convert, though likely it was hoped they would eventually. Gilbert, like Hinshaw, makes it clear that one of the main purposes of NGBS was to train up godly Quaker teachers who could spread out around the yearly meeting and open "guarded" schools all around the region. The aim was to improve the general state of education in North Carolina Yearly Meeting, train teachers and Friends leaders, and promote spiritual growth in the young people.[58] Over time this goal was fairly well accomplished.

Nathan Hunt and Joseph John Gurney were two important figures in the early development of NGBS and they had a significant impact on William Hobson's life. From the very beginning the influence of Nathan Hunt on NGBS was invaluable as an ardent promoter and supporter. After the boarding school opened, he served as a teacher and later in life as the campus grandpa. Hunt was definitely orthodox in his theology and was considered a prophet by North Carolina Friends. He also came down firmly on the Gurneyite side during the Wilburite controversy. Hunt contributed to the school financially as well as serving as an instructor and mentor to the young students.

---

57. Hobson, "Diaries," reel 2 of 2, notebook beginning 1/21/1868, 41 (Hobson's numbering).

58. Gilbert, *Guilford a Quaker College,* 13–16, 37–44, 52–63.

Likewise, according to Guilford College Quaker Librarian and Archivist, Gwen Gosney Erickson, Joseph John Gurney had a marked influence at NGBS,[59] though he was around for significantly less time than Hunt. In his book, *Memoirs of Joseph John Gurney*, Joseph Bevan Braithwaite notes that in late Eleventh Month 1837, "having returned to New Garden, North Carolina, he [Gurney] spent a few days at the boarding school for Friends' children at that place; with the view of encouraging the pursuit of scriptural knowledge upon the principles which had been so beneficially acted on at Ackworth."[60] William Hobson was in his first term at NGBS during Gurney's visit. It is very likely that charismatic Gurney helped William and his fellow students to solidify their trust in the authority of Scripture and to strengthen their understanding of the other orthodox evangelical influences they grew up with in North Carolina Yearly Meeting such as the importance of education in general and First Day Schools in particular. Later we will see that while living at Honey Creek, Iowa, William supported his son Samuel in an endeavor to organize a new kind of First Day School for the congregation. William does not mention meeting Gurney in his diary, but he does make a note, "Read from J.J. Gurney," on Tenth Month 1, 1872,[61] showing that even later in life he was still interested in what Gurney had to say.

While we can't know for sure the extent of Gurney's personal impact on William, his significant influence on NGBS as a whole can't be overemphasized. It's well known that his oratory skills were superlative and that he was an exceptionally inspirational speaker. His beliefs, writings, and lectures would have been discussed among teachers and students and his passion for Bible study adopted by leadership. Even though his stay at NGBS was short, his impact was huge. He inspired students and faculty alike, including Hunt, to pursue the things of God with new vigor. Gilbert tells us that Gurney also put his money where his mouth was and invested financially in the school.[62]

While at NGBS William was careful to exercise temperance in his diet and he chose to put healthy boundaries in place on the amount of time he spent studying, though he was very conscientious in keeping up with his lessons. He reports that he never drank alcohol and that he formed a habit of sleeping for about six and a half hours every night, a practice which lasted about a month and half. Apparently, he gave verbal reports without any trouble, but found writing compositions to be rather difficult, at first.

59. Gwen Gosney Erickson, telephone conversation with author, May 15, 2018.
60. Gurney, *Memoirs of Joseph John Gurney*, 103.
61. Hobson, "Diaries," reel 1 of 2, 10/1/1872.
62. Gilbert, *Guilford a Quaker College*, 52.

However, he persevered and he believed that writing compositions did him "more good than any thing else done at school and [it] soon became a pleasurable task to appear before the School with a composition And now I can compose letters to my relatives or friends with ease and much better I suppose than if I had never had the training which I got in this way at school."[63] His diary proves that he was a fairly good speller, however he paid little attention to capitalization and punctuation. This is understandable in a diary meant mainly for his own use, often written in haste. After his longer nine-month stint at NGBS William received no further formal education, though he was most certainly a life-long learner.

Along with going to school and teaching school, there was also physical labor. In fact, there was considerably more physical labor than school. At age thirteen his father put him in charge of the family's grist mill, and he worked there until he was about eighteen, except for, according to him, sporadic attendance at some other short terms of schooling,[64] probably referring to his first two terms at NGBS. As a teen he also worked at odd jobs around his father's industrial complex and was paid fifty cents a day for his labor.[65] When the water in the creek was low and the mill ran slowly teenaged William made or mended shoes, tended the garden patch, worked in the blacksmith shop, helped to full, color, or dress cloth, made linseed oil, or tended the store. However, at some point he decided he could no longer trade tobacco for his father and there were some dry goods he felt uneasy selling because they were not plain enough for his conscience.[66] William may have continued on at the mill in some capacity after his nine months at NGBS, though it seems he primarily worked in his father's mine after he turned twenty-one. He had learned mining and metalwork early on, for Stephen

> had his boys assisting in that line of business by halling [sic] wood, burning Coal digging ore, working in the Forge, or halling [sic] Coal or Ore. Father was much for having us to learn to do many things. That we might be handy to do anything that Occasion might require any time through life. We learned to milk the cows and to cook some. And the last art we found

---

63. Hobson, "Diaries," reel 2 of 2, notebook beginning 1/21/1868, 46 (Hobson's numbering).

64. Hobson, "Diaries," reel 2 of 2, notebook beginning 1/21/1868, 20 (Hobson's numbering).

65. Hobson, "Diaries," reel 2 of 2, notebook beginning 1/21/1868, 29 (Hobson's numbering).

66. Hobson, "Diaries," reel 2 of 2, notebook beginning 1/21/1868, 26-28 (Hobson's numbering).

useful to us straightway; as we had need often to cook for ourselves, when we burned coal dug Ore; or worked in the forge or dug mostly living in tents by our work. However I did not work but a little in a forge But when I became of age to do for myself; mostly dug Ore for 3 years.[67]

Young William learned how to engage in many different types of work, "but of all Business callings to make a living by [he] most desired to farm it."[68] The industriousness, versatility, and strong work ethic that William learned as a boy and young man translated easily into life as a pioneer-farmer.

Young William seems to have been especially sensitive to the leading and heart of God. We have seen that he received a calling to be a preacher in primary school and was very tender towards truth telling. He also felt that he was called to be a witness to God's righteousness among his peers by the way he lived his life. We know that he read Scripture and Friends literature and was deeply influenced by *Youthful Piety* at a raw time soon after his mother's death. All through his growing up years he was concerned with maintaining plain speech, plain dress, and simple living. He willingly took a share in raising his siblings with firm kindness, directing them to pursue a close life with God. During his formative years he was steeped in Quaker Quietism albeit of an orthodox, evangelical nature, and he remained, for the most part, an orthodox Quietist Quaker in adulthood. His whole life he avoided formal preparation for vocal ministry and was somewhat suspicious of music, believing firmly that unprogrammed worship was best.

We can get further insight into his views on the place of music in worship from a copy of a composition he wrote titled "Address to Our School Children on Music and Singing" a copy of which is preserved in the George Fox University Archives. He did not date the composition and there are no clues within it as to when he wrote it. However, his view on music seems to have changed slightly over his lifetime indicating the essay may have been written when he was older rather than younger and somewhat more forgiving in his views, though not by today's standards or even by the standards of Revival Friends. In his "Address" William reveals that at about ten years of age he sought "quiet and lonely places to sing aloud where none could hear" in spontaneous praise to God. Therefore, he was all for people of all ages singing freely and naturally like the birds that God also created. He believed that "no music is called for by God except what he gives us for full

---

67. Hobson, "Diaries," reel 2 of 2, notebook beginning 1/21/1868, 40–41 (Hobson's numbering).

68. Hobson, "Diaries," reel 2 of 2, notebook beginning 1/21/1868, 28 (Hobson's numbering).

expression of the feelings of the heart . . . but to learn tunes or make instruments is inconsistent with pure spiritual worship . . . same as if a minister choose his own subject and what words he will use in praying or preaching and prepare himself with his own fixing out beforehand." He leaves room for individual conscience in the singing and making of music, but also presents his viewpoint very clearly writing, "I want each one; however much their views may differ from mine to have liberty to worship God according to his or her own belief. But it always grieves me to hear people sing in a light manner." For William an individual singing in meeting was acceptable if not advisable, as long as the words were clear and the person sang out of the fullness of their heart; for singing, like preaching was for the edification of the church. However, William believed that congregational singing, in which worshipers sang a prearranged piece together, might force some to lie about their spiritual state and he feared such a situation for "God wants nothing of mans [sic] contrivings [sic] in his own will to worship him." Hobson was always very much concerned that worship be genuine and spontaneous.[69]

The Hobson family used to tell an anecdote about an incident at Honey Creek when William was middle aged. Goldsmith heard it firsthand from Leota Walton, a granddaughter of William Hobson. Goldsmith writes that

> according to a story told by the Hobson family, a minister from another denomination once visited the Honey Creek Meeting when it was at worship. Eventually the stranger stood to his feet, sang a gospel song and then proceeded to preach a message which was very acceptable to those present. William Reece arose and left the meeting when the singing began, but Hobson kept his seat throughout. After meeting, he went home and sat by the fire for a long time in silence, observing finally that he could not understand how anyone who would sing a song in meeting could still be such a good preacher.[70]

We learn a few more details about this incident from William's son Samuel. Samuel recalled a particular time when he was walking home from school in below-freezing weather and a stranger gave him a ride in his sled, whistling and singing the whole way home. William told Samuel he should not have accepted the ride because of the musical component and Samuel was indignant, thinking it better to bear with some singing than to freeze to death. The next day a visitor came to Honey Creek Meeting and was welcomed by William who told him to be free in the Spirit. The visitor took

---

69. Hobson, "Address to Our School Children."

70. Goldsmith, "William Hobson and the Founding of Quakerism in the Pacific Northwest," 211–12.

William's words to heart, sang a song, and preached a good sermon. According to Samuel, William Reece, a founding member of Honey Creek Monthly Meeting, walked out during the song but came back to hear the sermon. After meeting, Samuel asked William if he knew who the preacher was. His father replied, yes, that he was a Methodist minister and a good man. Samuel then revealed that the visitor who sang and preached was the very same man who had carried Samuel home in his sled the other day. Samuel triumphantly reports that after that William no longer reproached his son for accepting a ride from the preacher.[71] It appears that this may have been a pivotal experience in William Hobson's life concerning his understanding of the place of music in worship. Most Quietist Friends were like William Reece, completely opposed to music of any kind in a worship setting, and most likely when he was young this was also William's viewpoint. One can't help but wonder if the experience at Honey Creek with the Methodist minister and possibly other similar experiences, as well as revival later on, helped to move William out of a strict Quietist stance on music in his old age, since songs were sung regularly by members of the congregation in Newberg.

Before we explore the spiritual growth William experienced in his teenage years, we need to look more deeply into the affairs of North Carolina Yearly Meeting in the first half of the nineteenth century, for William was undoubtedly influenced by the spiritual climate of the yearly meeting. At the time of the Hicksite separation, North Carolina Yearly Meeting embraced the Orthodox position. Hinshaw reports that they wrote a paper during 1827 yearly meeting sessions titled "'On the Divinity of our Lord and Savior Jesus Christ, and the Authenticity of the Holy Scriptures'" and "directed that ten thousand (!) copies be printed and distributed."[72] Goldsmith adds that in the same year North Carolina Yearly Meeting addressed an epistle to every monthly meeting in North Carolina expressing a concern that all remain in the truth of Jesus, cautioning against reading unorthodox books, and testifying to the "full lordship and mediation" of Jesus. It also reminded the meetings of Fox's and Barclay's high esteem for Scripture and pointedly attacked "a volume of sermons by Elias Hicks as denying the divinity of Christ and his propitiatory sacrifice for sin, and ended by exhorting all parents to instruct their children in the doctrines of the Christian religion as contained in the Scriptures." Goldsmith goes on to say that "Stephen Hobson was a representative to North Carolina Yearly Meeting in the year the epistle warning against Hicksism was sent down. Whatever his part, if any, in the formulation of it may have been, his accord with it is clear, for

71. Hobson, "Memories" 28–30.
72. Hinshaw, *Carolina Quaker Experience*, 89–88.

his children were reared in an atmosphere steeped in the principles upheld by the epistle."[73] Both North Carolina Yearly Meeting and Stephen Hobson were expressing orthodox sentiments in no uncertain terms.

Hinshaw gives further insight into the effects and growth of evangelicalism in North Carolina Yearly Meeting. He writes that "it has been suggested that the great separation in Philadelphia Yearly Meeting drove Friends back to their Bibles in order to get their bearings in this controversy," and that the "Bible Association of Friends in America was organized in 1829, which began a tremendous program of printing and furnishing Bibles to people across the country."[74] The goal was to place a Bible in every Friends home. Branches of the association were established in North Carolina at New Garden and Deep River. Hinshaw goes on to report that, as best he can tell, the first Friends First Day schools in America were held by New Garden, Springfield, and Deep River Monthly Meetings. It seems that the initial First Day School was held at New Garden in 1818, the evidence of this being an inscription testifying to the fact on a marker erected at New Garden Cemetery.[75]

As time progressed, most members of North Carolina Yearly Meeting continued to embrace Gurney's evangelical orthodoxy, with all that it entailed: Bible study, justification separate from sanctification, emphasis on the importance of education, etc., and Wilbur's more traditional orthodoxy became highly suspect. However, a few embraced Wilbur's ideology and there was considerable uncertainty as to whether or not unity could be maintained within North Carolina Yearly Meeting. According to Allen Jay and Gwen Gosney Erickson, in the end, largely due to the strong convictions and personality of weighty Friend Nathan Hunt separation was avoided.[76] The 1845 minutes indicate that William Hobson was in attendance at these tense yearly meeting sessions during which Hunt held out against even members of his own family for what he considered to be the gospel truth. His lengthy, passionate verbal ministry on the floor of the meeting brought the meeting into unity under evangelical Gurneyite orthodoxy. Later during these yearly meeting sessions, Hobson and Hunt were appointed to a committee charged with writing a reply to epistles the meeting had read and

---

73. Goldsmith, "William Hobson and the Founding of Quakerism in the Pacific Northwest," 92–93.

74. Hinshaw, *Carolina Quaker Experience*, 246.

75. Hinshaw, *Carolina Quaker Experience*, 247.

76. Gwen Gosney Erickson, telephone conversation with author, May 15, 2018; Jay, *Autobiography of Allen Jay*, 120–25.

accepted from London, Dublin, and every other American yearly meeting, except New England Yearly Meeting which was not solidly Gurneyite.[77]

Picking up the thread of William's young life we return to the time when he started work at his father's grist mill at age thirteen. He enjoyed the work, but he was faced with some new spiritual challenges. The boys and men that visited the mill were accustomed to spending the time waiting for their flour by playing games like marbles. William considered this to be a sad waste of time, but he was sorely tempted to join them in their inane games. William acknowledged that his natural propensity towards foolishness was most likely greater than those who came by the mill. He struggled mightily to control the desire to waste time on what he believed were meaningless pursuits and "had what might be called a spiritual warfare to wage for years against the enemy of [his] soul who tempted [him] with some childish folly to which [his] proneness to sin was inclined to."[78] He felt the importance of living a holy blameless life deeply for one so young. Even though playing games wasn't necessarily sinful in and of itself, he was very concerned about spending his time in ways that were pleasing to God. He wrote that even though he

> wandered some from the path of holiness so as frequently to take part in play or foolishness Yet I [rarely] ceased to pray to the Lord to save me from going very far. Whilst playing at marbles or other sports my mind was seldom so much drawn away from thinking upon God; but what I seemed to feel that I could and ought to spend my time better. And as I felt the displeasure of the Lord as I continued the sport. I often wanted to end the fun or withdraw from it for I could no longer be happy in continuing; because the conviction was now forcible that I was not spending my time as one should who felt his their life continued, in part to set an example of holiness of life before men So I would gladly get myself back to the Mill, and see if it was doing as well as I could make it. And amidst the clatter of Cornmeal Seive [sic]; and the hum & buzz of many wheels &c. I would pray often vocally to be forgiven this time also. And the Lord knowing my my [sic] weakness and my sincere repentance was gracious still to forgive me for my childish folly.[79]

---

77. North Carolina Yearly Meeting, *Minutes of North Carolina Yearly Meeting 1845*, 4, 10–11, 17; Gwen Gosney Erikson, telephone conversation with author, May 15, 2018.

78. Hobson, "Diaries," reel 2 of 2, notebook beginning 1/21/1868, 21 (Hobson's numbering).

79. Hobson, "Diaries," reel 2 of 2, notebook beginning 1/21/1868, 22–23 (Hobson's numbering).

William experienced intense relief in repentance and oftentimes felt overwhelmed by God's great love and forgiveness. He sought solace in the Scriptures and did his best to put on the whole armor of God, living in the righteousness of Christ.

Strangely, William does not mention Deep Creek Monthly Meeting at all in his diary. Granted, he didn't begin writing his diary until a few years after moving to Iowa, but it seems odd that he never wrote about his home meeting. Goldsmith did some digging in the Deep Creek Monthly Meeting minutes and found that in 1839, at nineteen years of age, William was approved as a representative to the next quarterly meeting. According to Goldsmith, "regular appointments appear thereafter, examples of which are frequent appointments to assist the clerk in correcting and transcribing the Minutes, to attend a marriage and marriage entertainment to see if it were conducted in an orderly way, to determine the number of members using ardent spirits, to confer with those desiring membership, and the like."[80] Also in 1839, the quarterly meeting approved William as a representative to yearly meeting sessions, which showed the esteem in which he was held by his peers. During yearly meeting sessions he was assigned to a committee tasked with writing a summary of all the epistles written to the yearly meetings with which North Carolina Yearly Meeting corresponded and Goldsmith notes that this was the kind of work to which he was usually appointed to conduct at future quarterly and yearly meetings. Deep Creek Monthly Meeting assigned him some business that was typically given to ministers, though he was never recorded by Deep Creek as such.[81] Recording came later when he was living at Honey Creek, Iowa.

In keeping with the times, Deep Creek Meeting minutes are not especially informative about the feelings or experiences behind the facts recorded, but facts do tell us something. While carefully combing the minutes of Deep Creek Meeting Goldsmith was able to gather that the congregation experienced both its share of ministry and discipline, and to glean a few details that give us insight into the life of the meeting during William's growing up years. He notes that traveling ministers from both England and America visited Deep Creek including William Evans, Asenath Clark, Benjamin Cox, Hannah Backhouse, Benjamin Seebohm, and Robert Lindsey, among others. We must assume that worship at Deep Creek was much like Quaker worship everywhere at the time: in the Quietist mode.

---

80. Goldsmith, "William Hobson and the Founding of Quakerism in the Pacific Northwest," 106.

81. Goldsmith, "William Hobson and the Founding of Quakerism in the Pacific Northwest," 107.

Goldsmith also shares about the rougher side of Deep Creek. Marrying-out, by far, generated the most disownments. But Goldsmith points out several more transgressions committed by Deep Creek members. In the first half of the nineteenth century, some of the

> disciplinary actions at Deep Creek include, those involving fighting, dancing, attending muster, use of profane language, departing from plainness; neglecting meetings; being intoxicated and handling cards; distilling and trading in spiritous liquor; 'giving way to pashion [sic] & insulting a man and telling untruths'; 'taking too much Strong drink and taking of[f] his cloathes [sic] in an angry manner in order to fright'; 'being Intoxicated for Fighting and for having a child laid to his charge in an unmarried state'; 'keeping unseasonable Company with a woman so as to have a Child laid to his charge, and also for dancing,' and many others.[82]

Friends at Deep Creek seem to have been in a rather low state, like Friends in general at the time. However, there were certainly well-concerned Friends at Deep Creek while William was growing up, such as William's parents and grandparents.

Yearly meeting sessions in North Carolina were often spiritually rich and encouraging, with many inspirational ministers in attendance. Along those lines, Addison Coffin, in his short book *Early Settlement of Friends in North Carolina Traditions and Reminiscences*, tells of an experience during worship at Deep Creek Monthly Meeting when William was twenty-one and Coffin was about twenty-three. Coffin was a contemporary of William's who grew up in North Carolina and who also attended NGBS. Coffin describes a particularly stirring moment when Lindley M. Hoag interrupted his own sermon to give a prophetic word that Coffin believed was intended for William Hobson. Lindley M. Hoag was the son of Joseph Hoag and a well-loved traveling minister in his own right. Lindley was also known to exercise a distinct prophetic gift similar to his father's. Coffin places Hoag's visit to North Carolina Yearly Meeting in the year 1839 or 1840, but Goldsmith notes that the North Carolina Yearly Meeting minutes list Lindley M. Hoag in attendance during the 1841 yearly meeting sessions,[83] so he probably visited Deep Creek Meeting around that time. Coffin also misidentifies

---

82. Goldsmith, "William Hobson and the Founding of Quakerism in the Pacific Northwest," 88–90.

83. Goldsmith, "William Hobson and the Founding of Quakerism in the Pacific Northwest," 107.

him as William M. Hoag at first, though later correctly identifies him as Lindley M. Hoag:

> When William M. Hoag first visited North Carolina Yearly meeting in 1839 or 40, he went to Deep Creek in company of Dr. Nereus Mendenhall and held a religious meeting in the old–meeting house. His style of eloquence was well calculated to attract, and the minds of young thinking people, being in life's young bloom himself. William Hobson was at that meeting listening with deep interest to the wonderful flow of eloquence and spiritual life, which seemed to give new inspiration to all present; during the sermon the speaker paused for a few moments, then uttered this remarkable prophecy: "There is one sitting here, who shall pour oil on his feet, and go forth and plant the gospel in distant lands." Lindley M. Hoag subsequently settled and died in Iowa, William Hobson married and moved to Iowa, settling near Bangor, then on the extreme frontier. He soon became a prosperous farmer, a minister of the gospel, a valuable citizen in the community, earnest, active and persevering in all good works, that promised good to humanity. Near mid–life he had a clear definite call from the Lord to "Go forth and plant the gospel," and did not doubt or hesitate.[84]

Coffin believed that the word Hoag spoke came to pass when William obeyed the call to organize a Quaker community in Oregon.[85] There is no way to know for sure if William recognized this word from Hoag as a prophecy spoken over his life, since he never mentions it, but Coffin was convinced it was meant for William. Coffin goes on to explain how William settled in "Newburg" after searching for just the right place to start a Quaker colony, and established a regular meeting that became a monthly meeting, grew into a quarterly meeting, and eventually achieved yearly meeting status. Addison points out that Hobson

> lived to see it [Newberg] become a prosperous temperance town, to see a prosperous seminary established, and to see that changed to 'Pacific College'; lived to see the gospel 'planted' in a goodly land, lived to see the grant for a yearly meeting, lived to see a railroad built as he had foretold, then died in peace, full of joy and faith, had finished his work, and Oregon Yearly Meeting

---

84. Coffin, *Early Settlement of Friends*, 190.
85. Coffin, *Early Settlement of Friends*, 189.

will be his enduring monument, his name should be written on its first page of its history.[86]

Coffin clearly believed that William received an important call from God to establish a Quaker community in Oregon, which in his eyes was a fulfillment of prophecy. Coffin respected him for being true to the call, though it seems that he was a little surprised that God picked William for the job. Coffin remarked that Hobson was "noted for his unflinching conscientious performance of duty; was a marked character not only amusing his fellow students, but at his home among rude mountaineers with whom his early life was spent, yet few could have selected him as the one among his fellows who would be called of the Lord to a special work that was to influence the coming generations."[87] So, it seems that Coffin, like William's earlier classmates considered William to be a "stiff Quaker," though an affable yokel, that God, surprisingly, singled out for an unusual calling.

In spite of the fact that girls and boys were strictly segregated at NGBS, William met a young woman named Sarah Tulburt there, who was later to become his wife. William never mentions meeting Sarah and never writes about their courtship, marriage, or early life together in his diary, but Goldsmith became aware that they met at NGBS from a letter written to him by Laura Blair, one of William and Sarah's granddaughters.[88] Sarah was born Sixth Month 10, 1818, and so was about two years older than William.[89] Goldsmith gleaned a little more about Sarah from NGBS records and Deep Creek Monthly Meeting minutes. She was not a Friend while at school, but by the time she enrolled NGBS was accepting non-Friends students.[90] According to NGBS records, Sarah attended NGBS for two three-month sessions, one beginning in 1840 and one beginning in 1842,[91] for a total of about six months attendance in all. Therefore, William and Sarah were at school together in the winter of 1840–1841. She was born in Surry County, North Carolina, like William, and her family likely lived near Deep Creek, though when they moved to the area is unclear. Goldsmith found that the first mention of Sarah Tulburt in the Deep Creek Monthly Meeting minutes is a notation of her request to become a member, First Month 6, 1844. A

---

86. Coffin, *Early Settlement of Friends*, 191.

87. Coffin, *Early Settlement of Friends*, 189–90.

88. Goldsmith, "William Hobson and the Founding of Quakerism in the Pacific Northwest," 109.

89. Burial Records, notes on William and Sarah Hobson.

90. Goldsmith, "William Hobson and the Founding of Quakerism in the Pacific Northwest," 110–11.

91. "New Garden Boarding School Register: 1837–February 1842," 54–55, 60.

committee was duly appointed, the members approved her request, and she was entered into membership Second Month 3, 1844. Six months later William and Sarah told the men's business meeting that they wanted to get married. The women's meeting was informed a month later. Both meetings formed committees to determine whether the union would be suitable. By Eighth Month, William and Sarah had cleared both committees and on Eighth Month 7, 1844, they were married in meeting in the traditional Friends way.[92] William was twenty-four and Sarah was twenty-six, rather on the older side for matrimony in that time and place.

Did Sarah become a Friend in order to marry William? Was he enough of a "stiff Quaker" to refuse to marry-out regardless of an emotional attachment? Perhaps Sarah's convincement coincided with their desire to get married? It's hard to know what Sarah's true motivations were for becoming a Friend. William mentions her infrequently in his diary and almost entirely in a factual way (she was sick, she rode with him on an errand, or she accomplished some task). It seems that her parents were not Friends. For if they were, she would have been a birthright member and it would therefore have been unnecessary for her to apply for membership at Deep Creek. Had she belonged to another Quaker meeting she could have asked for a transfer of membership. Nothing is known about her upbringing or home life as a child. Goldsmith refers to several letters that William wrote to his in-laws, William and Mary Tulburt, while moving to and living at Honey Creek, but they are full of William and Sarah's news and don't reveal much information about the Tulburts. William and Sarah lived near Deep Creek for about three years before moving to Iowa.

So, we see that Hobson grew up in rustic and economically depressed rural Surry County, North Carolina towards the first half of the nineteenth century. His family had been Quaker for at least two generations on both sides and his parents were well-concerned Friends, industrious in their work, involved in their local meeting, and attentive to their children's education, both spiritual and academic. North Carolina Yearly Meeting was also concerned with the state of education in the entire region, a concern from which Hobson benefitted by the use of the Deep Creek library kept in his family home, and through his time at NGBS. At the time, North Carolina Yearly Meeting was made up mostly of orthodox evangelical Friends, Hobson's parents among them. He mentions specifically the good influence of his grandfather Bond and we also saw how weighty Friends like Nathan Hunt and Joseph John Gurney influenced Hobson's developing religious

---

92. Goldsmith, "William Hobson and the Founding of Quakerism in the Pacific Northwest," 110–11.

views. Hobson was conscientious, a hard worker, a loving older brother, and as his young schoolmates discerned, a "stiff Quaker." He felt called by God as a young child to be a preacher and to serve God as a reliable example of holy living. A steady diet of the Bible and Friends books helped him to grow spiritually, as did certain temptations to waste his time that he faced and conquered. He prayed out loud, at times, when no one else could hear him, and was grateful to God for taking away his sins through the sacrifice of Jesus on the cross. He struggled against sin and the temptation to withdraw from society in order to keep pure, but he recognized that desire as a tactic of Satan to keep him from living into his calling. As a young adult, he took his rich and vibrant spiritual life and his Friends convictions to New Garden Boarding School, where he continued to learn, grow, and solidify his commitment to God and Friends ways. There he also met his future wife, Sarah Tulburt, and shortly after marrying they left North Carolina for Iowa.

3

Pioneering on the Iowa Frontier

Trust in the Lord, and do good; so shalt thou dwell in the land, and verily thou shalt be fed. Delight thyself also in the Lord: and he shall give thee the desires of thine heart.

Ps 37: 3–4

FROM NORTH CAROLINA TO IOWA

About four decades after the fact, Hobson recorded in his diary a brief notation on the anniversary of the day he, Sarah, two-year-old Samuel, baby Rachel, and Sarah's sister, also named Rachel, left North Carolina to go west. He wrote, "1889 9 mo. 13&6 of the week . . . It is just 42 years to day since I left my home on logans [sic] Creek in Surry Co[unty]. N[orth].C[arolina]. to move westw[a]rd with a wife & 2 small Children. The youngest a little more than 8 months old. Also my wifes [sic] sister Rachel went with us first to Ind[iana]. & Also from Ind[iana]. To Iowa in the Spring of 1848."[1] Goldsmith notes that William and Sarah owned the land they farmed near

---

1. Hobson, "Diaries," reel 1 of 2, 9/13/1889; Goldsmith, "William Hobson and the Founding of Quakerism in the Pacific Northwest," 166 (footnote). Samuel was born 10/8/1845 and Rachel was born 12/30/1846.

Logan's Creek and that it may have been a gift from William's father.[2] Since Hobson either did not begin keeping a diary until 1859 or any diaries he may have written before that time are lost, we do not have a first-hand account of William and Sarah's life together in North Carolina, their journey west, or their early life in Iowa. Hobson also did not record their motivations for moving to Iowa, leaving us to make some educated guesses.

Like most Quakers moving west at the time, the Hobsons were probably partly motivated by the opportunity to escape the pervasive slave culture of the south. J. Floyd Moore in, *Friends in the Carolinas*, notes that "there was undoubtedly a combination of motives [for Quaker families moving west]--personal, economic, political, adventurous. The central fact remains, however, that the continued system of human slavery and the difficulties encountered by Friends in their attempt to abolish this practice, created the dynamics of social tension which produced the mighty exodus."[3] Most Quaker historians are a little more temperate than Moore, pointing out that slavery was not necessarily the main reason Friends migrated west, even while acknowledging it was one of the stronger motivations.

According to Hinshaw in *Carolina Quakers: Three Hundred Years 1672–1972*, another reason Friends moved west had to do with the poor quality of the topsoil in the southern states. Exhausted soil was certainly a reality in Surry County, North Carolina. After decades of questionable farming practices in the Yadkin Valley, the loam was stripped of nutrients. Commercial fertilizers were unheard of at the time and farmers could not raise quality crops in the worn-out earth in large enough quantities to make a profit. The only way to increase yields was to acquire previously uncultivated land. Unbroken acreage could be cleared without too much trouble, but it was in short supply, making opportunities to expand farms few and far between. Also, it was quite expensive to expand a farm in North Carolina, especially when compared with the low prices the government was offering for large parcels of virgin acreage out west. The challenges North Carolinian farmers were facing made abundant, inexpensive, and extremely fertile soil in the western territories very attractive,[4] despite the hardships associated with travel and frontier life. Goldsmith believed that Hobson's main motivation for moving west was economic, citing his passionate agricultural interests, as recorded in his diaries later in life, as well as the inference one can make from Hobson's writings that, as Goldsmith puts it, a "happy and

---

2. Goldsmith, "William Hobson and the Founding of Quakerism in the Pacific Northwest," 111.

3. Moore, *Friends in the Carolinas*, 9.

4. Hinshaw, *Carolina Quakers: Three Hundred Years*, 38.

useful life has an inevitable material and economic basis."[5] Perhaps his main reason for pulling up stakes in North Carolina was economic, but morale also had a part to play. Subsistence farming in inferior soil was not only disheartening financially, but also mentally and emotionally. For someone like Hobson who wasn't looking to get rich, but who did value prosperity earned by honest hard work and who, on top of it all deeply loved farming and horticulture, the unusually fertile soil of Iowa was a dream come true.

A potent mix of the lure of adventure and peer pressure may have also had a hand in prompting the Hobsons to leave North Carolina for regions west. Stephen B. Weeks, in his book *Southern Quakers and Slavery* makes much of the role of adventure in the mass migration of Quakers. He notes that they were of Teuton stock, migrating in "the same spirit that had led to the discovery and settlement of America... these Quakers, all unconsciously, were carrying out the spirit of their race."[6] He was writing in 1896, but this is still a troubling view when we consider the forceful removal of Native Americans from their ancestral lands in mid–America and elsewhere. The reality is that settlers were buying up land that the United States Government had wrongfully appropriated from Native American tribes and had no right to sell.

Whether or not there was a primal urge to move west throbbing in the breasts of Friends like William and Sarah Hobson, the whole endeavor certainly was an adventure. No doubt the Hobsons experienced a certain level of excitement, or at least William did as they contemplated the move and started out on their journey. It was a new beginning, a fresh start, and a quest for the perfect home in the great unknown where he could farm, be self-sufficient, prosper financially, and help to build up a new Friends community. One can't help but wonder how Sarah felt about starting over completely on their own in a new and wild place, far from civilization and her parents, with two children under the age of three–years–old. At least she had her sister with her. And it's hard to say for certain what Sarah may have felt. Perhaps, she dreaded the journey: the long days of walking or riding on a splintery wooden seat, cooking outdoors, sleeping on the ground or in the wagon, and leaving behind all the comforts of home. Or, maybe she was just as excited as William when they set out from Logan's Creek to pursue their piece of the American dream on the edge of the known world. Whether they counted the cost to the Native Tribes there before them, we'll never know.

---

5. Goldsmith, "William Hobson and the Founding of Quakerism in the Pacific Northwest," 117.

6. Weeks, *Southern Quakers and Slavery*, 291.

Peer pressure may have also influenced William and Sarah's decision to move west. Many of their friends, neighbors, and family members had gone on before them. Goldsmith notes that Friends from the Deep Creek area had been slowly trickling away west for about four decades. He also points out that Sarah's brother James Tulburt had recently moved to Westerfield, Indiana, with his wife Rachel, in the Spring of 1847. In their letters, since lost, the Tulburts likely at the very least gave a good report of their new surroundings and probably also urged Sarah and William to come settle near them, little knowing that Indiana wasn't far enough west for William Hobson. It's even possible that they had agreed together, before the Tulburts left that the Hobsons would join them in Indiana in the fall. It's a little strange they didn't travel together, but after all, in the spring of 1847 baby Rachel Hobson was just a couple of months old and mother and baby were likely not up for traveling when the Tulburts left. Ironically, after the Hobsons followed the Tulburts to Indiana, the Tulburts followed the Hobsons to Iowa in the fall of 1848.[7]

Louis Thomas Jones points out that between 1800 and 1860 about 6,000 Friends migrated to Indiana from four states: Virginia, North Carolina, South Carolina, and Georgia and that, like the Tulburts and Hobsons, many of these migratory Friends or their descendants later migrated further west to Iowa.[8] Friends and other family members who had grown up at Deep Creek and elsewhere in North Carolina Yearly Meeting probably wrote the Hobsons too, telling of the wonders of frontier life and inviting them to join them there. Also, when they reached Iowa, they were joined by William's uncle Elam Jessup and his cousin Abel Bond, as well as other Quaker families they were acquainted with.[9] They were likely in contact with these families before and during their journey to Iowa. Quaker communities were tight knit, interrelated groups and they took good care of each other, so there was definite incentive to join friends and family on the frontier.

William and Sarah did leave some family behind in North Carolina, though soon most would be scattered in other regions. Perhaps Hobson had hoped his brothers and father would follow him and Sarah to Iowa, but that did not happen. According to Thomas M. King, local San Jose historian, in his book *History of San Jose Quakers*, Hobson's brothers David and Stephen caught gold fever. They journeyed to the California gold fields in 1850, where they struck it rich, despite arriving a year too late to be called

7. Goldsmith, "William Hobson and the Founding of Quakerism in the Pacific Northwest," 117, 126.

8. Jones, *Quakers of Iowa*, 35–37.

9. Goldsmith, "William Hobson and the Founding of Quakerism in the Pacific Northwest," 148–49.

'49ers. Brother Jesse ended up spending several years in the gold fields as well. All three brothers finally settled in the Santa Clara Valley, near San Jose, California. They used their gold earnings to buy land and were quite successful in agriculture. The Hobson brothers were also instrumental in organizing San Jose Friends Meeting. Hobson's father Stephen moved to San Jose from North Carolina with his fourth wife, Eleanor "Ellen" (Adams) Hobson, much later in 1871.[10] We can safely assume that Sarah's parents remained in North Carolina for some time, because Hobson wrote letters to them there, though it seems that they, or at least Sarah's mother, joined them at Honey Creek before too long. Hobson first mentions "mother" in Third Month 1862.[11] We know he can't possibly be referring to his birth mother, since she died when he was young and he can't be referring to his stepmother, because she was still living in North Carolina with his father at the time. So, it seems most likely that Sarah's mother was living with them at Honey Creek by early 1862. At any rate, in the fall of 1847 William and Sarah were leaving behind his brothers, his father and stepmother, and Sarah's parents, which could not have been easy.

Hobson may have also had a strong personal reason for leaving North Carolina due to action taken against his father by Deep Creek Monthly Meeting. According to King, Stephen Hobson was in the habit of buying up mistreated slaves and then paying them a wage to work for him in various capacities, a practice that caused some friction with his neighbors[12] and with Deep Creek Monthly Meeting. According to Goldsmith, in late 1846 and early 1847 Stephen faced disciplinary action from Deep Creek Monthly Meeting. A notation dated Tenth Month 3, 1846, found in the Deep Creek minutes, proposed the removal of Stephen Hobson from the meeting and a second minute, dated Twelfth Month 5, 1846, gives the reason, as quoted by Goldsmith:

> Deep Creek preparative Meeting Complains of Stephen hobson [sic] for Demolishing a bridg [sic] leading from Benjamin Hutchens Coal yard to the forge for hireing a slave for refuseing the Council of Friends for useing Rough and unbecomeing language Wm. Tulburt *[author's note: was this William Hobson's father-in-law?]* Wm. Dobbins Thomas Benbow Daniel Huff are appointed to visit him on the occasion and report their care to the next meeting.[13]

10. King, *History of San Jose Quakers*, 3–6, 114.
11. Hobson, "Diaries," reel 2 of 2, 3/13/1862.
12. King, *History of San Jose Quakers*, 3.
13. Goldsmith, "William Hobson and the Founding of Quakerism in the Pacific Northwest," 118.

Goldsmith explains further that Stephen Hobson refused to write a letter of contrition, at the urging of the committee sent to deal with him, and was therefore disowned by Deep Creek Monthly Meeting, First Month of 1847. A committee from the quarterly meeting was able to persuade Stephen to write a letter of contrition and the quarterly meeting reversed the proceedings at Deep Creek in Fourth Month 1847, reinstating Stephen Hobson as an elder at Deep Creek. However, as Goldsmith notes, "It was done [reinstating Stephen], but apparently begrudgingly. In subsequent Minutes of Deep Creek Monthly Meeting, Stephen Hobson was never [again] appointed to responsibilities befitting his station as an elder."[14] It's hard to know how these actions against his dad may have affected William Hobson. He likely did not approve of his dad's disrespectful behavior and use of slave labor, even if Stephen paid the workers a wage, but William also most likely did not approve of the way his dad was treated by Deep Creek Monthly Meeting. He must have had mixed feelings about this incident, for his father had served the congregation at Deep Creek a long time in an exemplary manner. And if his father-in-law was involved in the proceedings against Stephen, that would have only complicated his family life more. Maybe the embarrassment of his father's actions and lack of remorse, coupled with the extreme disciplinary measures against his father undertaken by Deep Creek, provided just one more reason to leave North Carolina.

According to Goldsmith it took the Hobson family "no more than 26 days" to cross the Blue Ridge Mountains and arrive at Flatrock, Indiana, "and they had spent one day attending Indiana Yearly Meeting." He was also able to glean from a letter Hobson wrote to his in-laws William and Mary Tulburt that "it was a five hundred and thirty-eight mile journey, according to Hobson's computation, which cost them a total of about $13.00."[15] The route the Hobsons traveled is unknown. Likewise, the circumstances of their journey were never recorded.

Weeks reports that during this period Friends pioneers frequently traveled with a horse drawn wagon or cart and often traveled with other families. He describes how

> these vehicles [wagons] were usually covered with muslin or linen. Some had no paint, but were pitched with tar instead, while the horses were hitched to them with husk collars and rawhide traces. The movers took with them cooking utensils

---

14. Goldsmith, "William Hobson and the Founding of Quakerism in the Pacific Northwest," 118–19.

15. Goldsmith, "William Hobson and the Founding of Quakerism in the Pacific Northwest," 120; William Hobson to William and Mary Tulburt, October 1847.

and provisions, traveled in the day; camped out at night, and went singly or in companies. The women rode in the wagons or on horseback, and these companies were frequently followed at a short distance in the rear by runaway negroes who took this opportunity to make their way to the land of freedom.[16]

Samuel Hobson remembered that when the time came to leave, the family put everything they owned in a wagon drawn by a large white horse named John and started west.[17]

The Hobsons were traveling in early fall when the weather was consistently fair and the road at its best. The beauty of an Appalachian autumn must have been wonderful to behold as they tramped along. As noted by Goldsmith, a letter from James Tulburt to his parents dated Eighth Month 29, 1847, reads "'I suppose Wm. & his family & Rachel are on the road by this time. We expect to see them in the lane here about 4 weeks—tired enough.'" Sure enough, on Tenth Month 4, 1847, Hobson wrote a letter to his dad and stepmother informing them that the family had arrived in Indiana.[18] It must have been a happy meeting when the Hobsons pulled into the Tulburt's yard.

It is necessary to rely on Goldsmith for an account of the winter of 1847–48 during which the Hobsons stayed with the Tulburts in Westerfield, Indiana, as well as for the bulk of information about their early activities in Iowa, since Hobson wasn't keeping a diary at the time. Goldsmith in turn relied on several letters written by Hobson and James Tulburt which were loaned to him by a relative of Hobson, Effie Hadley Brindle, as well as monthly meeting records. According to Goldsmith, Hobson described Indiana in glowing terms as a "'highly favored portion of the world'" and as a large pastureland that made old Surry County seem small and insignificant, but he was already looking further west toward Iowa. Fairly soon after they arrived at the Tulburt homestead, he took off on a survey trip into Iowa, likely attempting to beat the worst of the winter weather. He returned to the Tulburts by mid-Twelfth Month and proceeded to write to North Carolinians strongly recommending that they emigrate to Iowa. His reasons: it would be easy to get a farm up and running quickly, the roads were well maintained, and supplies were cheap. Hobson's mind was made up. They were moving to Iowa where there was rich, cheap, and plentiful land. He hoped the Tulburts would come with them, but he was convinced

16. Weeks, *Southern Quakers and Slavery*, 247–48.

17. Hobson, "Memories" 5.

18. Goldsmith, "William Hobson and the Founding of Quakerism in the Pacific Northwest," 120.

it was the place for his little family regardless. After his preliminary inspection of Iowa Hobson taught a three-months school for which he was paid four dollars. The Hobsons stayed with the Tulburts about six months total, before departing for Pleasant Plain, located in southeastern Iowa in early Fourth Month 1848. The Tulburts were not yet ready to pull up stakes. They followed the Hobsons to Pleasant Plain later in the year, arriving in Eleventh Month.[19] The Hobsons would end up moving two more times before staying put for about twenty-five years on their Honey Creek farm in Hardin County, Iowa.

William Hobson did not describe the journey across Illinois into Iowa, but a contemporary account from William Evans gives us some idea of what it was like. William Evans and Joseph Elkinton, two American Friends ministers traveling with a concern to visit and encourage the fledgling Quaker meetings in Iowa, crossed the Illinois plains together in the summer of 1851, a few years after the Hobsons. Evans wrote about the crossing in his *Journal of the Life and Religious Services of William Evans*, giving good descriptions of the lay of the land and traveling conditions. He described the scene as they left Indiana and rode down into Illinois:

> This afternoon we crossed the Wabash River in a scow, where we saw evidence of a recent freshet, which had spread over the flats; and, we understood, had made crossing very difficult. A few miles from the river we came to an arm of one of the great prairies. Viewing the expanse appeared like looking out to sea; there being no object in the distance to rest the eye on, for miles, but grass. The thought of being out on such an extensive plain, which seemed to have no limit, and possibility of missing our way, was rather dreary.[20]

From Evans's continuing account of traveling across Illinois and into Iowa we learn that the journey was difficult and dirty. There was a sense of loneliness in crossing the prairie with few landmarks and few settlements. There was a real danger of getting stuck in a muddy slough or being swept away while fording rushing water. There also seemed to be some danger of being set upon by unscrupulous characters, or at the very least being taken advantage of by opportunists lying in wait near particularly difficult patches of swamp, who for an exorbitant fee would help stuck travelers out of deep mires. However, Evans and Elkinton were willing to undertake the arduous journey because of their serious concern to inspire Friends on the frontier.

19. Goldsmith, "William Hobson and the Founding of Quakerism in the Pacific Northwest," 120–23, 125–26.
20. Evans, *Journal*, 514.

After ferrying across the Mississippi River at Fort Madison, Evans and Elkinton traveled around Iowa visiting Friends meetings. It seems that the terrain in Iowa was similar to that of Illinois. Evans describes a journey to Richland, Iowa, where the Hobsons lived temporarily from about 1849 to 1852, in which their carriage became mired in the mud. Thankfully, some passing Friends were able to pull Evans and Elkinton out of the mire with their wagon.[21] Likely, they crossed paths ever so briefly with the Hobsons when they visited the meeting at Richland where the Hobsons were worshipping at the time. The Hobsons probably ferried across the Mississippi at Burlington, not Fort Madison, this being the easier route for travelers from Indiana.[22] However, it seems likely that as the Hobsons traveled across Illinois and into Iowa they encountered similar difficulties as those described by Evans. Samuel Hobson was apparently not impressed with the landscape, describing their journey to Iowa as "one big mud hole the whole way."[23] Being not quite three-years-old at the time, the journey must have made a big impression on him.

According to Louis Thomas Jones, the first Quaker family to settle in what would soon become the Territory of Iowa was that of Isaac Pidgeon. The Pidgeon family arrived in midsummer 1835 after an arduous journey from North Carolina, and settled near Salem in southeast Iowa. Shortly thereafter, Aaron Street and family arrived having traveled a shorter distance from Indiana. Isaac, Aaron, and another recently arrived Friend, Peter Boyer, together laid out the plan for the town of Salem using a grapevine for a tape measure.[24] Hobson once stayed overnight at Aaron Street's home near Winnishiek, Iowa, while traveling in the ministry and they later corresponded with each other about the history of Honey Creek Monthly Meeting.[25] The Friends community in Iowa was quite well connected even though they were spread out across the area.

Jones tells how Friends from many different regions flocked to Salem. Only three years after the arrival of the Pidgeon family Salem Monthly Meeting was opened in Tenth Month 1838, under the authority of Vermillion Monthly Meeting in eastern Illinois. This was the same month and year that Iowa was designated a territory. Jones points out that "In 1836 the population of Iowa numbered 10,531; while in 1840, only four years later, it

---

21. Evans, *Journal*, 516–21.
22. Jones, *Quakers of Iowa*, 49.
23. Hobson, "Memories" 6.
24. Jones, *Quakers of Iowa*, 38–41.
25. Hobson, "Diaries," reel 2 of 2, 1/31/ 1863, 3/17/1865.

had more than quadrupled and stood at 43,112."[26] While the population of Iowa was not exclusively Quaker, it is a fact that Friends played a prominent part in the settlement of the region. Iowa continued to grow in population and achieved statehood in 1846. According to Jones most Friends settled in the "fertile lands between the Des Moines and the Skunk rivers–a region of great fertility which extended almost without a break to the northwest for nearly a hundred and fifty miles into the very heart of the State," including communities like New Garden, Pleasant Plain, and Richland. Salem and the area around it became a gateway for Friends moving further west, as well as a safety net for those same settlers once they had pushed into the back country. As migrating Friends arrived in the Salem area, they found family or acquaintances with whom they could lodge while gathering supplies for moving on. After getting settled in the back country, these same Friends would return to the Salem area from time to time to replenish supplies, staying once again with family or acquaintances before returning to their land claims further west.[27] Likely, this explains the Hobson family's short stay at Pleasant Plain, as there is no evidence that Hobson bought land there.

The Hobsons arrived at Pleasant Plain, twenty-five miles northwest of Salem, sometime in the spring of 1848. According to Jones, Pleasant Plain became a monthly meeting in Twelfth Month 1842, and swiftly increased in membership. The meeting received 150 members from Ohio, Indiana, North Carolina, and Tennessee during the years 1842 to 1850. Pleasant Plain also absorbed Friends moving up from southern Iowa who were tired of being harassed by slave catchers infiltrating the state at the Missouri border.[28] In fact, as Elliot noted, "Salem, only twenty-five miles from the Missouri line, became a busy station on the Underground Railroad that led from Missouri northward to Canada."[29] Some also decided to move north to avoid Mormon settlements to the south. Though most, like the Hobsons, had moved from southern and eastern states.[30] Goldsmith tells how William and Sarah's certificate of removal from Deep Creek arrived at Westerfield Meeting in Indiana just in time to be forwarded on to Pleasant Plain.[31] The Hobsons probably camped on some obliging Friend's land near Pleasant Plain while scouting out the possibilities for buying their own land. They

26. Jones, *Quakers of Iowa*, 44, 48.
27. Jones, *Quakers of Iowa*, 49, 53–54.
28. Jones, *Quakers of Iowa*, 51–52.
29. Elliot, *Quakers on the American Frontier*, 120.
30. Jones, *Quakers of Iowa*, 51–52.
31. Goldsmith, "William Hobson and the Founding of Quakerism in the Pacific Northwest," 126.

may have paid a small fee or helped with chores around the farm as thanks for the favor. They ended up settling in Richland, about ten miles to the northwest of Pleasant Plain. According to *Iowa Yearly Meeting of Friends: 100 Years of History*, Richland Monthly Meeting was established at some point before 1852 when a request was made to Salem Quarterly Meeting for the formation of Pleasant Plain Quarterly Meeting, which included Richland. The Hobsons were most certainly active in the early days at Richland Monthly Meeting.

The first quarterly meeting in Iowa was held on Fifth Month 20, 1848, in Salem and included the following meetings: Salem, Cedar Creek, Pleasant Plain, Richland, New Garden, East Grove, Spring River, and three preparative meetings.[32] William Hobson was most likely in attendance at this event which included the first official use of a newly built, large brick meetinghouse erected especially for the occasion.[33] There is no doubt that he was present at the first Iowa Yearly Meeting, held at Spring Creek on Ninth Month 10, 1863.[34] The men met in a temporary shelter erected next to the Spring Creek Meeting House and the women met in the meeting house.[35] Hobson's is the first name listed as a representative from Bangor Quarterly Meeting (formerly Western Plains), of which Honey Creek Monthly Meeting was then a part. Lindley Hoag and Esther and Nathan Frame were also in attendance at the first Iowa Yearly Meeting. It can safely be said that significant ministry occurred during the worship and business meetings. Iowa Yearly Meeting was moved to Oskaloosa five years later, in 1865, and held in a new brick meeting house built especially for the event.[36] Iowa Yearly Meeting sessions took place in Oskaloosa until 1970 when they were moved to the campus of William Penn College.[37] Based on the record of his later involvement at the quarterly and yearly meeting level in Iowa, it's safe to say that Hobson was quite involved in the business of Iowa Friends in the early days.

Goldsmith reports that Hobson wrote his first letter from Iowa to his in-laws, William and Mary Tulburt. It was dated Sixth Month 26, 1849, and sent from Richland, so we know that the Hobsons were settled there by early summer 1849, at the latest. It may be that they arrived sooner, but he just didn't have time to write while putting in the spring crops. In his letter to the Tulburts he tells how he "purchased three parcels of prairie and timbered

---

32. Iowa Yearly Meeting, *Iowa Yearly Meeting of Friends*, 8, 81.
33. Jones, *Quakers of Iowa*, 54–55.
34. Iowa Yearly Meeting, *Iowa Yearly Meeting of Friends*, 9.
35. Elliot, *Quakers on the American Frontier*, 119.
36. Iowa Yearly Meeting, *Iowa Yearly Meeting of Friends*, 9, 12.
37. "History," *Iowa Yearly Meeting of Friends*.

land, totaling one hundred and sixty-seven acres, for which he had paid $209.58. He had also taken three choice forties of land by pre-emption, the whole cost of the properties being $330.00. He was busy cutting rails and fencing his spread, attempting the while to improve the cabin which had come with the land."[38] Goldsmith described further how the letter indicated that the cabin needed substantial work, but Hobson was "full of praise for his newly acquired land. Its rich soil, valuable timber and excellent water were beyond comparison with North Carolina's poor timber and soil he declared, and since claims were being taken up fast, he urged his Yadkin Valley relatives to hasten their coming while land was still available nearby." Sarah and William's second son and third child, Stephen was born Twelfth Month 22, 1849,[39] while they were living at Richland. Though he appeared quite pleased with their Richland farm, in just a few years Hobson was itching to move farther west.

Earlier assertions that a significant number of Friends were moving to Iowa are confirmed by the observations of Hobson. It also becomes apparent that Friends of substance were moving west. Goldsmith tells how Hobson noted in letters to the Tulburts, written in the early 1850s, that "'Friends are moving to Iowa fast'" and that "'Our last Quarterly Meeting was quite large.'" He was surprised at the number of resident ministers, reporting that "'we now have upwards of 25 [ministers] belonging to our Quarter Who either frequently or some times appear in public [preach].'"[40] Friends had moved to Iowa from predominately Gurneyite meetings, so the flavor of Iowa Yearly Meeting was predominately Gurneyite. However, there were some Friends who sided with Wilbur. Gurneyite and Wilburite Friends in Iowa Yearly Meeting were able to live and worship together, holding their differences in tension, until the 1877 revival at Bear Creek, which was the culmination of several years of renewal and awakening in that region. It seems that the exuberant worship experience at Bear Creek was the straw that broke the camel's back. Conservative Wilburite Friends flatly refused to join in what they considered to be overly emotional, un-Friendly worship innovations and by 1884 there were two Iowa Yearly Meetings, one Conservative which remained unprogrammed and one Gurneyite which embraced revivalist practices like singing and altar calls. The significant revival at Bear Creek occurred about a year after the Hobsons were settled in Oregon, so they

38. Goldsmith, "William Hobson and the Founding of Quakerism in the Pacific Northwest," 131

39. Goldsmith, "William Hobson and the Founding of Quakerism in the Pacific Northwest," 166.

40. Goldsmith, "William Hobson and the Founding of Quakerism in the Pacific Northwest," 135.

were not involved directly in the separation, though they were still under the authority of Iowa Yearly Meeting at the time. Hobson was a Gurneyite Friend, though one who preferred unprogrammed worship, and the new meeting he organized in Oregon applied to the Gurneyite Iowa Yearly Meeting for monthly meeting status. Later John Henry Douglas, a well-known revivalist and proponent of the pastoral system, visited Oregon meetings in his capacity as the Gurneyite Iowa Yearly Meeting Superintendent.

According to Goldsmith, in January 1850 Hobson, as part of a committee appointed by the yearly meeting, traveled ninety miles northwest of Richland to the Three Rivers Country to determine if a small meeting that had formed there was ready to become a preparative meeting. The Three Rivers Country, in central Iowa, was a fertile area about fifteen miles southeast of old Fort Des Moines where three small streams, the North, Middle, and South Rivers flowed into the Des Moines River. On this journey into the heart of Iowa, Hobson explored

> choice unoccupied land much more desirable than that upon which he had settled. The timber land near Richland, which he had depended upon for fencing and farm improvements, was two and one-half miles from his home, an undesirable situation when adjoining timber and prairie could be had by moving farther west. Under the latter circumstances, one could settle and improve a farm much faster, and due to the rising value of land around Richland, he saw that he could sell at a profit and settle to better advantage farther on.[41]

Hobson was no longer content at Richland after seeing some of the land to the west and he began looking for a place to resettle. Eventually, he decided to put down roots in what was called the Big Woods Country of Iowa, a sparsely populated area of "rolling prairies and heavily timbered bottom lands." The Big Woods Country was even farther out than the Three Rivers Country in virtually uninhabited, unbroken wilderness, "roughly sixty miles north by northeast of Fort Des Moines, and it represented the vanguard of northern Iowa settlements."[42] One can't help but wonder what Sarah thought when Hobson returned from his journey to the hinterlands west and told her the "good news"; they were moving again, even farther away from civilization. Hobson was able to convince some others to go with

---

41. Goldsmith, "William Hobson and the Founding of Quakerism in the Pacific Northwest," 143–44 (footnote on page 143).

42. Goldsmith, "William Hobson and the Founding of Quakerism in the Pacific Northwest," 144.

them, including her brother's family, so perhaps this helped to smooth over any objections she may have had.

Goldsmith worked hard to determine the exact date the Hobsons left Richland for the Big Woods Country. After carefully examining family letters, the accounts of Samuel Hobson and Abel Bond, Richland Monthly Meeting minutes, and *History of Hardin County*, Goldsmith concluded that the Hobsons departed for the Big Woods Country at the end of Third Month or first part of Fourth Month 1852. According to Goldsmith, the Hobsons started out that spring for regions further west with the James Tulburt family, his uncle Elam Jessup's family,[43] and though Goldsmith doesn't say, probably his cousin Abel Bond's family, as well. Sarah was pregnant and they had in their care three small children ranging in age from seven to three-years-old.

Goldsmith confirmed that the Hobson family stopped over at Bangor about a hundred miles northwest of Richland on the upper courses of the Iowa River where the Jessups and Bonds decided to settle. Hobson decided to seek out his own claim in the vicinity and he used the Bangor settlement as a base, camping on Jessup land for several months with Uncle Elam's family. During the summer of 1852 Hobson helped Uncle Elam build a cabin on his homestead, which the two families shared for a time.[44] The rich farmland at Bangor attracted more Friends and Bangor Monthly Meeting was established by 1853. Bangor Quarterly Meeting (formerly Western Plains) was established in 1858.[45] During the Hobsons' summer at Bangor, Sarah gave birth to their second daughter and fourth child, Mary, on Seventh Month 13, 1852.[46] According to Goldsmith, in the fall of that year, Hobson rode north scouting out the perfect piece of land to claim as his own. About five miles north of Bangor, he came across the Dobbins and Reece families settled on the south bank of Honey Creek, in what would later become Providence Township. Goldsmith noted, "these Quakers were at the edge of settlements, and as a prospective neighbor, Hobson was greeted with warmth. Not quite satisfied, he rode a mile and a half through heavily timbered bottom lands

---

43. Goldsmith, "William Hobson and the Founding of Quakerism in the Pacific Northwest," 144–47. Goldsmith considered Samuel Hobson and Abel Bond to be unreliable sources for the Hobson family's start date to Honey Creek and relied more on family letters, Richland Monthly Meeting minutes, and *History of Hardin County* to fix his date.

44. Goldsmith, "William Hobson and the Founding of Quakerism in the Pacific Northwest," 149

45. Iowa Yearly Meeting, *Iowa Yearly Meeting of Friends*, 8, 81.

46. Goldsmith, "William Hobson and the Founding of Quakerism in the Pacific Northwest," 166.

of Honey Creek and found a pleasing prairie to the north with fine timber adjacent. The neighbors to the south and the friends and relatives at Bangor came up to Hobson's claim and made short work of putting up a cabin. The Hobsons occupied it about January 1, 1853."[47]

Though very remote and separated from the nearest neighbors by about a mile and a half of timber, the land at Honey Creek fit Hobson's requirements for choice acreage, according to a letter he wrote to his father-in-law in the spring of 1851. The letter, summarized by Goldsmith, tells how quality timber grew right next to a large stretch of prairie, which meant less travel back and forth for lumber. Hobson was pleased that the Iowa River falls were not far off, which would be helpful in the running of mills and machinery. Limestone and coal were abundant. Hobson also listed sugar maples and wild game among the assets of the area, as well as a healthy climate and the fact that it was thinly settled. As Goldsmith points out, Hobson was looking for the perfect piece of land, not too close to his neighbors, but close enough to meet for worship together and to be able to help each other out as needed.[48] A letter to a newspaper written by Iowa Governor Eastman in 1869 and reprinted in the *History of Hardin County*, tells how difficult it was to cross icy Honey Creek in the early days. Several years before the Hobsons arrived, in 1844, Governor Eastman tried to ford Honey Creek. He broke a channel in the ice that had formed on top of the creek, but his oxen were swamped by the freezing cold water which had risen to eight feet. He cut them loose from the wagon, which drifted several yards downstream and then sank down in the creek bed. He was drenched through to his skin and his clothes froze, but he was able to walk two miles for help. The next day, with the aid of two men, he pulled his wagon out of the creek and drove home. The first ferry across Honey Creek, started sometime between 1844 and 1858, was located at Hadley's Mill,[49] making the crossing of Honey Creek much easier. This wonderful, yet wild and uncivilized spot, with its rich rolling prairie, well-watered by Honey Creek and its tributaries, and conveniently located timber would

---

47. Goldsmith, "William Hobson and the Founding of Quakerism in the Pacific Northwest," 149–50; Union Publishing Company, *History of Hardin County*, 845, 860. *History of Hardin County* states that the Hobson family arrived at Honey Creek in the winter of 1852, close enough to Goldsmith's move in date of 1/1/1853. Prior to this Sarah and the children stayed at Bangor while William worked on their cabin at Honey Creek, during which time he attended the first meeting of Honey Creek Preparative Meeting sometime in the fall of 1852.

48. Goldsmith, "William Hobson and the Founding of Quakerism in the Pacific Northwest," 147–48.

49. Union Publishing Company, *History of Hardin County Iowa*, 409–12, 865.

be the Hobson home for just over the next two decades, though it would not remain uncivilized for long.

Hobson's son Samuel described the process of moving to Honey Creek in more detail telling how William followed a stream on the south side of a belt of timber, varying from one to one and a half miles in width, northwest about twelve miles from Bangor. There he found some Quaker and Baptist families from North Carolina, near where he grew up, already settled. He ended up taking a claim on the north side of the timber from this little settlement and the neighbors agreed to help him build a log cabin near a spring branch of Honey Creek. According to Samuel, William returned to Bangor, reported his findings, and then returned north and built a small house at Honey Creek. The rustic log cabin was completed around Christmas time, after which Hobson fetched Sarah and the kids, bringing them home. There was snow on the ground and William had to build a sled to make the move. There was no road, so the horses broke a path through the snow and timber which took all day from Bangor. The family reached the cabin at sundown, William made a roaring fire, and they ate their second meal since early morning. The horses stayed out in the cold weather tied to saplings with snow for a bed in a sheltered place in the timber where the wind could not chill them.

Samuel remembered the floor of the cabin was frozen dirt that thawed in the heat of the fire and became sticky black mud. They laid a few clapboards down to stand on in one corner and made beds out of cord wood covered with hazel brush and spruce. Bedding was placed on top. He reported that the fire kept everyone warm that night, but Samuel did not sleep well on his makeshift bed. It seems that the first order of business was to lay down rough-hewn wooden floorboards, called puncheon, in the cabin and the second was to set up a sturdy windbreak shelter for the horses. Thankfully, Samuel noted, it was a mild winter. Hobson soon blazed a trail to their neighbors and then with their help carved out a wagon path across the timber, the only crossing for four or five miles up and down the stream.[50] The Hobsons could now settle in on their new homestead.

---

50. Hobson, "Memories" 10-13.

William Hobson.

HONEY CREEK, IOWA

Honey Creek was located within the boundaries of Hardin County which was created by an act of the Iowa General Assembly on First Month 15, 1851, though less than a dozen families were living there at the time. Census records show that by 1860, about seven years after the Hobsons arrived at Honey Creek, there were 5,440 individuals living in Hardin County and by

1870, about the time Hobson got the call to move further west, the population had increased to 13,684.[51] Honey Creek was a rural community, within Providence Township, flourishing along the banks and tributaries of a creek named Honey that flowed into the Iowa River.[52] The Dobbins and the Reece families were some of the first settlers at Honey Creek, along with John J. Thornton, arriving on Eighth Month 1, 1851. Friends continued to settle in the area and eventually made up the majority of the residents in Providence Township, including the Honey Creek community, which likely explains the fact that Providence Township was still a dry town when *History of Hardin County* was written in 1883.[53] This would have suited Hobson just fine.

The Hobsons were part of the first wave of pioneers to settle in Iowa, coming in wagons to tame the unmitigated wilderness. In fact, during his first trip to the Pacific Northwest while at Union Flat in remote and mostly unsettled Washington Territory, he wrote, "I have read much in the Bible to day. Was. Left alone a while. It caused me to recollect our loneliness of the first settling at Honey Creek in Iowa."[54] Unlike those who would come later on the railroad,[55] the Hobsons and their neighbors, who settled miles away from each other, lived "in a new country, far removed from the conveniences of civilization, where all [were] compelled to build their own houses, make their own clothing and procure for themselves the means of subsistence, [so] it [was] to be expected that their dwellings and garments [would] be rude."[56] The Hobsons certainly fell into this category, during their early days at Honey Creek.

According to *History of Hardin County* the typical Iowa log cabin built in the mid-1800s was daubed with a mortar of clay. Floors were either hard packed earth or puncheon. Stone or earth lined offset chimneys both provided warmth and were used for cooking. Doors were made of clapboards pegged to cross-boards and hung on wooden hinges. They were closed with a latch and hook catch and could be locked by pulling a buckskin strip inside the door through a hole drilled for that purpose. Most households owned a loom for making cloth, a rifle and ammunition, simple furniture, dishes and cooking utensils, washtubs, and washboards, as well as many other necessary household items. Clothes were hung on pegs fixed in the cabin walls

---

51 Union Publishing Company, *History of Hardin County Iowa*, 68, 233.

52. Goldsmith, "William Hobson and the Founding of Quakerism in the Pacific Northwest," 145.

53. Union Publishing Company, *History of Hardin County Iowa*, 866.

54. Hobson, "Diaries," reel 1 of 2, 4/23/1871.

55. Goldsmith, "William Hobson and the Founding of Quakerism in the Pacific Northwest," 150–51.

56. Union Publishing Company, *History of Hardin County Iowa*, 249.

and sheets hung over cords were used to partition off sections of the cabin when privacy was needed.[57] According to his diary, one of Hobson's chores was to daub the cabin with mud, chinking the cracks between the logs in hopes of keeping out the cold winter wind.[58] Samuel Hobson remembered that the family moved from their first cabin in the woods to a big double cabin over the high hill on the prairie, but William didn't mention in his diary when they left their old cabin behind. Perhaps, they moved to larger accommodations before 1859.

Hobson made notations in his diary about plowing, cutting timber and rails, cutting oats and wheat, building livestock pens and shelters, and butchering beef and hogs, along with sowing seed, tending his orchards, and numerous other choices required to keep up a farm. There was plenty of work to do from dawn to dusk and beyond. Of course, the children were expected to do their part as soon as possible. Samuel reported that starting at age ten he worked from four o'clock in the morning to sundown as a farm hand.[59]

Hobson raised enough beef and pork to be able to sell some of it. But the Hobsons kept sheep mainly for the wool.[60] Samuel remembered that his dad made Sarah a loom and that she made their clothes from the wool they raised. The itchy wool clothing gave Samuel sores. He also remembered feeding her wool as she made a bed spread on the loom.[61] *History of Hardin County* indicates that out of plain necessity every family did its own spinning, weaving, and sewing, using flax, hemp, and wool as raw materials.[62] Sarah and the children most likely carded and spun the wool themselves in the early days, so a spinning wheel must have taken up a corner of the cabin along with the loom, but by 1863 and possibly sooner, the family had other options. The wool could be sent out to be carded and spun mechanically.[63] The regular practice of shipping out wool to be carded and spun must have saved Sarah a lot of work. The nearest carding mill resided in Marshalltown, about twenty-five miles south of Honey Creek,[64] but even with the long trip it was a time savings overall. Sarah was not only responsible for carding and spinning the wool before the mill was up and running, but she was

---

57. Union Publishing Company, *History of Hardin County Iowa*, 250.
58. Hobson, "Diaries," reel 2 of 2, 1/4/1859, 11/5–8/1859.
59. Hobson, "Memories" 35–6.
60. Hobson, "Diaries," reel 2 of 2, 11/7–8/1861, 10/17/1863, 5/21/1859.
61. Hobson, "Memories" 32–33.
62. Union Publishing Company, *History of Hardin County Iowa*, 252.
63. Hobson, "Diaries," reel 2 of 2, 7/11/1859, 5/22/1863.
64. Goldsmith, "William Hobson and the Founding of Quakerism in the Pacific Northwest," 156.

also responsible for making all their clothes and other textiles. Perhaps she sewed everything by hand in the early days, but by the spring of 1865, at the very least, she had the use of a sewing machine.[65] Also, by this time Rachel and Mary, and even Anna at six years old, would have been old enough to help with the weaving, sewing, and mending.

At first, shoes may have been made at home. Hobson had learned how to make and mend shoes as a boy in North Carolina, so we can be pretty sure he owned cobbler's tools. Later, like with the convenience of sending out wool to be spun, ready-made shoes and fabric became available at the mercantile. However, these items were expensive and not to be taken for granted. Hobson mentions mending shoes and boots considerably more often than buying them. The earliest we see the family buying footwear is in Tenth Month 1863, when Hobson makes two notations about shoes, one at the first of the month and one at the end: "Bought Mary a pair of Shoes & B . . . to amount of [$]3.5" and "The children got back [from the store] got boots Dress &C."[66] It seems likely that ready-made dresses and other clothing, as well as shoes could be purchased at the store before 1863, but how much before is unclear from Hobson's diary. He does make a note, in a list of expenses written at the back of one of his notebooks, that he paid forty cents for muslin and buttons, so it's apparent that, at the very least, cloth and notions were available no later than 1859,[67] even if ready-made clothing and shoes were not. *History of Hardin County* indicates that a mercantile was established in Eldora, about eight miles northeast of Honey Creek in Twelfth Month 1853, and that general merchandise could be obtained in New Providence, about two miles away, near the north end of Providence Township, by 1856.[68] What exactly was on offer is difficult to determine. Certainly, stores became better stocked as time went on and the railroad pushed farther west. Eldora was finally connected to the railroad by 1868, which helped to not only stock the mercantile,[69] but also improved transportation options and made it much easier to ship crops to and receive goods from the east.

Beyond the daily toil of carving out a life in the wilderness, Iowa settlers also faced the twin hardships of sickness and injury. Doctors were few and far between, so home remedies and first aid procedures were important

---

65. Hobson, "Diaries," reel 1 of 2, 4/22/1865.
66. Hobson, "Diaries," reel 2 of 2, 10/13/1863, 10/31/1863.
67. Hobson, "Diaries," reel 2 of 2, see notations after 7/1860.
68. Goldsmith, "William Hobson and the Founding of Quakerism in the Pacific Northwest," 156; Union Publishing Company, *History of Hardin County Iowa*, 632, 870.
69. Union Publishing Company, *History of Hardin County Iowa*, 506–7.

skills to cultivate. Darius B. Cook in *History of Quaker Divide* indicates that "people were often sick in these early days. The prevailing acute diseases were pneumonia and typhoid. Extremely cold temperatures, shallow wells, and crowded homes all contributed to the instigation and spread of disease."[70] One might also wonder about the unsanitary nature of outhouses.

History of Hardin County describes an ailment singular to Hardin County called "chills and fever," "fever and ague," or the "shakes."[71] Samuel mentions that in the early days at Honey Creek the family suffered from chills and fever in the fall season as follows: "we would have a chill every other day, usually in the forenoon. Shake for 2 or 3 hours, and the shake was followed with a terrible headache and fever for the rest of the day. The next day we would mope around, get ready for a shake the next day. One with the chills and fever soon got poor, and pail [sic], and weak, good for nothing. I don't know why, but it seemed that everyone in a new plane [sic] had to have a round of chills and fever. As more people settled in our neighborhood the chills and fever faded out and we seemed to have a very healthy country from then on."[72]

Hobson mentions in his diary several different bouts of other sicknesses, during the years they lived in Iowa. He mostly suffered from colds, complaining of a sore throat and cough, or digestive aliments (food poisoning? viruses?) which involved vomiting to some degree. He also recorded three episodes of erysipelas, a streptococci bacterial infection of the skin. In Fifth Month 1865, he merely noted that the infection was spreading across his face. His second bout seems to have begun on the train a few days before he reached home after visiting the Pacific Northwest for the first time. He writes, while riding the train on Seventh Month 13, 1871, "My health is not as good as it was in the latter part of winter. I think there som [sic] erysepilas [sic] or else some other much hidden disease preying upon some unseen part of the body. As manifested by itchings [sic] about my head often with hot flashes about my ears and nose." He later notes on Seventh Month 17, 1871, just four days after arriving home, "have the Erysepelas [sic] So I have to stay in and try to cure myself. It is not a severe case as yet but is manifesting itself by hot flashes of feeling inwardly as well as outwardly on my face and nose with redness of skin and some little swelling." He was better two days later. His third bout occurred in First Month 1876, while he was living in Oregon. Erysipelas could be fatal in the years before antibiotics were

---

70. Cook, *History of Quaker Divide*, 22.
71. Union Publishing Company, *History of Hardin County Iowa*, 254–56.
72. Hobson, "Memories" 33.

discovered, but Hobson apparently had mild cases and was able to fight off the infection with rest and unrecorded home remedies.[73]

For the most part Hobson did not let illness slow him down, but, at the turn of the year in 1872, he had a bad cold. On Twelfth Month, 9, 1872, he noted "Halled [sic] 2 loads of wood was very unwell." By First Month 10, 1873, he had been sick for a month: "Have been unwell done no work but the chores for One Month ["One Month" written in big letters.]" Usually, he continued to work when sick. He couldn't afford not to, a common plight for pioneers. For example, in Eighth Month 1863, he reports, "killed a Beef, plowed &C I was very sick." The family had to eat, the crops and animals had to be tended, and chores had to be taken care of or long-term suffering would be inflicted upon them all. Sickness and injury were formidable foes on the frontier. If illness prevented the timely sowing or harvesting of crops, compromised the health of livestock, or prevented the preservation of food, families had no safety net to fall into and the survival of all was in jeopardy.

Hobson does not note that Sarah experienced any sicknesses apart from colds (sore throat, cough) and stomach complaints, though it's safe to say that pregnancy and childbirth were not easy in this setting. Sarah seems to have had no serious complications from giving birth to six children, however. Their third son and fifth child, Jesse, was born at Honey Creek Sixth Month 13, 1857. Their third daughter and last child, Anna, was born Fifth Month 4, 1859, also at Honey Creek. Hobson does not remark, beyond noting a cold or sore throat, on any ailment that their children experienced, though it seems likely that their kids endured several of the usual childhood diseases of the time, for which we now have vaccines. Samuel Hobson mentions a sickness he had as a child, a lung fever as he calls it (possibly typhoid or pneumonia) that almost killed him, as well as a time when he had the mumps and fell through some ice on the way to church. He was soaked through, but his clothes froze, so he suffered no adverse long-term effects. His sister Rachel helped him out of a twenty foot well he fell into by lowering a rope, and another time, he was flattened by a log that rolled down the skids as he and William were loading it onto a sled. Samuel also remembered an accident his brother Stephen experienced in the timber. Stephen fell while cutting a log with an axe and

> his left hand came down acrossed [sic] the blade of the ax acrossed [sic] the palm cutting all the leaders of the fingers except for the index finger. Also severing the big artery so that when his heart would beat the blood would shoot out in a great

---

73. Hobson, "Diaries," reel 2 of 2, 5/4–8/1865, 7/13/1871, 7/17/1871–7/19/1871; "Erysipelas," *Healthline*.

stream. I saw he would bleed to death the way it was running out. So I took his write in my left hand place [sic] the ball of my thumb on the artery in the wrist and with my right hand I led him home a quarter mile away. And there holding him by the wrist while father went two and a miles for a Dr. When he came he tied a knot in a strip of cloth placing the know [sic] where my thumb was tying it tight. This kept it from bleeding. He then took up the severed artery and put it together some way. I don't know what he did to hold it and with little strips of tape placed acrossed [sic] the cut in the hand to hold it together.[74]

His brother survived, but he never had good use of his fingers. Samuel also claims to have saved Stephen from drowning at some undesignated time and place.[75] Stephen's accident with the axe seems to be confirmed in Hobson's diary with the following laconic entry made Third Month 23, 1865: "Warm & (23) very Windy Stephen Cut his left hand very much. We all missed [fifth day meeting] on account there off [sic] Some Lambs & a calf come."[76] If this was the event Samuel described, he was twenty years old at the time and Stephen was sixteen. It seems that the Hobson family was made of stern stuff. All six Hobson children survived to adulthood, an unusual thing for the times, and both William and Sarah remained remarkably healthy during their years in Iowa.

The Hobsons produced most of their food, depending on stores in the surrounding towns only for things they could not grow or raise themselves, such as coffee and tea, though sometimes if they were low on supplies Hobson would purchase items such as bacon, cheese, or sugar at the store. Most of the acreage on the Hobson farm was taken up with wheat, oats, and corn. Hobson also planted sugar cane, flaxseed, and Timothy hay. Cook, explains the wheat sowing process:

> When time for spring farming came, the farmer might be seen plodding across the field, back and forth, with a grain sack slung across his shoulder, sowing wheat and other small grain by hand. Following him would be another man or one of his boys with the team hitched to an "A" harrow. This was a slow process, as the harrow had but one row of teeth, and if the ground was soddy or cloddy, the harrow was lapped half way.[77]

Cook goes on to describe the corn sowing process, as well:

74. Hobson, "Memories," 8, 30–31.
75. Hobson, "Memories" 39–40.
76. Hobson, "Diaries," reel 2 of 2, 3/23/1865.
77. Cook, *History of Quaker Divide*, 12.

Corn growing began in Hoosier fashion. Stirring was done with a left handed plow with a single line and jockey stick on the team. When the ground was ready it was marked both ways with the single shovel plow, the corn dropped by hand in the cross furrows and covered with a hoe. The corn was plowed with a single or double shovel. A single line was used, and the horse knew "gee and haw," some horses could be plowed "by the word" without a line. This method of planting was succeeded by the hand corn planter.[78]

Samuel Hobson reported that they used a single shovel for a plow pulled by a big white horse,[79] perhaps John who had started out with them from North Carolina, and Hobson broke raw prairie with help from neighbors using a plow pulled by oxen. *History of Hardin County* indicates that most pioneers in the area used a "bar-share" plow to break the earth. This type of plow had a point made from a bar of iron two feet long with a broad share of iron welded to it for cutting furrows. The handles were six or seven feet long and a wooden moldboard lifted and turned the soil over. Apparently, this plow worked so well a woman or even a young girl could guide it behind the horse. After plowing, the soil was harrowed with a wooden rake or a brush.[80] Hobson does not give details in his diary about how he plowed and harrowed. He merely remarks, laconically, "plowed" sometimes giving the location or the duration of this activity. Likewise, he does not tell how he sowed seed, whether grain, fruit, or vegetable, but merely states the fact that it was done.

Spring sowing and plowing was strenuous, but harvest time was even more back-breaking and the heat could be debilitating at times. Wheat and oats were cut with a cradle, a scythe with finger like rods attached that aligned the cut grain in neat rows. This made the grain easier to shock and stack. Later, a harvesting machine called the McCormick reaper was hired by several farmers in a neighborhood and they would take turns helping to harvest neighborhood fields.[81]

Hobson both cradled his grain crops and made use of a rented reaper. At the end of Seventh Month 1861, he made a note that he "Went & engaged for a machine to Cut Wheat," though later in the week he records that he "Cradled & bound about 4 ½ acres of Wheat 4 ½ acres of Wheat by 2

---

78. Cook, *History of Quaker Divide*, 12–13.
79. Hobson, "Memories" 21.
80. Union Publishing Company, *History of Hardin County Iowa*, 259.
81. Cook, *History of Quaker Divide*, 12–13.

Cradles & Jesse Martin, Daniel & Nereus Martin to help us Bind."[82] Maybe he and his neighbors were in transition from cradling grain to relying on the reaper or there may have been sections of land that were awkward to harvest with the machine. Hobson makes notations in his diary at the end of Seventh Month 1864, that show he was part of a group of neighbors that worked together to harvest their fields that year, using the reaping machine and likely pitching in on the cost. He records the names of hands and the hours each worked cutting wheat and oats, as well as noting who brought oil to lubricate the machine. At one point they had to stop and fix the machine before resuming cutting the next day. A few days later he reported that the wheat and oats harvest was finished on his farm.[83] Cutting the grain, whether cradled by hand or more efficiently cut with a reaper, was a familiar scene each year at the end of Seventh Month.

It seems that a large amount of wheat was threshed, or "thrashed" as Hobson called it, with a machine, after which it was taken to the mill to be made into flour. Smaller amounts were threshed throughout the year by hand, as needed. Oats were used mainly as feed for livestock and were threshed in the same way. Cook points out that there weren't many threshing machines available, so several neighbors would join in hiring them which prolonged threshing time in a particular region as each farm waited for their turn.[84] The harvest and processing of wheat and oats was a long, hot activity but it resulted in much needed flour, oatmeal, and livestock feed.

Corn was usually planted a little later than wheat and oats and gathered a little later in the season, by hand, as was sugar cane, which was boiled down into molasses in the fall. Corn was husked in preparation for a trip to the mill where it was ground into cornmeal. According to Cook, cornmeal was used for making mush eaten with milk, spoon cakes, cornbread, and cornpone, which was a mixture of cornmeal and water baked in a Dutch oven. "When done a pone was covered with a hard crust reminding one very much of a turtle shell, but the inside was good eating and would keep a long time. It differed from corn bread in being more solid and sweeter."[85] Corn could also be made into hominy, a dish made from corn kernels soaked in lye, or grits. Livestock was also fed with corn.

According to Samuel Hobson, before any mills were built, they pounded corn with a mortar and pestle made from a section of oak log attached to a spring pole. The wood was funnel shaped and could hold about a peck

82. Hobson, "Diaries," reel 2 of 2, 7/22/1861–7/27/1861.
83. Hobson, "Diaries," reel 2 of 2, 7/21/1864–8/3/1864.
84. Cook, *History of Quaker Divide*, 13.
85. Cook, *History of Quaker Divide*, 18–19.

of corn. Nails driven in the end filtered out fine particles of corn for bread. It's unclear as to whether this contraption was also used to mill wheat. It was Samuel's job to run this "mill," so he was happy when some neighbors got together and built a large windmill that could work two pestles when the wind was strong. Later, a water powered mill with large mill stones was built across the creek. Hobson was put in charge of this mill, because of his previous milling experience back home in North Carolina, though another man eventually took it over. This mill ran six days a week. When the Steamboat Rock Mill eighteen miles away on the Iowa River was established, the local milling operations ceased.[86] Hobson makes notations about going to the mill with either wheat or corn or both and returning from the mill with sacks of flour or meal numerous times. It took at least a day to go and come back from the mill and it cost a bit for the grinding service, but it was much more efficient than "milling" at home. He could often combine a trip to the mill with a trip to the mercantile or some other errand and wrote in his diary in the fall of 1871 how convenient it was to be able to go to the mill and market on the same day, indicating how much things had changed in the twenty years since the Hobsons had first settled at Honey Creek.

Hobson was not consistent in recording his grain crop yields, but he did note them from time to time. In one five-year period between 1859 and 1864, he saw an increase of 477 bushels of wheat and 306.5 bushels of oats.[87] For some reason Hobson did not record corn yields at all, merely noting most years in late fall, the fact that he had finished gathering the crop. Perhaps corn was used mainly as animal feed. He did buy about 400 bushels of corn in the fall of 1873 indicating a possible poor crop or a focus on other grain crops or apple production. He also bought corn, likely for seed or feed, in the spring of 1875.[88]

Settlers in the Honey Creek neighborhood engaged in a significant amount of trade and commerce with each other. In several of his notebooks Hobson kept records of who owed him money and to whom he owed money. Items such as wheat, corn, bacon, beef, apples, and other produce were sold to or bought from neighbors, often on credit. Neighbors borrowed from each other frequently and made up for what was borrowed in kind or with coin. When the arduous trip to the mercantile was undertaken, items were often traded with the storekeeper since cash was in short supply. Also, neighbors would help each other out by taking a load of grain to the mill,

---

86. Hobson, "Memories" 17–18.

87. Hobson, "Diaries," reel 2 of 2, 8/24/1871, 9/21/1859, 9/22/1859, 10/12/1861, 10/1863 see end of notebook, 11/16/1864.

88. Hobson, "Diaries," reel 2 of 2, 9/3/1873, 10/25/1873, 2/16/1875.

wool to the spinner, or making a trip to the store, if they were headed that way anyway. Occasionally, Hobson mentions paying off a note, but mostly, it seems, transactions were sealed with a Friendly handshake.

Often, Hobson was entrusted with money to pay for another settler's taxes or to buy a land deed for prospective members of the Honey Creek community. Samuel Hobson remembered that many potential settlers contacted Hobson for help with procuring acreage in the Honey Creek area. Hobson had encouraged several families to settle at Honey Creek by writing invitations which he sent back east, so he was a natural point of connection and a willing aide in the moving process for many settlers. After helping newcomers to choose property he was also quite willing to procure deeds for them by conveying funds and land claims to Fort Dodge. Most of the settlers that Hobson helped in this way were Friends and as Samuel noted, "it was greatly through my father's influence that they came."[89] Hobson was quite invested in establishing a strong Friends community at Honey Creek.

Over time, Hobson built up a large orchard on his homestead in which he planted mostly apples, some pears, a few peaches, a few cherries, and possibly other types of fruit trees as well. It seems that apples and pears did quite well at Honey Creek, and they were easier to store and transport than peaches or cherries, though peaches were his favorite. He planted several different types of each fruit and was continually trying new varieties. In the spring of 1862, he planted at least ninety trees, some pear and some apple, and he set out an undesignated number of unspecified types of trees in the spring of 1864. His orchard required a fair amount of upkeep, including the necessity for a good fence to keep out wild animals. In the spring each year he picked caterpillar eggs off the leaves of his trees by hand, trimmed the trees, and "washed" them, by which he meant he whitewashed the trunks. He painted his orchard to reflect heat and prevent sunburned bark. Whitewash also provided effective protection against boring beetles and moth larvae, pests that could easily damage bark, leaves, and fruit. Harvest generally began in late summer and ended in early fall. He mentions paying a man for grafting in the fall of 1863 and we can presume that grafting cuttings onto rootstock also became an annual task as he increased the size of his orchard. He even started some trees from seed. Around Twelfth Month each year, he mulched with manure, a task he called "littering" his trees. He first mentions "littering" in Twelfth Month 1859, and he first notes gathering a crop in Ninth Month 1863.[90] Since it can take up to ten years and as few

89. Hobson, "Memories" 18.

90. Hobson, "Diaries," reel 1 of 2, 2/25/1873, 3/14/1873, 4/24/1873, 5/15/1873, 5/4/1874, 6/1874, 8/11/1874, reel 2 of 2, 5/7/1859, 12/9/1859, 12/9/1861, 4/16/1862, 4/25-26/1862, 4/28/1862, 5/2/1862, 9/23/1863, 4/13/1864, 4/16/1864, 4/1/1865,

as seven years after planting bare root saplings for apple trees to produce a good crop, we can guess that he planted his first trees just a few years after arriving at Honey Creek.

Much later in Seventh Month 1871, after Hobson returned from his first trip to the West Coast, he ran an experiment to determine how long to leave apples on the trees before harvesting. He "weighted [sic] several different sorts of apples . . . And find that heaped measure will average 45 lbs to the bu [shel]. Have gathered one peck of Famouse [sic] Apples which weigh out well now and have been used by some for several weeks as cooking apples. I suppose they are not fully grown yet. I have placed one peck by to compare with those on same tree a few weeks [later]."[91] Though he did not record the results of this experiment, it's important to note that he was interested in improving his horticultural knowledge and crop yield. In 1871 a bushel of apples sold for $1.50,[92] but he does not record the total harvest. In the fall of 1872, he finished gathering apples from "the large orchard," as he called it, indicating that he had more than one section of his land planted with fruit trees. He gathered two hundred bushels of apples total that year. Assuming the going price for bushels was still $1.50 that would make $300 gross, or just over $6000 in today's money.[93] Though the total 1873 apple crop stands unrecorded, he gathered at least sixty-five bushels of fruit and was able to get $2.00 a bushel. He sold most of the crop, but also stored some apples in a root cellar, pressed cider, and made apple cider vinegar.[94]

The health and growth patterns of fruit trees was always noted by Hobson on his travels. He seemed especially interested in whether peaches grew well in various places, though he was also interested in the health of apples and other fruit. If a given area was not friendly to the cultivation of fruit trees, he pretty much wrote it off as poor country. Later, as he was in the process of looking for the perfect place to settle on the West Coast, he would not give a region much consideration if he thought fruit production was poor in that locality and he brought his love of growing fruit with him to the Chehalem Valley when he moved to Oregon.

So, we see that Hobson fed his sweet tooth with fruit, but there was something else almost as good that he loved to eat. What could be sweeter than a sun-warmed, ripe, and juicy peach? The answer: honey! And to

---

5/19/1862, 5/21/1864, 6/23-4/1864, 8/1864, 5/1/1865, 5/15/1865.
    91. Hobson, "Diaries," reel 2 of 2, 8/28/1871.
    92. Hobson, "Diaries," reel 2 of 2, 7/31/1871, 8/5/1871.
    93. Hobson, "Diaries," reel 1 of 2, 10/9/1872; *CPI Inflation Calculator*.
    94. Hobson, "Diaries," reel 1 of 2, 10/10/1872, 9/25/1872, 11/13/1872, 8/1/1873, 10/8-9/1873, 10/14/1873, 9/23/1874.

maintain a successful orchard and garden plot bees were a necessity. With Timothy hay, clover, and mustard growing in the rows between the trees, bees were attracted to the orchard, well fed, and happy, which would have assisted with both fruit and honey production. Apples and pears in particular require cross-pollination in order to set fruit well and bees facilitate that nicely. Certain other fruits and vegetables also produce better with increased numbers of pollinators, including crops like melons, squash, tomatoes, and cucumbers. It seems right that Hobson, who liked a touch of sweetness, settled in a region that took its name from a creek called Honey.

Samuel Hobson explains that the stream the Hobsons lived on was crossed by Honey Creek and Honey Creek received its name because of the large number of bees that lived in the timber flanking the steep banks of the small waterway. Samuel remembered that one time his dad cut down an old oak bee-tree growing in the timber, and they filled a washtub with honey from it. Another time his dad pulled up a stump with a hive in it, hitched up the horses to it, and dragged it back to their cabin. That old bee stump Hobson hunted produced two swarms the next summer and he hived them in bee gums, sections of hollow trees prepared to receive bees, likely placing them near his orchards.[95] Often in his diary he makes the notation "robbed the bees," by which he meant that he harvested honey from his hives. It seems very likely that he continued to increase the number of hives he tended, whether from wild bee hunting or further swarming of the hives he had already domesticated.

Serious-minded nineteenth century Friends were happy to live more simply and cleanly than many of their non-Quaker contemporaries, choosing to cultivate a healthy and wholesome family life free from the use of alcohol and tobacco, demoralizing novels, and what they considered to be time wasters like card games, theater, or playing musical instruments. Also, Friends at this period were still dressing, speaking, and living plainly. They valued frugality and good stewardship of their resources. The Hobsons were no exception to this kind of austere life, both out of conviction and necessity. Hobson as a strict Friend and as a recorded minister certainly led his family in the traditional Friends way. Their furniture, household items, and farm equipment were simple, plain, and useful. Hobson and other nineteenth century Friends did make use of new inventions like the McCormick Reaper and the sewing machine, that helped to lighten their workload, but this was considered good common sense and did not compromise their distaste for excess or show. Some examples of Hobson's dedication to simplicity are described by Samuel Hobson who tells of a time when, in his

---

95. Hobson, "Memories" 13–14.

estimation, his dad wrecked a new clock by removing strips of decorative molding and another time when William cut the red tops off a pair of boots Samuel had just bought. Samuel had a difficult time understanding why his dad would do these things and he chafed under what seemed to him to be excess diligence against the sin of pride. Samuel hints that his mother did not completely agree with Hobson's severity in these matters.[96] A certain level of sacrifice from all family members was involved in plain living.

Friends did enjoy reading even if they avoided novels,[97] and their libraries consisted of the Bible, Quaker classics like the *Journal of George Fox* or Barclay's *Apology*, various tracts, and reference books. Samuel confirms that he was kept busy reading George Fox, William Penn, Stephen Grellet, Robert Barclay, Joseph John Gurney, and other similar authors and that he had read the Bible through by the time he was six years old. A comment Hobson made to young Samuel echoes William Penn's *No Cross, No Crown*. Samuel was upset by a situation at school and his dad said "'If it is a cross to be made fun of, we must bear the cross [if] we expect a crown.'" Samuel had hoped that his dad would intervene at school, but he chose not to directly address the teasing Samuel was enduring.[98] Remember, Hobson himself had experienced ridicule when a young boy at school and had not complained. As a Gurneyite, it seems that Hobson was part of the group within Quakerism that began to study the Bible, instead of just reading it, though to what extent is unknown. He often quotes the Bible in his diary, so we can surmise he passed on his love for the Bible to his children, much as his mother had with him. Education was important to the Hobson family and all the children attended school.

Most nineteenth century Friends were concerned mainly with their small sphere of influence at meeting and among their neighbors. Jones states that beyond family life Friends' "chief interest was in church and neighborhood affairs" and "to the visitor from the world conversation among the Friends seemed limited, for rarely did they discuss topics of common political or social concern."[99] The Hobsons were no exception to this, until the call came to move west and even so Hobson expressed it as a desire to gather scattered Friends into a Quaker community. The legendary hospitality of Friends was one example of their concern for building and nurturing Quaker community. Traveling ministers were always welcomed with open arms and any traveling Friend was met happily. As Jones describes it "their

96. Hobson, "Memories," 35.
97. Jones, *Quakers of Iowa*, 280.
98. Hobson, "Memories" 15, 34.
99. Jones, *Quakers of Iowa*, 278–80.

hospitality was born of the long custom among themselves of frequent and uninvited visiting, especially in this western country [Iowa]."[100] In many cases a stranger at the door might be a relative, since Friends were so strict about "marrying-in." As part of his duties as a minister, Hobson visited all around the neighborhood, often staying for meals. He relied almost entirely on the hospitality of Friends and others during his longer trips in the ministry and to the West Coast, staying rarely at an inn. To be sure, the Hobsons themselves were hospitable to visitors. Jones gives insight into what hospitality during mealtime at the Hobson house may have looked like:

> With the abundance of simple but wholesome food and the good cheer that prevailed, the visitor was always welcome, whoever he might be. Little given to superfluity of any kind, the question of saying grace at the table was a serious one, for, thought they, better nothing said than that which came not from a reverent and honest heart. In consequence it was their custom when all were seated to observe a time of meditative silence, and if any one were moved to vocal utterance, he should prove obedient to his promptings. Not infrequently it occurred that for days or even weeks at a time no grace was said; but when it came, or come as frequently as it might, it was almost invariably sincere in tone and free from stereotyped expressions.[101]

When the family was gathered after the evening meal, as Jones also points out, "it was not uncommon, while sitting together for a long period of silence for religious reflection to occur, which often times ended with prayer or religious discussion without the slightest reserve." On the other hand, Friends also "had a wit and humor all their own, which not infrequently displayed itself." In other words, family life was not all reserve and hard work. Jones continues, "much of their humor concerned itself with amusing incidents known to have occurred—such as the story of the eccentric old Quaker who refused to allow his wife to grow red roses in her garden because they reminded him of the devil, while at the same time she might raise as many white roses as she wanted to.[102] This type of wry, self-deprecating humor, still characterizes the Friends sense of humor today. So, we see that Friends lived at home as they did in the world, seriously and deliberately by their convictions, but that they also took to heart George Fox's instructions to walk cheerfully over this world.

100. Jones, *Quakers of Iowa*, 278.
101. Jones, *Quakers of Iowa*, 281.
102. Jones, *Quakers of Iowa*, 263.

William and Sarah Hobson found many reasons for moving west from North Carolina. They hoped to escape the degradation of slavery, some of their Friends and family had already moved, it was a new adventure, they may have had personal reasons for wishing to leave Deep Creek Monthly Meeting, and, most importantly, the economic opportunities were so much more advantageous on the frontier. Once resolved to go, they made the trip to their final destination in stages, first stopping over in Indiana with Sarah's brother's family, then settling for a short time at Pleasant Plain, Iowa, slightly longer at Richland, and finally settling permanently at Honey Creek, in the Big Woods Country of Hardin County, Iowa, after a short sojourn at Bangor, a few miles to the south. Once settled at Honey Creek they began to improve their land, taming the rough country and surviving as best they could far removed from civilization. They built up a fine farm, grew grain crops and hay, produced garden vegetables and herbs, cultivated fruit and honey, raised livestock, and tended a large, productive orchard. They built a second home, several outbuildings, and miles of fence, as well as producing their own woolen cloth and other homemade articles like clothing and shoes. We have also seen how the Hobsons worked hard and lived simply, settling into a rhythm based on the seasons: plowing and planting grain crops, trimming fruit trees, and shearing sheep in the spring, tending the crops in the summer, harvesting and butchering in the fall, accomplishing indoor chores, and fertilizing the orchard in the winter. Winter was also the usual time for Hobson to travel in the ministry. Year-round chores included milking, tending the stock, mending boots and shoes, cooking, weeding the garden, laundry, and many other daily tasks. The Hobsons led the typical, wholesome Quaker family life free from "worldly" distractions. We also know that the Hobsons depended on their neighbors and their Quaker community for help with errands and for commerce until more people arrived and the railroad connected them with the eastern states. We have seen what it took physically to create a prosperous farm from scratch on the Iowa frontier and how important hospitality was to the fabric of the Friends community there. Now it's time to explore the spiritual side of life at Honey Creek.

HONEY CREEK MONTHLY MEETING AND TRAVELING IN THE MINISTRY

There is scant information about worship and business in the early days at Honey Creek because Hobson was not writing then and all the Honey Creek Monthly Meeting records prior to 1860 were lost when a tornado destroyed the home of the presiding clerk where the records were stored.[103] However, we can piece together some information from other sources. According to *History of Hardin County*, the first formal religious services in Providence Township consisted of a small gathering of Friends in the home of James Tulburt, Hobson's brother-in-law, sometime before the autumn of 1852, though most likely the Dobbins, Reeces, and a few other families had worshiped informally in their homes for some time previously. Soon after the meeting at the Tulburt home

> a preparative meeting was held at the house of William Dobbins, in the fall of 1852, at which time the Honey Creek Church was organized, composed of the following named: William Dobbins, Sr. and wife, William Dobbins, Jr. and family, Levi Reece and wife, William Hobson, an acknowledged minister; James Tulburt and family, Joseph Dillon and family, Samuel Dillon and wife, James Rawnsly and family. Among those who came soon after were Eleazer Andrews and family, Eli Jessup and family, John Andrews and family. The first minister was Wm. Hobson.[104].

Goldsmith adds the detail that Hobson and his cousin Abel Bond built benches to be used at this first official Friends meeting at Honey Creek.[105] During his journey in Iowa Robert Lindsey noted that all the meeting houses they had visited were "fitted up" with seats that were "nothing more than rough boards supported at each end by blocks of wood."[106] We can assume that this was the case at Honey Creek.

The first Honey Creek meeting house was a double wide log building constructed in 1854 and the first schoolhouse was built next to it soon after, with James Tulburt serving as the first teacher. It became a public school not too long after and by 1861 Honey Creek Meeting had decided not to hold their own school, but to lend their influence and support to the district school.[107] The meeting house later burned down and was replaced in 1859 with a new thirty-two foot by forty-eight-foot building. Levi Reece and

---

103. Goldsmith, "William Hobson and the Founding of Quakerism in the Pacific Northwest," 152.

104. Union Publishing Company, *History of Hardin County Iowa*, 860.

105. Goldsmith, "William Hobson and the Founding of Quakerism in the Pacific Northwest," 152.

106. Jones, *Quakers of Iowa*, 5.

107. Goldsmith, "William Hobson and the Founding of Quakerism in the Pacific Northwest," 154–55.

Hobson worked together to build the new meeting house,[108] a considerably larger project than building benches. The new meeting house was located about two miles southwest of New Providence. Honey Creek was approved as a monthly meeting on Tenth Month 1, 1856, by Pleasant Plain Quarterly Meeting, about two years after the first meeting house was completed and four years after achieving preparative meeting status. This means that the congregation at Honey Creek must have met in family homes for the first two years.[109] Meetings for worship were conducted in the traditional Quietist manner. Business was also conducted in the traditional way, with men's and women's meetings held separately. Honey Creek Quarterly Meeting was set off by Western Plains Quarterly Meeting (Bangor Quarterly Meeting) in 1865 and the first sessions were held at Honey Creek in Fifth Month 1866.[110]

History of Hardin County names Hobson as *the* minister at Honey Creek,[111] though he was not formally recognized as such until 1859, when the meeting recorded him. Goldsmith points out that, "due to the caution of Friends in recognizing ministers, it may be that he had been 'appearing in the ministry' for several years before he was 'recognized' [officially as a minister]."[112] In the early days, he may have been the only member of Honey Creek serving as a minister. Certainly, as time went on, other members were recorded, but there is no doubt that Hobson held a special position of authority at Honey Creek as the first minister. We might call him a lead pastor today, but he would shudder at the thought. He absolutely believed in the priesthood of all believers and felt that all Friends should help to carry the work of the church forward. He did acknowledge that some like himself were especially gifted to engage in vocal ministry, but he was also convinced that every follower of Jesus was gifted by God in some way and given the ability to engage in a corresponding ministry. Hobson felt it was his duty as a minister to set a good example of holy and righteous living, with the help of Jesus, as well as to do his best to help others live likewise. He spent a considerable amount of time visiting members of the congregation in their homes, visiting other meetings in the region, and engaging with Friends at the quarterly and yearly meeting level, despite demands placed on him at the homestead. Sarah and the older children took on more chores when he was gone and keep the farm running well. Hobson was never paid for

108 Union Publishing Company, *History of Hardin County Iowa*, 860.

109. Goldsmith, "William Hobson and the Founding of Quakerism in the Pacific Northwest," 154.

110. Iowa Yearly Meeting, *Iowa Yearly Meeting of Friends*, 84.

111. Union Publishing Company, *History of Hardin County Iowa*, 860.

112. Goldsmith, "William Hobson and the Founding of Quakerism in the Pacific Northwest," 162.

his work as a minister and would have been affronted at the suggestion. He supported his family solely with produce from their farm and orchard.

We will never know for sure what the Holy Spirit inspired Hobson to preach in meeting, though based on certain passages in his diary and notes in his memorandum some special areas of interest do emerge. He absolutely believed that Jesus died on the cross for the forgiveness of sins, that Jesus rose from the dead, and that Jesus would come again to judge the living and the dead. He believed that Jesus was the only way to the Father and the only foundation worth building a life upon and he wanted to communicate this truth to others. He also fully embraced the Quaker convictions that water baptism and communion were meant to be practiced for a short season following Jesus's resurrection, after which the necessity for these rites had faded away. According to Hobson, water baptism and the Lord's Supper had not been necessary practices since the first century church and had become stale and rote in other denominations. Spiritual baptism and spiritual communion were what mattered. He thought it was important to teach children, as soon as they could understand, to give their life to Jesus and to follow him. He was in favor of women preaching, he read the Bible as the authoritative and inspired word of God, he was interested in preserving traditional Quietist Quaker worship, though he appreciated the harvest of souls revival brought into the faith, and he enjoyed learning from George Fox, William Penn, Robert Barclay, and other early Friends. He studied the historical persecutions of Christians and noted other denominations that refused to take part in water baptism and communion. He made lists of Scriptures that were important to him and quoted articles or books in his diary and memorandum having to do with spiritual matters. A strong work ethic and the certainty that every person could learn to be useful in some occupation was at the core of his conviction that a simple life was best. He also took a firm stand against the production, use, or sale of tobacco and alcohol other than as medicine.

Surely, his convictions were communicated to the congregation during meeting or on pastoral visits in one way, shape, or form. Whether he exhorted, encouraged, or prophesied it is impossible to know, but it's clear that Hobson did not make any formal preparation for preaching, such as bringing sermon notes or an outline to meeting. He did engage in informal preparation for preaching, by reading and studing Scripture and Friends doctrine during the week, and he most certainly had conversations with God as he worked the land, trimmed trees, or fed the livestock. From the well-tilled soil of his heart the Holy Spirit put together sermons as Hobson sat in meeting and prompted him to speak in the Spirit's way and timing.

Later in life, he sometimes gave brief descriptions of sermons he and others preached at Newberg but did not go into much detail.

Once in awhile Hobson would note in his diary that he felt peace of mind for delivering a message God had given him. Hobson first wrote of such a "relief of mind," as Friends ministers often called it, on Ninth Month 21, 1862, when he recorded the following in his diary: "Attended Bangor Meeting. Was engaged in vocal supplication & testimony to the peace of my own mind. Held a meeting at night in the Methodist meeting-house. There was a Considerable gathering. I had a feeling of great emptiness much of the Meeting yet had some service [vocal ministry] several times with a degree of life that Brought peace to my own mind." The feeling of intense relief after delivering a sermon was a sentiment he expressed periodically throughout the rest of his life. For example, about ten years later in the fall of 1872 he wrote "spake by way of preaching to the meeting at H.C. to my relief. Meeting small but lively" and about three weeks later "Attended Honey Creek Meeting Gave or found relief in expressing some of my thoughts."[113] Much later towards the end of his life he was still using the same phrase to describe the liberation of delivering a Holy Spirit inspired message. He notes in Eleventh Month 1890, "attended with & spoke to the Y.M. [Young Men's?] Christian Association to the relief of my own mind and I reckon to good satisfaction of the audience: But found after speaking about 30 minutes I began to sweat very freely But I soon I believe found my right stopping place."[114] If he felt similar release at times prior to 1862, he did not record it. His diary in general was understandably terser during the years he was building up the homestead. But it is certain that Hobson practiced waiting on the Holy Spirit for a message and the measuring of a message his whole life long.

Samuel Hobson indicated that his father sat in front of the meeting at Honey Creek on the facing bench and timed it, the custom being to sit for one hour. Most meetings were held in complete silence when Samuel was a young boy. According to Samuel a stranger once sat through a silent meeting at Honey Creek and at dinner afterward Hobson "said to this stranger, 'What didst thou think of our meeting,' he replied, 'The meeting was alright, but the preacher didn't arrive.' Father look [sic] so funny he didn't know what to say, as he was supposed to be the preacher, but this stranger didn't know it." Samuel believed this conversation caused Hobson to think deeply about the responsibility that rested on him as a minister and leader of the meeting. He noted that not too long after that, silent meetings were a thing

113. Hobson, "Diaries," reel 1 of 2, 10/13/1872, 11/3/1872; reel 2 of 2, 9/21/1862.
114. Hobson, "Diaries," reel 1 of 2, 11/23/1890.

of the past,[115] indicating not so much that his father began preaching every First Day, though he may have preached more, but rather that the same Spirit of revival that swept through most of American Gurneyite Quakerism also reached Honey Creek.

The usual pattern of Friends was to hold two meetings a week, one on Fifth Day in the afternoon and one on First Day in the morning. Honey Creek followed this pattern and Hobson, as the minister, presided over both meetings faithfully week after week, except when he was traveling in the ministry or ill. The congregation also met once a month for business and sometimes attended special appointed meetings if a traveling minister was in the area. Various committees like elders and trustees met at unknown intervals. Hobson recorded minimal information about meetings, merely noting if they were favorable or large or small, so it's hard to know what the congregation he served was like. Goldsmith reports that Honey Creek often assigned Hobson to educational responsibilities such as the Committee on Education of the Meeting or the First Day School Committee. By 1860 he had "earned the reputation of one especially concerned for good education [and] . . . on his travels, he found it difficult to pass a school without stopping." Some of his education committee work included assessing the libraries of preparative meetings to see if they were up to standards.[116]

Based on diary entries, Hobson faithfully attended Bangor Quarterly Meeting, though he is not mentioned in the minutes, other than short approvals for some of his ministry trips. Goldsmith reports that Hobson attended the first Iowa Yearly Meeting sessions in 1863 and each Iowa Yearly Meeting after, up to 1875, except for 1867. He was appointed to committees like those at Honey Creek having to do with education. He also served on the Iowa Yearly Meeting Book and Tract Committee and the Iowa Yearly Meeting Correspondence Committee. However, as Goldsmith notes, "membership in the strategic Meeting for Sufferings is perhaps that which most indicates the regard of his Iowa Quaker contemporaries."[117] The meeting for sufferings was tasked with helping Friends who were bereaved, in financial trouble, or otherwise suffering. Hobson was a well-respected member and minister not only in his local Honey Creek congregation, but also in the wider Iowa Yearly Meeting.

First Day was almost always designated "Rest Day" in Hobson's diary during the 1860s and as the notation implies he was a stickler for not

115. Hobson, "Memories" 19.

116. Goldsmith, "William Hobson and the Founding of Quakerism in the Pacific Northwest," 185 (footnote 4).

117. Goldsmith, "William Hobson and the Founding of Quakerism in the Pacific Northwest," 186–87.

working on the Sabbath. By the 1870s First Day was usually marked with the following notation: "Attended Meeting & School," which also leaves the reader wanting more. However, it does show that, in true Gurneyite fashion, Honey Creek offered a First Day School to its members. Our only glimpse of what First Day School was like comes from Samuel Hobson. Reading between the lines, First Day School at Honey Creek initially followed the old Quaker pattern. All ages met together and didn't so much study the Bible as merely read it and possibly memorize some passages. Samuel apparently wasn't satisfied with this, so he spoke with his father suggesting they split up into four or five age-based classes, choose a superintendent, and then each class could choose their teacher. Samuel writes that it took some convincing, but Hobson eventually brought Samuel's idea before the congregation. They chose Samuel as First Day School Superintendent and new age-based classes were organized. The meeting house could be partitioned off into two rooms with shutters, creating smaller meeting areas. If they followed typical Quaker practice at the time, the shutters were opened at the end of First Day School and each class shared with the others what they had received from Scripture that morning as a closing exercise.[118] How much actual Bible study came out of this new arrangement is unknown, but if there was some it may have helped lead Honey Creek closer to revival. If nothing else, Samuel must have felt great affirmation from his dad and his church family.

Before describing revival at Honey Creek, it makes sense to look at Hobson's ministerial journeys, because he encountered revival stirrings while visiting Friends in Iowa, Kansas, and Missouri. Hobson traveled in the ministry close to home often and further from home a few times. His first recorded longer journey involved visiting the meetings of Salem and Pleasant Plain in the winter of 1859. According to Goldsmith, the minutes of Salem Quarterly Meeting show that he was accompanied by Eli Jessup, a Friends minister living at New Providence. Hobson had obtained a minute from Honey Creek Monthly Meeting indicating that "he was a minister with whom the Meeting had unity."[119] He was gone for about a month from Second Month 5, 1859, to Third Month 2, 1859. He gave no details about this trip except to note the day he left and the day he returned. The following spring he went on a journey to visit his friends and relatives in North Carolina.[120] Goldsmith found that Hobson traveled with the endorsement of Bangor Quarterly Meeting which was in unity with his concern. He may

---

118. Hobson, "Memories" 20–21.

119. Goldsmith, "William Hobson and the Founding of Quakerism in the Pacific Northwest," 162.

120. Hobson, "Diaries," reel 2 of 2, 2/5/1859, 3/2/1859, 4/21/1860–7/1/1860.

have engaged in ministry along the way there and back, but, probably, his main intention on this trip was to visit his father and other family still living at Deep Creek.[121] Hobson was gone a little over two months and once again he did not write down any of the details of the trip.

Hobson taught school during the winter of 1861–1862 which prevented long journeys in the ministry, though he did often visit other Friends meetings within the quarterly meeting.[122] In 1863 he undertook several journeys of varying durations. This may have been facilitated by the fact that his sons were now old enough to take care of the farm for longer periods of time. Hobson made notes during these two trips, which Goldsmith summarizes well. In January of 1863 Hobson and Robert King visited Fairview and Winneshiek Monthly Meetings to determine if they were ready to be given monthly meeting status. They were gone fifteen days. About two weeks later he made a short journey of a week "visiting homes, schools and Meetings not far from Honey Creek. On this occasion, he was especially concerned to find whether or not the homes he visited owned copies of the Scriptures, and if not to supply them. He also distributed tracts."[123] Hobson's third journey of 1863 was considerably longer than the first two beginning at the end of Fifth Month and concluding by the end of Seventh Month. Goldsmith notes that his traveling companion this time was John S. Bond, formerly of Indiana and the California gold fields, now a minister and member of Honey Creek. Hobson and Bond had developed a shared concern to visit and hold appointments at meetings in Iowa, Kansas, and Missouri. Appointments were special meetings arranged and publicized ahead of time. This concern was approved both by Honey Creek Monthly Meeting and Bangor Quarterly Meeting. Hobson kept a rather detailed record of their experiences during this journey. He recorded the miles they traveled, the people they stayed with, including relatives in Kansas and Missouri, the towns they traveled through, the meetings they attended and appointed, the lay of the land, fertility of the soil, the state of the grain and fruit crops (peach trees were hurt by a late frost), and livestock, as well as many other small details of the trip. The men distributed tracts and Bibles as they went, visited some schools and a Native American mission, and held appointed meetings at various locations along the way. Goldsmith notes that the biggest of these appointments was held at a courthouse in Savannah, Missouri, the Andrew County seat, in a region experiencing unrest due to tension between Confederate

121. Goldsmith, "William Hobson and the Founding of Quakerism in the Pacific Northwest," 163.

122. Hobson, "Diaries," reel 2 of 2, see 1862, 1863.

123. Goldsmith, "William Hobson and the Founding of Quakerism in the Pacific Northwest," 166.

sympathizing guerrillas and Union soldiers. Hobson reported that around four or five hundred people attended, including one hundred soldiers, noting that it was a favored meeting, and they were able to share the gospel with boldness. Previously, while in Kansas, both Hobson and Bond were laid low with some undiagnosed illness that involved vomiting. Bond was stricken enough to require a doctor's care, but they slowly recovered and continued with their visiting, while gradually working their way home. They were gone long enough that Hobson expressed a certain degree of homesickness, but apparently effective ministry was worth the discomfort.[124] He summarized the journey in his usual laconic fashion as follows:

> Got home about ½ after 9 P.M. Haveing [sic] been out 9 weeks & 2 days I & A traveled over 11 hundred miles. Some in Kansas, some in Missouri & Some in Iowa. Was at one time 350 m. Southwest from home. Had several good meetings in Kansas: Some in Missouri & Some in Kansas Iowa. Was detained by my own sickness & John Bonds Sickness 3 weeks in Kansas, Spent near 5 dollars this trip.[125]

He arrived home in time to help with the end of the wheat harvest, though he did not appear to have completely recovered physically from the trip.[126] For several months it was business as usual until he embarked on yet another journey in Twelfth Month of 1863.

Before we look at his next journey, it's important to note that it was during these second and third journeys of 1863 that Hobson first records a tiny bit more information about the nature of Friends meetings in the Midwest, indicating that worship was beginning to change. Before 1863 he merely notes that he attended a meeting, or that he spoke to good relief, with no further description. But, beginning in Second Month 1863, he uses the enigmatic term "favored" as a meeting descriptor several times. For example, on Second Month 25, 1863, he writes, "Went to David Masons to stay at night Attended a meeting at night. Had a small meeting but a *favored* [author's emphasis] one to day."[127] It's hard to know for sure, but he may have been referring to the precursor of a general meeting at which praying and singing were common. Night meetings were unusual in Quaker circles, though they were beginning to crop up here and there. During his longer trip down through Iowa, Missouri, and Kansas, with John S. Bond,

124. Goldsmith, "William Hobson and the Founding of Quakerism in the Pacific Northwest," 167–76, 220; Hobson, "Diaries," reel 2 of 2, 5/21–7/13/1863.
125. Hobson, "Diaries," reel 2 of 2, 7/25/1863.
126. Hobson, "Diaries," reel 2 of 2, 7/26/1863.
127. Hobson, "Diaries," reel 2 of 2, 2/25/1863

Hobson notes several instances of "favored" meetings and once refers to a meeting held to "good satisfaction." When he describes the large meeting, referred to above, that he and Bond appointed in "Savanna [Missouri] in the Courthouse" he notes that it "was largely Attended. I suppose 4 or 5 hundred. I guess a hundred soldiers was a quiet & a *favored* [author's emphasis] meeting we were *favored* [author's emphasis] to declare the word of life with boldness. A methodist [sic] preacher Spake [sic] in commendation of [what] had been spoken."[128] While we can't know for sure what was going on at "favored" meetings there is a sense that God's presence was real and palpable, that vocal ministry was occurring, that the gospel was being preached, that many were praying and giving testimony, and that possibly even some of the new worship practices, like altar calls and singing, were cropping up, though Hobson would not have approved of that. Bond on the other hand was not opposed to such evangelistic worship innovations.

In the winter of 1863–1864 Hobson, Bond, and a young minister named Stacy E. Bevan undertook a journey to visit meetings in the Bear Creek region about thirty or forty miles southwest of Des Moines. Hobson was the most conservative of the three. Bond and Bevan became movers and shakers in the Iowa Friends revival movement and Bevan went so far, later in his ministry, to embrace the doctrine and practice of water baptism. But during the winter of 1863–1864 things had not progressed quite so far in the spiritual lives of Bond and Bevan. True, the two ministers, as Goldsmith puts, it were "inclined to the bold abandonment of old and tried ways if new methods seemed more promising [and] Hobson appears to have let them take the lead in the visitation of the Bear Creek community, and they introduced methods which were as yet unusual among Friends... [like] the holding of night meetings and the holding of meetings especially for youth."[129] However, the revival movement was just beginning to gain momentum and Bond and Bevan had not reached their full force as revival leaders, nor were worship innovations widely accepted among Iowa Friends, as yet. This leads to speculation that Bangor Quarterly Meeting may have sent Hobson along to ride herd on these fiery revivalists in the making. Regardless, it seems that Hobson was pleased with the results of their visit to Bear Creek, even if the ministry methods were not entirely to his liking. They left around the 8th of Twelfth Month and got to Bear Creek in time to attend meeting on the 13th of Twelfth Month 1863. Starting on the 21st of First Month and running through the rest of their visit to Bear Creek, Hobson notes

---

128. Hobson, "Diaries," reel 2 of 2, 7/13/1863.

129. Goldsmith, "William Hobson and the Founding of Quakerism in the Pacific Northwest," 178.

one favored meeting after another. He also records an evening meeting with the youth at Bear Creek: "Was a very precious meeting." Later, on the 27th he mentions a favored meeting at which he, "Had a door of [utt]erance." He, Bond, and Bevan also held a youth meeting in the evening that same day at which, "John & Stacey were favored to speak largely to the people. I felt easy by delivering a few words near the close." Then on the 3rd of First Month 1864, the three men held an appointed evening meeting that, "Was a refreshing season. Several appeared in prayer & in testimony." Just once does he express discomfort, when he writes on the 28th of Twelfth Month, "Went to . . . Adell Had a meeting in the Courthouse Was not a very quiet meeting."[130] Hobson's use of words like "favored," "precious," and "refreshing season" coupled with the fact that a least one evening youth meeting was held, indicates that revival was stirring at Bear Creek. Hobson summarized the trip upon their return: "Reached home been out 27 days With John S Bond & Stacy E Bevans [sic] Had 17 meetings all in the limits of Bearcreek monthly meeting except 1 at Demom [sic] & 2 at four-mile. Most of which were seasons of great favor & manifestations of the Lords [sic] power. Spent \$7.15 Cents divided by 3 = 2.38 each."[131] Bond and Bevan returned to Bear Creek without Hobson in 1867. At that time, revival broke out in earnest and changes in the way Iowa Friends worshiped could not be checked. A decade later, in 1877, the revival at Bear Creek had gained so much momentum it precipitated a separation in Iowa Yearly Meeting which split into two camps, conservative and evangelical Gurneyite Friends. But, in First Month 1863, Hobson, Bond, and Bevan returned to Honey Creek with no understanding of what the future would bring.

The following winter Hobson made a short journey to Iowa's South River region in First Month 1865, giving very little detail about the trip in his diary.[132] Due to a gap in his diary there is no record of ministry trips he may have taken between Seventh Month 1865, and Eleventh Month 1870. Also, due to this break in his diary, it's difficult to determine how deeply he was involved in the revival movement that was beginning to build in Iowa Yearly Meeting during the late 1860s. We know he had a taste of revival during his visit to Bear Creek. And without a doubt, he was excited about spiritual renewal and awakening among Friends, but he was also suspicious of the new worship practices revivalists were introducing. Whatever Hobson's involvement in the awakening of Iowa Yearly Meeting may have been

---

130. Hobson, "Diaries," reel 2 of 2, 12/8/1863–1/3/1864.
131. Hobson, "Diaries," reel 2 of 2, 1/5/1864.
132. Hobson, "Diaries," reel 2 of 2, 1/7/1865–1/16/1865

between the summer of 1865 and the fall of 1870, it is clear from his diary that by the winter of 1873–74 revival had come to Honey Creek in full force.

Unfortunately, it's hard to tell exactly what revival looked like at Honey Creek. For one thing, Hobson was writing in two separate notebooks during the early 1870s. He may have mislaid one for a while and started another, but it seems as though he used one for a summary log and one like his usual diary. So, there is some overlap of entries in separate notebooks while revival was gathering momentum at Honey Creek. For another thing, entries in Hobson's diary up to the advent of full-on revival at Honey Creek give very little indication that spiritual renewal for the whole community was on the way. It comes as a surprise therefore when he writes about significant revival meetings at Honey Creek in First Month 1874, meetings that brought in a large harvest of new believers. Looking back carefully, we can glean some signs from his diary that revival had been stirring in the region for several years. One enigmatic entry in the winter of 1865 reads "Attended Monthly Library at night," indicating that Honey Creek Friends were getting together outside of meeting to talk about religious books or tracts or even the Bible, and possibly praying together.[133] Also, Hobson began attending general meetings in different locations around the quarterly meeting and down in Oskaloosa. General meetings began as a means of teaching youth about Quaker faith and practice, but slowly morphed into prayer and Bible study groups, conduits through which renewal and awakening moved with great vigor. According to Goldsmith,

> Iowa Yearly Meeting had begun a cautious experimentation with General Meetings in 1868 by appointing a committee to arrange for no more than three such meetings to be held in the ensuing month, and report to next Yearly Meeting . . . in 1872, the Yearly Meeting appointed William Hobson to its Committee on General Meetings.[134]

It seems the yearly meeting was playing catch up, because Hobson reported attending a youth meeting during quarterly meeting sessions as far back as Fifth Month 1864. On Tenth Month 4, 1872, about a year after his return from the West Coast, Hobson noted, "Attended Select meeting Had a favored time" and then on the 5th, "Attended Honey Creek Quarterly Meeting, had a favored time. Many were engaged vocally to the satisfaction of the Church," while on the 13th, they enjoyed a "small but lively," time. While Hobson didn't specifically name these as general meetings they had the

---

133. Hobson, "Diaries," reel 2 of 2, 1/28/1865.

134. Goldsmith, "William Hobson and the Founding of Quakerism in the Pacific Northwest," 214 (footnote).

same flavor about them. Honey Creek did hold at least one general meeting as noted by Hobson in Sixth Month 1873.[135]

Also, as a member of the Iowa Yearly Meeting Committee on General Meetings, Hobson likely felt it his duty to attend general meetings at other locations, too. Several of the general meetings he attended in this capacity were very moving. Hobson attended one at Bangor that elicited an unprecedented response as noted in his diary: "Attended a General Meeting at Bangor Had a Cementing time. Toward the conclusion of the meeting many became wrought upon and many found relief by words. Some could not utter all they wanted to say but had to stop in their attempt. I frequently had some part in vocal service. And felt much peace & joy and thought I was in my true place." Another time Hobson noted, "Rose before 4 am & made ready for going to Oskaloosa General Meeting. Arrived at Oskaloosa about 3 P.M. Attended one session 3 meetings Next day[s] & 2 the next Having a Crowning finish with much joy and gladness to go home under." After yet another general meeting at New Sharon, he reported feeling a similar sense of great joy.[136] Hobson's experiences at general meetings give us a glimpse of how the revival movement was gathering steam in Iowa Yearly Meeting.

It also seems that Hobson was experiencing some degree of personal renewal. About a year before corporate revival broke out at Honey Creek he had an encouraging spiritual experience in the middle of the night:

> Waked before 2 a.m. Although I had gone to bed after 9--And as I waked & soon after I found my mind receiving afresh a lesson from many scriptures showing that Christ is the life lights way of salvation That He is all in all to him that believeth That through Christ Salvation is free. That he came to destroy the works of the devil and to set us free. His yoke is easy & burden light The Christian Religion designed for mans [sic] good now and forever Through Christ the Savior man is brought into the Religion which brings glory to God & good to men. At the Birth of the Savior A light shined round about the shepherds And an Angel appeared unto them and said fear not for I bring you glad [sic] of great joy which shall be to all people & suddenly There was a multitude of the heavenly host with the Angel praising God & say [sic] Glory to God in the highest and on earth peace & good will to men. Good to man. Yes. Evidently Our Wise loving heavenly Father designs to relieve men from all unnecessary burdens. In Christ we shall be made free. Surely it is the Lords [sic] pleasure to make man happy. Or else he would not have

135. Hobson, "Diaries," reel 2 of 2, 5/29/1864, reel 1 of 2, 6/8/1873.
136. Hobson, "Diaries," reel 1 of 2, 3/16/1873–3/18/1873, 3/22/1873, 5/25/1873.

made such large & perfect provision for it. And chiefly in that he had given him a Savior Who is our life &.[137]

This was an opening that he likely communicated in some manner to his congregation during First Day worship. He may not have been a full-on revivalist, but he was most certainly a Renewal Friend and an evangelist.

Clearly, Hobson was thinking seriously about corporate revival (how it happens, and what's involved with it) based on another entry in his diary written at the end of Twelfth Month 1873. He copied information about early Friends worship from an article submitted to the *Christian Worker* by John Henry Douglas, the well-known Quaker revivalist. He quotes a paragraph from the article describing how early Friends were not against sighing, groaning, and singing during worship, so long as everything occurred in an orderly fashion, as follows:

> Concern [sic] Singing Groaning and sighing It hath been, and is our living sense and consistant [sic] testimony, according to our experience of the divine operations of the Spirit of God in his church; that there hath been and is serious sighing, sensible groaning and reverent singing, breathing forth an heavenly sound of joy, with grace, with the spirit, and with the understanding, in blessed unity with the brethren, while they are in the public labor and service of the Gospel, whether by preaching, praying or praising God in the same power and spirit, and all to edification, and comfort in the church of Christ; which is therefore not to be quenched or discouraged by any. But when any do or shall abuse the power of God, or are immoderate, or do within immitation which rather burdens than edifies; such ought to be privately admonished unless rebellious for that life, power, and spirit is risen in the church which doth distinguish and hath accordingly to judge. The foregoing was written in Third month 1675 and signed by George Whitehead Wm. Penn and 62 other friends [sic] John H Douglas from Christian Worker 12 mo: 15 1873.[138]

It seems as though Hobson was seriously contemplating the idea that revival comes as a gift through the power of God and therefore, the Holy Spirit must not be quenched regardless of the outcome. How much he gave himself over to this in practice is up for debate.

It's clear that Hobson remained uneasy with congregational singing, even after revival came to Honey Creek. According to Goldsmith, most of

---

137. Hobson, "Diaries," reel 1 of 2, 11/12/1872.
138. Hobson, "Diaries," reel 2 of 2, 12/19/1872.

the Friends in Iowa Yearly Meeting were convinced that music had no place in public worship as late as 1868,[139] so at that time Hobson fit right in with most of his contemporaries. But was that majority predisposition against congregational singing beginning to dissolve by the early 1870s? Even as early as Seventh Month 22, 1871, Hobson noted in his diary, "Artistic Music seems to be gaining in places. As at Chestnut Hill & some other places (information)."[140] Did worship at Honey Creek slowly become more vibrant and vocal, as well? Were revival innovations creeping in while Hobson was on the Pacific Coast? Did Friends at Honey Creek eventually embrace singing, sighing, praying, preaching, and the giving of testimonies? What about the mourner's bench and altar calls? Hobson does not describe the Honey Creek revival in enough detail to answer these questions definitively.

Along with library nights that became Bible studies and prayer groups, general meetings, and individual renewal, traveling ministers also helped to set the stage for revival in Iowa Yearly Meeting. Goldsmith points out that in 1873 several evangelists visited monthly meetings in Iowa, including Honey Creek. John S. Bond, as a member of Honey Creek, likely preached there often,[141] as well as at other meetings in the area. Remember he had played a part in the Bear Creek Revival and was by this time a fervent revivalist. Elwood Scott, described by Hobson as a "'young man . . . valiant for the truth'" visited Honey Creek towards the beginning of Ninth Month 1873,[142] and engaged in vocal ministry among them. Towards the end of Ninth Month 1873, Honey Creek Monthly Meeting "heard a great Sermon from W. Haworth from the Text Simon son of James lovest thou me more than these (Fishes) He brough it home to us individually whether Christ was not asking us whether we love him more than our farms our cattle our hogs our property of [whatever] kind more than him."[143] Here was a challenge to put Jesus above all else. Yet another young revivalist, Elwood Osborne who, as Hobson reported, "preached well," visited towards the end of Eleventh Month 1873, spending about two weeks at Honey Creek.[144] These revivalists may have primed the pump, so to speak, for the next set of evangelists who visited Honey Creek to bring a flood of souls into the Kingdom of God. We cannot know for sure if ministers like Bond, Haworth, Scott, and Osborne

---

139. Goldsmith, "William Hobson and the Founding of Quakerism in the Pacific Northwest," 213.

140. Hobson, "Diaries," reel 1 of 2, 7/22/1871.

141. Goldsmith, "William Hobson and the Founding of Quakerism in the Pacific Northwest," 215.

142. Hobson, "Diaries," reel 1 of 2, 9/2/1873.

143. Hobson, "Diaries," reel 1 of 2, 9/27/1873.

144. Hobson, "Diaries," reel 1 of 2, 11/16/1863, 11/20/1863–11/30/1873.

were utilizing new methods of worship to help usher in revival at Honey Creek and elsewhere. But we can know for sure that Hobson was wrestling with the reality of the changes to traditional, unprogrammed Friends meetings that were sweeping through Iowa Yearly Meeting and indeed through American yearly meetings everywhere.

Hobson reported a series of "favored" meetings over the next few months after Osborne's visit. He was also corresponding with Bond who was traveling in the ministry. Then, shortly after the turn of the new year, revival broke out in earnest at Honey Creek. First Month 3, 1874, Hobson wrote, "Attended Quarterly Meeting Had a very precious Meeting Many Short sermons and a few prayers," and on the 4th, "Attended a good meeting at Honey Creek at usual hour Also one at night James Haworth & others present." Then a few days later on the 17th he noted that the congregation had just "Closed a series of Revival Meetings held at H[oney] Creek by Jacob Henshaw and Joel Stewart in which by Invitation by Jacob Henshaw about 90 persons came forward who had decided for Christ during this series of meetings. Being about ¼ of the audience present." Meetings had been held twice daily for about a week, by Henshaw and Stewart.

In this same diary entry Hobson also quoted from an account of a revival in Stockton, England that occurred the previous year in which

> a very important feature was the Absence of Noise ["Absence of Noise" written in large letters] in the meetings; we dwell on this more particularly, because some good brethren believe that loud prayers and singing are essential to a good meeting; and in carry[ing] out their convictions they unfortunately prevent or make uncomfortable the attendance of those who believe that noise and fervor are not synonymous. The experience of the past few days will we think, have convinced them that the best and most successful prayer meetings ever held in Stockton have been the quietest, reminding us of the old ladys [sic] description "God Almighty was so near that nobody had to shout to him." Extracted from an account in the S[unday].S[chool]. Times of a great Revival in Stockton England in 1873 in which between one and two hundred decided for Christ.[145]

While Hobson did not want to quench the Spirit, he continued to be uncomfortable with too much noise and activity in meeting. He was apparently willing to push through his discomfort, writing in the same diary entry as above, "We are having Blessed meetings Since our late revival. Some new ones are still born into the Kingdom. There is probably about 120 new born

---

145. Hobson, "Diaries," reel 2 of 2, 1/17/1874.

babies in Christ within the limits of Honey Creek Monthly Meeting. May we be vigilant now to nurse them; lest some perish."[146] It seems that Hobson was able to hold in tension a genuine excitement that so many had become new believers in Jesus with his anxiety over the new innovations revivalists were using to bring in the harvest. He gives a recap of the revival at Honey Creek later in his diary noting that

> to our Quarterly Meeting in this month [First Month 1874] came Jacob Henshaw from Lyon County & Joel Steward [sic] from Montgomery Co Ministers & after laboring at each place of our meeting in this vicinity Held a series of meetings at Honey Creek for near 2 weeks in which time there was many (about 100) made public confession that they had found acceptance with the Lord and still up to 5 of second mo[nth] we are continuing to hold additional meetings, and to get round to our meetings [in the vicinity] to try to keep all alive and widen and increase and confirm the work.[147]

Goldsmith points out that according to Honey Creek Monthly Meeting Minutes "forty-two new members were received into the Meeting by recommendation of the overseers, and Hobson and others were appointed to give them information and instruction."[148] That's a big new members class! Hobson was "much concerned lest many converts will not understand baptism aright,"[149] which indicates that most, if not all the new believers at Honey Creek and elsewhere in Iowa Yearly Meeting were not well acquainted with Friends beliefs. Shortly after all the new members were added at Honey Creek, while attending meeting at New Providence on his fifty-fourth birthday Hobson was "drawn out by way of Tes[timony] . . . To Show the simplicity and Blessedness of the gospel dispensation of the spiritual gifts through Christ Of Christs [sic] Baptism and of progress even in the apostolic time by getting rid of externals, That the design of the according to the Scriptures is that light should advance upon the understandings of men until the Church will be satisfied with enjoying the substance, for in Christ we are complete."[150] He continued to believe that external rites were

---

146. Hobson, "Diaries," reel 2 of 2, 1/17/1874.

147. Hobson, "Diaries," reel 1 of 2, page 15 of notebook titled on catalog card: "Diary of William Hobson Tenth month, 1872 to Seventh month, 1875 Includes second trip to Calif. & Oregon," (1/1874).

148. Goldsmith, "William Hobson and the Founding of Quakerism in the Pacific Northwest," 216.

149. Hobson, "Diaries," reel 1 of 2, 2/18/1874.

150. Hobson, "Diaries," reel 1 of 2, 2/4/1874.

not necessary because the sacraments were internal and spiritual. He dwelt much on the subject of peace during this time, as well, another testimony unique to Friends.[151] Hobson and others had their work cut out for them teaching new believers what it meant to follow Jesus as a Friend.

While Hobson was obviously happy with the results of revival at Honey Creek and was seriously thinking about how to disciple the significant number of converts, he continued to prefer the old manner of quiet Quaker worship. It was a strong preference that he retained until the day he died. Hobson was certainly excited about renewal and awakening among Friends, but nothing could shake his belief that the Spirit of God communing directly with a person's heart could bring them to a saving knowledge of Jesus without all the hoopla of revival fervor. He found an article in the *Friends Review* agreeing with his view that singing and loud verbal ministry should not be a part of Friends worship, which he tacked on to the end of the above diary entry from First Month 17, 1874. It's safe to assume that he was not a fan of altar calls, mourner's benches, and other revivalist innovations either, though he remained close friends with Revival Friends like John S. Bond and Stacy E. Bevan. On the other hand, he was also friendly with Joel Bean, the clerk of Iowa Yearly Meeting, who publicly opposed the revival movement, indicating Hobson could get along with most everyone. As Hobson's friend Jesse Edwards once said:

> There is one thing I want to mention: William Hobson has been spoken of. He is one of the conspicuous figures of that time. He was a peculiar man in a way. One would not think to look at his children here that he was anything but an ordinary man. I wish we had his picture here today--I supposed it would be here. I think he was the only man that God ever made of the kind. He had his place and he filled his place. If all of us had filled our mission and our work as full as he did in his life Christianity and Quakerism would be stronger today. He was a man absolutely true to his convictions. And I want to say that while he had some peculiar convictions and his way he was a mixer. William Hobson was a mixer. He would go among all classes and all classes respected him. I think everyone who knew William Hobson will justify me in making that statement. He was pronounced in his views--in what he believed--but he was not so narrow but that he could see good in every person he met and in that way I consider him (what we would call in present day phrase) a 'mixer.'"[152]

151. Hobson, "Diaries," reel 1 of 2, 3/21/1874, 4/13/1874, 5/31/1874.
152. Hobson, "Twentyfifth Anniversary," 4.

What a rare thing to get along peaceably with people from all walks of life.

It's noteworthy that even after the revival at Honey Creek, which, reading between the lines was pretty lively, Hobson remained not only willing to attend general meetings, but also that he got something out of them. He was able to set aside personal discomfort for the good of the whole church body. He tells of one general meeting at New Providence in the spring of 1874, "a glorious meeting" that consisted of nine sessions over three days and another about a month later at which "The last 3 Sessions of the Meeting were remarkably Blessed seasons to many. Many of the youth renewed their covenants with their Lord to be his children Many of the Old people spake a little to the general comfort of all."[153] Hobson also mentioned a series of favored meetings at Honey Creek and elsewhere in early 1874 and notes in Third Month 1875, "We are Having a Joyful Meeting A series of meetings held by Jacob Henshaw Barclay Jones Melinda Baldwin & others."[154] So, it seems that renewal and revival at Honey Creek were still going strong a year later, a few months before he embarked on a second trip to the Pacific Coast.

The two decades during which the Hobsons lived in Iowa were full and significant. The young pioneer family arrived in the early 1850s and, starting from scratch, developed a prosperous homestead along the banks of Honey Creek, growing various grain crops, corn, vegetables, and fruit and raising livestock. In the early days they were subsistence farmers, but as time went on the neighborhood became more developed and trade improved. The Hobsons raised their six kids at Honey Creek and provided the kind of steady home life Friends are famous for, instilling biblical values and the Quaker Testimonies in their children. Hobson, as a minister of Honey Creek Monthly Meeting, was active in the life of the congregation, as well as an important part of the yearly meeting, with a special concern for education. He traveled in the ministry helping to build up Friends all around the region and down into Kansas and Missouri. When revival came, he was pleased with the resulting harvest of souls, if not the changes in worship practices, and he continued to work towards the encouragement, support, and spiritual growth of Iowa Friends. By the early 1870s, the Hobsons were living a comfortable life. Their farm was large and productive. The railroad provided an improved means for the exchange of goods. Honey Creek school and meeting were well established and thriving. God was on the move among Iowa Friends and it was a great blessing to participate in the spiritual awakening that was taking place. The neighborhood was made up mostly of Friends and believers of other denominations and the community

---

153. Hobson, "Diaries," reel 1 of 2, 5/9/1874, 6/8/1874.
154. Hobson, "Diaries," reel 1 of 2, 3/15/1875.

reflected their moral values. In the midst of simple comfort and prosperity, a settled ease in his neighborhood, a profound sense of belonging within a reviving Iowa Yearly Meeting, and service as an anointed minister at Honey Creek, Hobson received the call to go west, making his sacrificial obedience to God that much sweeter.

4

To the Pacific Northwest and Back Twice, Then to Stay

Being confident of this very thing, that he which hath begun a good work in you will perform it until the day of Jesus Christ.

PHIL 1:6

RELEASED FOR MINISTRY ON THE WEST COAST

The first mention of the West Coast in William Hobson's diary occurs on Third Month 17, 1865. On this day he received a letter from his brother Jesse Hobson who wrote, "Desiring [a] good Ministering Friend to Come to Cal[ifornia] and gather the lost sheep."[1] Hobson's brothers David, Stephen, and Jesse, as well as several of his half-brothers and cousins had been settled in San Jose, Santa Clara Valley, California, for several years. Other Friends had joined them there and the small settlement was in the process of establishing a preparatory meeting. Hobson did not immediately act upon his brother's request by going out west himself, but he probably communicated Jesse's request to their cousin Abel Bond, with whom William was in regular correspondence.

---

1. Hobson, "Diaries," reel 2 of 2, 3/17/1865.

According to *Abel Bond's Foot Travels* an autobiographical account of Bond's life, he was able to oblige Jesse almost immediately, though it took some time to get out to San Jose from Kansas where he was living. He took no money with him, relying on God to provide what was needed, and walked or hitched rides the entire way. Bond arrived at San Jose late in 1865 staying several months with various relatives and hospitable Friends, going on pastoral visits, distributing tracts, and attending meeting. Led by the Spirit towards the end of the year 1866, he took a steamship up the coast from San Francisco to Portland. It seems the spiritual hunger there was great, for he noted,

> When I got to Portland, Oregon, the wind was favorable for me to distribute tracts. The platform was covered with people from different parts of the country and state. . . .I would throw up a handful of tracts and they would scatter around the people who would pick them up and motion for more. . .They would go for them like ducks for corn.[2]

Bond traveled around the Willamette Valley for about three months making contacts with Friends and former Friends, as well as ministering to complete strangers, and then returned to San Jose by the overland route early in 1867. Before journeying home to Kansas Bond helped to organize and carry out the erection of a meeting house in San Jose, the first Friends meeting house west of the Rocky Mountains. He also encouraged and strengthened the growing Quaker community there, leaving religious literature with every family he visited. Bond wrote in his autobiography that he "believed if the Friends would keep on praying there would be meetings established in various places along the Pacific Coast."[3] Though no correspondence between Bond and Hobson is known to have survived we can be sure that Abel kept his cousin William apprised of his activities in California and Oregon and communicated his hopes for the establishment of Friends meetings all up and down the West Coast.

There had been a small but promising Quaker presence in Oregon for a little over twenty years before Hobson first visited the state. Beebe tells how the first Friends to settle in Oregon were the Lewelling brothers, Seth and Henderson, back when Oregon was still part of the Northwest Territory, "who brought 700 grafted fruit trees and shrubs by oxen over the Oregon Trail in 1847."[4] Goldsmith adds that the brothers hailed from Salem, Iowa, and that Henderson was an Abolitionist. His home in Iowa was a key

2. Bond, *Abel Bond's Foot Travels*, 36.
3. Bond, *Abel Bond's Foot Travels*, 21–44, 47.
4. Beebe, *Garden of the Lord*, 27.

stop on the Underground Railroad. The Lewelling brothers settled near Milwaukie and operated a nursery, "thus making an important contribution to the horticulture of the Pacific Northwest."[5] Beebe points out that the first Friends First Day School held in the Pacific Northwest was organized at Ashland in the early 1850s, and that "other Friends in the Northwest during that decade included the families of Hiram Bond, James Whinstone, Mary Stroud, Edwin Comfort, and William Mills."[6]

A small handful of Friends ministers visited the West Coast before Hobson, as well. British traveling ministers Robert and Sarah Lindsey were appointed by London Yearly Meeting as missionaries to the West Coast of America in 1859. They ministered first in California and then in Oregon's Willamette Valley, holding meetings at Eugene City, Corvallis, and Oregon City.[7] After appointing meetings and visiting families west of Portland the Lindseys held a few meetings in Portland proper and concluded their tour of the Willamette Valley, First Month 1860.[8] They went on to Washington Territory for a brief visit and when they left America to return home to Great Britain "they had contacted at least eighteen adult Friends in Oregon and Washington and approximately thirty-seven former Friends who had placed their membership with other denominations, because of there being no Friends Meetings in the Pacific Northwest."[9] Abel Bond noted that "their [the Lindseys'] missionary work ahead of me was a great help to me."[10] The Lindseys had paved the way wonderfully for further Friends missionary work in the Pacific Northwest.

Two female Friends ministers from Ohio likewise had concerns to minister on the West Coast. Rebecca Mendenhall Lewis and her husband David, settled in Portland in 1864 and their home became a headquarters for traveling ministers.[11] Also, according to Rayner W. Kelsey in "Quakerism Beyond the Mississippi," an article written for *The American Friend*, Mary B. Pinkham was released for religious service in the Far West at the same time Hobson was released by Honey Creek for the same purpose. She

---

5. Goldsmith, "William Hobson and the Founding of Quakerism in the Pacific Northwest," 219.

6. Beebe, *Garden of the Lord*, 27.

7. Goldsmith, "William Hobson and the Founding of Quakerism in the Pacific Northwest," 221–23.

8. Goldsmith mistakenly gives the date as 1/30/1861 (see Goldsmith, page 224). For correct date see Lindsey and Lindsey, *Travels of Robert and Sarah Lindsey*, 152.

9. Goldsmith, "William Hobson and the Founding of Quakerism in the Pacific Northwest," 224–25.

10. Bond, *Abel Bond's Foot Travels*, 36.

11. Beebe, *Garden of the Lord*, 28.

and her husband Thomas left shortly after receiving approval from Ohio Yearly Meeting in Ninth Month 1870, and ministered for a brief time in the Willamette Valley before Hobson's arrival there, returning home after only three months.[12] Hobson and Mary Pinkham were in correspondence with each other and she agreed with him that a Friends settlement should be established somewhere on the West Coast.[13] Kelsey reports that the Pinkhams returned to the Willamette Valley in 1873 while Hobson was back in Iowa between journeys to Oregon, ministering among the settlers there for about two years while staying mostly at Eugene.[14] By the time Hobson returned to Oregon there were still more Friends settled in the Willamette Valley, some near Salem, some at Dayton, and others scattered throughout.

Hobson made no diary entries between Fifth Month 1865, and the autumn of 1870 when he left on his first trip west, making it difficult to determine the manner in which his concern to visit the Far West developed. A minute issued by the Honey Creek women's business meeting in Sixth Month 1870, releasing Hobson to undertake a religious visit to the West Coast is equally enigmatic. It gives no insight into Hobson's discernment process or the motivation behind his calling to service. The minute is recorded as follows by Goldsmith: "'Our beloved friend William Hobson informed that he believed it right for him to stand resigned to visit in the love of the Gospel some of the people West of the Rocky Mountains by appointing meetings or otherwise, with which this meeting fully united, and he was liberated and encouraged to attend to said services as Best Wisdom may direct.'"[15] Goldsmith noted further that the "Yearly Meeting of Ministers and Elders reported to Iowa Yearly Meeting that it had liberated William Hobson for religious service in the Far West."[16] These records, while releasing Hobson for ministry among Friends on the West Coast, do not say anything about his intention to look for a place to form a Quaker settlement.

However, it seems likely that establishing such a settlement was on his mind from the very beginning. It becomes apparent later that he hoped to

---

12. Goldsmith, "William Hobson and the Founding of Quakerism in the Pacific Northwest," 227; Kelsey, "Quakerism Beyond the Mississippi," 424–25.

13. Hobson, "Diaries," reel 2 of 2, 12/29/1870, 12/31/1870, reel 1 of 2, 5/26/1876. From section of diary missing from microfilm. For more information see Goldsmith, "William Hobson and the Founding of Quakerism in the Pacific Northwest," 266–68; Paul, "Extracts," 14–15.

14. Kelsey, "Quakerism Beyond the Mississippi," 469.

15. Goldsmith, "William Hobson and the Founding of Quakerism in the Pacific Northwest," 227.

16. Goldsmith, "William Hobson and the Founding of Quakerism in the Pacific Northwest," 227.

both gather scattered and lapsed Friends into meetings and to establish a central Friends center for immigrating families. But he may not have been ready to communicate the full scope of his concern to Honey Creek in 1870, or perhaps it was still coming into focus. It's clear that from the start he intended to explore further up the coast into Oregon and Washington, using his family and the small Friends settlement at San Jose as a home base. He hoped to visit many different regions in California, Oregon, and Washington Territory in order to assess their merit and find the perfect place for his own Friends settlement. Hobson's concern to locate somewhere in the Far West with the intention of establishing a Quaker community waxed and waned as he traveled up and down the coast. It was not until his return to Iowa that Hobson's concern solidified into a compelling calling he could not ignore.

FIRST JOURNEY TO THE WEST COAST

For the moment let's turn our attention to the details of Hobson's first journey to the West Coast. Hobson enjoyed a considerably faster and more comfortable journey than his cousin Abel Bond had experienced just five years previously, for on Fifth Month 10, 1869, the Transcontinental Railroad was completed with the driving of the Golden Spike at Promontory Summit, Utah. According to Martin W. Sandler, in *Iron Rails, Iron Men and the Race to Link the Nation*, with the connection of the Central Pacific and Union Pacific railroads, Sacramento, California, and Omaha, Nebraska, became stops on a continuous railroad running from coast to coast.[17] Track had previously been laid between Sacramento and San Jose,[18] so Hobson was able to ride the "cars" from Union Station in Iowa to San Jose, California, with ease. He boarded the train in Union, approximately ten miles southeast of Honey Creek, Eleventh Month 21, 1870, and arrived at San Jose, Eleventh Month 30, 1870, completing a journey of ten days. Along the way he enjoyed conversation with fellow travelers from whom he gathered information about the inhabitants, geography, industry, and climates of various western regions, including areas in California, Oregon, and Washington Territory (California became a state in 1850, Oregon in 1859, and Washington in 1889). He was especially interested in soil types, geography, available land, and the crops specific to each region he visited. He also engaged in spiritual conversations with several folks on the train. He probably stood out from the crowd in his plain Quaker clothing and with his plain Quaker speech.

17. Sandler, *Iron Rails*, 170–71, 193.
18. "History of the Niles Passenger Depot."

Hobson likely spent a significant amount of time looking out the window, for he remarked often on the landscape noticing how barren, rocky, and hilly it became, once the plains were crossed and they entered Utah. He took great interest in the different layers of sediment in the banks, the lay of the land, rock formations, and the sparse vegetation he could see from the train, which consisted mostly of sage and bunch grass at this stage of the journey. He noted that the rocky, arid soil was not good for farming and that "The Earth & Stones of these Mountains are mostly Reddish" adding also that "There is very little timber of any kind to be seen yet." He bought provisions at Ogden, Utah, and changed "To better Cars. A long train We are without water because the conductor had not time to put it in the Cask—got water from the Engine a Cask full of Mountain water." Later they took on fresh water from a fountain at Humboldt Station.[19] Hobson was very interested in the coal diggings that cropped up here and there along the tracks in Utah and amazed at the lack of trees. On Eleventh Month 26, after about five days of chugging along he remarked "There is a thousand miles of this route without a good sized tree in sight of the [rail]road. And only a very little amount of shrubs & Brush." The next day, he wrote "last evening we passed a small evergreen tree standing on the south side of the [rail]road a little before we came into the Salt Lake Valley with a sign Board on it thus 1000 Mile Tree. As we pass through the valley we see it snowing a little on the Northside of some of the mountains."[20] According to Stephen E. Ambrose in *Nothing Like It in the World: the Men Who Built the Transcontinental Railroad 1863–1869*, this tree keeping watch in Weber Canyon, Utah, was "a tall, ancient pine [which] marked precisely the point where the tracks were a thousand miles from Omaha. It surely deserved to be memorialized, so a sign reading '1000 Mile Tree' was hung from its lowest limb. Andrew Russell took a picture, often reproduced, and the base of the tree became a picnic spot for tourists."[21] It seemed a small and lonely tree to Hobson in that barren, rocky landscape.

After crossing the border into Nevada, the country became more mountainous, and a few inches of snow covered the ground. Hobson spent the time conversing with a family of Methodists traveling to Mendocino, California, and a family of Baptists who had lived in Oregon for sixteen years, noting that they liked it, "because of the climate. The woman says And the man likes it because he raises Cattle and horses without feeding

---

19. Hobson, "Diaries," reel 2 of 2, 11/21/1870, 11/26/1870, 11/28/1870, 11/30/1870.
20. Hobson, "Diaries," reel 2 of 2, 11/26/1870–27/1870.
21. Ambrose, *Nothing Like It in the World*, 328.

And is so good for Apples."²² As we know, Hobson had a special interest in fruit growing and this conversation may have piqued his interest in Oregon as a possible location for a settlement of Friends. The next day, on Eleventh Month 28, he got his first hot meal, breakfast, since the train had stopped in Omaha three days earlier. He spent the day talking with his fellow passengers "about Iowa Kansas California Oregon & other States About Religion &C And about the ground we are passing."²³

The train then passed some busy silver and lead works just before skirting Humbolt Lake and running through the alkali flat "a desert destitute of vegetation except scattering bunches of grease brush which is about the size of [illegible] a rolling Careless weed But harder And some what resembling a small scrubby dead Cedar."²⁴ On the 29th the cars began to climb up the Sierra Nevada Mountains and finally here were some trees: "The mountains now have much Excellent timber of the narrow kinds of the evergreens. Tall and every size desirable. Saw mills near the road in some places."²⁵ As the train descended the western slopes of the Sierra Nevada Mountains the weather changed to snow and rain mixed. Hobson expressed some nervousness at the length and speed of the train after several lumber cars were added, but all was well. The vegetation was getting progressively greener as they sped along, and he noticed several mining operations along the tracks remarking "I suppose a large portion of the western slope of the Sierr[a] Nevada Slpe [sic] for great many miles has pay dirt near the surface; if they could have water to wash it. We are past the steep[est] parts of the mountain I suppose Saw mining operations along the Roadside all the way down nearly to Sacramento," where the train arrived in the evening.²⁶ The cars continued to roll on through the night arriving at Niles Station south of Sacramento at dawn. While waiting for the connection to San Jose, Hobson took some time to reflect on his journey as follows:

> I am now sitting in the shade on the north side of the [station] house writing & feeling comfortably warm with out hat or mittens on. It is partly cloudy, The wind from the south. I feel very thankful that I have arrived safely and in good health. Did take some Cold about 3 nights ago But am getting better. Having traveled west about [illegible] 2000 miles. I prove by the sun and my watch that the earth is near 25,000 mi round. May The people

22. Hobson, "Diaries," reel 2 of 2, 11/27/1870.
23. Hobson, "Diaries," reel 2 of 2, 11/28/1870.
24. Hobson, "Diaries," reel 2 of 2, 11/28/1870.
25. Hobson, "Diaries," reel 2 of 2, 11/29/1870.
26. Hobson, "Diaries," reel 2 of 2, 11/29/1870.

of this country Be industrious & feel their responsibility to their maker, is the desire of my heart. Try to live right and Help to get others to do so. That our Heavenly Father may bless us. And give us much joy, and gladness of heart in this life, make our lives a blessing to this and succeeding generations and transmit us to the realms of eternal Bliss is the prayer of my soul.[27]

Hobson boarded the cars again at about half past eleven o'clock and arrived in San Jose in time to eat dinner with his cousin George Hobson shortly after noon. Then they walked over to see Hobson's brother Jesse and the next day he visited his brother David.[28] Hobson's three living full brothers David, Jesse, and Stephen owned prosperous farms in the Santa Clara Valley. The three months Hobson spent at San Jose were very full. He visited family, made pastoral calls, attended and appointed meetings, visited schools, and gathered information about the region.[29] Several of his extended family members also lived in San Jose and the outlying areas including some half-brothers and many cousins. Hobson made the rounds, staying now with one family member and then with another, engaging in ministerial visits as he went. Just a few days after arriving at San Jose on the 4th of Twelfth Month, he wrote, "Last night I thought much about going to my religious work waked before 3 oclock [sic] yet lay thinking." He took his duties as a traveling minister seriously, meeting with many people in their homes and passing out tracts. He often went out of his way to visit people on distant farms, sometimes walking, riding, or taking the train.

Hobson also continued to hold a special interest in education. As a part of his spiritual care for the people of San Jose he visited several schools, at which he spoke and distributed tracts. For example, when at Gilroy on the 12th of Twelfth Month, a community a few miles outside of San Jose, he "had an opportunity to speak to the School children in 5 different School-rooms was well received And I had a very relieving opportunity 5 minutes or so in each place There were altogether perhaps 250 Children." He often visited the schools in whatever community he found himself in.

Hobson was active in meeting at San Jose, speaking when the Spirit moved and lending his support to the formation of a First Day School. He also held a few appointed meetings in the area. Hobson was ecumenical to a certain degree, often attending the Methodist First Day School before

27. Hobson, "Diaries," reel 2 of 2, 11/30/1870.
28. Hobson, "Diaries," reel 2 of 2, 11/30/1870–12/1/1870.
29. Hobson spent three months in San Jose and environs before departing for Oregon. I have summarized his time there from his "Diaries" (11/30/1870–3/2/1871: reel 2 of 2), giving specific dates for quoted entries within the body of the work.

the organization of one among Friends. Once during a short trip north of San Jose on the 19th of Second Month, he "Went School at the Baptist MH Thence to the Methodist Meeting & School Thence to the Baptist meeting. At Methodist And the Baptist Meeting. But there was one Thing which seemed rather to take from The Solemnity of the worship because of so much sound without of music without life both of Instruments and voices." So, while finding some common ground with Methodists and Baptists, he still felt most comfortable in Friends unprogrammed worship.

Hobson's concern for finding a good place to form a Friends settlement on the West Coast plus his natural fascination for all things farming related resulted in a keen interest in the agricultural prospects at San Jose. On the 5th of Twelfth Month he noted, "I Saw fig trees of large size at Kings Also Almond trees which bear a nut perhaps as good as a Hickory nut. Saw Parsnips Carrots Turnips Cabbage lettuce and many other garden productions of various ages. This is certainly one of the countries of great variety of production. And If one has land enough ought to be an easy place to make a living in Still I do not see as I like it upon the whole better than Iowa." Apparently, he was not overly impressed with San Jose agricultural prospects as compared to those back home.

He was also not overly impressed with the healthfulness of the climate in the Santa Clara Valley. He caught cold after cold while at San Jose and experienced considerable hoarseness, which made engaging in public speaking difficult. This somewhat hampered his efforts at ministry. On the 6th of First Month, 1871, he wrote, "Have a deep cold I seem to take fresh colds often since I came to Cal[ifornia] . . . That I am never without a hoarseness so much that It . . . is very hard to speak much publicly this much discourages me from seeking opportunities for public meetings." So, poor health hampered his religious work. He later remarked that the lack of "cutting sea or bay breeze[s]," to which he attributed his hoarseness while at San Jose, was one of the positive things about settling in Oregon.[30] At various times, while down with colds he copied into his diary several glowing accounts of the land and climate of Walla Walla, Washington and Eastern Oregon that stirred his interest to visit those localities.

When Hobson felt released from his religious work in the Santa Clara Valley, he boarded the cars at San Jose Station bound for Sacramento.[31]

30. Hobson, "Diaries," reel 1 of 2, 5/26/1876. From section of diary missing from microfilm. For more information see Goldsmith, "William Hobson and the Founding of Quakerism in the Pacific Northwest," 266–68; Paul, "Extracts," 14–15.

31. Hobson spent about three months traveling by stage north through the Willamette Valley to Portland, Oregon, from there steaming up the Columbia River to Walla Walla, in Washington Territory, where he stayed for several weeks, and then traveling

After arriving at Sacramento, Third Month 3, 1871, he bought a ticket for the stagecoach to Portland, Oregon, scheduled to leave at two o'clock that afternoon. He had the option of taking a steamship from San Francisco up the coast, following in the footsteps of his cousin Abel Bond, but presumably he wanted to look over the land as he rode along in the stage. He sacrificed comfort and expediency for exploration. The coach road, though picturesque, was rough and uncomfortable. Goldsmith notes that the "Oregon Stagecoach Company was advertising 'Through In Six Days To Sacramento,' in 1871, but no human being could have endured the through trip."[32] Apparently, the through trip was an express option with few halts, but Hobson chose a journey of longer duration which included several stopovers at inns along the way. This was probably less taxing on the body, but maybe not significantly. The stage often left very early in the morning at first light and drove far into the night.

At first, the weather was very warm and the land was similar to what he had seen at San Jose. However, when they came to Scott's mountain in northern California he met with a disagreeable change. Hobson and several other passengers were transferred from the stagecoach to an open wagon. The trip over Scott's Pass, lasting from 5 o'clock in the morning until 2 o'clock in the afternoon, was therefore, extremely uncomfortable. Blowing rain and snow saturated Hobson's clothes. The wind was like a knife. He was waterlogged, chilled to the bone, and exhausted by the time they came down off the mountain. Because of this, he chose to spend the night at the Callahan Inn as opposed to riding far into the night on the stage while wringing wet and frozen. He intended to try to stave off a cold while drying out in front of a roaring fire and continue his journey in the morning after a good night's rest.

He wrote in his diary, on Third Month 7, 1871, a lengthy account of how hospitable and warm the inn was, but also of the rough crowd in the corner of the main room, a group of shady characters playing cards, drinking, and taking the Lord's name in vain. He had a few of his tracts out on the table and was prepared to engage in conversation with some of these rude characters. Soon he got his chance. He answered a few inquiries about Iowa, and then, "a considerable time elapsed without much being said in the room except by the players near the further end of the room. When some drew near us and took seats. One of which I took to be a rough infidel and

---

back to California by steamship from Portland, Oregon. I have summarized this portion of his visit to the West Coast from his "Diaries" (3/2/1871–6/10/1871: reel 2 of 2), giving specific dates for quoted entries in the body of the work.

32. Goldsmith, "William Hobson and the Founding of Quakerism in the Pacific Northwest," 234.

commenced conversation. By saying that there were so many pick pockets and robbers back east that he was afraid to live there." Hobson replied at length saying that there were many honest jobs people could do and the world would be a better place if we all attended to our own vocations and didn't meddle in the lives of others, which the men agreed with. Then someone asked a pointed question: "But I [was] Questioned what I thought of Christ. To which I answered all the Scriptures say of him That he had made an atonement for us for our sins Sins [sic] as we have all sinned and could never fill up the lack ourselves he had suffered for us us [sic] our brother and in his infinitude for all the world of mankind and had thus opened a door of salvation to all men who will come and be saved by faith in Christ." He went on at length speaking of humility before Christ, and repentance, coming to Jesus like a little child, the work of the Spirit, listening for God's voice, praying for the Kingdom to be realized on earth, living a simple lifestyle, and the importance of both the Old and New Testament. He also pointed out that as wise as Solomon was, Jesus has done more for us. And when questioned as to the usefulness of ministers after this long sermon he likened his calling to preach to any other vocation, adding that he must be obedient to do the will of God regardless of what man thought. The "rough infidel" was apparently not yet ready to put his trust in Jesus, but Hobson had been faithful to present him with the opportunity.

The next few days as Hobson passed through northern California and southern Oregon, he made notes on the timber and crops, as well as spoke with several people about various localities known for good farmland, including Walla Walla, Washington. He noticed the timber, mostly pine and cedar, was getting thicker the closer they got to Eugene. It was probably getting progressively wetter and muddier, too. One early morning after riding through the night the horses and coach got stuck in a bog and had to be dug out, a delay of three hours. As is typical in the spring, it was raining heavily in Eugene, but this did not seem to trouble Hobson. He considered the land to be rich and not likely to wear out, as he put it. However, the widespread rain in the Willamette Valley made travel a little more difficult. He had to wait at Corvallis for the swollen river to go down before proceeding and cross several deep waterways to reach Albany, where he purchased a train ticket to Salem. Apparently, he was fed up with the stagecoach. He was favorably impressed with the rich farmland he saw in the Willamette Valley and thought it a healthy, wholesome place to live.

Hobson spent the next few days visiting in and around Salem. His cousin Hadley Hobson was living on an expansive farm with his large family near Sublimity, a small settlement about fifteen miles southwest of Salem. While in the Salem area Hobson wrote to his brothers in San Jose and to his family back in Iowa. He also took down the names of several people who were apparently either Friends, lapsed Friends, or interested in becoming Friends, perhaps given to him by Hadley. It continued to rain incessantly, but as he rode through some of the country around Salem he was impressed with the soil, crops, and timber. The general consensus of those living there was that the climate was advantageous, except that people might be more prone to rheumatism due to the damp. He priced the farmland at about thirty dollars an acre and the timber land around ten dollars an acre.

After visiting in the Salem area for approximately a week, Hobson boarded the cars for Portland on Third Month 22, 1871, arriving late in the afternoon. Hobson was so eager to see Walla Walla he spent only one day in Portland. At half past four o'clock in the morning on the 24th he boarded the *Oneonta*, a steamship headed up the Columbia River. In those days, long before Bonneville Dam was built, passengers had to portage around the Cascades, since steamers could not navigate the rapids. Hobson reported disembarking from the *Oneonta* at the Lower Cascades, traveling by rail for five miles, and then boarding the steamship *Idaho* after bypassing the rapids. Upon arrival at The Dalles, on the evening of the 24th, he noted, "There is but little rain yet evevery [sic] thing seems healthy and We are thus from 3–5 in the Morning to 5 in the evening Transferred from a damp rainy climate of Ocean Shore messiness and damp lowlandness to a pleasant healthy dry [illegible] atmosphere invigorating the whole frame into a happy courageous feeling." The next day on the 25th of Third Month he wrote, "Pretty well and in good heart feel happy & resigned to the will of the Lord. I really feel glad that I have Favored to overcome every obstacle and feeling of discouragement Which several times have closely proved my faith & energ[y] My hopes are that The Lord will gather a great Harvest in this country from a willing people." But he also expressed some doubt as to his ability to follow through on what he believed God was calling him to do, writing on the 26th of Third Month, "I am apprehensive if I should fail to get along by suffering any discouragement to hinder me from filling my whole mission to this country." It is understandable that Hobson might feel a little discouraged being so far from home and the support of his family and friends. Nonetheless, he was determined to continue on the course in which he believed God was guiding him.

Though Hobson does not describe it in his diary, Goldsmith tells how in those days a second portage around Celilo Falls was necessary in order for passengers to continue further north up the river. Goldsmith believes, and it makes perfect sense, that Hobson must have taken a train upriver to a point above Tumwater Falls, where he boarded a third steamer, the *Owyhee*, which customarily traveled that portion of the river. Hobson stops recording river travel after passing Umatilla, "but would normally have continued to Wallula, on the Washington side of the river, and then journeyed overland to Walla Walla."[33] He reached Walla Walla on the 28th of Third Month, 1871, about six days after leaving Portland.

Hobson was much impressed with the Walla Walla region, the Touchet River Valley, and the Palouse. He spent about a month and a half traveling in and around these sparsely settled areas. Here Hobson heard good reports from residents about the prospects for plums, pears, and other fruit, as well as continual praise for the climate, grain crops, and the ease of raising livestock. On the other hand, he met a man on the 29th who "had 'rather live down in Webfoot [Willamette Valley] than up here for there the people live for enjoyment and here to make something There have the finest summers And winter they mostly set in the house until the rain is mostly over. Here they can raise much more grain but after all webfoot is a good country.'" This is the first use by Hobson of the term webfoot as shorthand for the Willamette Valley. The plural "webfoots" was used to refer to the valley's residents. The University of Oregon Library's Special Collections blog explains that "the nickname, however, was not a synonym for a duck. It was rather a term that had originated in Massachusetts during the 1700s to describe locals who lived in wet conditions. The term was proliferated by miners coming northward from California as a pejorative descriptor of the locals of the waterlogged Willamette Valley and had grown in popular usage by the 1860s.[34] Walla Walla residents bragged that they could raise considerably more grain, fruit, and garden produce compared to "webfoot" and that the land was clear of trees and rocks, making it much easier to work. Obviously, it also rained considerably less. Hobson would have to decide for himself which region was better suited to his needs and, more importantly, where God was directing him to settle.

Toward the first part of Fourth Month, Hobson toured the area around Waitsburg near the Touchet River. He visited two schools, several farms, and walked over to view the timber on the lower reaches of the Blue Mountains remarking on the 7th of Fourth Month, "as I wearily ascended the last hills [before reaching the home of Joseph Hammer] I cheeringly remembered David Mor remark in the yearly meeting of ministers And Elders Speaking of his confidence that I might reach some upon the heights with staff in hand not easily of access by those not able to go on foot." He held a meeting for the family of Goldsmith Hammer who apparently lived higher up in the

---

33. Goldsmith, "William Hobson and the Founding of Quakerism in the Pacific Northwest," 237.

34. Bigalke, "The Oregon Mascot Part 1: The Webfooter Years."

mountains than Joseph and then returned to Waitsburg. He was tired from hiking the steep hills, but very impressed with the beauty and productivity of the region and the friendliness of the people. It seemed a good prospect for a settlement of Friends. He returned to Waitsburg by the 9th and after attending the Methodist worship service in the morning, he held an appointed meeting in the afternoon at which he "found relief by speaking to the people."

Hobson was seriously considering this area for a settlement of Friends. He was not yet satisfied with his survey of the larger region, however. He was determined to be thorough, so he set out northeast from Walla Walla into the mountains once again with the intention of looking out over the Touchet River Valley. He rode part of the way with a teamster and came upon a timber operation where men were making rails and shingles for two dollars per hundred. Later he came to a sawmill where he stayed the night. Up in the mountains it was cold and wet with both snow and rain at times, but he was impressed with the variety and endless supply of cheap lumber. The view of the Touchet Valley was favorable. By the 16th of Fourth Month 1871, Hobson had walked down the slopes into the valley on the other side of the Blue Mountains where he "Attended Scripture School And A meeting appointed by Wm Adams a Colporteur. Said a few words near the Conclusion Also appointed a meeting at 4 oclock [sic] And had a favored meeting Preached from the text Blessed are the Peace makers for they shall be called the children of God." From there he continued on towards Lewiston, noting the richness of the land around the Touchet, Patite, and Tucannon waterways even remarking that this area around the Touchet would be a good spot for his father and others to settle. He then returned to Walla Walla without much more comment.

Still, he wasn't completely satisfied with his land look. On the 21st of Fourth Month he wrote, "It is 5 months to day since I left home. To day I am middling well And with borrowed horse & Saddle am On my way towards Union Flat Country North of Snake River to look at it." He didn't want to return home without a glimpse of the Palouse, an area in southeast Washington and Idaho known for its extraordinarily rich rolling hill land especially well suited to the production of wheat. As he approached the Palouse his thoughts turned towards the good prairie land along the Touchet, so rich and fertile, with a nearby band of timber quite similar to the layout at Honey Creek. In fact, the remote, wild, and unsettled area around the Touchet reminded him of his and Sarah's first years at Honey Creek. He favored the Touchet region, but when he saw the Palouse he was awestruck with the quality of the soil. He thought the Palouse was wonderful and would also be a great place to settle. However, on the 26th he was ready to wrap up his land survey and head for home.

Upon his return to Waitsburg he held an appointed meeting on the 30th that was not especially well attended, and he was unable to speak to the good relief of his mind. He seemed to be having doubts about the effectiveness of his ministry. On the 1st of Fifth Month he wrote, "I have the headache a little to day [sic] But feel peace within, and a little measure of the Lords upholding [power] to Strengthen me. My trust is in Christ who strengthened me. I felt very happy all day to day I trust in him To day with Strong hope that He will make his power known through his servant to the edification of the people here and for his own praise & glory." It was also disappointing to find only one letter at the Walla Walla Post Office, a message from his brother David. He was hoping to hear from his father, Sarah, and others he had written to. He was certainly feeling homesick, but he also felt it was his duty to hold an appointed meeting at Walla Walla the next First Day. He ended up holding two: one at the Methodist Church in the morning and one at the United Brethren Church in the afternoon. The day after he returned to Wallula where he waited for the steamship that would take him back down the Columbia. Before embarking he received news of three letters waiting for him at the Walla Walla Post Office. There was no time to retrace his steps, so he sent a message asking for his letters to be forwarded to him at Salem. Missing those letters by such a small margin must have been disheartening, but now he had something to look forward to upon reaching the Oregon State Capitol. Hobson boarded the steamship for Portland on the 8th of Fifth Month 1871, beginning his long, circuitous journey home.

Hobson steamed down the Columbia to Portland and then down the Willamette, arriving at Salem on the 11th of Fifth Month. He decided to stick around awhile and wait for the letters that were hopefully coming from Walla Walla. The next day when they still hadn't arrived he was feeling rather low: "To day I am trying to Bring my deeds to the Light to be tried I have been feeling so small Is it right Or am I falling below my place. Was not Paul Bold. Did he not strive to preach Christ even where he had not been named. And do not the wicked fleas [sic] when no man pursue them. And are not the Righteous bold as a Lion[?]" He decided to keep busy and held an appointed meeting at Sublimity on the 14th. It was a small meeting "held to pretty good satisfaction." He borrowed a horse and visited some families living in the area as well as the school at Aumsville where he held an appointment. He appointed another meeting about five miles northeast of Salem in a schoolhouse on the 23rd and yet another at a schoolhouse in Salem on the 26th. He visited with several ministers from different denominations and made several notations about his views on certain Scriptures. It seems he had a renewed sense of his calling to reach people with the good news of Jesus Christ.

On the 27th he received his anticipated letters, one each from his brothers Jesse and David and one from a friend living in Iowa, Caleb Baldwin. If he was disappointed not to hear from his family in Iowa he didn't say. He held a final appointed meeting at the courthouse in Salem on the 28th at which there was "pretty full attendance And feel pretty well over what I was instrumental in giving The people." He spent some more time visiting in the vicinity, but by the 30th he expressed the desire to move on. He noted, "This morning I am Looking towards leaving pretty soon. Yet I have filled but a small portion of my prospect of religious prospect in this valley but I have found it somewhat difficult." On the 31st Hobson took the train for Portland noticing from the cars that the young grain looked good and the fruit trees were setting blooms. But something had changed in his view of the Pacific Northwest. After he reached Portland he wrote, "I have now seen And Collected information [smudge] of The soil, Climate & productions of the Pacific States and am able to compare them with Iowa Missouri and some other corn growing States. And am of the opinion that mostly people will or can still do about as well without crossing the plains." Had his opinion of the Far West and especially the wonderful land available in Washington Territory truly changed or was this just fatigue and homesickness talking?

Hobson was compelled to wait at Portland a few days for the departure of the *Oriflamme*, a steamship bound for San Francisco. He climbed up into the Portland West Hills where he had a spectacular view of Mt. Hood, the Willamette Valley, and the city. In this atmosphere he wrote a rather lengthy section in his diary, indicating more about his frame of mind at the time noting,

> to me some portions of these Countries on this Coast appear to me very good: *But as a whole it lacks much of being equal to the Old Northwest My estimation of the NNW [New North West] is not quite as great as before I saw it.* Yet I have a height [sic] estimation of it still. There is some good prairie Some has lately been but now more or less covered with small growth not hard to Clear off. Much of it is hills and mountains too steep or too high to be of much value There is some gold and other metals. The large rivers are very high now Covering the low bottoms & thees [sic] so much water at this time of the year prevents some good land from bearing crops to much profit if at all [italics added].[35]

35. Hobson, "Diaries," reel 1 of 2, 6/5/1871.

It seems Hobson was cooling off on the idea of establishing a Friends community in the Pacific Northwest. As Goldsmith points out Hobson "considered California unsuitable for what he had in mind [a settlement of Friends], and apparently never gave that state further serious consideration. He found the Pacific Northwest, however, immensely attractive, yet at the conclusion of nearly three months of extensive travel in Oregon, [and Washington] he suddenly was ready to abandon the entire project. The new Northwest was too mountainous, and subject to flooding and other ills that had not troubled him earlier." Goldsmith believed that "the religious depression which gradually crept over Hobson's mind in the Willamette Valley was the cause of his loss of enthusiasm for a Far West settlement. He became lonely after weeks without mail and depressed at the lack of apparent results from his preaching." This "religious depression" as Goldsmith called it, seemed to be creeping over Hobson even before he returned to the Willamette Valley from Washington Territory, back when he was traversing the region near the Touchet. Perhaps he felt like the Methodists and Brethren had things well in hand. Goldsmith also notes correctly that "Iowa Quakerism was caught up amidst the fervor and excitement of religious revival when [Hobson] left in 1870, and he found it difficult for one man to pack up all the new enthusiasm and warmth and carry it west. Failing, he concluded that the Middle West was perhaps the best place for Friends, after all."[36] Failing is a strong word. While it is reasonable to say that Hobson was homesick, down in the dumps, and feeling ineffective in his ministry, it is less reasonable to say that he completely gave up on his concern to form a Friends settlement in the Pacific Northwest. Vocations unfold in complicated ways sometimes and while the discouragement he experienced towards the end of this journey almost snuffed out his desire to form a Quaker settlement on the West Coast, his original concern remained, a tiny spark in his heart. Perhaps this was one of the spiritual "baptisms" Friends often referred to, a mission refining bout of melancholy.

The *Oriflamme* left Portland on the 7th carrying Hobson to San Francisco without incident, except for some light sea sickness.[37] He disembarked at San Francisco the morning of the 10th and attended an agricultural meeting in San Jose that afternoon. He visited in the neighborhood, attended meeting, and wrote letters. He also received a large package of tracts from

36. Goldsmith, "William Hobson and the Founding of Quakerism in the Pacific Northwest," 246.

37. This time Hobson stayed about a month at San Jose and then returned home. I have summarized this portion of his journey from his diary (6/10/1871–7/13/1871: "Diaries," reel 2 of 2), giving specific dates for quoted diary entries in the body of the work.

Friends back east that encouraged him greatly as a sign of support for his ministry. On the 20th he seemed to be coming out of the gloominess he experienced in Portland:

> To day [sic] I am Much of my time alone in one of my brother Jesses [sic] upper rooms in Sanjose with [illegible] 80 kinds of the Tracts spread over the room. Many of which I know and have shed tears tears [sic] of joy because they Have reached me and the good letters from my wife daughter & daughterinlaw [sic] & my friends Caleb B . . . & Wm. Reece . . . And more We had a much larger attendance than usual at Friends meeting last first day. And a favored meeting Some served in forepart by by [sic] 3 ministers including myself and again through me in such a manner as I trust to all present there there [sic] was acknowledgment that the pure gospel stream is a gift from the Lord. And I one of his mouthpieces had again some fullness of joy in preaching The gospel. And again have happy days & favors abound After feeling some times of leanness and loneliness. But I am thankful for all that a I have passed through.[38]

After more visiting and more ministry among San Jose Friends, including the distribution of the tracts he had received, Hobson said his goodbyes. He took the cars to Sacramento on Seventh Month 7, 1871, and from there got on the east bound train. He arrived home just in time for the wheat and apple harvest which was early that year. The family must have taken good care of the farm and orchard in his absence for he "found things in pretty good order" and that was that. After a journey of about eight months he resumes his diary in his accustomed manner recording daily events with no further remarks about his adventures on the West Coast.

BACK HOME AT HONEY CREEK

Hobson returned to regular life at Honey Creek apparently forgetting all about his concern to form a Quaker settlement somewhere on the West Coast. He was much preoccupied with farm work and ministry, diving right back into all his responsibilities at home and at Honey Creek Monthly Meeting. But he must not have completely forgotten about his experiences on the Pacific Coast. Toward the end of Eighth Month 1871, he sent letters to some of his acquaintances living on the Palouse in Washington Territory.[39] He also sent Iowa Yearly Meeting minutes to Friends in California, Oregon, and

---

38. Hobson, "Diaries," reel 2 of 2, 6/20/1871.
39. Hobson, "Diaries," reel 2 of 2, 8/26/1871.

Washington Territory towards the end of 1872 and 1873.[40] Hobson noted on the 31st of First Month 1873, that he "Talked with N. Williams giving information about the New north West."[41] Williams eventually moved to the Walla Walla area. So, internal deliberations concerning whether or not Hobson truly was called to the Pacific Coast had evidently been simmering on the back burner. Over the next three days, directly after Hobson spoke with Williams, John S. Bond held a series of "favored" appointments during which Hobson's calling to the Far West was in some way confirmed. After the first meeting Hobson wrote, "Today I am fully and was almost yesterday given up to move to the far West yet not decided where to Locate: But believe it will be in Was[hington T[erritory]." The next day he noted, "Surrendered myself to become a Missionary in the far West. If all needful things work favorably thereto." After the third meeting he remarked, "felt courageous & we had a highly favored Meeting at Honey Creek."[42] So, something significant must have been happening spiritually over the last year and a half that he did not commit to paper until this pivotal experience in Second Month 1873, when he made the decision to go back to the West Coast and find the place God had in mind for a settlement. About a week later, he gave information to some others who asked him about Washington Territory and in Third Month 1873, he gave a lecture at Honey Creek about missions and the New Northwest.[43]

John S. Bond was liberated for religious service on the Pacific Coast at Iowa Yearly Meeting Sessions in 1873[44] and at the end of Twelfth Month 1873, Hobson received a letter from his friend with a "good account of the far West." Hobson collected $34.50 for Bond from the congregation at Honey Creek and sent it to him to help with ministry expenses.[45] When Bond returned in Third Month 1874, the two men got together twice, perhaps to discuss the Far West.[46] It seems that Hobson was now determined to follow through with the concern God had placed on his heart to form a Friends settlement on the West Coast and serve as a missionary there. Why then did it take him until Fifth Month 1875, to act on his resolve and journey west for a second time?

40. Hobson, "Diaries," reel 1 of 2, 12/28/73, 12/15/1873.
41. Hobson, "Diaries," reel 1 of 2, 1/31/1873.
42. Hobson, "Diaries," reel 1 of 2, 2/1/1873–3/1873.
43. Hobson, "Diaries," reel 1 of 2, 2/10/1873, 3/11/1873.
44. Goldsmith, "William Hobson and the Founding of Quakerism in the Pacific Northwest," 247.
45. Hobson, "Diaries," reel 1 of 2, 12/24/1873–25/1873.
46. Hobson, "Diaries," reel 1 of 2, 3/4/1874, 3/23/1974.

There are several possible reasons Hobson delayed returning to the Pacific Coast including financial, physical, emotional, and spiritual considerations. It had cost Hobson about $400 to visit the Far West the first time of which Iowa Yearly Meeting had kicked in $150.[47] And while his sons kept up the farm and orchard well in his absence they were deprived of his labor and expertise while he was gone. It must have taken some time to recover financially from the outlay of around $250 which was close to about $5000 in today's money.[48] Hobson probably felt a sense of urgency to be on his way once he had made up his mind to return to the Pacific Northwest, but he was held back by a lack of funds. He ended up borrowing money from his brothers, David and Jesse. This enabled him to return right away instead of saving up money in Iowa over time which would have delayed his departure for years. Once in San Jose for the second time he noted, "Went to Brother Davids [sic] gave a note for two hundred & 21 dollars & 50 Cents. At States Gold Coin with ten per cent per annum until paid Also to Brother Jesse two hundred & 61. Dollars with 10 percent Due in 12 months from date." Oddly, his brothers charged him interest. Also, as Goldsmith points out somewhat melodramatically, David Hobson "received his start in California as a gold miner during the days of the Gold Rush, [so] it can therefore be said that a link exists between the discovery of gold in California and the founding of Quakerism in Oregon."[49] This was true of Jesse as well. Was gold strike money tainted? Perhaps some Quakers may have thought so, but apparently it didn't bother William.

Hobson borrowed heavily in order to move to Oregon and at times wondered if he and Sarah would ever get out from under the substantial burden of indebtedness to his brothers, as well as the relentless weight of their mortgage.[50] At one point during Sixth Month 1876, he worried, "For 3 or 4 days last week my mind was somewhat in trouble with an uneasy feeling about how I am to succeed in getting my next payment ready towards my land It will take 12 hundred dollars on the 7 of next first mo. Besides, considerable of other debts and means to go home [to Iowa] on. But this morning I feel more easy and trustful that as hitherto some way will work out for me." The sale of his property at Honey Creek in the Fall of 1876 provided enough funds to meet this payment. Eventually, much to his relief, Hobson was able to pay off his debt to his brothers. Early in 1886, he wrote,

---

47. Hobson, "Diaries," reel 2 of 2, 1/8/1882.

48. *CPI Inflation Calculator*.

49. Goldsmith, "William Hobson and the Founding of Quakerism in the Pacific Northwest," 270.

50. Hobson, "Diaries," reel 2 of 2, 1/8/1882.

"L[etter] [from Bro] David [illegible] fully paid & will send my note So after a little more than ten [years?] By diligence I have got My old debts paid off at Length [Made] by Borrowing money to [travel] on in the year 1875." A few days later he wrote, "Received a letter from my Brother David including my last note which he held against me for money borrowed of him to bear expense in traveling in the ministry in the year 1875 & 1876 on this Coast A. paid 1381.90 C[en]ts [written vertically in the margin the following:] Paid to bro D. H. 13.81.90 Cents." Hobson must have borrowed from his brother several times in order to be indebted to the tune of $1,381.90, even with interest. After clearing his obligation to his brothers, it took him another four years, until Tenth Month 1890, to pay off his mortgage, shortly before Sarah's death and about eight months before his own.[51] So, we see that the Hobsons spent pretty much the remainder of their lives after leaving Honey Creek, approximately fifteen years, in debt. It was a sacrifice in more ways than one to follow God's calling to the Pacific Northwest.

After all, the Hobsons were quite comfortable on their homestead at Honey Creek both physically and financially. They had put a lot of sweat equity, not to mention cold, hard cash into improving their homestead and were heavily invested at Honey Creek, having built it up over the last two decades into a prosperous, going concern. In fact, in the late summer of 1874 just under a year before he returned to the Pacific Coast, Hobson was inexplicably engaged in the process of building a new house. He noted on the 17th of Eighth Month, "Commenced a House Repaired west fence Halled [sic] Stone & Brick." Over the next several days he hauled a total of 1,100 bricks and several loads of lumber to a building site on his homestead. By the 26th he was able to write, "I now have my lumber for my house as far as I know except the doors (& besides the bill for one Load which seems to be misplaced) Cost [$]347.96," nearly what it cost him to travel to the West Coast the first time. He then bought eleven doors for the new house and a large load of lime. It's hard to understand why he spent so much money on a new house when he might have saved the funds for a return trip west. By the end of Ninth Month, he was busy plastering the house with a mixture of lime and water. He took a break from construction in order to attend Iowa Yearly Meeting Sessions, but started up again shortly after his return from Oskaloosa. Work on the new house was completed on the 7th of Tenth Month 1874.[52]

Why did Hobson spend so much time and energy building such a large, fancy new home at a significant expense just months before he

51. Hobson, "Diaries," reel 1 of 2, 6/26/1876, 3/11/1886, 3/16/1886, 10/24/1890.
52. Hobson, "Diaries," reel 1 of 2, 8/17/1874–10/10/1874.

returned to the west? Was he wavering in his commitment to the Lord's calling? Was he still trying to discern God's direction or timing? Did he feel it would be impossible to raise the needed funds for missionary work in the west, so he might as well go on with life at Honey Creek? It's possible, but not likely, that the Hobsons considered such an endeavor a capital improvement which would make the homestead more saleable. It's much more likely that Hobson was influenced by the fact that Sarah was not on board with his concern to serve as a missionary in the Pacific Northwest and she was hoping he might change his mind. In fact, during the summer of 1876 Hobson wrote how her reluctance to leave Honey Creek made him question his resolve and held him back from returning to the West Coast sooner. He even remarked, when reflecting on the process of his calling, that for a time he entertained the idea of helping other Friends get started in a settlement somewhere on the Pacific Coast, but not living there permanently himself. Late in Fifth Month 1876, he wrote, "But my mind was impressed from the very first that part of my duty was to Obtain a good knowledge of the countries [sic] hereaway [Willamette Valley] So as to be able to give important information to others especially to the Friends whose duty it might be to settle here. And this last time I was the more forcibly impressed with this latter part of the work That I must find a Locality for a Friends settlement, and help some to get it started; even if for the main part my home remained in Iowa."[53] If he was still toying with the idea of returning to Honey Creek after helping others to form a Friends settlement in the Pacific Northwest, that might explain why he built the new house, especially since Sarah was reluctant to leave Iowa.

Another reason Hobson may have delayed leaving Honey Creek had to do with spiritual matters and his ministry among Iowa Friends. After all, Iowa Yearly Meeting was in the middle of a significant revival as he was working out his calling to move west. As a minister he may have felt a responsibility to the congregation at Honey Creek, as well as to Iowa Yearly Meeting at large to help lead during this exciting time. Emotionally it would have been very difficult for him to pull away as the revival progressed and gathered momentum. He likely felt torn between his ministry in Iowa and the stirring in his soul that he recognized as a word from God compelling him to serve as a missionary on the Pacific Coast.

Clearly, Hobson wavered back and forth about heading up a settlement of Friends on the West Coast, but he was not being intentionally disobedient to God. Goldsmith criticizes him for what he categorizes as a lack of resolve

---

53. Hobson, "Diaries," reel 1 of 2, 5/26/1876. From section of diary missing from microfilm. For more information see Goldsmith, "William Hobson and the Founding of Quakerism in the Pacific Northwest," 266–68; Paul, "Extracts," 14–15.

stating, "He [Hobson] had now twice resolved that Friends should emigrate and begin new settlements in the Far West, and twice given up the project. Yet in his Diary of Fifth Month 26, 1876, he declares that the responsibility to work for such a purpose had weighed upon him since 1870."[54] Sure, it took him a while to follow through on God's leading, but this was no small undertaking Hobson was being called to. We have seen the things he had to disengage from at Honey Creek, including his faith community and the disapproval of his wife, as well as financial considerations and the great geographical distance to be covered. He was also in his mid-fifties and though in good health, no longer a young man. Though it took time and he encountered a few bumps in the road, in the end Hobson chose to say "yes" to God in spite of Sarah's disapproval and all that was still attractive about staying at Honey Creek.

SECOND JOURNEY TO THE WEST COAST

Once he made a firm decision to return to the Pacific Coast Hobson followed through fairly quickly. Fourth Month 12, 1875, he notes, "liberated by Honey Creek Monthly Meeting in 3 mo. [1875] And by H[oney] Creek quarterly Meeting in 4 mo. [1875] To perform religious service on the Pacific Coast."[55] The Honey Creek Monthly Meeting Minutes back this up.[56] So, with the affirmation of Iowa Friends and the promise of a loan from his brothers, Hobson was finally ready to depart.

On Fifth Month 11, 1875, almost four years since returning from his previous journey west, he boarded the cars at Union Station headed once again for San Jose, California.[57] And though he does not mention it, John S. Bond traveled with him.[58] The return trip took one week: back over the buffalo grass plains, through Weber Canyon and past the 1000 mile tree, along the Great Salt Lake and through the Alkali Flats, over the Sierra Mountains, beyond Humbolt Canyon, and down to San Jose via Sacramento and Niles Station.[59] This time he wrote considerably less about the journey, likely be-

---

54. Goldsmith, "William Hobson and the Founding of Quakerism in the Pacific Northwest," 248.

55. Hobson, "Diaries," reel 1 of 2, 4/12/1875.

56. Goldsmith, "William Hobson and the Founding of Quakerism in the Pacific Northwest," 248.

57. Hobson, "Diaries," reel 1 of 2, 5/12/1875.

58. Goldsmith, "William Hobson and the Founding of Quakerism in the Pacific Northwest," 249; Hobson, "Diaries," reel 1 of 2, 5/18/1874.

59. I have summarized Hobson's second journey west from his "Diaries" (5/11/1875–9/20/76: reel 1 of 2) giving specific dates for quoted entries in the body of

cause he was not seeing everything for the first time. He did feel it was a blessing to be able to ride on the train especially over the Alkali Flats and found the company pleasant. The trip was pretty uneventful, except for the forty-mile-an-hour descent down Humbolt canyon, which, thankfully, everybody survived without incident.

When Hobson reached San Jose on the 5th of Fifth Month he immediately mailed a letter to Sarah, most likely letting her know he had arrived safely. He was happy to see his father, Stephen Hobson, who had moved to San Jose from North Carolina and he enjoyed visiting with other family and friends. John S. Bond stayed at San Jose, too. Apparently, he had planned to accompany Hobson further north into Oregon since their departure from Honey Creek. Shortly after Bond and Hobson arrived at San Jose, Perry C. Hadley and his wife Hannah, Quaker neighbors from Iowa, and David J. Wood, the former clerk of New Providence Monthly Meeting (Iowa), his wife Maggie, and their young daughter also arrived. Hadley and Wood joined Hobson and Bond in the search for a perfect location for a Friends settlement while their wives remained behind in California.[60]

Hobson's hoarseness returned almost immediately upon his arrival at San Jose. His ill health and a poor show of wheat due to drought contributed to a marked dissatisfaction with the area. He wrote on Fifth Month 25, 1875, "I cannot recommend Iowa folks come here for settlement unless is should seem to be their duty." If he had entertained any doubt before, Hobson was now firmly convinced that San Jose was not the place for his Quaker community. On his previous trip Hobson had stayed three months at San Jose. This time he stayed only three weeks, just long enough to spend some time with his father, other family, and friends, and to secure the loans from his brothers. He was a man on a mission. He was eager to find the location for a Friends settlement that God had in mind and begin his Kingdom work there.

By the 7th of Sixth Month 1875, Hobson, Bond, Hadley, and Wood were riding the cars on their way to San Francisco. From there they boarded the steamship *Empire* bound for Empire City in the Coos Bay, Oregon. Hobson reported sighting sea lions on the 8th and whales the next morning, bright spots during a tedious time in choppy water. All were seriously seasick as they traveled up the coast. Their nausea was severe enough that it took the four men a few days to get over their queasiness even after disembarking from the ship. However, they were well enough to appoint two meetings at Empire City on the 13th after which they steamed twenty-five

---

the work.

60. Goldsmith, "William Hobson and the Founding of Quakerism in the Pacific Northwest," 249–50; Kelsey, "Quakerism Beyond the Mississippi," 469.

miles through the bay further inland to Coos City. From there they got on the stage to Roseburg. Early in the morning on the 14th Hobson wrote, "We have had sickness 4 days on Sea and a heavy expense to Roseburg of 33 dollars now paid out Yet with all discouragements met with by the way I feel pretty well and joyful that I am here Even so happy That since before 1 oclock [sic] I could not sleep for joy and heavenly meditations I am Thankful that I am so near my anticipated field of Labor." Hobson felt relieved to be about God's Kingdom work even in the face of certain difficulties.

Hobson's description of the seemingly endless forest on the way to Roseburg is reminiscent of a romantic idyll in a gothic novel, though he would hate to hear it. They

> set off from Coos City at ½ after 6 a.m. and arrived at the 31 mile-house toward Roseburg about 5 p.m Some were on a wagon & some on horseback. W[e] passed dense Forests all day very tall; many very long trees of many kinds of evergreen averaging as we suppose nearly or quite 200 feet. Saw a few cleared patches of from one to 10 acres or so by the way and a few settlers Their little farms were mostly in Timothy looking pretty well. We passed many beautiful mountain Streams. In afternoon we came to rocky mountains and high enough by 4 oclock [sic] to be among the rain and clouds A little before we arrived to this place we pass [sic] a little rich Valley Called Brewsters Valley said to be about 1 by 2 12/ miles. This little spot almost exclusively a Forest very valuable timber for furniture of soft Maple & Myrtle, Chiefly Myrtle. Some Alder are large [enough] for saw logs is [sic] these mountains There is some Ash But probably 95 hundredths of all the Timber and it is almost wholly set thick by with tall timber from 150 feet tall and upward for about 50 miles from the Coast towards Roseburg. Consists Chiefly of Red yellow & white Fir of which there are many trees. 6 to 8 feet in diameter set [close] and 200 or more feet long There is also much hemlock. And much better There is quite a scatter of White and Post Cedar Very valuable.[61]

On the 15th as they continued on their way towards Roseburg, Hobson met "an Iowa man [at] Looking-glass Prairie . . . [who] would not live through Iowa winters for very much again. No one after staying here awhile wants to endure Iowa winters again." More confirmation that it was good to settle in the temperate Pacific Northwest.

After passing through Roseburg the four travelers met another Iowa man, a Baptist minister named George W. Bond, who also preferred the

---

61. Hobson, "Diaries," reel 1 of 2, 6/14/1875.

Willamette Valley to Iowa, praising the quality and high yield of fruit in the valley and declaring he would much rather live near Eugene than in Iowa. They also received a glowing report of the Willamette Valley from a woman named Alice Macy whose hospitality they enjoyed while at Eugene. On the 17th they held a meeting in the Methodist Church at Eugene and the next day traveled on to Hobson's cousin Hadley Hobson in Sublimity. Hobson continued to gather testimonials about the superiority of the Willamette Valley as he traveled around the countryside noting on Sixth Month 19, 1875, "Stopped at James Wisners Who had been here about 23 years likes Oregon well. I have asked 3 women to day whether they prefer living in Oregon or back in Iowa or Missouri. They having tried [smudged out] the Latter for many years And now Oregon for many years do greatly prefer Oregon. Say it is easier living here than any country they ever lived in; and would not exchange Oregon for any other place. all things considered I feel Cheerful to day and pretty well and very much at home in this state." He may have been specifically asking women what they thought of the Willamette Valley in order to report favorably about the area to his wife from a female perspective.

Now at this point in his journey things really began to fall into place as to where to settle, but we need a little background to see certain connections. According to Goldsmith, in the fall of 1874 some Friends from Kansas arrived at Salem, Oregon. They were Nathan and Elizabeth White with their young children, Elizabeth's mother, a Quaker minister named Rebecca Clawson, several families with the last name of Haines, the William Adairs, the John Townsends, and possibly others. In the spring of 1875, the Whites moved to Dayton, a small, but lively town about twenty miles northwest of Salem on a bend of the Yamhill River, a tributary of the Willamette. At about the same time two other Friends families from Indiana, the John Fusons and Macy Hadleys, also settled at Dayton, but Rebecca Clawson apparently stayed in Salem awhile with another daughter. Clawson was in the habit of visiting prisoners and holding meetings at the state penitentiary and in the course of one of her calls she met a prisoner there named Thomas Markham.[62] Rayner W. Kelsey describes it as follows:

> Sometimes she [Clawson] spoke to the convicts at the State penitentiary, and at the close of one such service a prisoner came forward desiring to speak with her. He had known something of Friends, and was attracted by the Quaker bonnet. He told Rebecca Clawson the sad story of his imprisonment, and pleaded

---

62. Goldsmith, "William Hobson and the Founding of Quakerism in the Pacific Northwest," 251–52.

with her to visit his sorrowing wife and children, still living upon the farm in the Chehalem Valley. The winter of 1874–75 was severe, and as Rebecca Clawson was not rugged in strength, Nathan and Elizabeth White went upon the errand of mercy. They took the boat from Salem to Roger's Landing (present day Newberg). They climbed the steep embankment at the landing, slippery with rain and melting snow. After sheltering themselves from the storm for a time in an old shack, they made their way slowly along under the dripping branches that over hung the untraveled road. They found at last the lonely family, and comforted the wife and children as best they were able.[63]

Markham was convicted of arson toward the end of April 1873 and sentenced to ten years in the Oregon State Penitentiary[64] along with two other men from Yamhill County, one named John Russell who got one year for arson, as well as William Bruce who was sentenced to ten years for "attempt to kill."[65] It seems the three men may have been partners in crime. At any rate, Markham must have been desperate to avoid transfer to the prison after his conviction. According to the *Albany States Rights Democrat* he tried to commit suicide in jail directly after receiving his sentence. The paper reported that "Markham, last week convicted of arson at Lafayette, tried to kill himself in jail with a jack knife last Sunday. One or two digs in the ribs with it persuaded him that the process was too painful for Sunday amusement, and he let up."[66] This wretched character happened to be the husband of Hobson's cousin Esther who was living on a leased farm eight miles east of Dayton near Newberg. After leaving Hadley Hobson's in Sublimity, William Hobson and Perry C. Hadley stayed with Rebecca Clawson at her home. She must have told Hobson about Thomas Markham, for Hobson visited him at the penitentiary on the 24th of Sixth Month. During this visit Markham probably asked Hobson to check in on his wife and family in the Chehalem Valley. Goldsmith sternly warned against making too much of Kelsey's quixotic description of a "Quaker bonnet" leading to Hobson's acquaintance with Markham[67] and subsequently to his later property acquisition in the

---

63. Kelsey, "Quakerism Beyond the Mississippi," 470.

64. "Pacific Coasters," *States Rights Democrat* (Albany, OR), May 2, 1873, accessed March 23, 2020, https://oregonnews.uoregon.edu/lccn/sn84022644/1873-05-02/ed-1/seq-2/.

65. Convict Records, Oregon State Penitentiary.

66. "Pacific Coasters," *States Rights Democrat* (Albany, OR), April 25, 1873, accessed March 23, 2020, https://oregonnews.uoregon.edu/lccn/sn84022644/1873-04-25/ed-1/seq-2/#words=digs+One+ribs+two.

67. Kelsey, "Quakerism Beyond the Mississippi," 470.

Chehalem Valley. Goldsmith preferred a more pragmatic view of Hobson's land choice based on his geographical and crop surveys, but there is no denying that both a Quaker bonnet and a felon interred at the Oregon State Penitentiary played pivotal roles in Hobson's choice of where to settle.

The day after his visit with Markham, Hobson and Bond traveled to Dayton with Elizabeth White, a woman Hobson admired greatly. According to Rayner, "the new company brought good cheer to the Friends at Dayton, and as the wagon drove up, Nathan White [Elizabeth's husband] could exclaim with spirit, 'Well, if here isn't a whole wagonload of Quakers!'" The next day Nathan took Hobson and Bond to visit Esther Markham. They had a pleasant visit and Hobson got his first look at the Chehalem Valley where he would soon reside. As they went along he

> saw good Old Orchards generally except that the Peach trees have nearly dwindled out largly [sic] I think by age and overbearing. The land was all good which we passed. Crops of grain and [some] grass all good. Considerable of the land is covered in a mixture of Oak and fir mainly fir with some other kinds A few large firs and large Oaks but chiefly brush and pole timber. In some places there several acres together of oak timber chiefly pole or brush but there are plenty of large Oaks for posts, wood or for wagon making or coopering if needed It is White Oak I see ten times as much White oak Timber as I remembered seeing when here before red Clover & Timothy grows every where here where [illegible] had been given it and that luxuriantly.[68]

Hobson seemed to be favorably impressed with the Chehalem Valley, but not overly enthusiastic and he certainly did not immediately decide to dwell there. He liked the area and there were already Friends nearby at Dayton, but he wasn't satisfied, yet. He still wanted to keep his options open.

Upon returning to Dayton he held two appointments and then stayed overnight with Joel Palmer, the town founder. According to William L. Lang, author of the "Joel Palmer" page in the online Oregon Encyclopedia, Palmer's parents were Quakers which may have predisposed him toward his roles as the "Oregon Provisional government peace commissioner to the Cayuse, Superintendent of Indian Affairs in 1848, and Superintendent for Indian Affairs for Oregon Territory in 1853–1856." Later he served as Speaker of the Oregon House of Representatives in 1862 and for two terms in the Oregon Senate (1864 to 1866). He was popular enough with Oregon Republicans to be endorsed for a seat in the U.S. Senate, a race he withdrew from out of loyalty to the state government, and for Governor of the State

---

68. Hobson, "Diaries," reel 1 of 2, 6/26/1875.

of Oregon in 1870, a race he lost by a small margin to the Democratic candidate. After his death Palmer was remembered as a "defender of Indian people."[69] It's a pity that Hobson did not record any of his conversation with Palmer.

After visiting in Dayton the four companions from Iowa traveled to Portland where they put John S. Bond on the stage headed for San Francisco. Then Hobson, Hadley, and Wood embarked on the steamer *Neonta* for a trip up the Columbia to Walla Walla. Much to his dismay Hobson found many of the orchards at Walla Walla severely damaged or dead noting on the 4th of Seventh Month 1875, "The fruit Trees are much injured Some peach trees are killed Dead. There appears to be no Peaches this year in this locality," and the next day on the 5th, "Made a visit to Philip R[itz] Visited his Orchard and Beheld the effect of last winters [sic] coldness on the Trees. Peach Trees were nearly all killed. Many of the Apple & Pear trees are damaged very much and some of Both are killed w even some plum trees are killed." This devastation wrought by an unusually cold winter apparently changed Hobson's former good opinion of the region. Dead and injured peach trees, especially, were a real tragedy. The three men visited Waitsburg and went to see N. Williams their former neighbor from Iowa who had moved to the region after hearing Hobson's glowing reports from his previous visit. Hobson admired Williams's land and the Pataha Prairie near where Williams had settled, but his enthusiasm for the Walla Walla area seemed to have waned. Hobson and his traveling companions spent only two weeks in Washington Territory before steaming back down the Columbia to Portland and on down the Willamette to Dayton.

Hobson spent the next several months continuing his search for a place to settle. He first explored Yamhill north of Dayton and Clackamas south of Portland. He then took a short break and worked an ore deposit at Oswego where he camped for a couple weeks living in a tent or sometimes a rough cabin. He looked around Dayton some more and at land between Yamhill and the Willamette River. Then he, Hadley, and Wood looked over the burnt woods near Clackamas. Hobson remained hopeful that he would find the right parcel of land writing on Ninth Month 12, 1875, "I have been to Portland twice and to Oregon City several times to get Posted up with information and descriptions Preparatory to Taking a land look understandingly. I am expecting several others to accompany us in this attempt to Settle in Oregon." Perry C. Hadley, David Wood, Joseph Almond, Nathan Hobson, identified as Almonds's nephew, but likely Hobson's half-brother who was visiting from California, and William Macy went together on an excursion

69. Lang, "Joel Palmer (1810–1881)."

to Silverton, the Clackamas burn (again), Soda Springs, Molalla, on through the valley, and back to Dayton. Then Wood, Almond, and Hobson decided to look at land in Clark County, Washington Territory. While at Vancouver Hobson made an important decision:

> At Vancouver in Wash[inton] Ter[ritory] ... where I can look out on the Great Columbia 1 mile in width at this place I am seriously thoughtful now in regard to Holding with other friends a meet[ing] soon at Dayton after the order of Friends twice in the week I think my head has improved somewhat perhaps as much as any way through my long sweats at the Ore-bank There are like to be about 20 or more at Dayton Oregon this winter. I believe I will take my things from the Orebank and make my home at Dayton perhaps until Friends there can do without me.[70]

Apparently, he was narrowing his search for property to the northern Willamette Valley.[71]

After returning to Dayton he presided over the first of what were to become weekly First Day meetings at Dayton on Ninth Month 26, 1875. He traveled out Clackamas and Silverton way yet again. Then he went to get his belongings from the ore bank at Oswego, taking them to John Fusons's house at Dayton, where he was to stay for a time. On the 14th of Tenth Month he went to the Oregon State Fair, staying over with cousin Hadley Hobson at Sublimity. While at the fair he had a spiritually uplifting experience at a camp meeting; a taste of the revival that was going on back in Iowa.

Hobson returned to the Dayton area for several days helping the Whites and Fusons on their farms. At this point he expressed some of his inner feelings about his current ministry. He was

> feeling this morning a necessity laid upon me to seek out the religious person talke [sic] with them some on religious subjects. I have seriously and I thing [sic] profitably pondered over this scripture "Be not righteous over much neither make theyself [sic] over wise why shoudest [sic] thou destroy they self "neither be not thou over much wicked neither why shouldest thou die before thy time." Much study is a weariness to the flesh. Now I want [illegible] what I may be able in the Lords vineyard; But I think right to tell my younger friend honestly and in greatest of humility as regards myself. That I feel to be a servant as far as

---

70. Hobson, "Diaries," reel 1 of 2, 9/19/2875.

71. I have summarized Hobson's first year living in the Willamette Valley from his diary (9/18/75–9/1876: "Diaries," reel 1 of 2), giving specific dates for quoted entries within the body of the work.

I am able But I want you to be careful not to depend too much upon me. For I often feel wearied and worn and have not much physical or mental force. I seem to need much rest and some time for my worn body to patch up lest I fail to be of much more use in the world. I fear in looking over my life since my childhood days that with all my care to live temperately and in moderation That I have failed some what of taking rest enough. And that Both my small physical and mental capacities have been over taxed.[72]

Hobson was feeling weary and maybe beginning to despair of ever finding the right place to establish a Friends community. He may have been feeling his age, too. After all, he was fifty-five years old at the time and had been traveling hither and yon for many months. He missed his wife and children and was both physically and mentally tired. He hoped to meet some mature Christian with whom he could discuss some of the deeper things of the faith and his current spiritual state. There is no evidence from his journal that he found such a one. However, his search for where to settle was almost over.

LAND PROCURED IN THE CHEHALEM VALLEY

After several weeks in the Dayton area working on surrounding farms, Hobson decided to visit his cousin Esther Markham on the 13th of Eleventh Month 1875. The next day was First Day, but on the 15th he returned mainly because Esther was so sick she required nursing. Three neighbor girls came to help. The next day after staying over to help nurse Esther back to health, he took some time out to explore his surroundings. It was

> nearly clear till near day. Then clouded up and, snowed an inch or two During which time I went round and looked at the piece of land that cousin lives on. It is a good lot said to be 320 Acres. South quarter enclosed one hundred and 75 fruit Trees Old Orchard of Appletrees [sic] on the place a well and poor house with 3 little out buildings. And 3 lots fenced together at the house and one lot on the opposite side of a few acres rather meadow or Oats land The land belongs to a Blacksmith at Bridgport [sic] by the name of Wm. Greenwood The land is held at 6 ¼ dollars per acre. There is a little mountain creek of living water crosses the North-end. There are many acres on this place that is with but little Brush. A few good timber trees of large size both of Fir and also of Oak. Some small Ash Some little oak generally among

72. Hobson, "Diaries," reel 1 of 2, 10/25/1875.

the Fir and some small clumps of Oak Brush Some Clumps of Hazel Brush and several acres of good swale lands, and a few acres of Beaver Dam land. Esthers [sic] P.O. is Newberg.[73]

A few days later, Hobson looked over his cousin Esther's farm again on the morning of the 23rd of Eleventh Month 1875, and then went to see William Greenwood in the afternoon. Greenwood, who lived at Bridgeport (modern day Tualatin) about twelve miles northeast of Newberg, owned the land Esther was living on. Hobson must have made an agreement to purchase the property from Greenwood, though strangely he does not record it. He does mention visiting with a previous tenant of Greenwood's who had favorable things to say about the land, including an affirmation that he could successfully grow peaches there which must have made the deal with Greenwood that much sweeter.

Proof that he purchased the acreage comes the very next day, on the 24th, when Hobson records laconically "stepped off different parts of the place I have bought." With no fanfare he had finally made his choice deciding to settle in Newberg at the eastern end of the Chehalem Valley on the land his cousin Esther had been leasing. If his agreement with Greenwood was indeed $6.25 an acre, as he had written on the 16th, he committed to buy about 320 acres, or half a square mile, for around $2000. Later, on First Month 5, 1876, it becomes apparent that he initially put only twenty dollars down, 1 percent of the purchase price, to show that his intentions toward purchasing the land were serious. Seeing as how Hobson was a Quaker, one wonders if a handshake and a small sum were enough to seal the deal for both parties. Greenwood must have been willing to work with Hobson because he accepted several small payments into Fourth Month of 1877, totaling $512.[74] After this, Hobson doesn't mention further payments to Greenwood so it's unclear who held his mortgage. After transacting business with Greenwood on the 23rd, Hobson quickly went to the Fusons, gathered his things, and brought them to his new home. A few days later he walked over to Lafayette, the Yamhill County seat, and got information from the Yamhill County Clerk about procuring a title to his land.

It seems that his half-brother Nathan Hobson, who was visiting in the Dayton area at the time, was in some way involved with his decision to buy and possibly with the ability to put money down on the Greenwood land. Nathan helped Hobson look over acreage in the eastern Chehalem Valley towards the end of Eleventh Month including perhaps a portion of

73. Hobson, "Diaries, reel 1 of 2, 11/16/1875.

74. Hobson, "Diaries," reel 1 of 2, 8/30/1876, 2/25/1876, 1/8/1877, 1/18/1877, 4/10/1877.

the property Hobson bought soon after. Nathan may also have backed him financially for a second payment of twenty dollars to Greenwood that secured the deed and mortgage for a total outlay of forty dollars. On Twelfth Month 1, 1876, Hobson noted, "Talked with Brother Nathan about our land trade with Greenwood. Received of Nathan Hobson the sum of 130 dollars in Gold Coin." It's unclear as to whether Nathan loaned William the money towards the down payment on the Greenwood land or gave him the money in return for a small parcel of land of his own. It seems likely that it was a loan because, while Hobson did not note the day when Nathan Hobson returned to California, the next mention of his half-brother involved a postcard he sent to him the 13th of Fifth Month 1876. If Nathan was living nearby William would have just walked over. Apparently, Nathan Hobson returned to California sometime between First and Fifth Month 1876. Also, Hobson probably used the remainder of the $130 for living expenses, tools, seed, livestock, and other items necessary for setting up house that he would not have otherwise had money to buy.

On Twelfth Month 2, 1875, William sent a letter to Sarah, likely informing her that he had finally found the location for a Friends settlement in the Chehalem Valley and agreed to buy property there. Though there is no solid evidence in his diary it's possible he purchased this large acreage with the intention of selling off parcels to family and Friends who wanted to immigrate to the Chehalem Valley and become part of the community there. At the end of First Month 1876, he mentions sending a deed to his son Samuel Hobson and it seems he may have prepared a deed for his son Jesse on the 15th of Fourth Month 1876. Since both sons ended up living on farms near Hobson's it seems likely he sold them part of his property. On the other hand, his cousin Esther Markham seemed perfectly happy to leave behind the acreage Hobson had bought. He helped her move to Portland and by Second Month 1876, she was in the process of looking for a farm near Salem where she could set up house with her sons, presumably in order to be closer to her husband who was still serving time in the state penitentiary.

Hobson began to write letters, lots and lots of letters, to friends and family in Iowa. He sent maps of western Oregon to several people including his wife and his son–in–law Henry Austin, their daughter Mary's husband. He had found the perfect place for a Quaker settlement in Oregon, now he set out to encourage everybody to join him there. However, his excitement was a little dampened due to serious misgivings about Sarah's possible reaction to the news that he had bought property in the Chehalem Valley. The first hint of anxiety over Sarah's state of mind came on the 1st of Twelfth Month 1875, the same day he received the cash from Nathan Hobson, when he wrote "I want to get some advise [sic] from Justice or lawyers about the necessity of the wife signing a Mortgage." About a month later, on First Month 5, 1876, Hobson "Paid over 20 dollars to Wm Greenwood to wards the Walker Donation making with twenty paid on the 23 of 11 mo last 40 dollars. Now paid towards this ½ Section Township 3 S Range 2 West from Portland Oregon." The next day, on the 6th of First Month he lamented "Raining Yesterday as I rode along the road I thought much about my wife will she ever become a true helper in the Lord. Or will she refuse to sign a mortgage for a tract of Land in Oregon which I have purchased." He was not sure Sarah would agree to sign the mortgage, but he went ahead with the acquisition of the Greenwood land anyway. The next day, on the 7th of First Month he returned to the county clerk's office in Lafayette and paid a small fee for a copy of the deed and mortgage for his new land.

Hobson now owned the original Oliver J. Walker land donation claim. The Walker claim was located north of the Portland Road or what is currently East First Street, and east of North College Street in the northern part of current day Newberg. It's difficult to locate the exact boundaries of Hobson's property since maps showing the Walker claim are hard to translate to modern maps. However, it seems likely that his homestead was a little north and possibly east of where George Fox University stands now.[75] Jennie Miller in her compilation of Newberg history tells how two land donation claims, the Joseph Rogers claim south of the Portland Road and the Deskins claim north of Portland Road, later became the site of early Newberg.[76] Furthermore, according to information in *Old Yamhill* compiled by Ruth Stoller, "although Daniel Deskins had acquired 640 acres just north of [the] Rogers [claim] in January of 1848 his claim was not formally determined until August of 1851. Because he was not married soon enough, he was entitled to only 320 acres, so the northern half was sold to Oliver J. Walker who gave the date of settlement on his claim December 1851."[77] C. J. Edwards revealed a little more information about the location of the Deskins claim when he noted that "Mrs. Deskins' home on the north side was located near where Meridian street leaves First street to the north."[78] Placing the De-

75. "Digital General Land Office Maps," (Quadrant 1 index, 3s 2w); Fuller and Van Heukelem, *Images of America Newberg*, 12; United States Department of the Interior, "Newberg Quadrangle, 7.5 [map]," (7.5 minute series, 45122–C8–TF–024). I compared a land donation claim section map from the University of Oregon collection, a hand drawn section map in Fuller and Van Heukelem's book, and a modern map of Newberg in order to try to pinpoint the exact location of Hobson's property, but was successful in finding only the general area in which he lived.

76. Miller, "History of Newberg," 1.

77. Stoller, *Old Yamhill*, 61.

78. Edwards, "Newberg as it was Fifty Years Ago," *Newberg Graphic* (Newberg, OR) 50th Anniversary Progress Edition, April 1939.

skins claim helps us to see that the Walker claim did not reach down to the Portland Road. This is confirmed by local Yamhill County historian George P. Edmonston Jr., in his compilation of newspaper articles *Newberg: Stories from the Grubby End*, when he states that "the location today [of Hobson's land] would be three-fourths of a mile north of E. First Street."[79] Jesse Hobson, Hobson's youngest son, said in a speech which was later printed in the *Newberg Graphic* that his father's lands were "lying just north of the Deskin's [sic] lands and one-half mile north of First street [sic] in Newberg."[80]

A few more clues as to the location of his land came from Hobson himself, though they rather confuse the issue. When describing the proposed site for the first Monthly Meeting House, he wrote, on Tenth Month 14, 1877, "At the [close] of the meeting The Subject of A meeting house & place to have it was taken up The place preferred near my [west] gate." In his senior research paper "History of the Newberg Monthly Meeting, 1878-1893," Stephen Z. Perisho notes that "this means that his [Hobson's] west gate was probably close to the Portland Road since according to C. J. Edwards the meeting house was built on "a three-quarter acre site, on the south side of the Portland road [sic] just outside Newberg,"[81] near where Villa Road intersected with the Portland Road, a location close by the homes of "'Uncle' Wm. Hobson and two or three of his sons and daughters; David J. Wood, Dr. Elias Jessup and several [other Friends]."[82] This would seem to indicate that the southern border of Hobson's property was the Portland Road, even though that was impossible due to the location of the Deskins claim. Perisho wrote "west gate" but it's hard to decipher the faded and blurry word in Hobson's diary. It might not be "west" at all. Edmonston Jr., claims that the first Friends Church was "located on the same ground as occupied today by the Friends Cemetery on Everest Road,"[83] but does not share how he came to that conclusion. It makes sense that the church would be located close by the cemetery or vice versa, but it's hard to see how Hobson's land could have reached so far south as to be adjacent to the church land if it was located next to the cemetary. Perhaps after consideration the congregation decided not to build the church near Hobson's gate.

79. Edmonston Jr., *Newberg: Stories from the Grubby End*, 36-37.

80. Hobson, "Looking Backward: A Paper Read by Jesse Hobson at Last Sunday's Anniversary Meeting," *Newberg Graphic* (Newberg, OR) November 14, 1912, https://oregonnews.uoregon.edu/lccn/sn96088233/1912-11-14/ed-1/seq-1/.

81. Perisho, "History of the Newberg Monthly Meeting," 19.

82. Edwards, "Newberg as it was Fifty Years Ago," *Newberg Graphic* (Newberg, OR) 50th Anniversary Progress Edition, April 1939.

83. Edmonston Jr., *Newberg: Stories from the Grubby End*, 39.

Another clue to the location of Hobson's property appears in his diary on Sixth Month 27, 1876, when he noted that the eastern part of his property contained a creek that never failed. Based on the comparison of old land donation claim maps and modern maps of the Newberg area this was probably what we call Hess Creek today. Based on another old map of Yamhill County from 1879 it appears that if Hobson's parcel was north of the current site of George Fox University it may have included an eastern leg running along the edge of the Deskins claim, leading to the Portland Road. On the map a notation, "Friends CH," is scrawled to the south of the leg.[84] Could that mean Friends Church? As George Edmonston Jr. tells it in an article published in the *Newberg Graphic*,

> the location of the [Friends] church, long a discussion among local historians, Woodward [Ezra H. Woodward owner of the Newberg Graphic 889 to1921] remembered as on 'the outer edge of Newberg, on the south side of the road (Portland Road/ Highway 99W) opposite the Henry Ehret residence and in the rear of the McGary residence.' Where did the Ehrets and McGarys live? He doesn't say, although he shares the church was built where the old road 'angled to the northeast.' Today, this would be in the vicinity of Walgreens, where Villa Road intersects with Highway 99W. Church Street is near this location. Makes you wonder.[85]

Whatever the exact boundaries, it's apparent that Hobson's acreage was located north of the Deskins claim in the north section of present–day downtown Newberg.

After squaring away the paperwork for his parcel of land Hobson immediately sent a letter to Sarah with the mortgage enclosed. Then he had to wait for her reply. When he didn't hear from her in over a month, he began to get impatient, but on the 25th of Second Month 1876, he noted, "Received Some important News & the mortgage." Thankfully, Sarah had agreed to sign the papers. A couple days later Hobson filed the deed in the Yamhill County Clerk's office at Lafayette and everything was official.

Even before the formalities were completed and Sarah signed the necessary papers, Hobson began to improve his new acreage and home. The pace at which he worked indicates that he was over his previous weariness and, of course, the disappointment at not finding a location for settlement was resolved, since he had now found the place. He was also working hard

---

84. Lawrence et al., Map of Yamhill Co., Oregon, 1879, ¾ inch to 1 mile, 15338102.

85. Edmonston Jr., "Where there is a church, there is a town," *Newberg Graphic* (Newberg, OR) January 20, 2016.

to bring the homestead up to snuff for Sarah. While helping his cousin Esther move, he fit in some shopping and spent "20 dollars in Portland for Tools, Seeds, Nails, &c," on the 9th of Twelfth Month 1875. That same day in the afternoon he planted six hundred peach seeds, presumably placing them in a sheltered area where they could grow into saplings. Over the next several weeks he worked on fixing up the house inside and out with boards he cut himself from his own timber, building furniture including a bookcase and bedstead, harvesting and drying apples from the existing orchard, fixing up the chimney, and grubbing brush, along with daily chores like cooking, sweeping, and laundry. After the sale became official, Hobson planted more fruit trees of an unnamed variety in a nursery, trimmed and tended the apple orchard, fixed old and built new fencing, and looked over his land deciding where to plant various crops. Towards the middle of second month Hobson sowed some oats. It seems that despite his misgivings about Sarah's willingness to sign the mortgage he was pretty sure that things were going to be resolved favorably and they would soon be settled permanently in Oregon. After receiving the signed mortgage from Sarah, he bought a yoke of oxen. There was no turning back now.

At the end of Fifth Month, Hobson's daughter Mary and her husband arrived with their baby daughter and so did his son Jesse and family. They planned to settle in the Chehalem Valley, and they stayed with Hobson a while before settling on their own property. Eventually, four of the Hobson's six children settled near him in Oregon. Samuel and his wife Mary Ann (Hunicutt), Mary and her husband Henry Austin, and Jesse and his wife Mary Charlotte (Blair) all found property near Hobson. William and Sarah brought their teenage daughter Anna with them to Newberg in the fall of 1876. Anna met Alpheus T. Blair in Newberg and they were married in 1880.[86] According to Davis and Wiles, Rachel (Hobson) and her husband Elkanah Reece remained at Honey Creek and Stephen Hobson and his wife Clara (Owen) most likely did as well, though the records concerning him are incomplete.[87]

After the arrival of the Austins and the Jessie Hobsons, Hobson planted some more oats, wheat, and corn, and still more vegetables with the help of his son. He acquired a horse with which to plow the garden and cleared a path from a gate towards the Portland Road. He and Jesse did a fair amount of plowing at the end of Seventh Month and continued weeding the crops already planted. By the first of Eighth month Hobson was already harvesting oats and towards the end of the month he and Jesse shocked the late

---

86. Hobson, "Diaries," reel 1 of 2, 2/1/1877, 11/27/1890; Miller, "History of Newberg," 14.

87. Davis and Wiles, *Hobson*, 292–95.

wheat. After working hard to improve his house and land, he was now ready to leave it in the care of capable Jesse, return to Iowa, sell his place at Honey Creek, and bring Sarah and Anna back with him to their new home in the Chehalem Valley.

Before we return to Iowa with Hobson, let's take a deeper look at the first several months Hobson spent on his new property. Several aspects of this season in his life reveal valuable insight into his mental and spiritual state at the time. He was very busy repairing his house and working his land, but against the backdrop of strenuous physical labor important social, emotional, and Kingdom work was playing out. His new home near Newberg was not nearly as remote and lonely as the early days at Honey Creek had been, so he was already feeling a sense of community. He called on neighbors, neighbors called on him, and he enjoyed an almost constant stream of visitors from more distant regions. However, when Hobson did have time alone, he took the opportunity to reflect on the validity of God's calling on his life, to work out some of his feelings about Sarah's reluctance to join him in Newberg, and to communicate with distant friends and family by writing letters. Hobson also organized First Day meetings near Newberg shortly after settling there. He dived right into the spiritual work God had set before him. Hobson was an enthusiastic accomplished farmer *and* a deeply committed, conscientious Quaker minister on a mission.

The Oliver J. Walker claim was definitely rural and fairly undeveloped, but it was not completely isolated or unimproved. And it was considerably further along than their homestead at Honey Creek had been in 1853. A small house that needed some repair and a few ramshackle outbuildings came with the property and there was already an established apple orchard. However, it is true that God had directed him to a homestead in what was considered the backwoods section of the Chehalem Valley. According to an online article written by George Edmonston Jr. for the Newberg Downtown Coalition, "folks living in and around Newberg referred to this section [eastern Chehalem Valley] of Yamhill County as the 'Grubby End.' Simply put, the soil wasn't as good for farming as, say, over around Lafayette or McMinnville or across the Willamette River in French Prairie. At least that was the perception."[88] Edmonston Jr. adds in a different article written for the *Newberg Graphic*, "the land around Newberg (aka the 'Grubby End'): Shrubs and fir stumps choked the soil. Stumps proved formidable to remove. Farmers complained of the 'staying power' of the roots and held the roots responsible for 'delaying the progress of the region.'" Hobson did spend a significant amount of time grubbing out brush and stumps on his acreage. In fact, he

---

88. Edmonston Jr., "Yamhill County's Most Interesting City."

mentions grubbing as a regular chore right up to Fourth Month 1891, just about two months before his death.[89] Also, in the beginning the roads were poor, filled with tree stumps and potholes that easily became deep puddles. But there was a post office and a store not too far away, as well as a district school[90] and Portland was a short steamship ride up the Willamette.

As for a sense of community and belonging, we know that Hobson had neighbors only eight miles away at Dayton who were Friends, including the Whites, Fusons, and several other families. This must have boosted Hobson's morale significantly and, at first, he continued to attend meeting in Dayton. Some of his more prominent neighbors closer to home in the Grubby End were his old traveling companion David J. Wood, who eventually settled near Hobson's property, and William P. Ruddick, a Friend from the Midwest, who was mentioned briefly a few times by Hobson in his diary. Wood and Ruddick became famous for platting the eastern half of Newberg several years later.[91] Nearby neighbor William Clemmens[92] opened his home for First Day School and meeting multiple times and Hobson briefly mentions several other neighbors living on homesteads in the area during his early days in the eastern Chehalem Valley. These were mostly transplants, for as Edmonston Jr. put it, "the 'Grubby End' had already been settled before their [Friends] appearance, meaning the Quaker 'migration' to the area must be characterized as a 'displaced settlement,' that is, someone had to sell-out or move-out for the new arrivals to move in."[93] Some of the old-timers still living there included the Deskins, Everests, and Hageys, making the east end of the Chehalem Valley more populous and civilized when Hobson settled there in 1876 than Honey Creek had been upon arrival in 1853. But the area was not at all as crowded or developed as Honey Creek was in 1876. After all, in 1870 there were only 5,012 inhabitants living in all of Yamhill County.[94] But before long the area began to see significant growth. It seems that Perry C. Hadley and John S. Bond chose not to relocate to the Pacific Northwest, but soon significant numbers of Friends began to trickle in from Iowa and other midwestern states. This migration occurred largely in response to the many letters Hobson wrote inviting Friends to join him out west, some of which were published in the *Friends Review* and other Friends

89. Hobson, "Diaries," reel 1 of 2, 4/24/1891.
90. Hobson, "Diaries," reel 1 of 2, 4/3/1876.
91. Edmonston Jr., *Newberg: Stories from the Grubby End*, 40–41.
92. I have standardized the spelling to "Clemmens" since it varies in Hobson's diary.
93. Edmonston Jr., "Newberg at its beginnings," *Newberg Graphic* (Newberg, OR) November 18, 2015.
94. "Yamhill County, Oregon" (1870).

publications. The coming of Friends combined with the migration of other new settlers attracted to the area by cheap land and the temperate climate caused the population of the Grubby End to increase quickly.

Not only was the neighborhood fairly well populated, but Hobson also enjoyed a steady string of visitors at his house. Some were just passing through, but others were exploring the valley as a possible place to settle. Some of the most notable visitors included his half-brother Nathan Hobson from California, his old traveling companion Perry C. Hadley, Solomon Hockett from Bangor, Iowa, Joseph Almond from Washington Territory, and Nathan Talbert and family from parts unknown, who stayed with him for several months. Talbert helped Hobson considerably with work around his place before moving on to California.

Hobson was so used to having visitors that when left alone for a spell he became rather introspective:

> Nearly Clear At ½ past 6. a.m. just finished my mornings work, Which Takes me a good while now for I am alone; and have had the new experience yesterday and to day of doing all the out-door work and the in-door work necessary to a living for man. It takes me a long time. Yet I suppose I am over all this nearly by the time some careless sleepy folks are up and washed and ready for breakfast. I would not swap conditions with [them] in the day when we shall give an account of our stewardship. But I remember the Lord said. "It is not good that the man should be alone; I will make him a help meet for him." I am every day desiring the Lord may make of my wife a help suitable to my present need. Has not enough come to pass already to inable [sic] her to believe That I am in the work of the Lord in trying to make settlement here. And like Israel of old say "It is enough" This is no imaginary or crazy freak of the brain of Wm. Hobson. What the Lord lays has laid upon Wm. Hobson. The arduous work of selecting a suitable location and the commencing of a settlement of Friends in Oregon this part of the world. The Selection is made. A settlement has already begun to form David J Wood has purchased a home near Wm mine the selection is generally thought to be a very favorable one by those who have see[n] it. Some are on the way to this place and many others have their thoughts this way. I hope my wife will soon see it her duty to enter in as my helper in this thing because it is of the Lord; and he will surely prosper the work if his servants prove faithful under all trials.[95]

---

95. Hobson, "Diaries," reel 1 of 2, 5/24/1876.

In this diary passage we get a glimpse of Hobson's emotional and spiritual state. It's obvious that he missed Sarah and longed for her agreement with the calling he was certain he had received from God. This was not something he had just dreamed up, no "crazy freak of the brain." He hoped that the unity of their marriage would be restored so they could labor side by side in the work God was calling them to. He was sure now that he was meant to dwell in the Chehalem Valley and not return to Honey Creek to live. The next day on the 25th he wrote "I like Oregon and my place here rather better still I think if my wife were here she would like it too for it is seldom Cold or hot I conclude that before now S[amuel] Hobson is resolved to move any how to Oregon next fall."

On the 26th he wrote a rough draft of a letter in his diary that he planned to send to his brother Jesse. Hobson hoped Jesse would share the letter with other relatives at San Jose and then forward it on to a friend, Caleb Baldwin, at Honey Creek. In it he describes his vision for ministry in the Chehalem Valley. This is arguably the most famous passage from his diary in Northwest Friends circles since it contains the famous phrase "garden of the Lord," from which Ralph Beebe took the name for his well-known history of Northwest Yearly Meeting. Strangely enough Edward P. Thatcher, Quaker journalist and University of Oregon librarian, who microfilmed Hobson's diaries mistakenly omitted a section of this passage, but Goldsmith who also held the actual diaries in his hands transcribed the entire entry. Mercedes J. Paul's transcription from the early part of the twentieth century corroborates Goldsmith's as far as it goes, though she like Thatcher omits certain sections including the "garden of the Lord" passage, replacing them with ellipses. Here I have combined the incomplete microfilmed diary entry with Goldsmith's transcription for a complete rendition of the passage as follows:

> 6 a.m. mer[cury] at 57 just finished my mornings work lastly by sweeping my house and Kitchen. There is not much dirt to sweep up where there is but one to carry it in. Last night was the third night in the which I Have stayed here alone. I slept well and feel comfortable this morning And as I have been finishing up my indoor work for the morning I have afresh thought over how I have been pressed for more than six years that some settlements of Friends ought to formed in these parts for the good of the race of mankind. That It was laid on me to work for it as the Lord should direct and make way for I came once to this field of labor for a while & went home. But I found I could not rest in Iowa with the Load which continued to grow heavier upon me. But I must go again when I could. And not seeing how I could,

early as it ought to be with my own means at my command. I wrote to my brothers at Sanjose whose work is in the [Lord who thought it their duty to advance the means and thus without further delay way was made for me and for John S. Bond to visit Oregon religiously: But my mind was impressed from the very first that part of my duty was to Obtain a good knowledge of the countries [sic] hereaway So as to be able to give important information to others especially to the Friends whose duty it might be to settle here. And this last time I was the more forcibly impressed with this latter part of the work That I must find a Locality for a Friends settlement, and help some to get it started; even if for the main part my home remained in Iowa. My wife seeing or feeling little or nothing with me in this work has seemingly come nigh causing me to fail going on but I rejoice this morning that I have not suffered even this to hinder me from apprehended duty. This is party [sic] a work of Faith and for my help just now I call to mind Mary Pinkhams [sic] similar impressions relative to settlement of Friends here; and her earnest efforts under unfavorable circumstances at a great cost to do her part. I have performed some religious labor in many places on this Coast in which I had peace. I have Obtained much knowledge of the countries over this Coast There are many localities hereaway some in California, Many in Oregon and Wash. Ter. which which [sic] are favorable for making happy homes and for the rearing a light which will shine far into the world. With the knowledge which I have Obtained; and the favors still granted to me I feel thankful to all my brothers and friends who in the Providence of God had some little hand in this work which I feel to be a work of great importance. And is now well and firmly begun. I have Obtained a Title to 1/2 sec. and D.J. Wood to 3 forties in a central part of one of the best small Valleys in Oregon. Where to our surprise; land with considerable of improvements, Often including old Orchards is only rating around us at about ten dollars per acre. I can now speak of Oregon and this Valley by certain knowledge. Last was the pleasantest summer I ever passed through. Last the wettest winter that I ever saw. But no cutting sea or Bay breeze here. For it is Broken off twice by the mountains and large hills; and thirdly by the scattering old Fir trees, many of which have reared their heads above one hundred and fifty feet above [sic] my land at H.C. Iowa. There are a few Old white Oak trees too. good for timber or for fire. The more I am able to see this place and to know it the better I like it. I did not see it all which I took hold here. Therefore It was not all of me; But in the Providences of God] Rather that this selection is made. For which I thank the Lord and give him the praise in this too. The climate seems favorable to my health here. Probably Therefore I might be able to live a few years longer to do good among men here than in Iowa. I think including upon the whole of winter and Summer I like the climate of this Locality best of any that I have tried. It is seldom cold or hot. I think if my wife were here she would like it too. And I think it would especially suit our Son Samuel who has once been so near sun struck in Iowa, and who frequenly [sic] has such hard attacks of headache Probably this climate might prove a great Benefit to him. Hope now Our dear friends at Honey or Elsewhere will not try to hold us all to any one place. But will rather possess missionary Spirit enough to gladly let some suitable members go to form a settlement there and make it a garden of the Lord. I think I have not time to write more to send out by next mail Therefore. I send this to Brother Jesse that my Relatives there may hear it with the Request that it be forwarded next to Caleb Balwin at Honey Creek New Providence Hardin Co. Iowa who will take an interest in letting my friends and family there have the reading of it. It seems to be such a good time to work this morning that I would take time to write this letter But with the hope I will do good faster with the pen thus this forenoon than with my plow or other tools here alone.[96]

Much has been made of Hobson's gem-like phrase, "garden of the Lord." In fact, there is a famous and beloved anecdote often duplicated in local histories and repeated at public events describing how Hobson wrote about the Chehalem Valley as a "garden of the Lord" directly after taking in the glorious view from the top of Chehelam Mountain or Bald Peak, depending on who's telling the story. Unfortunately, this romantic narrative, usually told to celebrate a supposed prophetic vision Hobson received concerning God's future Eden-like spiritual blessing on the valley, is inaccurate according to his diary. He very well may have received a prophetic word from God, but probably not on Chehelam Mountain. The mountaintop vision narrative seems to have originated with a paper housed in the George Fox University Library Archives written by John H. Rees simply called "History of Friends Church, June 6, 1906." In this paper Rees gives a brief history of William Hobson and in the process relates the following with no citations: "Looking from Chehalem's summit he [Hobson] saw, not the unbroken forest of that day, but a beautiful valley of happy homes

---

96. Goldsmith, "William Hobson and the Founding of Quakerism in the Pacific Northwest," 266–68; Paul, Extracts," 14–15. Goldsmith's transcription is contained within brackets.

connected with the outside world by railroad and telegraph, quarterly and yearly meetings established, a flourishing town with a Friend's College, and a strong Christian community."[97] Perhaps Rees was writing down oral history, but was he accurately reporting what Hobson truly did or thought? Rees wrote about Hobson's "vision" after quoting the diary passage in which Hobson notes that planting a Friends settlement was "no imaginary freak of the brain," not in connection with the "garden of the Lord" diary entry at all. Apparently, over the years the repetition of Rees's questionable account of Hobson's "vision" on Chehalem Mountain became paired with the phrase "garden of the Lord" which resulted in misinformation becoming accepted as a true story.

It's clear that Hobson wrote the above diary entry early in the morning just after finishing his housework. He mentioned at the end of the passage that it was a good morning to labor outside, but he chose to put pen to paper instead, indicating that he took precious time out from working his land to sit indoors and write. He didn't have plans to climb a mountain that day and there is every indication that after taking the morning off to write he worked around his place in the afternoon. Further evidence that he didn't climb the mountain on the 26th comes the next day on the 27th when he remarked, "A fine day Yesterday for work But I spent it mostly in fixing out a letter to my folks." Hobson certainly had faith that God would bring great spiritual blessing to the Grubby End. But most likely this vision did not come to him as he stood looking out on the valley from a perch in the mountains. Hobson's vision for ministry was a much more pragmatic undertaking developed in the valley. He was busy enjoying his neighbors and visitors, working hard at improving his land and house, leaning into his calling, inviting others to join him in ministry, and trusting God to provide what was needed to keep him on the mission field in the Grubby End.

FRIENDS MEETING STARTED AT NEWBERG AND A BRIEF RETURN TO HONEY CREEK

The last aspect of Hobson's life that bears looking into during this busy time before his return to Iowa, involves the organization of a Friends meeting in the Grubby End. He enjoyed the meeting at Dayton, but the distance was beginning to take a toll. Attending meeting in Dayton involved a round trip of sixteen miles and it was not an easy hike, especially in the dead of winter. On Twelfth Month 19, 1875, he wrote, "Walked up to Dayton to Meeting and Back late in the evening coming 5 miles after night. It had rained all day

97. Rees, "History of Friends Church," 2.

and heavily throught [sic] the night so it was pretty hard on me and on my boots to trudge 16 miles through the mud and and [sic] numerous branches of water and in addition 5 miles of it through the darkness." It was forty-seven degrees Fahrenheit that evening, quite damp and chilly and the next day he was forced to clean, stretch, and re-grease his boots. He continued to attend meeting at Dayton sporadically, which was not like him. His pattern at Honey Creek was to go to meeting every First and Fifth Day without exception unless he was too sick or was traveling in the ministry. Sixteen miles in the rain and mud was a difficult obstacle to overcome, even for William Hobson. However, when he did attend, the meetings at Dayton were favored. On Second Month 27, 1876, he wrote, "We had a blessed meeting to day. Several strangers were present. I was largely drawn out in gospel love to the people in a comforting lively testimony." Nonetheless, he was ready to begin holding meeting closer to home.

The first recorded Friends meeting in the Chehalem Valley was held at William Clemmens's house on the 19th of Third Month 1876. After this Hobson alternated between holding meeting in Dayton, at the Clemmens's home, and in his own home. Occasionally, meeting was also held at "David Everets." This was probably a misspelling of Everest, the surname of one of the first families to settle in the Chehalem Valley. The Everests owned a land donation claim to the southeast of Hobson's property. Surprisingly, according to a section in *Old Yamhill*, the "Richard Everests, who lived next to the Rogers, were from England and also belonged to the Episcopal Church." Episcopal services had even been held previously for a short time at Roger's Landing near the Willamette several years before Hobson arrived in the area.[98] Amanda Woodward told how William Clemmens lived on "part of the old donation land claim of the Hess family, situated about one-half mile northwest of Newberg."[99] Also, based on a short entry in Hobson's diary on the 4th of Eighth Month 1876, in which he noted, "Cleaned off a place in the Firgrove [sic] for Meeting place," it seems that meeting was sometimes held outside in nice weather. Meetings continued to be held sporadically in the neighborhood, until a more regular pattern was established after Hobson returned from Iowa.

At the end of Eighth Month 1876, Hobson and his son Jesse each got a smallpox vaccination, perhaps along with other family members. Unfortunately, Jesse and his dad reacted strongly to the inoculation. Hobson noted on the 21st of Eighth Month that they were "having a serious time with

---

98. Stoller, *Old Yamhill*, 59.

99. Woodward, "Reminiscences of an Editor's Wife," *Newberg Graphic* (Newberg, OR) 50th Anniversary Progress Edition, April 1939.

[their] vaccination," but by the 29th they had recovered enough to harvest the late wheat, after which Hobson got ready to return to Iowa.[100] Jesse dropped him off in Portland where he caught a steamer for San Francisco on Ninth Month 1, 1876. He arrived at San Jose on the 5th of Ninth Month and stayed just under a week. On the 7th he noted, "pleasant visits with my relatives and friends here," but he was eager to be on his way. He boarded the cars at San Jose on the 11th, chugged swiftly over the mountains, desert, and prairie and arrived at Union Station, Iowa on the 20th. He had been gone a little over sixteen months. Perry C. Hadley took him home and then several silent weeks passed with no diary entries during which Sarah must have become fully convinced it was time to move to Oregon. Perhaps the fact that two of their children were already settled there and their son Samuel intended to settle there, helped her to make a decision. Hobson's entry on Tenth Month 10, 1876, reads: "To day I had a Sale ["Sale" written in large, dark letters] and sold my loose property amounting with Some sold before and after the day of sale to $1500.00." By the end of the month William, Sarah, and Anna were packed up and ready to leave. Loose ends would be tied up after they left by their son–in–law Elkanah Reece. The Hobsons attended meeting at Honey Creek one last time and then boarded the train the very next day on Tenth Month 30, 1876, bound for Oregon "with 3 boxes checked to Sanjose Cali. Placed ony [one] extra Baggage Box of 175 lbs under way to Portland and paid on it to Sanfrancisco. Also on 6 boxes which are behind called 700 lbs."

Four unnamed families went with them, also heading for Oregon. Hobson described the trip very briefly in general terms and before long was recording their arrival at Sanjose on Eleventh Month 9, 1876, a journey of ten days. They visited with friends and family there for about a week. Hobson recorded the highlight of the trip on the 15th of Eleventh month when he wrote, "Yesterday [we] were present at Fath[er's] All his living children were present 11 sons & one daughter." On the 18th the travelers visited the San Francisco Mint and on the 22nd they boarded the steamer *G.W. Elder*. Hobson reported another bout of seasickness on the journey up the coast but, was feeling better by the time they reached Portland on the 26th. At this point in the journey it becomes apparent that his son Samuel, Samuel's wife Mary Ann, and their sons were with them, since Hobson noted how much tickets cost for the steamship *Occident* to take them all down the Willamette. He still did not name the other families traveling with them. On Eleventh Month 27, 1876, the Hobsons reached their new home in the Grubby End

100. I have summarized Hobson's second return journey to Iowa from his diary (9/1/1876–11/27/1876: "Diaries," reel 1 of 2), giving specific dates for quoted entries within the body of the work.

of the Chehalem Valley. After almost six and a half years since Honey Creek had released him the first time for religious service in the Far West, the Hobsons were finally settled in the place God selected for a Friends mission: Newberg, Oregon.

5

Planted in a Garden of the Lord

Blessed is the man that walketh not in the counsel of the ungodly, nor standeth in the way of sinners, nor sitteth in the seat of the scornful. But his delight is in the law of the Lord; and in his law doth he meditate day and night. And he shall be like a tree planted by the rivers of water, that bringeth forth his fruit in his season; his leaf also shall not wither; and whatsoever he doeth shall prosper.

Ps 1:1–3

The Hobsons were now planted in a garden of the Lord near Newberg, Oregon, in the Chehalem Valley. The life experience they had gathered during their time at Honey Creek, Iowa, both in the building and sustaining of a productive homestead and in the building and sustaining of a spiritually sound, growing monthly meeting, helped them immensely as they embarked upon their new life as missionaries in Oregon. With a few modifications to cultivation techniques and some changes in crop selection they were able to carry on agricultural and horticultural pursuits in the Chehalem Valley quite successfully. Farming remained Hobson's profession and the produce of the land was still their only means of financial support. The setting and people were different in Oregon, but Hobson's spiritual beliefs and practices remained largely the same. He took his calling to the Chehalem Valley seriously. The spiritual health of the growing Quaker community at Newberg and throughout the region, as well as outreach to their non-Quaker neighbors remained the center of Hobson's ministry focus for the rest of his life.

The Hobsons were not required to change their way of life significantly once settled in Oregon, but it was necessary to make some adaptations to their new environment. For example, Hobson grew fewer grain crops in Oregon and concentrated more on fruit cultivation, since orchards could return a better profit on less acreage than grain and corn. This was important because clearing land in the Grubby End was a real chore. Also, Hobson could now grow larger, more diverse orchards with less effort and better results than in Iowa due to the temperate climate. Since he loved growing fruit this was not a disappointment but a pleasant change.

Another difference the Hobsons encountered in their new home had to do with the fact that they were now inhabitants of a region with a generally wilder and more uninhibited ethos than that of the Midwest. Not so long ago, Oregon had been the home of the enigmatic Native Tribes, the solitary mountain man, and the rugged fur trapper. Many early inhabitants of Newberg and the surrounding area were rough-and-ready unrefined frontier folk who liked to drink, dance, and organize horse races, pastimes which were not exactly compatible with the Quaker way of living. It's interesting that it took approximately forty years for any kind of organized religion, which just happened to be established by Hobson, to take hold in the Chehalem Valley since the first settlers arrived there, and not all the inhabitants of the Grubby End were pleased with the strong Friends influence over the neighborhood as the Quaker community grew. John H. Rees, writing in 1906, remembered what the district was like when Friends first came to Newberg:

> The moral conditions of the country were not of the best, drinking, horse-racing, and dancing were common amusements. The nearest church was at Dayton, eight miles distant . . . Some of the old settlers so disliked the new-comers, they sold out and moved away. Others received them kindly, and the scattering [sic] few earnest Christians welcomed the Friends as co-laborers in the Lord's work.[1]

Amanda Woodward, wife of Ezra Woodward, long-time owner and editor of the *Newberg Graphic* and a notable Newberg Friend, reminisced in the 50th Anniversary edition of the *Graphic* published in 1939 in much the same way writing that

---

1. Rees, "History of Friends Church," 3–4.

the old settlers were very kind and neighborly to the Quakers, notwithstanding the fact that we spoiled some of their good times. A neighbor came to our home one Sunday morning to borrow a gun to go hunting. He said, "It used to be here, that we would all pile into a big wagon on Sunday morning and go visiting, and have a big dinner and a horse race, and a dance, and if there happened to be a preacher around we'd have a sermon. Now if we go anywhere we don't find anybody at home. They all go to church since Quakers come."[2]

Yamhill County historian and librarian Jennie D. Miller, also writing in the 1930s, pointed out that in the mid–1860s "some wet goods [liquor] were also dispensed at [Rogers Landing], but later a more profitable location for this was found in connection with the mile race track south of the present Oaks Barbecue, east of Newberg, which was a regular Sunday rendezvous for many near and far."[3] It seems that William Everest, Hobson's not too distant neighbor, was partly responsible for some of these distractions. According to Doris Jones Huffman writing in the centennial publication of the *Newberg Graphic*, "by 1872 he [Everest] was operating a saloon on the old Dayton–Portland Road." Everest made his own home brew from hops imported from his native England. Apparently, Everest's saloon was right across the street from the racetrack which was located at the present site of the 99W Drive–In Theater and which he also owned. Huffman notes that the "track attracted the best jockies [sic], racers and trotters in the Willamette Valley."[4] It must have been quite a busy place and even on the Sabbath no less. It's easy to see why Friends cramped the style of the original inhabitants of the Grubby End.

Things were also a little different in Oregon for the Hobsons simply because of William and Sarah's stage in life. They were no longer a young couple with small children just starting life together as they had been when they left North Carolina for Iowa so many years ago in 1847. When the Hobsons left Iowa for Oregon their children were mostly grown and married. Only Anna, their youngest, was still living at home but she married soon after arriving in Oregon and set up her own household near Newberg. William and Sarah were still strong and fit, but they were pushing sixty years old when they first arrived in the Chehalem Valley.

2. Woodward, "Early Days of the Quakers in Newberg," *Newberg Graphic* (Newberg, OR) 50th Anniversary Progress Edition, April 1939.

3. Miller, "History of Newberg," 2.

4. Huffman, "A Tale of Gold, Saloons and Race Horses," *Newberg Graphic: A Century to Remember, Newberg, 1889–1989* (Newberg, OR) 1989 special edition, 24.

They were also transplanted into a community that was about a decade behind Honey Creek in development. There were some local businesses, mills, and a post office in those early days, but no established religious institutions in the immediate area and the educational offerings consisted of sporadic schools formed without a dependable overarching organization. During the little over a decade that William and Sarah lived near Newberg they organized and helped to grow a thriving Friends Church, they experienced a rapid increase in population (not only Friends transplants), and the infrastructure of the town grew by leaps and bounds. The times they were a-changing.

However, Hobson's vocation did not change at all. His service as a Friends minister, his strong commitment to spreading the gospel, his support of First Day schools, and his enthusiasm for the Gurneyite Friends expression of what it meant to be a believer in Jesus Christ, remained steady as he leaned into his calling to establish a Friends meeting and presence in Newberg. He was also fully invested in the Friends missionary spirit. As Ione Harkness points out in her Master of Arts thesis "Certain Community Settlements of Oregon," "in the early days, the Friends conception of missionary work was not so much the sending of teachers to the foreign fields, as that a few strong characters should go into a new and thinly settled region to start a nucleus which would tend to build up that neighborhood by attracting other Friends from adjacent settlements."[5] This was exactly what Hobson accomplished.

The ministry experience Hobson developed at Honey Creek helped him to organize and lead Chehalem Monthly Meeting[6] and he continued

---

5. Harkness, "Certain Community Settlements of Oregon," 26.

6. Chehalem Monthly Meeting approved a name change to Newberg Monthly Meeting of Friends Church on Seventh Month 9, 1889, according to the Chehalem Monthly Meeting Minutes (see Book 2, June 4, 1889–April 5, 1898, 13). Newberg Friends Church came into general use several decades later in the 1930s according to church bulletins, though the official name for the congregation remains Newberg Friends Monthly Meeting of Friends Church to this day. The name was originally changed from "Chehalem" to "Newberg" in order to avoid confusion about location. Later "monthly meeting of" was dropped from daily use because those without Quaker connections were confused by the term "meeting." The use of Newberg Friends Church was likely intended to help with outreach and evangelism by identifying the congregation more closely with mainstream evangelical Christianity. The change from "meeting" to "church" was widespread throughout Oregon Yearly Meeting in the early part of the twentieth century. In the interest of clarity, I use Chehalem Monthly Meeting to refer to the Friends congregation at Newberg up until 1889, and Newberg Monthly meeting after that. When I write about the congregation's more recent years, I will refer to it as Newberg Friends Church. Many thanks to Rachel Thomas, University Archivist at George Fox University, for her help figuring out these details from historical records.

to serve faithfully as a beloved and respected minister in that congregation until his death. Hobson also traveled in the ministry a few times and continued to serve as a trusted agent of Iowa Yearly Meeting under whose authority Chehalem Monthly Meeting remained during his lifetime. He preached often during meeting and was deeply involved in the day to day activities of the Friends community not only in Newberg, but also elsewhere in the region. Pastoral care and the support of educational endeavors were two special interests Hobson continued to pursue in Oregon as part of his vocation. And though he did not explicitly state it in his diary, he must have prayed and worked towards revival in their new neighborhood, for revival did come to Chehalem Monthly Meeting more than once. Hobson's capability as a strong spiritual leader, refined after many years of dedicated service in Iowa, carried over beautifully to Newberg. But before we go on to explore in more detail the Hobsons' new life near Newberg, let's take a quick look at the bigger picture and delve into the geography and climate of the region in which they settled.

WILLAMETTE VALLEY

The fertile Willamette Valley is nestled between the Coast Range and the Cascade Mountains in western Oregon. This was the "promised land" destination for thousands of intrepid pioneers who braved the many hardships and dangers of the Oregon Trail in search of a better life. By the time the Hobsons arrived the Willamette Valley had been occupied for roughly thirty years by settlers who had come in migratory waves since the mid–1840s. The journey west was considerably easier by the mid–1870s. Supplies, livestock, and household goods were readily available, and roads were much better. Trains and steamships also helped to make travel faster and more convenient.

The Willamette Valley runs almost the full length of the State of Oregon. William Robbins writing for the online Oregon Encyclopedia tells how the Willamette Valley is "part of the Cascades geological province that extends from British Columbia to northern California, the valley is an elongated, relatively flat body of land extending approximately 150 miles from the Columbia River south to the Calapooya Divide."[7] According to Warren Dupre Smith in his article "Physical and Economic Geography of Oregon," the Calapooya Divide in southwestern Oregon marks the division between the Willamette River watershed to the north and the Umpqua River watershed to the south. The state capitol, Salem, located near the center of the

---

7. Robbins, "Willamette Valley."

valley on the Willamette River is almost exactly halfway between the equator and the north pole. The valley is named for the Willamette River which has carved it out flowing, notably, from south to north.

Smith goes on to say that during the early days of Willamette Valley settlement, before the railroad was established, the river was used extensively as a means of transportation with steamboats traveling between Eugene and Portland regularly.[8] Boats passed the Willamette Falls through the use of a canal and a series of locks now closed. The Willamette twists and turns as it makes its way north and most of the major cities in the western part of the state are located on a stretch of the Willamette from Eugene to Corvallis and from Salem to Portland, with many smaller towns strung out along the river in between the larger cities. As it happens, Newberg is located just north of a stretch of the Willamette River in the Chehalem Valley. In fact, Rogers Landing just south of Newberg, served as a steamboat stop for the Newberg area and Hobson mentioned river travel on both the Willamette and the Columbia in his diary.

CHEHALEM VALLEY

The Chehalem Valley runs east to west in the northern part of the Willamette Valley in a four-mile-wide by ten-mile-long stretch. This small valley within a larger valley is "closed in at the north end and east by the Chehalem Mountains, at the south by a northward bend in the Willamette River, and west by the Red Hills of Dundee."[9] John R. McBride, an early pioneer, described the view from the Chehalem Mountains at the end of summer in the mid-1840s:

> We could see the valley stretching to the south, prairie and timber, sunshine and shadow, hills and streams, while the coast Range on the west and the lofty Cascades with their glittering snow peaks on the east bounded all. The French prairie just at our feet on the left, with fields of stubble, houses, fences, and barns, allowed us that we had arrived in the land of homes as well as of beauty. We halted, took a short noon meal, and my heartache was cured. I had seen the "promised land," and felt henceforth it was home.[10]

---

8. Smith, "Physical and Economic Geography of Oregon," 41, 138.
9. Perisho, "History of the Newberg Monthly Meeting," 7.
10. McBride, *Overland to Oregon*, 45.

The town of present-day Newberg, which occupies land McBride spied from the top of the Chehalem Mountains, is located in the east end of the Chehalem Valley and lies about twenty-five miles west of Portland. Newberg was incorporated in 1889. Bald Peak to the north of Newberg is the tallest spur in the Chehalem Mountains range at 1,629 feet.[11] Parrott Mountain, also a significant spur, rises east of Newberg reaching 1,247 feet.[12] The Chehalem Valley is well watered with springs and creeks, though not particularly prone to flooding, and the soil is especially well suited for growing tree fruit, nuts, grapes, nursery stock, and other specialty produce.

About thirty years before the Hobsons first set foot in the Grubby End, three Quaker families settled in this eastern end of the Chehalem Valley that would later see a much larger influx of Friends. George P. Edmonston Jr. mentions that "Jacob Shuck and his family, his son-in-law David Ramsey and Levi Hagey, all of whom were here by the late 1840s and who established Provisional Land Claims just east of Dundee were Quakers," based on a study of Yamhill County inhabitants in the 1850 census. These families settled "along both sides of Dayton Avenue in southwest Newberg clear to the Dundee city limits. In both places, Shuck, Ramsey, Hagey and others helped established [sic] what became known as the 'Quaker Community,' a location responsible for all subsequent development of the Quaker influence in the 'Grubby End.'"[13] No record of these families worshipping together has been found, so they may not have been dedicated Quakers. It wasn't until the 1870s that regular Quaker worship was instituted in the area by William Hobson. And it wasn't until significant numbers of Friends moved to the Chehalem Valley from the Midwest that the Quaker community exerted much influence in and around Newberg.

By the time the Hobsons arrived in the Grubby End most land claims had changed hands many times, and others had been broken up into smaller parcels, with only a few of the early settlers' families still remaining in the area. Families such as the Hageys, and a few other original families like the Daniel Deskins family, Richard Everest family, and Sebastian Bruschter family continued to live near Newberg. In the 1870s and 1880s incoming Friends did not buy virgin land, but rather bought land sometimes from original settlers or more likely from families that were one, two, or even more times removed from the original claim holders.

---

11. "Bald Peak State Scenic Viewpoint."
12. "Parrott Mountain."
13. Edmonston Jr., *Newberg: Stories from the Grubby End*, 37.

AGRICULTURE AND HORTICULTURE IN THE CHEHALEM VALLEY

Hobson did not record temperatures consistently in his diary during his years in the Chehalem Valley, but he did make enough notations for us to get a general idea of weather patterns.[14] Weather in the Chehalem Valley was quite different from weather at Honey Creek. From about Tenth Month to Sixth month the weather was very wet, with lots of rain and rare snow falls. Temperatures almost never dipped below zero. The gloomy overcast skies and heavy rains typical of a Webfoot winter, which often extended far into spring, likely took some getting used to for Hobson accustomed as he was to Midwest weather patterns, as did the fluctuation year by year between severe and mild winters, a pattern noted by Samuel and Emily Dicken in *Making of Oregon*.[15] Summers were hot and dry, with temperatures rarely reaching over ninety-five degrees. According to Smith this was challenging to farmers, requiring them to provide both drainage and irrigation systems for good crop production.[16] The soil in the Grubby End, mostly rich clay loam was quite fertile. Once cleared of scrubby trees and brush, the ground was good both for agricultural and horticultural pursuits, though it did tend to hold water. Obviously, due to the difference in climate, flora, and soil composition farming was quite different in the Willamette Valley as compared to farming in the Midwest.[17]

One of the major differences about farming in the Chehalem Valley had to do with methods for getting the land ready for cultivation. It was certainly harder to prepare the soil for planting in the Grubby End than at Honey Creek. Before the plow could be employed several steps were required to clear the land: slashing, burning, and grubbing. Slashing and burning was taken up again by farmers during Hobson's time after the original settlers, who learned how to clear the land from the Kalapuya, let the ancient tribal practice lapse for several decades. This was a practical if strenuous way to clear and fertilize land that had reverted to brush and small trees. As John H. Rees described it,

> in East Chehalem, where the principal colony of Friends was located, the land, excepting a few small fields had become

---

14. In this chapter specific dates for quoted entries from Hobson's diaries will be given in the body of the work and can be found on microfilm reel 1 of 2, unless otherwise noted. Summarized sections in this chapter are footnoted.
15. Dicken and Dicken, *Making of Oregon*, 83.
16. Smith, "Physical and Economic Geography of Oregon," 161.
17. Dicken and Dicken, *Making of Oregon*, 92–93.

covered with a very dense growth of fir trees from three to six inches in diameter and forty to seventy-five feet high, fir brush as it was usually called, with occasionally an old fir tree three to seven feet in diameter and 125 to 200 foot high. The growth was so dense that no other vegetation except hazel, willow and grub oak was seen and even these in places all gave way to the rapidly growing fir timber. This had grown up since the original settlers who came between 1842 and 1854 kept down the fires which the Indians had formerly allowed to keep the land clear of timber. Through these young forests were numerous small streams or creeks, usually in rather deep canyons fed from fine never-failing springs on the hillsides. There were also narrow stretches of wet or swale and, usually carrying a dense growth of grass, wild rose and other shrubs, generally styled buckbrush . . . Five, ten or twenty acres were slashed during the Winter and Spring, then in August or early September this slashing was burned, making a terrific fire which left only the charred straight poles. These were then piled and burned and grain was sown on the mellow ashy surface and covered either by brushing in or with a shovel plow and jumping cutter, or the land was sown to timothy or other grass. An abundant crop of the highest quality was a sure reward.[18]

Harkness also described the slash and burn process:

The progressive Quakers, during the winter and spring would "slash" down twenty or thirty acres of this "second growth" fir, letting it dry out during the summer. The task of the settler in the fall after the first rains was the burning of these "slashings." The method of disposing of the huge old firs was to bore a hole into the center from two different angles, using a large inch and a half auger. A live coal was then pushed into the intersection of the angles and encouraged to blaze by a hand bellows. Thus the monarch of the forest was soon laid low. The tree trunk was then divided into short lengths by a similar process, piled and burned.[19]

Hobson certainly participated in his share of slashing and burning. In his diary Hobson mentions several instances of cutting brush for neighbors, especially before he bought his property. He also notes slashing for himself on his own land, and hiring others, including his son Jesse and grandson Franklin, to help him clear acreage. He made at least one brush fence, but he

18. Rees, "History of Friends Church," 3.
19. Harkness, "Certain Community Settlements of Oregon," 38.

also mentions burning piles of brush, briars, and piled up poles otherwise known as tree trunks. In general, his notations concerning slashing and burning were not specific, so it's difficult to determine how extensively he slashed and burned on his homestead. He also burned trimmings from his orchard. He rarely mentioned amounts of acreage cleared and exact locations are impossible to figure out. Hobson most often wrote something like "Slashed around the little Spot of B[eaver] dam land" or "mowed some briars slashed some." Other times he merely reported "Slashed," or "In afternoon I piled & burned (Stumps Grubs)."[20] These references are not especially frequent, so it seems that he cleared just enough to grow his large orchards plus some grain crops and Timothy. Though he did not strictly follow a schedule of slashing in the winter and spring and burning in the fall, he mostly kept to that pattern. It was an ongoing process, for there was always new land to clear and he mentioned slashing and burning right up to the time of his death, along with grubbing out roots and stumps which was also an endless chore. Slashing, burning and grubbing, was a considerably longer and more strenuous soil preparation process than that of plowing smooth, rich furrows in the treeless prairie sod of Hardin County, Iowa.

However, Ezra Woodward notes in a letter to the editor printed in the *Newberg Graphic* in the fall of 1922 that Hobson had an unusually positive attitude about grubbing. One time

> an Iowa man who had been brought up on prairie land complained to Uncle William Hobson, who, always an optimist, answered by saying, "Well, it is a great blessing to always have something to do." Uncle Ben Heater was said to have remarked that while "never" was a long time, the roots of an old fir stump would never rot, and he had been here a long time. The staying qualities of these stumps has had much to do in delaying progress in this section, but a lot of daylight has been let in during these years.[21]

The difficulties of clearing land in the Grubby End likely contributed to a regional focus on growing fruit and other specialty crops that took less acreage than grain or corn.

According to Perry D. Macy, a local historian and Pacific College professor speaking to the Newberg Chamber of Commerce in 1929, as the

20. Hobson, "Diaries," reel 1 of 2, 3/12/1877, 6/13/1887, 5/4/1886.
21. Woodward, "Newberg Citizen in Reminiscent Mood Tells of Atending [sic] First Church Service in Newberg Forty-Two Years Ago," *Newberg Graphic*, (Newberg, OR) September 14, 1922, letter to the editor, https://oregonnews.uoregon.edu/lccn/sn96088233/1922-09-14/ed-1/seq-9/.

switch from beef, wheat, and potato production was made in the Grubby End to specialty agricultural and horticultural crops during the California Goldrush in the mid-1840s, the Chehalem Valley became increasingly known for quality fruit production, much of which was exported to California where miners paid top dollar for fresh produce.[22] This included both orchard crops and berries, but Hobson focused mostly on growing tree fruits after his arrival in Oregon.

In an article published in the 50th Anniversary Edition of the *Newberg Graphic*, C. J. Edwards credits Hobson and the two Hoskins brothers with introducing new varieties of fruit to the Chehalem valley. He remembers how

> when we came [the Edwards family in 1880] to the Chehalem Valley, apples and pears were about the only fruits being raised, there also being wild blackberries, raspberries and strawberries in abundance. Uncle William Hobson was introducing peach, apricot, plum and prune trees which he felt would be adapted to this climate. A little later Cyrus and Louis Hoskins were very active in the production of the prune and plum trees of various kinds. Cyrus especially was interested in many varieties of the prune. From their effort it was but a few years until many acres of prunes were planted along the side of Chehalem mountain and from the development of the prune industry the question of marketing fruit arose. The first effort to operate a cannery (unsuccessful) was during the fall of 1886.[23]

William Hobson and the Hoskins are again credited with introducing "much fruit" to the Grubby End in a second article in the 50th Anniversary Edition of the *Newberg Graphic*.[24] It seemed to be generally accepted that Hobson was one of the first to expand the varieties of fruit grown in the valley and that he promoted the cultivation of fruit as a favorable crop. In yet another article the Chehalem Valley was praised as a location especially well suited to the growing of fruit. The writer thought it would probably develop into a fruit growing center like San Jose. The article stated further that "already the numerous small farms set to fruit, especially prunes, pears, plums, peaches and apple, attest the faith of the people in the fruit business. Some of these farms have already realized handsome profits to their owners." The article went on to say that raising fruit in the Chehalem Valley was

---

22. Edmonston Jr., *Newberg: Stories from the Grubby End*, 30–31.

23. Edwards, "Newberg as it was Fifty Years Ago," *Newberg Graphic* (Newberg, OR) 50th Anniversary Progress Edition, April 1939.

24. "Springbrook Cooperative Minded Community," *Newberg Graphic* (Newberg, OR) 50th Anniversary Progress Edition, April 1939.

"an investment that is paying annual dividends sufficient to satisfy any one, and from comparatively nothing at the start can show acres of apples, pears, plums, prunes, peaches, cherries, grapes, and berries of all kinds, that find ready sale at high prices."[25]

It's fitting to place peaches at the top of the list of fruits grown by Hobson in the Chehalem Valley, for after all peaches were Hobson's favorite fruit. He was not the first to grow peaches in the area, but it seems he had better success with peaches than some. In the Grubby End peaches had a much more prominent place in Hobson's orchards than they had enjoyed at Honey Creek. Peaches were mostly eaten fresh or canned, but a few were dried. In fall 1890, he described an experiment in which he

> brought away the remnants of Peaches from my East Orchard. Mostly Clings. Put some Peaches in my Dryer [sic]. Took the fruit, put in yesterday; out 1 pulled & weighed 15 lbs of my favorite Peaches (freestone & just ripe barely now 8 of 10 mo.) I put them in the Dryer [sic]. I want to know how good a dryed [sic] peach they will make & how much they will loose in drying. Well the 15lbs made 3 lbs of well dryed fruit & gained by [absorption] ½ lb.[26]

Some of the varieties of peaches mentioned in his diary include Early and Late Crawfords, Clings, Freestones, Hale's Early, and something called "Hobson's Best," which was likely his own hybrid. He continued to plant seed and set out saplings each year until his death in 1891. In fact, just about two months before the end of his life he received four peach saplings from New Jersey, perhaps a special cultivar he wanted to try growing.[27] Hobson was continually expanding his peach orchard and experimenting with different varieties.

While peaches were certainly his favorite, Hobson still grew the old apple and pear standbys, both of which did quite well in the Chehalem Valley and probably brought in considerably more money. There was already a small apple orchard established on his land which he expanded over time. He also experimented with a few other fruits including plums, prunes, nectarines, apricots, cherries, and something he called a peach plum. He first became interested in peach plums on the 7th of Seventh Month 1875, when he learned from a farmer living near Oregon City that this kind of fruit, measuring about two inches in diameter, could earn about eight or ten

25. "Impressions of Newberg in An Early Day," *Newberg Graphic* (Newberg, OR) 50th Anniversary Progress Edition, April 1939.
26. Hobson, "Diaries," reel 1 of 2, 10/8/1890.
27. Hobson, "Diaries," reel 1 of 2, 4/7/1891.

dollars a tree or about $800 an acre. But apparently, Hobson planted only a few peach plums, noting one time setting out ten and another time setting out four.[28] He also experimented with almonds, noting on the 1st of Fourth Month 1890, that the almond, apricot, and peach bloom was out.

The amount of land planted out in fruit trees on Hobson's homestead is impossible to determine. He does not give the acreage of his orchards, probably because he held the numbers in his head and he did not think it important to write them down. He merely noted locations in the briefest of ways, such as "little orchard," "young orchard," "orchard east of garden," "peach orchard," "old orchard," "east orchard," and in 1890, "new peach orchard."

Hobson listed orchard maintenance tasks similar to those he performed in Iowa. He pruned his trees in the late winter and also into the spring to encourage better yields and to prepare trees for horticultural fruit propagation techniques like grafting or budding. He also "littered" his trees with manure in the winter, just like at Honey Creek. However, some notable differences concerning orchard care in the Chehalem Valley included the following: Hobson never mentioned picking caterpillar eggs off his trees, never mentioned whitewashing their trunks, and instead of grafting he budded his trees, sometimes hiring that job out.

Hobson exported large amounts of fruit, mostly apples and pears, dried a fair amount, especially prunes, and sold smaller amounts to local families. He also liked to give fruit away to his children, to those who were experiencing financial difficulties, and to school children when he visited classes. It took a lot of time and care to maintain a successful orchard and the *Newberg Graphic* praised his efforts, noting at the end of summer 1920 in an article titled "Thirty Years Ago" that "Uncle William Hobson brought to this office the first of the week [in Eighth Month 1890], samples of apples, pears, apricots and peaches. Several years ago when others were skeptical regarding peach raising here William said he intended to prove to the people that peaches could be successfully grown here and he has done it."[29]

Of course, in order to produce a worthwhile fruit harvest, Hobson continued to keep bees in Oregon, just as he had in Iowa. He mentions "robbing" his bees several times between Eighth Month 1876, and Seventh Month 1890. Hobson had at least four hives and quite likely several more. On Fourth Month 4, 1890, he tells how an apiculturist, "Poppleton of Layfayette stayed with us last night. He is round fixing our Bees with lb [sic] section Boxes. Fixed 4 of mine. Did not Charge for the first two; Because

---

28. Hobson, "Diaries," reel 1 of 2, 4/13/1876, 2/1877 or 1878.

29. "Thirty Years Ago," *Newberg Graphic* (Newberg, OR) August 19, 1920, https://oregonnews.uoregon.edu/lccn/sn96088233/1920–08–19/ed-1/seq-4/.

I did not Charge him for staying a night with me & feeding him & horse the night. And only charged me 50 Cents for the next two." So, we see that beekeeping was just one more task added to the wide array of chores that must be performed to keep the Hobson farm running smoothly.

Farm work in Newberg took on a comfortable rhythm for the Hobsons. Fruit trees were planted, trimmed, budded, and fertilized in late winter and early spring. A large vegetable garden was planted in late spring and early summer. Clover and other cover crops were planted between the rows of trees in the orchards. Fruit and vegetables were harvested in late fall and early winter, and sold, dried, and otherwise processed into late winter. Wheat, oats, rye, buckwheat, and other crops like sugar cane and sorghum were sowed in moderate amounts throughout the cooler seasons of the year and harvested at the appropriate times. Timothy and corn sown in spring and harvested in late fall were used mostly as animal feed. Trimmings and slashings were burned in the fall and more brush was cut in the winter and spring, increasing Hobson's cleared land bit by bit. Interwoven in this melody of seasonal farm routines, was the undergirding harmony of tending livestock, milking, butchering, caring for bees, maintaining fences and outbuildings, and all the myriad of other daily chores necessary for keeping up a prosperous farm.

HOBSON FAMILY TIES

Throughout this all, the Hobson family remained close-knit and helpful to each other. Reading between the lines, Sarah and William enjoyed a loving and happy relationship with each other and were good parents to their children. There was a notable bump in the road of marital bliss when Sarah did not want to leave Honey Creek for the Chehalem Valley but, in the end, she agreed to move to Oregon seemingly with a good will. There are no indications of serious marital discord before or after this recorded in Hobson's journal, though even the healthiest marriages have their moments. He says next to nothing about their day to day interactions, so we'll just have to be content with the knowledge that William and Sarah remained married until Sarah died, for a total of forty-six years together. Their sons Samuel, Stephen, and Jesse helped immensely on the farm back in Iowa, especially when Hobson traveled in the ministry. Their daughters Rachel, Mary, and Anna must have also been useful around the farm, helping Sarah with her chores. All six children were provided with the best education available during their growing up years and received a solid Quaker spiritual upbringing from which it seems they did not stray.

After Hobson bought his land in the Chehalem Valley, the volume of letters between him and his third son Jesse increased significantly, and Jesse sent some large sums of money to his dad. It seems that Hobson was scouting out land for Jesse to settle on. When Jesse arrived with his sister Mary's family, they all stayed with Hobson for awhile. Jesse helped out some with the farm work and also looked after his father's land when Hobson traveled back to Iowa to bring Sarah and Anna out to Oregon. It's unclear when Jesse settled on his own land, but likely it was soon after his father's return from Iowa, if not before. In an article Jesse wrote for the *Newberg Graphic* he gave an account of his journey west from Iowa with the Austins in which he described the approach to Newberg from Portland:

> A lovely trip it was up the Willamette the next day, on one of the river steamers that plied to up-river points, and was carrying us to our new home place that we had read so much about and had looked forward to with unbounded interest. It was a perfect day in June, such as no other country can excel. The scenes along the route which greeted the eyes of the prairie accustomed immigrants were novel but intensely interesting. The water was as clear as crystal and the woods came down to the river's edge where "The lithe willow bend in graceful mien and sees its likeness in the depths all day." By two o'clock in the afternoon we were at the top of the bluff near the foot of the present River street, in the town of Newberg. The surroundings there did not look then as they do now. At the end of the steep climb from the water's edge was only a small clearing.[30]

Jesse went on to explain how it took a while to locate his father's house through the thick, sparsely inhabited timber. After arrived at Hobson's they spent several days viewing real estate, but sadly Jesse does not say where he ended up settling. He did wax eloquently about the valley writing

> here was the Chehalem Valley, a beautiful place, sheltered on the north and east by the mountain of the same name, and the Red Hills to the south and west, with the navigable waters of the Willamette at the foot. A natural pass had been left in the mountain formation to the east, to be occupied as a gateway for railroads to and from the great city that Portland was to be. Here the land was rich and in its virgin state, for only a few acres on each large tract had been cultivated, although having been settled for more than thirty years. From an observation point on

30. Hobson, "Looking Backward: A Paper Read by Jesse Hobson at Last Sunday's Anniversary Meeting," *Newberg Graphic* (Newberg, OR) November 14, 1912, https://oregonnews.uoregon.edu/lccn/sn96088233/1912-11-14/ed-1/seq-1/.

the mountain side, then only a small clearing could be seen here and there in the eastern portion of the valley. It was veritable sea of living green, but in a few short years the woodman's ax and the constant stream of accessions to the inhabitants made a striking change. New highways had to be established to accommodate the demand of the increasing settlement and oftentimes against the protest of the older residents. There were only three schoolhouses in this territory, and these old, dilapidated buildings. I could count on my fingertips and not use them all, the painted houses then in this portion of the valley. The habitations were uninviting on the outside, with their roofs overgrown with moss, but were occupied by a cheerful, kindly and hospitable people.[31]

Jesse was obviously pleased with his new home and his place must have been fairly close by his father's. According to his obituary in the *Newberg Graphic*, Jesse attended Pacific University in Forest Grove soon after arriving in Oregon and served on the board of Friends Pacific College (now George Fox University) in Newberg for many years. He was married to Mary Blair in 1881 and they raised their children in Newberg. Jesse and Mary were active members of Newberg Monthly Meeting, right from the beginning.[32] Besides farming Jesse was involved in multiple business enterprises during his years in Newberg, including warehouse ownership, sawmill ownership, ownership of a couple of general stores, and the real estate industry, as evidenced by numerous advertisements in the *Newberg Graphic*. Jesse and William continued to help each other out with work, finances, and gifts of produce or fodder for their animals. Hobson notes visiting when Jesse was sick and taking gifts of food to the family. He also notes hosting Jesse's family for supper and going over to their house for dinner. Likely this was a more frequent occurrence than he noted in his diary. It appears that Jesse moved to Portland in the spring of 1891[33] shortly before his father's death, where, as noted in his obituary, he lived for a number of years until his own death, Tenth Month 13, 1927, at age seventy.[34]

31. Hobson, "Looking Backward: A Paper Read by Jesse Hobson at Last Sunday's Anniversary Meeting," *Newberg Graphic* (Newberg, OR) November 14, 1912, https://oregonnews.uoregon.edu/lccn/sn96088233/1912-11-14/ed-1/seq-1/.

32. ; "Jesse Hobson," *findagrave.com*.; "Pioneer Man of This Section Passed Away: Jesse Hobson Died in Portland Thursday Was Member of First Academy Board," *Newberg Graphic* (Newberg, OR) October 20, 1927.

33. "Jesse Hobson came up from Portland Tuesday Evening," *Newberg Graphic* (Newberg, OR) May 1, 1891, https://oregonnews.uoregon.edu/lccn/sn96088233/1891-05-01/ed-1/seq-3/.

34. "Pioneer Man of This Section Passed Away: Jesse Hobson Died in Portland

Hobson's oldest son Samuel also settled on land not too far away from his father and brother Jesse. In the same edition of the *Newberg Graphic* containing Jesse's reminiscences, there is a short article telling how "Samuel Hobson who in the early days of Newberg lived at the end of the bridge where the B.R. Bass home now is, and who was Newberg's first photographer, was here last Sunday in attendance at the anniversary meeting and took some group pictures of those in attendance."[35] It's impossible to tell from this account just where Samuel lived, but it must have been fairly close to Newberg and the rest of the family. Hobson kept up a regular correspondence with Samuel, just as he had with Jesse, until Samuel, his wife Mary Ann, and their children came west with William, Sarah, and Anna. Samuel and William helped each other out with planting, harvesting, tending livestock, and other aspects of farm life, as well as with financial transactions, in a way similar to William's interactions with Jesse. They also ate meals with each other periodically and the Samuel Hobsons were charter members of Newberg Monthly Meeting.

The *Newberg Graphic* reveals from the above quoted article that Samuel had a successful photography business in addition to working his land. In fact, on Hobson's seventieth birthday, Second Month 4, 1890, Samuel presented Hobson with a large portrait he had taken of his dad at the request of a friend by the name of Allen Craven. Also according to the *Newberg Graphic*, after Samuel moved to California in the early 1900s he spent several summers at Yosemite taking photographs of the scenic wonders there.[36] While still living in Newberg, Samuel became the third owner of the *Newberg Graphic*, purchasing it from Will Hiatt, the son of the original owner John C. Hiatt, previously of Whittier, California. Samuel's son Franklin edited and published the *Newberg Graphic* for a time with O.V. Allen until future President of the United States Herbert Hoover's brother, Theodore Hoover, took over the paper.[37] Samuel's older sons Franklin and Oliver, and sometimes younger Murray, often helped their grandfather with farm work, especially toward the end of his life when Hobson's strength was failing.

Thursday Was Member of First Academy Board," *Newberg Graphic* (Newberg, OR) October 20, 1927.

35. "Samuel Hobson," *Newberg Graphic* (Newberg, OR) November 14, 1912, https://oregonnews.uoregon.edu/lccn/sn96088233/1912-11-14/ed-1/seq-1/.

36. "Samuel Hobson, who with Mrs. Hobson," *Newberg Graphic* (Newberg, OR) December 19, 1918, https://oregonnews.uoregon.edu/lccn/sn96088233/1918-12-19/ed-1/seq-5/;"Mrs. Samuel Hobson of Portland," *Newberg Graphic* (Newberg, OR) October 26, 1905, https://oregonnews.uoregon.edu/lccn/sn96088233/1912-11-14/ed-1/seq-1/.

37. Kelly, "The Graphic: A Century of News," *Newberg Graphic: A Century to Remember, Newberg 1889–1989* (Newberg, OR) 1989 special edition, 55.

Samuel was one of two first co-clerks (the other being Maggie Wood) of Chehalem Monthly Meeting when it gained approval as a monthly meeting under the authority of Honey Creek[38] and he served at least one term as Mayor of Newberg beginning shortly after his dad died in 1891.[39] Around the end of 1905 Samuel and his wife moved to California, living in various locations in that state, until he passed away in Whittier on Tenth Month 18, 1944, at the ripe old age of ninety-eight.[40] At any rate, it's clear that Hobson and his nearby sons, Samuel and Jesse, their wives, and children enjoyed a rich and loving family relationship with William and Sarah during their time in Newberg.

According to her obituary in the *Newberg Graphic*, William and Sarah's youngest daughter Anna went to school at Sunnycrest in Newberg, then Tualatin Academy in Forest Grove after which she taught school for a while at Chehalem Center. In 1880 she married Alpheus T. Blair, another Quaker transplant from Hardin County, Iowa, and they raised three children on their farm near Newberg. Both were active members of Newberg Monthly Meeting. Anna died in 1951 at age ninety-one, outliving Alpheus by almost two decades.[41]

Sadly, three of William and Sarah's children preceded them in death. Mary (Hobson) Austin died in 1887 at age thirty-five, after living about a decade in the Chehalem Valley. Unfortunately, there is no obituary on record for Mary Austin, since the *Newberg Graphic* was not started until 1889, but the year of her death can be fixed by a reference to it in her husband Henry Austin's obituary (he died in 1912),[42] and by the inscription on her grave marker in the Newberg Friends Cemetery, which gives only the year and not the day she died. Strangely, Hobson does not mention her death in his diary. The last mention of Mary in Hobson's diary comes on the 21st of Eleventh Month 1886, when she accompanied him on a visit to Middleton Meeting. Then on First Month 1, 1888, Hobson notes "Went to Henry As' [sic] to dinner & home early." The lack of reference to Mary stands out ominously in this notation, indicating that by this time Henry was a widower, but for how long is unclear.

38. "Chehalem Monthly Meeting Minutes," 1.

39. Miller, "History of Newberg," 120, 124.

40. "Deaths: Samuel Hobson," *Whittier News*, (Whittier, CA) October 19, 1944, http://digi.cityofwhittier.org/awweb/main.jsp?flag=browse&smd=2&awdid=2#.

41. "Mrs. Anna Blair, Pioneer Resident, Dies Tuesday," *Newberg Graphic* (Newberg, OR) January 25, 1951.

42. "Obituary, Henry Austin," *Newberg Graphic* (Newberg, OR) October 31, 1912, https://oregonnews.uoregon.edu/lccn/sn96088233/1912-10-31/ed-1/seq-9/.

Hobson also does not refer to their son Stephen's or their daughter Rachel's deaths directly in his diary. Stephen remained in Iowa and the last letter Hobson recorded receiving from him arrived on the 21st of Seventh Month 1876. Quaker genealogists Wiles and Davis do not report a date of death for Stephen, but they do note that his wife remarried in 1882.[43] A photograph of his grave marker in the New Providence Cemetery posted on findagrave.com indicates that he died in 1879.[44] He was only twenty-nine or thirty years old. Rachel (Hobson) Reece, who also remained in Iowa, died eight months before her mother on Third Month 2, 1890, at the age of forty-three.[45] There is indirect evidence of this in Hobson's diary on the 14th of Fourth Month 1890, when Hobson writes, "Received a letter from Elkana [sic] Reece [Rachel's husband], Saying they [the bereaved family] are well and getting along as well as could be expected. He informs me that the Teleagram [sic] sent me was Started about 10 a.m. It was handed to me about 11 (And our time about 15 minutes too fast) here in our meeting in Newberg Oregon. It seems only about 3 of an hour coming And yet as it takes about 2 hours for the Sun to come. Therefore about 2 ¾ hours." Reading between the lines, Elkanah sent his father-in-law a telegram with the news of Rachel's death almost immediately after she passed and then followed it up with a letter later on.

Toward the end of his life, Hobson gifted his children property in the Chehalem Valley. On Tenth Month 1, 1888, Hobson noted "walked over the Land which I gave to My Children Samuel, Stephen, Rachel & Mary." He may have been reassessing since two of the named children were already deceased. Later in Second Month 12, 1891, he gave Samuel and Anna some parcels of land as follows: "To day I have deeded to my daughter Anna Blair 10 Acres of my land. And to Samuel Hobson my son 10 acres & 25 rods of my land & I have made a written Will in case I should die in regard to the whole rest of my property." Why Jesse is not mentioned by name in connection with a gift of land is unclear. What is clear is that William and Sarah had mutually loving and beneficial relationships with their adult children. This was a tight-knit, healthy family that farmed together, went to meeting together, celebrated and mourned together, and helped each other in times of need or sickness. And each one contributed in their own way to the building up of Chehalem Monthly Meeting, as well as to the development of the larger Newberg community to which they belonged.

43. Davis and Wiles, *Hobson*, 295.
44. "Stephen G. Hobson," *findagrave.com*.
45. "Rachel Hobson Reece," *findagrave.com*.

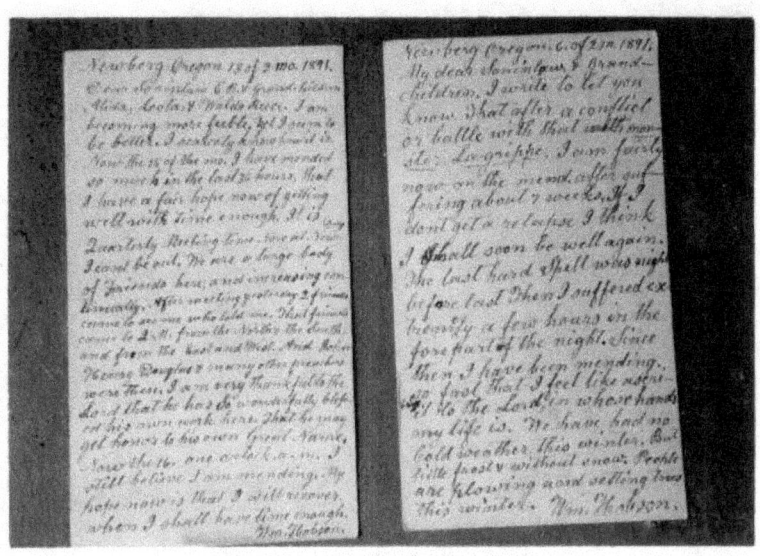

A sample of William Hobson's writing and William and Sarah Hobson (left) with two unidentified people.

William and Sarah Hobson.

RISE OF NEWBERG, OREGON

Newberg was growing right along with Hobson's orchards. The population was exploding, businesses and services were increasing, schools were improving, and Chehalem Monthly Meeting was thriving. The 1880s were a time of great expansion as more and more Friends families arrived in the Grubby End. Most came in response to letters Hobson wrote and sent back east asking for Friends to join him in his mission work at Newberg. Some of his appeals had even been published in the *Friends Review* and *Christian Worker*, reaching a wide Friends audience. In an article written for the *Oregon Historical Quarterly* called "Friends Come to Oregon: I, Newberg Meeting," H.S. Nedry notes that Hobson "wrote numerous letters to Friends and relatives in Iowa and Indiana urging them to come to Oregon to settle near him. Hobson also wrote a circular invitation to be passed around the churches in Iowa."[46] Amanda Woodward tells about the correspondence between her husband Ezra and Hobson in her "Reminiscences Given at the Fiftieth Anniversary of Newberg Monthly Meeting of Friends":

> We had heard a great deal about what a fine country Oregon was, through Elwood C. Siler, a minister who had visited the

---

46. Nedry, "Friends Come to Oregon," 199.

Friends here, and through other sources, so my husband wrote to William Hobson to know of some of the drawbacks. William answered very promptly, telling all about the advantages and good things about the country. He could see nothing wrong with it, so well did he like it, and he closed his letter by saying: "If thou wants to know the drawbacks of Oregon thou had better write to someone else."[47]

Many Quaker families responded to Hobson's encouraging description of the Chehalem Valley by pulling up roots in the Midwest and moving out to Oregon. Jesse and Mary Edwards, Friends from Indiana arrived in 1880 with their four children Clarence, Walter, O.K., and Mabel. Ezra and Amanda Woodward the future owners of the *Newberg Graphic,* no doubt convinced by Hobson's optimism, traveled with them. Several other prominent Friends families also arrived in the mid-1880s from the Midwest including Henry J. and Laura Minthorn, with their young nephew, the future President of the United States, Herbert "Bertie" Hoover.[48]

Jesse Edwards is commonly known as "the Father of Newberg" because it was his plat of the town that was finally adopted after two previous tries that didn't take, first by Rogers and later by the team of Ruddick and Wood. After their arrival in Oregon, the Edwards family wintered in Dayton and then bought the 184 acre Hagey farm in the spring of 1881, later adding smaller parcels to their holdings finally totaling about 360 acres in all. The Hagey land was worn out from over farming, so Edwards sold off plots for a business district that continues to stand as the downtown core of Newberg to this day. Edwards also engaged in several business ventures that helped to build up the town including a store in partnership with William Hobson's son Jesse Hobson, a warehouse also in partnership with Jesse Hobson, a sawmill, and several other useful enterprises. Eventually, the section of town to the northwest of Edwards's town that Ruddick and Wood had platted previously and, which had vied unsuccessfully for prominence, was joined to the Edwards's section through natural urban growth, and the two rival halves of Newberg became one. Jesse and Mary Edwards were also influential members of Chehalem Monthly Meeting, as well as enthusiastic early supporters of Friends Pacific Academy.[49]

Because of Jesse Edward's influence and vision the city blocks were quickly laid out and government buildings and businesses sprang up.

47. Woodward, "Reminiscences," 1.
48. Edmonston Jr., *Newberg: Stories from the Grubby End*, 42.
49. Miller, "History of Newberg," 16; George P. Edmonston Jr., *Newberg: Stories from the Grubby End*, 40–43.

According to notes compiled by Jennie D. Miller, by the winter of 1888 there were "about 15 business houses, representing nearly every line of business there are near Newberg, five good sawmills, one flouring mill, three grain warehouses, two fruit drying houses, a nursery, a brick and tile factory, and another brick yard to start soon, a company organized to buy a fruit cannery and the prospect of a new roller process flouring mill and other manufacturing establishments."[50] According to the Newberg Downtown Coalition Historical Walking Tour Guide the current City Hall building erected in 1913, replaced an earlier building of an unknown age that housed both City Hall and the fire department.[51] Miller reports further that the first jail once stood facing College Street on the corner of Hancock and College, but was moved to the middle of the block bordered by First, Second, Center, and Meridian in 1889. The Chehalem Valley Mill was built in 1880, though the old Ramsey mill still continued to grind. The *Newberg Graphic* was established late in 1888 and the United States National Bank was established in 1889 the same year the city was incorporated. A narrow-gauge railroad with limited freight and passenger service which ran three times a week linked Newberg with Oswego and thus Portland, beginning in 1884.[52] According to Leslie M. Scott in his article "History of the Narrow Gauge Railroad in the Willamette Valley," this track was part of a larger system that ran through much of western Oregon linking Newberg to the southwest with Airlie in Polk County, as well as with Portland to the east.[53] The depot was located on North Main Street and several small businesses sprang up nearby. Daily passenger and freight service to Portland on the river continued to be offered at this time, as well.[54] Edmonston Jr. adds that by 1877 the narrow-gauge was converted to standard rails by the Southern Pacific Railroad Company and "the neighborhood along Main Street saw a surge of growth, including several hotels, a train depot, drug and furniture stores, a tobacco shop and other small businesses."[55] Passenger and freight traffic increased considerably with the change to standard rails and expanded service, which made it much easier for people to move to Newberg, for students to travel back and forth from Friends Pacific Academy, and for friends and family to travel there and back again on visits.

50. Miller, "History of Newberg," 119.
51. "Newberg Downtown Coalition Historical Walking Tour guide."
52. Miller, "History of Newberg," 2, 55, 64.
53. Scott, "History of the Narrow Gauge Railroad," 142.
54. Miller, "History of Newberg" 2, 58, 64.
55. Edmonston Jr., *Newberg: Stories from the Grubby End,* 43.

As the 1880s progressed Newberg approached the level of development the Hobsons had enjoyed at Honey Creek and even surpassed it in some ways. Travel and trade on the river boomed and the railroad chugged directly to and from town, a luxury they did not experience at Honey Creek. And mostly due to the railroad, the population of Newberg had increased significantly by 1890. Hobson noted in his diary on the 17th of Second Month 1890, that "Andrew Picket is said to have found 603 persons residing with in the town Corporation of Newberg. And 100 more near by by [sic] about as much in town as other[s] So I venture to place the Population of Newberg at 680" Newberg was becoming a lively and thriving community, rural still, but growing more urban every day.

As more and more people arrived in Newberg, many with no Friends or even any religious background at all, the opportunities for evangelism increased. It only remains now to tell the story of how the Quakers of Chehalem Monthly Meeting, led by William Hobson, helped foster spiritual growth in Newberg, shaping the town and surrounding areas in positive ways. While Hobson does write more about Chehalem Monthly Meeting than he did about Honey Creek, he cannot be relied upon to give a full history. However, we can piece things together fairly well using other materials in conjunction with his diary. Chehalem Monthly Meeting Minutes handwritten in notebooks and housed in the George Fox University Archives are an important primary source for the history of the meeting. Several valuable secondary sources also help to tell the story of Chehalem Monthly Meeting including Stephen Z. Perisho's senior research paper "History of the Newberg Monthly Meeting, 1878-1893," various items of interest in the *Newberg Graphic*, and certain other short papers, and journal articles housed in the George Fox Archives.

FIRST FRIENDS IN THE VICINITY OF NEWBERG

Two of the earliest well-concerned Friends in the Newberg area, ministers Rebecca Mendenhall Lewis and Rebecca Clawson, were active in service several years before Hobson arrived. Their impact on early Friends in the region was significant. Lewis and Clawson may not have directly influenced the formation of Chehalem Monthly Meeting, but they certainly exerted a general influence over the spread of Quakerism in the the upper Willamette Valley.

According to the *Newberg Graphic* and Joseph Gaston in *Portland Oregon Its History*, Rebecca Mendenhall Lewis was especially well loved and respected as the first Friends minister to settle permanently in Portland where she had lived with her husband since 1864. The Lewis home was always open to traveling Friends and while Lewis did not organize a meeting, she was held in high esteem by her peers.[56] She placed her membership with Chehalem Monthly Meeting soon after it was established.[57] It was the nearest Friends meeting for many miles, but she was not required to transfer her membership. That she chose to do so was likely seen as an endorsement of the work at Newberg. How much she contributed to the establishment and later life of the meeting is negligible, living at a distance of twenty-five miles from the Grubby End. Lewis passed away in Eighth Month 1901, and was memorialized fondly during the 1902 Oregon Yearly Meeting sessions. She was well known for her strict adherence to Friends ways and for her purity of spirit.[58]

The other Friends minister named Rebecca living in the vicinity was equally important to Willamette Valley Friends in the early days, and certainly vital in the history of Chehalem Monthly Meeting. The tale has already been told how Rebecca Clawson connected William Hobson with Thomas Markham, an inmate at the Oregon State Penitentiary, and thus with Markham's wife Esther in the Grubby End and how the very farm Esther was living on became the property Hobson bought and settled on. In addition to holding meetings at the penitentiary, Clawson also held meetings periodically for law abiding citizens in Salem and vicinity, including at Dayton. Hobson became acquainted with Clawson when he visited Salem during his second journey to the Pacific Northwest and with the Whites through her, which in turn brought him to Dayton and subsequently to Newberg. Elizabeth White's obituary in the *Newberg Graphic* notes that "Uncle Wm. Hobson and the seven pioneers from Iowa who organized Newberg Friends meeting made their home [the White's home in Dayton] headquarters,"[59] while they searched for a perfect location in which to settle and build up a Quaker community. Certainly, David J. Wood, John S. Bond,

---

56. "Quarter Century Event Celebrated," *Newberg Graphic* (Newberg, OR) November 14, 1912, https://oregonnews.uoregon.edu/lccn/sn96088233/1912-11-14/ed-1/seq-1/; Gaston, *Portland Oregon*, 542–43.

57. Kelsey, "Quakerism Beyond the Mississippi," 520.

58. "The first part of the afternoon was a 'Memorial Service,'" *Newberg Graphic* (Newberg, OR) July 18, 1902, https://oregonnews.uoregon.edu/lccn/sn96088233/1902-07-18/ed-1/seq-2/; "Mrs. Nathan White Went Down," *Newberg Graphic* (Newberg, OR) September 6, 1901, https://oregonnews.uoregon.edu/lccn/sn96088233/1901-09-06/ed-1/seq-3/.

59. "Mrs. Elizabeth White Passes Away After Long Life of Activity," *Newberg Graphic* (Newberg, OR) October 15, 1914, https://oregonnews.uoregon.edu/lccn/sn96088233/1914-10-15/ed-1/seq-1/.

and Perry C. Hadley were among the seven mentioned, but it's not clear who made up the balance.

Hobson did indeed use the small community of hospitable Friends at Dayton as a base from which to scout out the perfect location for his Quaker settlement. And while he is generally credited with beginning the first regular meeting of Friends in the northern Willamette Valley, there is clear evidence to the contrary. As Perisho states "Quaker meetings for worship were held at Dayton for several months before William Hobson arrived. Rebecca Clawson had started them earlier in Salem, and after she moved to Dayton to be near her daughter and son-in-law, Elizabeth and Nathan White, they continued to be held under her leadership, even after Hobson arrived."[60] Elizabeth White confirms this, though with more emotion than accuracy, during a short address at the quarterly meeting twenty-fifth anniversary celebration in the fall of 1912, as recorded by O.J. Hobson who was taking notes. During the gathering "Mrs. Lizzie White arose and remarked: I just wanted to say that my family--my mother Rebecca Claussen [sic] came out here in 1874. When she came there were no Friends here. We were the very first friends [sic] inOregon [sic]. William Hobson came to our house--we lived in Dayton--and he held meetings invarious [sic] places--in school houses and other places."[61] Obviously, Rebecca Clawson and the Whites were not the first Friends in Oregon, though they may have been the first Friends in Yamhill County and they did arrive shortly before Hobson settled in Newberg. It seems that Lizzie White did not want the significant contribution her mother made to the organization of Friends in Dayton and Newberg to be overshadowed by the erroneous idea that Hobson was the first to hold regular meetings in Oregon.

Regular First Day meetings at Dayton were logged in his diary for several months after his acquaintance with Clawson and the White's, and some were presumably conducted under his leadership, though Rebecca Clawson likely led when she was not traveling in the ministry. Fifth day meetings were not held with regularity, or at least Hobson was not in attendance, due to the fact that he was traveling hither and yon, trying to find a place to settle. He noted in his diary attending meeting at White's several times in the fall of 1875 and early winter of 1876, but in the spring of 1876 this pattern changed. Hobson began to alternate between attending meetings in Dayton and holding meetings nearer to home. Most likely Rebecca Clawson continued in a leadership position at Dayton.

60. Perisho, "History of the Newberg Monthly Meeting," 6.
61. Hobson, "Twentyfifth Anniversary," 2.

According to John H. Rees, the roads in and around Newberg were so poorly maintained in those days that most everybody went to meeting on foot because it was easier than driving a wagon over a stump choked track. As he put it, "after jolting over a mile or two of stumps in an old lumber wagon, the worshiper on reaching church sometimes longed for other than spiritual blessings. We may here note that four years after the Monthly meeting was established no Friend rode to meeting in a Spring Vehicle. The people became accustomed from necessity to walking, and a habit was formed which is yet very noticeable to persons from elsewhere."[62] It was at some point during this time that Hobson made a way for some distant neighbors to attend meeting. At the quarterly meeting twenty-fifth anniversary celebration "Mrs. Matilda Hoskins told of she and her husband locating on a piece of timberland at Springbrook... Soon after they located there William Hobson came over one day and invited them to his home to attend a meeting for worship. Said he had cut out the brush and blazed a way through the timber so they could reach his home without getting lost."[63] Hobson never mislaid his determination to get people to meeting.

CHEHALEM MONTHLY MEETING ESTABLISHED

After bringing Sarah and Anna home to Oregon, Hobson began holding meetings regularly at Newberg, alternating between his own home and that of William Clemmens's or David J. Wood's. He no longer led or attended at Dayton on a regular basis and even noted on Fifth Month 27, 1877, that some Friends from Dayton were in attendance at the Newberg meeting. An entry in his diary on the 6th of Third Month 1881, indicates that a few Friends were still meeting in Dayton since John Henry Douglas was holding evangelistic meetings in the small town. There is no way of knowing how Rebecca Clawson, the Whites, the Fusons, and other Friends at Dayton felt about Hobson abandoning them and starting a new meeting at Newberg. Would they have preferred that Hobson settle closer to their already established community? Perhaps, but it's a matter of record that Rebecca Clawson, Elizabeth and Nathan White, W. Macy Hadley, and Elizabeth M. Fuson, all of whom were Dayton Friends, were accepted into membership at Chehalem Monthly Meeting about the same time as Rebecca Mendenhall Lewis, in First Month 1879.[64] This would seem to indicate that they were

62. Rees, "History of Friends Church," 3.
63. "Quarter Century Event Celebrated," *Newberg Graphic* (Newberg, OR) November 14, 1912, https://oregonnews.uoregon.edu/lccn/sn96088233/1912-11-14/ed-1/seq-1.
64. Kelsey, "Quakerism Beyond the Mississippi," 520.

joining in solidarity with the growing Friends community near Newberg. However, according to John H. Rees, Rebecca Clawson was not at Chehalem Monthly Meeting much. Apparently, she felt called to preach and give temperance speeches at various regional meetings, which resulted in significant traveling in the ministry. She lived in Oregon for only nine years, mostly in Portland, and died in Indianapolis in 1883 while traveling to Philadelphia as a delegate for the Women's Christian Temperance Union (WCTU). Rees tells how Clawson's "occasional visits [to Chehalem Monthly Meeting] were always hailed with joy by the entire membership, her kind words, her saintly bearing, and her earnest exhortation endearing her to every one with whom she came in contact."[65] One would expect that all meetings she visited felt the same.

Perhaps most Dayton Friends eventually moved closer to Newberg, since there is no record of an official monthly meeting in Dayton. Perisho believed this to be the case stating that "many of those families still living in Dayton were soon to resettle near Hobson, and Dayton, then the center of Yamhill County Quaker worship, would give way to Newberg."[66] Though William Hobson has generally been given all the credit for bringing Quakerism to the Pacific Northwest, it's clear that Friends like the two Rebeccas, the Whites, and others before them, were already engaging in noteworthy ministry before he came. However, Hobson used his experience and gifts to organize and build on the nascent ministry that was already in place and the significant growth of Friends influence in the Chehalem Valley was mostly due to his vision and leadership.

By First Month 1877, the congregation at Newberg had grown to about forty-five persons and by Tenth Month of the same year the need for a meeting house was mentioned in business meeting.[67] A few weeks later on the 4th of Eleventh Month, Hobson wrote, "Held meeting in our old house was much Crowded David J Wood offered the upper room of his house for Meeting [place]." So, the congregation began meeting at David and Maggie Wood's in the large upstairs room of their newly built home. By the next month there were about sixty people at meeting,[68] proving the need for an even larger meeting space. After this Hobson made a few entries in Twelfth Month, none of which referred to Chehalem Monthly Meeting, and then there is a gap of about seven years in Hobson's diary from Twelfth

---

65. Rees, "History of Friends Church," 6.
66. Perisho, "History of the Newberg Monthly Meeting," 7.
67. Hobson, "Diaries," reel 1 of 2, 1/28/77, 10/14/77.
68. Hobson, "Diaries," reel 1 of 2, 11/11/77.

Month 1877, to Eleventh Month 1885, so we must turn to other sources for the early history of the meeting.

It's unclear exactly when the name Chehalem Monthly Meeting was chosen, but the first recorded use appears in the official opening minutes of the meeting. Grubby End Friends had applied to Honey Creek Quarterly Meeting for monthly meeting status, Honey Creek being the closest established quarterly Friends meeting at the time, and Honey Creek readily approved their request on the 6th of Fourth Month, 1878. Chehalem Monthly Meeting was approved just over two years after Hobson held the first meeting of Friends in Newberg, in the spring of 1876. The minutes show that Samuel Hobson and Maggie Wood were chosen as temporary clerks for the day. The lack of separate men's and women's minutes plus two clerks, one a woman and one a man, and the fact that men and women were appointed to committees together, indicates that the meeting was integrated from the start. After choosing the clerks, the meeting got right down to business. A committee was appointed to find clerks to serve for the next year and William Hobson was officially appointed as correspondent, probably because he was already doing that job so well. A committee to nominate individuals to serve as overseers was appointed which included Sarah Hobson, David Wood, Samuel's wife Mary Ann Hobson, and Mary (Hobson's) husband Henry Austin. David Wood was appointed treasurer and another committee was formed to select a site for the new meeting house plus a graveyard. This committee included J.T. Smith, Sarah Hobson, Samuel Hobson, S.E. Smith, Jesse Hobson, J.L. Carice, Cyrus Hoskins, Mary Austin, Matilda Hoskins, and Byron Morris. At the next business meeting Samuel Hobson and Maggie Wood were approved as clerks for the year, a site for the new meeting house was approved as was the price for the land: five dollars, and J.T. Smith, William Hobson, and Samuel Hobson, were approved as trustees. Smith and William Hobson also served on the finance committee with Zimri Mendenhall. Obviously, Hobson and his family were prominent founding members of Chehalem Monthly Meeting.[69]

Rayner Kelsey points out that Chehalem Monthly Meeting was the first to be officially approved as a monthly meeting on the West Coast, though San Jose Friends had been meeting longer. He notes several names of charter members as follows: "Wm. Hobson, Samuel Hobson, John T. Smith, Henry Austin, Zimri Mendenhall, David J. Wood and Cornelius Davis. The list included 29 names. But the minutes of the first meeting mention also Rebecca Clawson, Cyrus and Matilda Hoskins, and Byron Morris, whose certificates were soon received from their meetings in the Eastern States. There were

---

69. "Chehalem Monthly Meeting Minutes," 3–7.

probably others whose names are not given who were present and took part from the beginning."⁷⁰ Kelsey goes on to list more Friends who had joined the meeting either by certificate or otherwise by First Month of 1879, "Rebecca M. Lewis, Rebecca Clawson, Mary Emily Clawson, Edwin D. Pool, W. Macy Hadley, Elizabeth M. Fuson, Daniel Morris, Nathan and Elizabeth White, Abner B. George, Albert M. Hoskins, William Ruddick, Thompson Hutchens, Marcus Blair, Riley Smith, Jane Crator, and John Townsend. Other members continued to be received almost monthly, twenty-four being accepted at one meeting, Second month 1, 1879."⁷¹

This core group of dedicated Friends continued to meet together consistently on First Days and then later beginning in the fall of 1885 on Fifth Days, as well.⁷² They also met monthly for business and some of the younger ones formed a "reading meeting" which functioned much like a prayer meeting. The congregation soon out-grew the upstairs room at the Woods's and moved to a larger building east of Newberg, that was owned by John T. Smith. Kelsey tells how it was described to him "recently [in 1910] by the owner as a shack about 15 feet by 20 feet in dimensions, so low that a tall man could not stand upright in it, with a large, rock-built fireplace and a chimney of sticks and mud."⁷³ It's easy to see why the congregation hoped to build a proper meeting house as soon as possible, but it took some time to accomplish.

FIRST REVIVAL AND GROWTH AT CHEHALEM MONTHLY MEETING

While they were gathering funds to build, the congregation continued to meet in Smith's ramshackle cabin, and it was in this less than ideal meeting house that spontaneous revival broke out during the winter of 1878-79. Kelsey tells how

> in the old moss covered shack described above, broke out the revival movement among Oregon Friends. Many of the Friends had seen religious revivals in the Society in the Middle States, and no doubt the spirit of the movement was carried West by those who built up Chehalem Monthly Meeting. There was no visiting minister present and no professional evangelist. In that respect it was quite a "Friendly" revival meeting. A reading

70. Kelsey, "Quakerism Beyond the Mississippi," 520.
71. Kelsey, "Quakerism Beyond the Mississippi," 520.
72. Hobson, "Diaries," reel 1 of 2, 11/26/85.
73. Kelsey, "Quakerism Beyond the Mississippi," 521.

meeting had been established in addition to the regular meeting for worship, and this developed spontaneously into a religious revival. Many indifferent people and now a few hardened sinners declared their allegiance to Jesus Christ and made application for membership in the local meeting. The accession of 24 members at one monthly meeting, as mentioned above, was one of the results of this first religious revival among Oregon Friends.[74]

Friends were apparently orderly in their religious expression during this outpouring of God's grace on their congregation, but some in the neighborhood were not so decorous in their response to it. Anna (Hobson) Blair recounted her memory of strenuous resistance to the revival during a Newberg Monthly Meeting of Friends Church fiftieth anniversary celebration as reported in the *Newberg Graphic* in 1928. Anna remembered how the congregation persevered through some difficulties

> in the winter of 1878–79 in the old moss–covered shack the revival movement broke out against much opposition by many outsiders who thought to break up the meeting by building bonfires and making stump speeches near the [meeting] house and even going so far as to throw clubs on the roof. But the revival continued and the stump speeches ceased. One result was the addition of 24 members at one Monthly Meeting.[75]

Here are two fond references to the "old moss–covered shack" where so much good ministry and vibrant worship took place, as well as two references to the large number of new members the revival brought into the church. Such corroboration lends credibility to the strength of this early out–pouring of God's grace on Chehalem Monthly Meeting.

Traveling ministers may have helped to till the soil for the planting of the gospel seed. Robert W. Douglas, the brother of John Henry Douglas, a minister and powerful preacher in his own right was present at the second business meeting of the new congregation. The minutes state "His [Robert Douglas's] Gospel labors and teachings have been edifying and encouraging to this meeting."[76] Kelsey noted that Robert Douglas had just returned from a religious visit to Australia and that he stayed at Newberg for several weeks before moving on. Kelsey also noted that "John Scott, of Deer Creek Monthly Meeting, Maryland, was present at the opening of Chehalem

---

74. Kelsey, "Quakerism Beyond the Mississippi," 521.
75. "Early Days in Newberg Given," *Newberg Graphic* (Newberg, OR) June 21, 1928.
76. "Chehalem Monthly Meeting Minutes," 6

Monthly Meeting"[77] and, he also presumably stayed on a few weeks preaching powerfully and encouraging the congregation mightily.

It seems, however, that this early revival was mainly a spontaneous movement, led by several members of a "reading group," who were praying and listening to the Holy Spirit and not by one or two individuals. John H. Rees explained further how

> reading meetings were instituted as an auxiliary work which developed into a great soul-saving revival, the results of which are seen in many staunch Christian lives. Among those actively engaged in this [reading] meeting were Byron and John Morris, William Hobson, Cyrus E. Hoskins and others, but no visiting minister. Of those converted in these meetings thirty united with the Friends Church, among these were Thomas W. Atkinson, now a prominent minister of the M.E. Church, N.L. Wiley, J.H. and Carrie Hutchens. The meeting had now grown in membership and attendance until the need of building a good-sized log house, the material for which was all too plentiful, but the more progressive favored commencing a good frame house, which might be completed later, for few of our pioneer Friend's had very much capital, but willing hands and cheerful hearts.[78]

Doctor Byron Morris, one of the founding members of Chehalem Monthly Meeting, was instrumental in this early revival movement and during the quarterly meeting twenty-fifth anniversary celebration he shared his conviction that Hobson was called by God to lead the gospel work in the Chehalem Valley:

> There is no doubt in my mind, friends, that the Lord separated out William Hobson. I am persuaded that the Lord was in it from the start just as much as he was in those times described in this lesson, [Acts, Chapter 13] when he [Holy Spirit working through church leaders] came to those Jews and laid his hands on some of them and said to "Go to a new country and establish the gospel. That's what William did--he came out to establish the gospel and now we are here to celebrate it, and no celebration is complete if it leaves out the name of William Hobson for it was by and through his efforts that it was accomplished.[79]

Morris was articulating a general understanding among Pacific Northwest Friends that Hobson's obedience to God's call to establish a Friends mission

77. Kelsey, "Quakerism Beyond the Mississippi," 521.
78. Rees, "History of Friends Church," 2.
79. Hobson, "Twentyfifth Anniversary," 1.

in the Chehalem Valley was blessed by God, resulting in revival and spiritual growth in Newberg and beyond. Later during the meeting Morris reminisced about the 1878–79 revival remembering that

> up to this time we had no night meetings. We had a meeting in the morning and that would do us for the next few days. Some of the younger members thought it was about time to hold a revival meeting. I do not know whether it started by the Bible meeting or by the revival started by some of the younger people. We finally got permission to hold Bible Meeting in the church. That was the best we could do. We started in. My recollection is that we did not do much Bible reading. It was a wide-open meeting. That is we were all private soldiers and no leaders at these meetings. It would be hard to say who was leader. We prayed and sang and it was so fine we had another one next night. We had a leader to follow the singers. There was not a preacher in sight. When the fire got to burning that way the older people began coming. Why they did not start in when the balance of us did I am not able to say, whether it was on account of the roads being so muddy or not. Revivals were not so much in evidence in those days. At any rate Uncle "Billy Hobson" as he was familiarly called came in and apologized like a man. There were two incidents to show that he could rise to any occasion showing his tact and fitness. To start a new church in the "Wild and wooly West" he was smart enough to not try to runit [sic]. One evening we would appoint Samuel Hobson and John Smith the next night and when it came Uncle William's time he would take his turn. We were there many times when there was not a preacher around. I think it does us good to do a little praying by ourselves sometimes and do our own leading. I tell you it can be done. Some of those who were converted wanted to join some church. Among the number were Presbyterians and Methodists. They said we cannot join the Quakers for they do not baptize. Uncle William told them if they wanted to be baptized if they would get some one to baptize them we would go down to the creek and we did and they came back and joined the Quaker Church. These two incidents to my mind show his broad-minded-ness. We cannot pay a better tribute to "Uncle Billy Hobson": He rose to the occasion. Thank you.[80]

The Reverend Thomas Atkinson also stood during the quarterly meeting twenty-fifth anniversary celebration and told how the revival changed his life with the

---

80. Hobson, "Twentyfifth Anniversary," 8.

first alter [sic] service that was given--I do not know which one of these brothers was leading the meeting that night, but I think is was Brother Morris. I remember I tumbled down right at the end of the alter [sic]. I did not know just how to come to Christ or anything of that kind. There was a good sister I believe it was his mother--I did not look up to see--put her hand on my head and said "Brother, if you ever prayed, pray now." I did not care whether men, devils or angels heard me. In less than five minutes I was one of the shouting kind and ever since then--some twenty-five years have passed since I have been along this line and I have seen hundreds of people brought to Christ through my ministry and my work and I praise God for that revival.[81]

Atkinson went on to thank Friends for discipling him when a young Christian, especially thanking Samuel Hobson and family for their acceptance of him. He told how the meeting sent a letter to his parents' church, a Methodist Episcopal congregation, that resulted in a license to preach, after which he traveled all around Oregon, Washington, and Idaho holding revival meetings. He ended his remarks with the following assertion: "Only eternity, brother Morris, will reveal the extent of the spiritual influence of that little revival that was held in that little building."[82]

While remaining a conservative, Gurneyite Friend in his convictions and practices, Hobson loved the results of the revival movements he experienced. He was thrilled to see people putting their trust in Jesus and was willing to join in with what the Holy Spirit was doing. Even if he was not exactly on board with the *way* in which people were being led to Jesus, he was glad to see so many find salvation. He was also willing to allow those transformed by the living God to respond in ways contrary to Friends practice, such as engaging in water baptism, if they were truly following their conscience. However, Hobson never personally practiced or endorsed water baptism or communion with the elements. Notice how Morris reported that Uncle William said he was willing to let converts be water baptized if they could find someone else to do it for them. He was not willing. Whether he went and watched the process down at the river side we'll never know. While the "stiff Quaker" had unbent a little, allowing for "reading meetings," spontaneous singing, and altar calls, he remained uneasy with the outward expression of inward spiritual truths.

This first revival at Chehalem Monthly Meeting did much to strengthen the spiritual life of the congregation and added to their numbers several

81. Hobson, "Twentyfifth Anniversary, 8-9.
82. Hobson, "Twentyfifth Anniversary," 8-9.

converts who now needed to learn Quaker ways. Traveling ministers likely helped with discipling, so the burden did not fall completely on resident ministers. Kelsey notes that "during 1879 and 1880 the frontier community was visited by four Friends from Indiana: Elwood C. Siler, a minister, with his companion, Josiah Morris, and Jared P. Binford, a minister, with his companion, Amos H. Hill."[83] The Chehalem Monthly Meeting Minutes note that Siler was a minister of the gospel of Christ and Morris was an elder in good standing. The meeting felt that "their Gospel labors and teaching have indeed been very instructive and encouraging to us."[84] A list of resident ministers from this time in Chehalem Monthly Meeting's history has yet to be discovered, though we see from the meeting minutes that ministers Jesse and Mary Edwards deposited their certificates with Chehalem Monthly Meeting in the fall of 1880 and minister Dr. Elias Jessup's certificate was received soon after.[85] According to Rees, Jessup was "a minister, doctor, statesman, and financier who came with his family from Honey Creek, Iowa" and Jesse and Mary Edwards came with their family "from Plainsfield Indiana. With the accession of these three ministers, all in the prime of active, energetic life, the meeting could not fail to feel a great impetus in aggressive work. Brother and sister Edwards preached the gospel in every church and school-house within a radius of fifteen miles. Mission sabbath-schools were organized and great good was accomplished."[86] Amanda Woodward mentions several resident ministers from before and after the pastoral system was implemented. Some of those listed by Woodward who were contemporary with Hobson included H.J. Minthorn, Martin Cook, Rebecca Lewis, Rebecca Clawson, Albert Dixon, Lindley M. Haworth, Jane B. Votaw, Louisa Painter Round, and Elizabeth Miles.[87] Statistics provided by Stephen Perisho show between six and nine recorded ministers attending Newberg Monthly Meeting in the years 1882 through 1889. There were fifteen in the year 1890, and nine in the year 1891.[88] Certainly, the ministry of both traveling and resident ministers was instrumental in the building up of Chehalem Monthly Meeting.

While the spiritual life of the meeting was robust, the financial resources of the meeting were rather anemic. Most of the members were just starting out in the Grubby End and in those early days had not seen much

83. Kelsey, "Quakerism Beyond the Mississippi," 521.
84. "Chehalem Monthly Meeting Minutes," 27.
85. "Chehalem Monthly Meeting Minutes," 45, 47.
86. Rees, "History of Friends Church," 4.
87. Woodward, "Reminiscences," 2.
88. Perisho, "History of the Newberg Monthly Meeting," 76.

return yet on their investments in land and crops. There was also a certain off-the-cuff approach to church business, both in the formation of committees and in the fiduciary workings of the meeting. As Perisho put it

> the "Minutes" for that day, although somewhat bound, stylistically, give evidence of an informal way of doing business, a certain "ad hocness," if you please, that characterized the Chehalem (Newberg) Monthly Meeting for much of these first fifteen years, and that became less noticeable as the church approached the twentieth century.[89]

Perisho tells how "during the first few years of its existence, the Newberg Monthly Meeting approached its financial matters with a casualness that would appall the modern accountant." He goes on to explain how the Treasurer (David Wood in the first year) often paid routine expenses himself out of his personal funds, as opposed to paying out of funds already collected, and then reported at the next business meeting how much he was owed by members. After his report members were assigned to pay a share of what the Treasurer had already spent, based on their assessed ability to do so. Needless to say, it was difficult to get all the families to contribute their assigned shares. This ad hoc way of dealing with meeting finances continued until the early 1890s when understandable frustration within the finance committee resulted in the change to a subscription plan, which according to Perisho "faintly resembled a budget system."[90] So, these two things, lack of funds and a disorganized approach to the gathering and spending of meeting monies, delayed the building of a meeting house. Since this took place during the gap in Hobson's diary, we don't know how he felt about the delay or what frustrations he might have felt while serving on the finance committee.

Finally, after a few fits and starts enough money was raised, with the help of Siler and Morris soliciting funds from Friends back east, to build a brand-new spacious framed meeting house. The new meeting house was erected near the old moss-covered shack in the summer of 1880 and was apparently in use before the finish work was completed. C.J. Edwards who visited Newberg with his parents Jesse and Mary in late 1880 prior to settling there described how during their trip they "found the Friends meeting house, located on the Portland Road, just opposite Villa road. This building had been in use only a few weeks prior to our arrival. The studding was bare on the inside, having only a roof and rustic floor. Boards were laid on blocks of wood for seats."[91] Amanda and Ezra Woodward also arrived in Newberg

---

89. Perisho, "History of the Newberg Monthly Meeting," 12.
90. Perisho, "History of the Newberg Monthly Meeting," 12–14.
91. Edwards, "Newberg as it was Fifty Years Ago," *Newberg Graphic* (Newberg, OR)

just after the completion of the new meeting house. Amanda's assessment of the building was similar to Edwards's based on her description of

> the new church building, which was the first to be erected in Yamhill County, northeast of Dayton and Lafayette, was located east of the bridge on the south side of the road opposite the Henry Ehret place. The new building had just been inclosed [sic], with rough planks laid on blocks of wood for seats, which were soon replaced by substantial seats, and the pulpit was afterward built by David J. Wood. Several years ago Evangeline Martin and I were wandering around in the college basement and found this old pulpit in the discard, ready to be split up into kindling wood. We could not bear the thought. Too many precious memories clustered around it. As we gazed upon it we could visualize dear old William Hobson giving his earnest messages from behind it: Dr. Elias Jessup holding the people spellbound by his powerful sermons: Dr. H.J. Minthorn, Jesse and Mary Edwards, Martin Cook, and many others so the old pulpit was rescued and placed in the college museum.[92]

The old pulpit constructed by David Wood was used for many years in an "Extemporaneous Speaking Contest," otherwise known as "The Old Pulpit Contest" at what is now George Fox University[93] and currently resides at Newberg Friends Church where it is sometimes still used during worship.

Perisho notes that "when the Quakers first arrived, there was not a single church building on the Dayton—Portland road. When the Chehalem meeting house was actually constructed, it not only captured the Dayton—Portland Record, but was the very first Friends meeting house in the Pacific Northwest, as well."[94] This singular meeting house served the congregation well for about a decade until they outgrew it, after which they met for several years in the lower room of the boys dormitory at Pacific College,[95] otherwise known as the gymnasium, while waiting for the current brick meeting house to be erected.[96] The finish work on the new, larger house was completed shortly after the first Oregon Yearly Meeting which was held in the summer of 1893. Newberg Monthly Meeting officially moved into this new building after the first yearly meeting sessions were completed.

50th Anniversary Progress Edition, April 1939.
- 92. Woodward, "Reminiscences," 2.
- 93. Woodward, "Reminiscences," 2.
- 94. Perisho, "History of the Newberg Monthly Meeting," 19.
- 95. Hobson, "Diaries," reel 1 of 2, 11/24/89.
- 96. Perisho, "History of the Newberg Monthly Meeting," 62–64.

According to the *Newberg Graphic* it cost $15,000 to erect and put the congregation into debt. It took until Fifth Month 1903, to pay off the loan, mainly because of financial obligations to Pacific College.[97]

Unsurprisingly, Hobson was not thrilled with the design of the new, larger house. According to Della Osburn, a long-time member of Newberg Monthly Meeting with whom Perisho spoke, who in turn heard it from her Sunday school teacher, Hobson thought the building plans were too elaborate and the steeple was much too extravagant. "It aroused in him, evidently, the old polemic against 'steeple-houses,' fancy buildings that indicated to seventeenth century Quakers a lack of spiritual life within. However, in keeping with his commitment to speaking the truth without forcing it upon others, Hobson admitted that there was nothing intrinsically evil about a steeple. He reluctantly agreed to a steeple just so long as it didn't house a bell. So, the plans which were drawn up at the request of John Henry Douglas by Pearson and Tate went forward with no more opposition from Hobson."[98] Church historians agree that during the 1880s Chehalem Monthly Meeting absolutely did not lack spiritual life within, regardless of the steeple, but rather took an active interest in three main areas of ministry: education, temperance, and evangelism. These were also areas of personal interest to Hobson and so are pertinent to his story.

EDUCATION, TEMPERANCE, AND EVANGELISM

Providing a solid, guarded Quaker education for the Newberg community was important to Hobson and to Chehalem Monthly Meeting as a whole. They firmly backed the establishment first of the Friends primary school, then the academy, and later the college, but Friends were not the first to establish educational opportunities in Newberg. In her book *From Then 'Til Now: 1879/2015 Schooling in Newberg, Oregon*, Barbara Doyle states that early settler Josiah C. Nelson erected a school building on his acreage as early as 1846. It was probably located near North Valley Road "between what is now Hwy. 219 and Ribbon Ridge Road—pretty much the center of the Chehalem Valley. The school was funded by subscriptions from the neighboring families which included Bailey, Hess, Welsh, Noble and Nelson."[99] After this "the historical record pertaining to Newberg area schools is blank

---

97. "Friends Church Now Free From Debt," *Newberg Graphic* (Newberg, OR) May 22, 1903, https://oregonnews.uoregon.edu/lccn/sn96088233/1903-05-22/ed-1/seq-1/.

98. Perisho, "History of the Newberg Monthly Meeting," 69.

99. Doyle, *From Then 'Til Now*, 3.

for about the next three decades."[100] Classes were organized sporadically for short durations in varied locations throughout the 1850s, 1860s, and 1870s, but as the population in and around Newberg increased more consistent schooling was needed.

Doyle goes on to explain how in 1881 Newberg's first public school building was built on the northeast corner of Main and Illinois streets. It was a typical one room schoolhouse and it opened with a total of thirteen students who were not placed in grades. Horace Cox, a Friend, served as the first teacher.[101] Evangeline Martin, also a Friend, likewise taught public school in the early days. Martin served on the Visiting Committee,[102] a committee appointed by Chehalm Monthly Meeting that was tasked with making sure excellent educational standards were upheld at Friends Pacific Academy. Martin later served on the board of Pacific College for several years until her death in 1928, as recorded in the *Pacific College Oregon [Handbook], 1891–92*.[103]

Later, in 1889 a much larger public school designed to accommodate 200 students was built on the site of present-day Central School which has become the Chehalem Cultural Center, located where Howard Street terminates at Sheridan. N.E. Deskins sold part of his land to the school district for this new school building. The large new school was divided into eight grades, and the building quickly became overcrowded. By 1890, with 603 school age children living in the city limits and about one hundred more in outlying areas, the need for another school building became apparent, however funds were lacking. In 1892 the community decided to remodel the old building to accommodate more students, but now we're moving past any involvement Hobson might have had since he died in 1891.

Doyle reiterates the well-known story that the first continuously functioning school in Newberg was opened by Friends in 1877. This small school was first taught by Maggie Wood, David Wood's wife, and her first classes totaled under twenty children.[104] School was held in her kitchen in less than ideal circumstances. According to C.J. Edwards who visited in 1881, class was still being held in the Wood's kitchen, though taught by Horace Cox, and "there were 10 or 12 students sitting on benches made of rough lumber

---

100. Doyle, *From Then 'Til Now*, 3
101. Doyle, *From Then 'Til Now*, 4–7.
102. Friends Pacific Academy, *Catalogue, 1886-7*, 3.
103. Pacific College, *Pacific College Oregon [Handbook], 1891–92*. See bound volumes of Pacific College catalogues housed in George Fox University Archives for further dates of Martin's service to the institution.
104. Doyle, *From then 'Til Now*, 4, 8–11.

and tables made in a similar manner."[105] Students may have received splinters along with their lessons.

As the first classes of children to attend the Friends school grew older and progressed in their studies, the need for secondary education became apparent and in 1885 Friends Pacific Academy, what we might call a high school today, was organized through the local Chehalem Monthly Meeting. Dr. Henry J. Minthorn served as the first principal[106] and his young nephew, Bertie was the first student enrolled.[107] Later, the need for a next level of education was met when Pacific College was added to the Friends educational menu in 1891. At first the college, now known as George Fox University, was located in the vicinity of the 300 block of College Street where Newberg Friends Church is located today. It was moved to its present site north of First Street and east of Meridian Street by 1893. Newberg Quarterly Meeting assumed responsibility for the college in 1892 and subsequently transferred responsibility to Oregon Yearly Meeting after it was formed in 1893.[108]

Naturally, Hobson was involved in the promotion and support of education in Newberg from the beginning. And, unsurprisingly, it's readily apparent from his diary that he was a supporter of both the public school and the Quaker school in Newberg. Once settled in the Grubby End, Hobson continued to exhibit the habitual interest in learning institutions he had shown at Honey Creek and during his travels. His life-long interest in all things educational was fostered by a family that valued education, early school experiences, teacher training at New Garden Boarding School, and personal experience as a teacher. Hobson served on Chehalem Monthly Meeting's [School] Visiting Committee, as noted in his diary on the 5th of Twelfth Month 1885. From the end of 1885 to First Month 1891, Hobson recorded several visits to both the public school and Friends Pacific Academy. It's extremely likely that he was involved in education in Newberg before 1885, but the gap in his diary from Sixth Month 1878, to Eleventh Month 1885, makes it impossible to know if or how often he was visiting the two schools in Newberg.

Despite ill health the last eighteen months of his life, Hobson continued to take an active interest in the schools. On Second Month 14, 1890, he "Visited Our Schools in afternoon Newberg Both the Academy & Public

105. Edwards, "Newberg as it was Fifty Years Ago," *Newberg Graphic* (Newberg, OR) 50th Anniversary Progress Edition, April 1939.

106. Doyle, *From Then 'Til Now*, 4–12.

107. Kidd, "Hoover: A Rags and Riches Saga," *Newberg Graphic: A Century to Remember: Newberg 1889–1989* (Newberg, OR) 1989 special edition, 64.

108. Perisho, "History of the Newberg Monthly Meeting," 36–40.

School We have the care of many Children & youth The sum of them is about 250." By the 17th of Second Month 1890, he amends this to 270 children. In the spring of 1890, Hobson visited the public school on the 21st of Third Month. Then on the 5th of Fourth Month he preached about the necessity for Christian education during meeting. Very likely when Hobson visited both the public school and Friends Pacific Academy, he was cheerfully given time to speak to the students about spiritual matters, along with listening to lessons and watching presentations. He also attended the opening and closing ceremonies of both schools when he could. Walter C. Woodward, a former Friends Pacific Academy student remembered Hobson fondly: "The intelligent and sympathetic interest manifested in the school by the founder of the settlement was indicative of the attitude of Friends toward education. One of the earliest of the writer's schoolboy recollections is that of Uncle Wm. Hobson visiting the school, always bringing a sack of apples which he happily distributed among the boys and girls."[109] On the 25th of Tenth Month 1890, Hobson subscribed one hundred dollars to the Friends Pacific Academy endowment fund which he was to "keep myself & pay 6 percent therefore [sic] Annually. So 6 dollars will be due the 25 of 10 mo. 1891." Sadly, he did not live long enough to make the first payment, but this shows that he was willing to support the Friend's school financially. Hobson was an avid devotee of education in all its forms not only in theory, but also in practice.

Focused spiritual education was just as important to Hobson and Pacific Northwest Friends, as reading, writing, and arithmetic, or later scientific, and liberal arts instruction at the college level. The Friends school of course wove spiritual instruction and Scripture learning in with other subjects. In those days, even district school classes began with prayer and the Bible was used as part of the curriculum, but a more concentrated effort at learning Scripture, for children and adults alike, could be obtained by attendance at First Day school once a week. Hobson rarely, if ever, missed First Day school. He even attended Sunday school, though he would never call it that, at Methodist and other churches during his travels when there were no Friends meetings close by. At this time study of the Bible was probably quite limited among Friends but, reading and memorizing was a step towards analysis and application. Hobson wasn't just promoting First Day school as a matter of course, but he truly believed that familiarity with the Bible was necessary for healthy spiritual growth to occur.

Goldsmith notes further that when Hobson began regular meetings for worship in the Chehalem Valley there was no question of whether or not to hold First Day school. It would be held, and attendance was expected. The

---

109. Woodward, "Quakerism Beyond the Mississippi," 601.

Planted in a Garden of the Lord   231

first recorded official action taken by Newberg Monthly Meeting concerning the establishment of a First Day school system and the appointment of a First Day school superintendent occurred in Twelfth Month 1886, but as Perisho emphatically notes "in the light of Quaker penchant for Scripture Schools, it would be preposterous to suggest that no Sabbath Day school was organized in the Newberg vicinity until ten years after William Hobson settled in Newberg for the final time."[110] Preposterous indeed, since Hobson recorded in his diary that he habitually attended First Day school beginning in the winter of 1876, just after his return from Iowa.[111] This was back in the days when Chehalem Valley Friends were still meeting in private homes, so it's clear that First Day school was a priority for Hobson from the very beginning. However, organizing the school in the late 1880s was a positive and necessary step since attendance had increased significantly. By Eighth Month 1888, three classes were formed "that were keeping thirty-seven officers and teachers busy in the instruction of an average of 172 pupils."[112] Goldsmith tells how, "in his declining years, he [Hobson] was still attending First Day school conferences, and occasionally addressing the Children [sic] at Newberg Friends Meeting,"[113] showing that Hobson not only attended First Day school, but also held a long-term leadership role in the organization of classes. Hobson's influence on the establishment of a First Day school at Chehalem Monthly Meeting was strong, undeniable, and long lasting.

We now turn to the second main area of ministry embraced by Chehalem Monthly Meeting: temperance. It practically goes without saying that William Hobson was a dyed-in-the wool teetotaler. Growing up in the Society of Friends it was a given that he would avoid alcohol like the plague, and he was likely not even exposed first-hand to its use or evils. Both his family and his Quaker culture of origin regarded the making, selling, or drinking of alcohol as a grievous sin. Friends believed that drinking was not only a waste of money, but that it opened the floodgates on a host of sinful activities including but not limited to, swearing, fighting, domestic violence, adultery, card playing, "entertainments," and other moral degradation.

While at New Garden Boarding School Hobson made a conscious choice to avoid liquor then and in the future. He noted in the autobiographical section of his diary, "And as for drinking what is called Spiritous [sic]

---

110. Perisho, "History of the Newberg Monthly Meeting," 29.
111. Hobson, "Diaries," reel 1 of 2, 12/3/76.
112. Perisho, "History of the Newberg Monthly Meeting," 29–30.
113. Goldsmith, "William Hobson and the Founding of Quakerism in the Pacific Northwest," 281; Hobson, "Diaries," reel 2 of 2, 12/25/70, reel 1 of 2, 1/1/88.

Liquors I never knew the taste of in the raw state."[114] He happily adopted the injunctions against liquor with which he had grown up. His interest in temperance was a life-long thing, though it was not a central part of his mission or calling in life. His interest in education, for example was a much more prevalent concern.

Hobson first mentions attending a temperance meeting while visiting at San Jose on First Month 11, 1871. Later during the journey north to Oregon he noted, "There are many Boarder[s] at this Hotel. All But A few drink drams & smoke cigars Some drink often & Many seem to have a cigars in their mouths much of the time. So it is quite a money trap at this office for Board & lodging Liquors & Cigars."[115] And just a few days later he preached the good news to rough characters drinking drams in the inn on Scott's Mountain. Hobson was pleased when the hotel they stopped at the next day didn't have a "drinking bar." A few months later on Fifth Month 11, 1871, Hobson noted while traveling down the Willamette,

> My mind is deeply thoughtful this morning because of the bondage under which so many are now living. The world under the influence of fashion & Pride Suffers much; Some by the use of Oaths Taking our Makers name in vain Some by the use of strong drink & Tobacco Some by following fashions for show rather than for utility. And for the Religious world that they are so generally under bondage to more or less of Types and Fig[ments] instead of that freedom which they might enjoy were they Enlightened to see fully that glorious liberty there is to be attained to & enjoyed in Christ. Who was given for our Salvation & to set us free from every yoke of bondage. Enabling us to live in this world to the Lords glory & for the happiness of man.[116]

Later still during the same journey, this time while waiting in Portland to catch the steamer back to San Francisco, he wrote on Sixth Month 2, 1871, "It makes me feel sorry to see men using tobacco other than as medicine. And a great many Smoke cigars and pipes and some chew. And more some drink dram[s] One man who lodged in same room where I did was sick & vomiting says he is drunk got among his friends and got too much whiskey."[117] On the train traveling back to Iowa Seventh Month 6, 1871, Hobson expressed regret over miners who were addicted to tobacco and alcohol noting

---

114. Hobson, "Diaries," reel 2 of 2, 1/21/1868, 42 (Hobson's Numbering).
115. Hobson, "Diaries," reel 2 of 2.
116. Hobson, "Diaries," reel 2 of 2.
117. Hobson, "Diaries," reel 2 of 2.

and sorrowful I feel for many [miners] who are already in the habit of using much Tobacco & Strong drink until I fear unless timely met with true friends who in love & sympathy for them should assist them to live a more temperate and safer life and let intoxicating drinks alone lest they go down under this habit they like many other have done. In less than 20 years more thousands of these. [illegible] dram drinkers yearning strength to [illegible]strong But in less than 20 years [ye] will lye I the drunkards grave. I do not say you will all die drunkards But I do say that unless you leave off drinking that I expect more than one for every 12 of you will. Let the Query eby [sic] in your hearts severally is it I. And may the good Shepherd follow you up by his grace manifesting to your hearts the necessity of a better example. And may Some of you this day be induced here after to refrain [from smoking and drinking].[118]

These life experiences merely deepened Hobson's belief in the evils of alcohol and tobacco. He wrote a short statement emphasizing his convictions at the end of his 1871 diary as follows, "Corrupting Influences Drinking, Idleness, Using Tobacco. Plays Musical instruments Novel reading. And the selling of Novels and corrupting papers And all whatsoever That has not for its object the benefit of man These ought to be met by meekly instructing those who thus oppose themselves. So as to answer that of God in man."[119] This was an idea he was likely considering conveying in a sermon since a very similar undated phrase written, almost word for word appears towards the beginning of his next diary notebook, probably jotted down sometime in early 1872. The only meaningful change to the above phrase was the addition of lottery sales to the list of corrupting influences. After returning to Honey Creek Hobson noted attending temperance meetings from time to time during the years 1873 and 1875.

Once in Oregon Hobson recorded his attendance at several temperance meetings, in 1877, 1885, 1889, and 1890. After a meeting at which the national WCTU lecturer gave a rousing speech, Hobson wrote on Tenth Month 6, 1889, that "On hearing her. [sic] I am confirmed that the time has now come for temperance people to vote one way all together, and for those who will go for putting away the Liquor Traf[fic] in intoxicating drinks." On another occasion, Tenth Month 20, 1889, he attended a temperance meeting at lunchtime and again at three o'clock, but decided that he was too old and tired to go back for the evening meeting. Newberg Monthly Meeting must have been holding a special temperance conference.

118. Hobson, "Diaries," reel 2 of 2.
119. Hobson, "Diaries," reel 2 of 2.

One might think that alcohol use was not a big problem in Newberg due to the proportionately large population of Friends. However, in the early days Grubby End Friends experienced some unpleasantness associated with the imbibing of spirits. That William Everest ran a saloon at his racetrack just east of town and that the Newberg area had a long history of liquor fueled carousing has already been established. In addition, according to Perisho, "the [Newberg] area was plagued with repeated attempts on the part of liquor interests, to set up saloons just outside the city limits. Not even the local west-end drug store was above suspicion." Perisho also relates a story written by Walter C. Woodward, son of Ezra and Amanda Woodward, in a lost paper called "Son of the Pacific Border" about how drunken men were in the habit of racing their horses on the road that ran along his family's orchard. One time, an intoxicated man miscalculated the curve in the road and his horse jumped the Woodward's rail fence throwing him in the process. Woodward noted drily that the man got up shaken and sobered, and that he as an observer was also sobered.[120] Alcohol was definitely a problem and in the minds of Newberg Friends temperance was the answer.

However, the movement was just beginning to gain momentum towards the end of Hobson's life. Perisho points out that officially Newberg Monthly Meeting was not heavily involved in the temperance movement at the end of the nineteenth century. A standing temperance committee was not even established until 1892, the year after Hobson's death, though the meeting did send delegates to the State Temperance Alliance in 1883 and 1885. Monthly temperance meetings were held First Day afternoons beginning in the Fall of 1880. Amanda Woodward described how "on one Sabbath of each month we took big baskets of dinner to meeting, and the whole day was spent at the church. In the afternoon enthusiastic temperance meetings were held, and right here may be discovered the foundation of the strong prohibition sentiment which has always characterized this neighborhood."[121] By 1890 an ad hoc committee was tasked with the job of working with other area churches to gather and pool funds in order to combat Newberg area liquor interests. However, Perisho notes that "as a rule, commitment to the elimination of intemperance was an individual matter, not a corporate one." In this he may be correct, but there is no denying the powerful influence Friends had whether as like-minded individuals or in a corporate way.

---

120. Perisho, "History of the Newberg Monthly Meeting," 41.

121. Perisho, "History of the Newberg Monthly Meeting," 42; Woodward, "Reminiscences," 4.

Perisho also points out that several influential friends were active in the temperance movement. Rebecca Clawson, as already mentioned, was president of Portland's first WCTU, her daughter Elizabeth White served as the Vice President of the Oregon WCTU, Evangeline Martin served as the President of the Yamhill County WCTU in 1887, and Mary Edwards served as the district and state organizer of the Oregon WCTU, was the WCTU national delegate from Oregon in 1885 and 1887, and "the founder of unions in Dayton, Amity, LaFayette, Dallas, and Corvallis, among others."[122] Clearly Friends in Newberg had considerable influence in matters of temperance, with the involvement of these and other key members of the congregation in the temperance movement at local, state, and national levels. The Newberg WCTU was largely controlled by Newberg Monthly Meeting and even the children were asked to sign pledges not to drink liquor.[123] Quaker influence was certainly brought to bear on civil government when it came time to make the town of Newberg an official municipality. Amanda Woodward explained how

> when the town was incorporated a temperance clause was put in the charter, prohibiting the sale of intoxicating drink. A saloon was started just west of town, and a "gallon house" across the river, and a drug store down on Main Street was selling drinks. They were all labored with, but to no avail until the temperance people employed detectives and caught them. There were saloons in most, if not all the nearby towns, and not a single newspaper in the county, excepting the Newberg Graphic, raised its voice against them. The editor of the Graphic [Ezra Woodward, Amanda's husband] stood alone, so far as editors were concerned, but he decided to stand by his principles if he had to close up shop. He didn't have to, but the saloons did. The stand Friends took in temperance, and their interest in education and public enterprises, have help to make Newberg what it is today.[124]

At the quarterly meeting twenty-fifth anniversary celebration Jesse Edwards stood and shared that "Newberg was the first and is now the only town of its size in the state having absolute prohibition under the law. Hon. George H. Himes, the Oregon Historical Society worker told me just recently that the first distillery in this state was located right down here near the river on the banks of the Chehalem creek. It is a strange co-incidence that

---

122. Perisho, "History of the Newberg Monthly Meeting," 43–44.
123. Perisho, "History of the Newberg Monthly Meeting," 44–45.
124. Woodward, "Reminiscences,," 4.

the first distillery and the first prohibition should be here in this town."[125] Newberg remained a dry town well into the 1960s. It's supremely ironic that Newberg is now at the center of the burgeoning Chehalem Valley wine industry with numerous vineyards and wineries bringing significant trade and tourism dollars into the area.

This brings us to the last area of Newberg Monthly Meeting influence we will explore, that of evangelism. Since his earliest days the heart of an evangelist beat within William Hobson's breast. How remarkable that he witnessed to his fellow school children even before he turned ten, so that still as they teased him, they recognized his calling and predicted he would become a preacher. This was a thing he was not quite ready to own up to publicly, but secretly he had already embraced his vocation. His tender heart and the spiritual education he received from his grandparents, parents, and the congregation at Deep Creek guided him in the calling he felt to preach God's word and to live a godly, sanctified life as an example to others. He grew into his calling through Bible study and obedience to the word of God, through the influence of books like *George Fox's Journal* and *Barclay's Apology*, through repentance and holy living, by praying out loud in secluded places, and, later, by speaking to gathered meetings as the Holy Spirit led. At Honey Creek he was recorded as a minister showing that the community there recognized his vocation. And while traveling with Bevan and Bond his eyes were opened to the beauty of spiritual renewal and revival. Even before this his consistent message to Friends at Honey Creek included a call to trust Jesus Christ as Lord and Savior. This desire to lead others to Jesus was also behind his calling to the Pacific Northwest.

Hobson wasn't called merely to create an insular colony of Friends at Newberg, but to go as a missionary to people of all walks of life and share the good news that Jesus had died for the forgiveness of their sins, resulting in eternal life and reconciliation with the Father. As Perisho puts it, Hobson exuded a "settled commitment to the gospel. [His] original vision extended far beyond those who were Friends already, to include men and women in the West who had already lost touch with the ultimate significance of spiritual values. And it was in keeping with this concern that one of the major themes of early Newberg Monthly Meeting history was evangelical outreach."[126] But it even went beyond "spiritual values." Hobson genuinely wanted people to come to trust in Jesus Christ as their Lord and Savior and to introduce them to the transforming power of the Holy Spirit through the Baptism of the Spirit. Several sections in his diary prove that he was not

---

125. Hobson, "Twentyfifth Anniversary," 9.
126. Perisho, "History of the Newberg Monthly Meeting," 25.

just interested in spiritual things, but deeply believed that the only way to the Father was through the Son and that it was important to share this with others in order that their souls might be saved. He felt so deeply about this he encouraged Friends from back east to join him in his Kingdom work at Newberg. He wanted to include his spiritual family in the amazing things he knew God was about to do there.

How do we know what Hobson really believed about the person of Jesus Christ, about the Holy Spirit, and about the Father? Did he believe in the Trinity? Did he hold traditional evangelical views on Jesus's deity and humanity? And what did he believe about the death and resurrection of Jesus? What did he believe about the Bible and sin? First, it's clear that Hobson believed Jesus was both divine and human from a notation he made Eleventh Month 21, 1873:

> Notes taken from the Ministry of Elwood Osborne Christs [sic] body from the virgin not corruptible & not proper to call him human (quoting George Fox for it) yet was made flesh, to wit the Word Is now at the right hand of God. Will come again. Will be a general judgement [sic] But I, Wm Hobson, do not well see any impropriety in speaking of him as having humanity as well as Divinity since he was made of the seed of David and Abraham according to the flesh Made a little lower than the Angles for the suffering of death. Took on him the Nature of Angels but: the seed of Abraham and made in all points like unto his brethren yet without sin.[127]

Around the same time he noted his belief that little children who cannot yet understand what sin is are automatically admitted to heaven, indicating that he did believe in the existence of sin and the need for a Savior as follows:

> It is a plain Scripture that Jesus owns them [little children] as of the King[dom] . . . of God I suppose every infant is through Christ a member of the Kingdom [here written in the space between two sentences in larger letters "Jesus died for all mankind"] of God are innocent & clean through Christ before they go astray We don't believe any such go to hell. We believe Christs [sic] death covers their case as well as ours who have sinned. And he is the propitiation for our sins; and not for ours only: But also for the sins of the whole world 1 John 2.2. Infants and little children are a part of mankind and of the world. And at birth

---

127. Hobson, "Diaries," reel 2 of 2.

> and until they wilfully [sic] disobey God certainly are stand acceptable with the Father through Christs [sic] offering made.[128]

Notice how he writes that Jesus died for all and for the sins of the whole world, citing 1 John 2:2.

He also indicated that the Father sent Jesus to die so humans who trust in Jesus can be made right with the Father. Hobson writes in several different places in his diary about the need to trust Jesus for salvation, pointing out that

> Jesus is the way we enter into the Holiest of all. He has bought us with his precious blood therefore we ought to glorify Him and hold his name above every other name, for Christ is all in all. Other foundation can no man lay;" Therefore we should take heed how we build there upon . . . My objector brings to view the practices of the Apostles. But it will not do to build on those practices wherein the Apostles were not redeemed from Judaism. As an evidence that the Apostles had weaknesses, it is recorded that Peter was to be blamed." But many of us have more failings than Peter. Our faith and building should be founded on the Rock: for other foundation can no man lay than that is laid which is Jesus Christ. Paul, who was the Apostle to the Gentiles said Christ sent me not to baptize, but to preach the gospel . . . They will then preach that the Father sent the Son to redeem us from all iniquity, and from the curse of the law.[129]

Here he has indicated that Jesus has all authority in heaven and on earth.

Hobson expressed his deep conviction that Jesus is the only way of salvation even more clearly on Eleventh Month 12, 1872. Shortly before surrendering to the call to go west, he was reminded during a wakeful time in the night that "through Christ salvation is free."[130]

Later in life, he approved a message given by a minister at Newberg Monthly Meeting, showing that his views had not changed as follows:

> Services by George N Heartly All the above will & lively Seeming to be with the Lords [sic] authority And all on the same line & agreeing together Proving that Man is both Spirit & flesh that he never ceases to exhist [sic] somewhere We are only saved by Jesus Christ By what He has done for us without us & what he doth in us We believing Repenting & Obeying This That He the Savior give us reliable evidence by Spirit of our standing before

---

128. Hobson, "Diaries," undated notation towards beginning of reel 2 of 2.
129. Hobson, "Diaries," undated notation towards beginning of reel 2 of 2.
130. Hobson, "Diaries," reel 2 of 2.

God. And if we have become, & are now the Lords [sic] accepted
Children We know it. Because we have the evidence of it His
Sprit being with our Sprit that we are the children of God.[131]

Several other such passages could be quoted here, but this seems sufficient to prove that Hobson believed in Jesus Christ as his Lord and Savior. These passages also prove that Hobson believed in the Trinity, in the dual deity and humanity of Christ, and in the sinful nature of humankind. These were core convictions he held his entire life.

In true orthodox, Gurneyite, evangelical style, it was not enough for Hobson to merely hold onto belief in Jesus for himself. He was compelled to share the good news of Jesus Christ with others and as a Friends minister of the mid–to–late nineteenth century he was in a good position to do so. As early as Twelfth Month 2, 1871, while at San Jose Hobson showed a concern for spreading the gospel noting, "At Brother Jesse's Waked before 2 did not sleep much afterwards My thoughts were nearly taken up dwelling upon The Kingdom of God & feeling desirous that the people should be in it now in this life and this day."[132] On Sixth Month 4, 1872, while in Portland, Hobson wrote favorably about a sermon delivered by a Methodist minister speaking on missions during which, "He spake very well Spake of his own [calling] to This Coast Commencing 25 years ago of the Missionary Spirit in general. It is the spreading the gospel. By sending Ministers round among the people. The Bible among them. Living the life of a Christian before man so as to influence them to Into the fold of Christ."[133] Once safely back at Honey Creek he made several remarks, on Ninth Month 17, 1873, about another inspiring sermon he heard, this time from a Quaker minister.

> at Honey Creek Heard a great Sermon from Wm. Haworth from the Text Simon son of James lovest thou me more than these (Fishes) He brought it home to us individually whether Christ was not asking us whether we love him more than our farms our cattle our hogs our property of [whatever] kind more than him. Said these things were needful and he did not want to be under[stood] as finding fault for having and acquiring property But it was right to do so and to love these things by which we have a lawful and honest living But the question is to each one of us Do we love these things more than Christ. If we love Christ most we will serve him first. Now we are known by the fruit which

---

131. Hobson, "Diaries," sample of a service from 1890 with no month, day 13, reel 1 of 2.
132. Hobson, "Diaries," reel 2 of 2.
133. Hobson, "Diaries," reel 2 of 2.

we bear. And it is plainly seen that many neglect much of their *religious duty for the saving of Souls* and are busy attending first to the lesser matters of providing first for the bo[dy] and thus are making it manifest that they love some thing else more than Christ. Because they omit his work to do theirs [Italics added].[134]

Later still, on Fifth Month 1, 1887, he noted, "Rose at 4 a.m. And believe I have arisen in the Strength of the Lord for his work to go forth in his power to direct all to the Savior who is the light of the world." Hobson was called to share the good news of Jesus Christ with both Friends and strangers, not only through his preaching, but through the example of his life lived in obedience to Jesus.

True to Friends doctrine Hobson believed that Baptism by the Holy Spirit was more important than water baptism and that physical communion with the elements was also unnecessary. In fact, these two ordinances were to him but an empty form without the accompanying immersion in or communion with the Holy Spirit, and therefore superfluous. He also believed that no one could come to Jesus without the aid of the Holy Spirit. The instruction of children at a young age in the things of God was important to Hobson and in one passage in his diary written in the early 1870s he shares some of his views about baptism and the Spirit in a rough draft of an article to be published in the *Christian Worker* and the *Friends Review*. Here is one paragraph of that article:

> I believe it is the duty of Christian Parents and also of the Church to acknowledge this Birthright [of children] to the kingdom of God and extend a diligent and fostering care to these lambs of God: so many, as come by duty under our charge to feed and to shepherd that they go not astray. *They should however be taught very early the necessity of experiencing that of being born again– born of the spirit cleansed and made new in Christ by the operation of his Spirit upon them as the[y] willingly submit themselves unto Him.* [Italics provided][135]

Hobson writes with the same sentiment in several different passages in his diary. He does not address the Lord's Supper as much in his diary, merely indicating on Seventh Month 25, 1875, that "a few selections from History of those who used neither Bread nor wine or Baptism with water as Church rites Christians of different centuries down to us, who held that The [illegible] rites which were probably preached considerably in some way by the

---

134. Hobson, "Diaries," reel 2 of 2, 9/17/1873.
135. Hobson, "Diaries," reel 2 of 2, undated near beginning of reel.

disciples for a time. And probably even in the infancy of the Church only a little or not at all by some. That these rites were only to continue for a time." He expands on this thought about the "bread and wine," with an extensive list in his memorandum of other Christian groups which historically did not practice communion.[136] But it's safe to say he saw physical communion in the same light as water baptism. Neither Honey Creek nor Chehalem Monthly Meeting practiced communion with the elements, further proof of their pointlessness to Hobson. Another diary section from the early 1870s gives scriptural backing to Hobson's belief that the ordinances have passed away and the current work of the Spirit is more important that outward gestures,

> for as many of you as have been baptised [sic] into Christ, have put on Christ As many of you as have been baptized with water have put on water. This is the difference: one is of the Spirit and the other of the flesh. I do not find that God sent any to baptize with water but John the Baptist, and his was a shadow of the holy baptism. John buried the bodies of those who received his baptism with water. So ought we to be buried with Christ. John was sent before to lead to Christ John said to his disciples and the jews [sic] : "Ye yourselves bear me witness that I said I am not the Christ But that I am sent before him." "He must increase, but I must decrease." John did not want his baptism increased. There are some now trying to increase John's baptism but it is Christ's baptism that purifies the heart; But the natural man receiveth not the things of the Spirit of God for they are foolishness unto him; neither can he know them for they are spiritually discerned. [see Gal 3:27, John 3:28, John 3:30, 1 Cor 2:14][137]

Around the same time he notes, "God is a Spirit No man can say Jesus is Lord but by the Holy Ghost [see 1 Cor 12:3]."[138] He kept this viewpoint his entire life writing on Tenth Month 26, 1887, "Christs [sic] Church built on the revelation of Jesus Christ by Spirit to our Spirit[s]," and on Second Month 2, 1890, "Attended meeting [I] Preached Christ & his Spiritual Baptism for salvation." Several other passages from his diary and from his memorandum book could be cited to show over and over again his conviction that Baptism by the Holy Spirit led a person to salvation in Jesus Christ, not water baptism, which to him was an obsolete and meaningless practice, as was communion.

---

136. Hobson, "Memorandum," 6–10.
137. Hobson, "Diaries," reel 2 of 2, undated near beginning of reel.
138. Hobson, "Diaries," reel 1 of 2, undated near beginning of reel.

All of Hobson's convictions rested on a firm bedrock of Scripture. Hobson believed the Bible was living, authentic, and authoritative. A few notations from his diary will be sufficient to show his love and respect for Scripture. At some point in the early 1870s he wrote, "Believe, and do as the Holy Bible Teaches. In the Bible we are taught to obey Christ; And that means happiness and Salvation is in; and by him."[139] While in the Walla Walla area he noted, "I have had a few intervals through the day in which I richly enjoyed reading Having both my Bible and Browns small concordance with me. Now the work is over for to day I have some more time to freshen up some of my store of knowledge of the Scriptures, feeling After and moving in the will of God. Indeed I feel that I walk with him to day."[140] Later in life while at Newberg he noted one First Day on Fifth Month 16, 1886, "Attended Meeting Preached from the words first Seek the Kingdom of God [see Matt 6:33]." On the first microfilm reel of his diary an undated notebook full of Scripture references and verses written by Hobson is headed by microfilmer Edward P. Thatcher as "Sermon Notes," which is not entirely accurate. Hobson was obviously reading and studying Scripture during the week and it almost certainly came out in his sermons, but he did not prepare specific notes or speeches. Remember, Quaker ministers of this time relied entirely on the movement of the Spirit for what to say, or even for direction on whether or not to speak. These several pages of Scripture notations show only that they had meaning for him and are not necessarily an indication of what he preached about. Regardless, Hobson's diaries show he held an orthodox, Gurneyite, evangelical view of Scripture.

Hobson held strong convictions and he lived them. Newberg Monthly Meeting as a whole held the same convictions and also lived them. The majority of Friends joining the Hobsons at Newberg from the Midwest were also orthodox, Gurneyite, evangelical Quakers. But the congregation was not just made up of Friends transferring their certificates from meetings back east. The early revival added a significant number of convincements and there was a steady influx of non-Quakers into the congregation over the years until the first of many revivals led by John Henry Douglas in the winter of 1890 and 1891 brought even larger numbers into the fold. Perisho includes a helpful chart in Appendix A of his paper that gives detailed statistics for Newberg Monthly Meeting from 1878 to 1893. The chart shows an increase in membership by request of thirty persons and by certificate of thirty-two persons in the year 1879, a roughly equal amount. This was a result of the early spontaneous revival. The numbers of convincements are small the next

---

139. Hobson, "Diaries," reel 1 of 2, undated near beginning of reel.
140. Hobson, "Diaries," reel 2 of 2, 5/5/1872.

few years, with only three requesting membership from 1880 to 1884 and twenty-nine accepted by transfer of certificate. However, in 1885 sixty-four joined by request and only sixteen by certificate. This may have had something to do with, as John H. Rees reported, "Samuel Lloyd, a minister, from Berkely, Kansas, and Mahlon Stubbs his companion, [holding] a series of meetings lasting two weeks. His [Lloyd's]preaching was greatly blessed of the Lord in many convertions [sic], and the upbuilding of believers in the most Holy Faith."[141] Following this in a three year span from 1886 to 1890, seventy-three persons joined by request and one-hundred-twenty-six joined by certificate. The years 1890 and 1891 ushered in a large number of new converts largely due to the efforts of Douglas. The chart shows fifty-three convincements in 1891 and ninety-eight in 1892, truly remarkable numbers. On the other hand, growth by certificate during that time, though not insignificant was considerably less at sixty-nine in 1890 and forty-six in 1891. By the time Hobson died in 1891, membership totaled 510, an increase of roughly 400 members since 1878 (a few by birth), and only about a hundred more transfers of membership than members by request.[142] The numbers do not lie. Newberg Monthly Meeting was invested in evangelism.

According to Perisho, the members of Newberg Monthly Meeting played a significant part in attracting new converts, but a series of traveling ministers played a bigger part. Most likely the congregation exuded a steady influence of the gospel truth which attracted their neighbors and traveling ministers "reeled them in" so to speak. Members of the congregation at Newberg would then be responsible for discipling new believers after traveling ministers moved on. Traveling ministers were well cared for and appreciated by Newberg Monthly Meeting as much needed support in their ministry.

Several members of Newberg Monthly Meeting were themselves liberated for service in different areas of the Pacific Northwest and California, including Jesse and Mary Edwards, Elias Jessup, Elkanah S. Craven, Rebecca Clawson, and William Hobson. This outreach resulted in the planting of several new meetings all across the region, which later led to formation of quarterly meetings, and eventually Oregon Yearly Meeting, the predecessor of Northwest Yearly Meeting of Friends. A formal Evangelistic Committee was formed at Chehalem Monthly Meeting in 1883, but a Missionary Committee wasn't established until much later after Hobson's death.[143] This isn't to say that missions were not important to the congregation. In fact, Hobson

---

141. Rees, "History of Friends Church," 5.

142. Perisho, "History of the Newberg Monthly Meeting," 76, see chart for statistical information.

143. Perisho, "History of the Newberg Monthly Meeting," 15, 26–29.

mentioned taking several bushels of apples to a neighbor to be dried for "the Alaska Mission," on Tenth Month 1, 1889, and noted that "Elwood Weesner & wife at meeting to day from The Alaska Mission," on Third Month 1, 1890. He also mentioned taking up a collection after meeting on Eleventh Month 9, 1890, for his cousin Abel Bond to do a little tract distribution. The congregation gave $14.50 so Bond could "go to the Sound & to Vancouver's Island & back," as Hobson put it the next day. These were likely only two examples of several opportunities to support missions in those days.

TRAVELING IN THE MINISTRY

Hobson mostly traveled locally after moving to Oregon, though he did take two longer trips in 1888. It seems that his focus at this time was mainly on building up Chehalem Monthly Meeting. He was also getting older. In the fall of 1886, Hobson noted in his diary a couple of day trips to nearby Middleton, a small preparative meeting started by Jesse and Mary Edwards about seven miles northeast of Newberg. He may have been visiting to see if they were ready for monthly meeting status, for they were established as a monthly meeting in 1887.[144] During the last half of Sixth Month 1887, Hobson described a ten–day round trip to Alder Monthly Meeting in Wallowa County, Oregon in the far northeastern part of the state. He visited this remote congregation which had just recently been established as a monthly meeting with the intention of inviting them to join Middleton, Rock Lake (in Washington Territory), and Newberg Monthly Meeting in forming a quarterly meeting. He took the train from Portland to La Grande then the stage on to Wallowa where he lodged with Friends. After visiting families in the Wallowa Valley he returned home with the good news that Alder Friends felt clear to form a quarterly meeting with the other Friends meetings in the region.[145] Later in the fall of that same year, Hobson visited the Rock Lake Settlement in eastern Washington Territory. Rock Lake had been established as a monthly meeting in Fourth Month 1887. This time Hobson was gone for just under a month. While at Rock Lake he held appointments and visited families. Hobson didn't record a purpose for the visit in his diary, but it's clear he went to speak with Rock Lake Friends about forming a quarterly meeting. With all meetings in unity a request was sent to Honey Creek Quarterly Meeting back in Iowa, which was approved with a good will. Newberg Quarterly Meeting was officially established on Eleventh

---

144. Hobson, "Diaries," reel 1 of 2, 10/31/86, 11/21/86; Rees, "History of Friends Church," 7.

145. Hobson, "Diaries," reel 1 of 2, 6/13/1887–25/1887, 6/27/1887.

Month 25, 1887,[146] about nine years after Chehalem Monthly Meeting was given monthly meeting status.

Hobson's last expeditions consisted of two long trips very close together: a visit to Iowa in the late summer of 1888, during which he attended Iowa Yearly Meeting, and a visit to San Jose Friends on Iowa Yearly Meeting business, in the fall and early winter of 1888. Hobson was able to take the train directly from Newberg to Des Moines, Iowa, arriving in four days, even though the train was delayed by a car wreck as it was entering the Blue Mountains. He attended the State Fair at Des Moines and then traveled on to Oskaloosa for Iowa Yearly Meeting sessions where he was happy to see many old friends. After yearly meeting sessions, he spent considerable time at Honey Creek visiting with friends and family and appointing meetings. He also attended Honey Creek Quarterly Meeting and likely gave a report about Friends in the Pacific Northwest. In all Hobson spent seven weeks in Iowa. His return trip home took six days since the train was delayed again by a wreck, this time near Yellowstone.[147] The time saved and relatively comfortable travel conditions, as compared to the days when the train must be caught in San Jose, were considerable.

Though it's only hinted at in his diary, Hobson was tasked with a delicate mission by Iowa Yearly Meeting leadership having to do with the former Iowa Yearly Meeting Presiding Clerk, Joel Bean. Unbiased information on Joel Bean is hard to come by. Most evangelical Friends publications ignore the fact he existed, while the publications of other Quakers hail him as a spiritual hero. Thomas M. King explains certain hard to dispute facts concerning Joel Bean, based on Bean's diaries. According to King, Bean served Iowa Yearly Meeting as presiding clerk for eleven terms spanning 1867 to 1878, except for 1872 when he was visiting in England. He and his wife Hannah, both recorded ministers, traveled to Hawaii in the ministry, as well as England, Rhode Island, and other destinations in New England. However, they were opposed to the revival sweeping through Iowa Yearly Meeting for several reasons. Like Hobson, they did not approve of the widespread changes to worship that the revival brought, preferring the traditional unprogrammed mode of worship. However, unlike Hobson they were opposed to revivalist theology, especially the idea of instant justification and sanctification upon belief in Jesus Christ. Bean was also troubled by the doctrine that only the "saved" received the Holy Spirit. Bean believed that the "inner light" was in all people, just waiting to be tapped into. He wrote several articles, the most famous of which were "The Issue" in which he described the tensions in Iowa

---

146. Rees, "History of Friends Church," 8; Hobson, "Diaries," reel 1 of 2, 11/25/87.
147. Hobson, "Diaries," reel 1 of 2, 8/29/1888–10/16/1888.

Yearly Meeting from his perspective and "The Light Within" in which he expounded on his unorthodox view of "The Light."

What happened next is a little muddied by one-sided reporting, but in fairness to Bean, he was giving voice to objections many Friends in Iowa held at the time. Iowa revivalists who believed Bean was standing in the way of the work of the Holy Spirit and denying the work of Christ on the cross could not tolerate his views. Because he spoke up and held his ground, Bean was soundly thrashed in Friends publications by fervent revivalist ministers like Dougan Clark and David B. Updegraff. Some merely considered him unsound, while others went so far as to say he was trying to revive the old Hicksite heresy. His revivalist peers certainly believed he did not preach the full gospel. As King puts it "as a Quaker leader, Joel sought to define and limit Christian Evangelicalism and enthusiasm of Quakers and outsiders who were new to Quakerism."[148] To this day the spiritual descendants of Quakers who did not embrace the evangelical revival believe Joel Bean was persecuted by revivalist Friends and by them forcefully driven out of Iowa Yearly Meeting. Perhaps this view has some merit, for Evangelical Friends barely acknowledge Bean existed. Louis T. Jones in his definitive history *Quakers of Iowa* mentions Joel Bean only once in an endnote as a member of a committee formed to visit Friends at Harper's Ferry who were not acting peaceably.[149] That he was not recognized by Jones for his long service as clerk of Iowa Yearly Meeting shows how Bean was persona non grata to revivalist Friends. Self-proclaimed "mystical" Rufus Jones, who did not participate in evangelical Quakerism, described Bean in retrospect as having a "beautiful character," a "saintly soul," and as a "favored Minister of the Gospel."[150] Obviously, there was a sharp theological division in Iowa Yearly Meeting.

King tells how the Beans decided not to prolong the fight against Iowa revivalists and thought it best to move out of state. They arrived in San Jose California in 1882 hoping to put the conflict behind them and were welcomed by Friends there with open arms. It had been touch and go as to whether their home Springdale Monthly Meeting (Iowa) would issue them a certificate of removal in good standing, but in the end, it was granted. Unfortunately, the Iowa unpleasantness followed them to San Jose in short duration. Honey Creek Quarterly Meeting wrote to Friends at San Jose warning them about Bean's unsound beliefs. By 1885 the small congregation at San Jose had split into Morse Street Friends (Santa Clara), who later became the independent Friends College Park Association, and Stockton

---

148. King, *History of San Jose Quakers*, 41–72.
149. Jones, *Quakers of Iowa*, 195, 324.
150. Jones, *Later Periods of Quakerism, Vol. 1I*, 931.

Street Friends (San Jose), who were loyal to Iowa Yearly Meeting and were later made a monthly meeting under Pasadena Quarterly Meeting (Evangelical Friends) in 1889.

So, how was Hobson involved in all this? While in Iowa during the summer of 1888 Hobson was asked by Honey Creek Quarterly Meeting to find out firsthand what was going on with Friends in San Jose, determine if either meeting was ready for monthly meeting status, and report his findings back to them.[151] Hobson was probably appraised of Honey Creek's reservations about the Beans by the quarterly meeting, but he weighed the evidence carefully. He had read Bean's article "The Issue" while in Iowa just after yearly meeting and before Honey Creek Quarterly Meeting met. He had also read some British commentary on Bean's work which presumably defended his views and some American works which did not. He jotted down the need to think on this carefully. After he arrived in San Jose, he read several articles from the *Friends Review* and the *Christian Worker* which likely spoke against Bean and then he read Bean's article "The Light Within." Hobson seemed troubled by the conflicting viewpoints and took his responsibility to report back to Honey Creek seriously.[152] He had not yet made up his mind one way or the other before visiting Friends at San Jose.

There must have been some sympathy between Hobson and Bean, since they both preferred the traditional form of Quietist Friends worship over revivalist innovations and the pastoral system. Also, Bean stayed with the Hobsons on a visit to Oregon in the fall of 1887, according to a short entry in Bean's diary.[153] Hobson makes no mention of the visit and there is no way to know what the men talked about. After visiting with the Beans in San Jose and attending Stockton Meeting and Morse Street Meeting several times each Hobson felt he had enough information to report back to Honey Creek Quarterly Meeting. On Twelfth Month 12, 1888, Hobson recorded that Bean's Morse Street congregation was in favor of applying to Honey Creek for monthly meeting status and they hoped to be called Santa Clara Monthly Meeting. Hobson was favorably impressed by Bean's meeting, as it was called locally. He recorded his observations while beginning the return trip to Oregon on the cars as follows:

> Went into their meeting house [Santa Clara] for it was not locked. I reckon about 75 persons could be seated possibly [sic] 100 by Crowding. All the floor is [fixed] the room carpeted is furnished with Chairs A Stove stands near the middle of the

151. King, *History of San Jose Quakers*, 60, 72–73, 97–136.
152. Hobson, "Diaries," reel 1 of 2, 9/13/1888, 12/4/1888.
153. King, *History of San Jose Quakers*, 144.

room & a large table in front of where ministers commonly occupy with a large Book Lying on the table I did open it but I should not hesitated had I been impressed with a duty thereto: But My Master was with me; and with my friend there manifestly in vocal service with joy in serving him. Bro. David came to this meeting. came in after it was near half out; Heard Joel Bean Preach a short sermon. & some words from several others said a few words himself An Open Library of Friends Books are open to view in this Meeting house. A Library which I looked over joyfully Because of its variety of authors & of its rareness. Here a little body of valuable friends mostly in easy walking distance of their own Meeting house large enough to make a Monthly Meeting of. I would not know where to find a truer sample of genuine Quakerism then I believe to be in this place And I believe Lord amonst [sic] Friends. I have tryed [sic] to write plainly in their behalf to honey Creek Monthly & Quarterly Meeting on their behalf. I have spent near two days in a long letter as b[e]st I could to suit the occasion. Have mailed it at Sanjose [sic] to Wm Reece New Providence Iowa.[154]

Hobson was pleased with the plain meeting house, traditional style of worship, and the expansive library well stocked with Friends books at Bean's meeting. Apparently, he was also satisfied with Bean's theology at the time. In an 1899 letter to Rufus Jones, Hannah Bean noted that "Will Hobson, a dear veteran Minister of Newberg, wrote a touching letter asking Honey Creek Mo. Mtg. to relieve our situation but they gave his letter into the hands of a Com., & it was not read in the Mo. Mtg." So, Hobson's favorable recommendation that Santa Clara Friends be given monthly meeting status stalled out in committee and they never achieved monthly meeting status under Honey Creek or any other established meeting, blocked from approval as they were, by the Gurneyite Iowa Yearly Meeting.[155] Obviously, Iowa Friends did not share Hobson's leniency with Bean's theology. In their defense the direction Bean's theology took later in life was a radical departure from that of orthodox, Gurneyite, evangelical, Friends. There is no way to know for sure how Hobson would have reacted to Bean's later forays into Unitarianism and Bahai, two religions that teach there are many valid paths to God, since Hobson died not too long after his visit to San Jose. However, we can say for sure that Hobson, while preferring traditional Quaker worship like Bean, was certainly not a Universalist like Bean. Hobson remained an orthodox, Gurneyite, evangelical Friend all his days. As has already been established, he

154. Hobson, "Diaries," reel 1 of 2, 12/15/1888.
155. King, *History of San Jose Quakers*, 153.

believed and taught that trust in Jesus Christ was the only way of salvation. The evidence of this has played out in the separate yearly meetings each man is credited with founding. Bean's Pacific Yearly Meeting and Hobson's Northwest Yearly Meeting are indisputably widely divergent in belief, purpose, and practice. However, at the time, Hobson was happy to make his report endorsing monthly meeting status for Santa Clara Quakers to Honey Creek Quarterly Meeting and even happier to return home to Oregon.

MINISTRY AT NEWBERG, DOUGLAS REVIVALS, AND THE PASTORAL SYSTEM

Hobson's remaining time on earth was spent in Newberg focused on his own Quaker community. Worship at Newberg Monthly Meeting remained unprogrammed, with the exception of some of the later revival services held by John Henry Douglas and other evangelists, until shortly after Hobson's death when the pastoral system was adopted in earnest. Strict plainness was also enforced by Hobson. King tells how Walter C. Woodward remembered David Martin's description of Hobson presiding over services: "We did not know the gallery and facing benches (of meeting houses farther east) but looked up instead at a pulpit on a raised platform. Dear old Uncle William sat head of the meeting, and we recall having seen him reach forward after the meeting had "set" and remove from the pulpit a little bouquet of flowers which some adventuresome soul had placed there."[156] However, unprogrammed and plain did not mean dull and lifeless and it seems that most meetings for worship were full of vocal ministry. As he got older, in a departure from the laconic style of his early days in ministry, Hobson began to write more details about what took place in worship. For example, on Ninth Month 1887, he wrote "All recorded Ministers away to day But EM & Myself I was favored with a lively flow of gospel to a pretty large Audience for about 35 minutes as well as an early prayer And with some service from John Edwards & from Elizabeth Miles and a prayer by [unnamed person]."[157] Later in the 1890s, shortly after the first revival meeting held by John Henry Douglas, Hobson lists the order of service on several different occasions. He was of course writing down what took place in real time, not planning an order of service ahead of time. Often there would be lengths of silence broken by vocalized prayer, songs started individually that some joined in with, Scripture readings, sermons, testimonies, and announcements. The meeting was variously ended with a Friendly handshake

156. King, *History of San Jose Quakers*, 11.
157. King, *History of San Jose Quakers*, 49.

or a benediction.[158] In light of the first early and more spontaneous revival in the winter of 1878–79, it seems reasonable to believe that this was not a new pattern of worship, but that something similar had been occurring in services since the meeting was established, though singing was probably a later addition and only tolerated not encouraged by Hobson.

Hobson did not explain how John Henry Douglas's revival meetings were conducted, but we can guess. John Henry Douglas was chosen as the first Iowa Yearly Meeting General Superintendent of Evangelistic, Pastoral, and Church Extension Work a position he held from 1886 to 1890. Jones described him as "keen of mind, eloquent in speech, magnetic, and tireless."[159] Douglas was raised in a traditional, strict Quaker home, but at eighteen he experienced a conversion event which led to his preaching ministry. He was one of the first to embrace the revival movement among Iowa Friends. He believed that the old ways and forms were empty and what was needed was fresh vigor and new life in the Society of Friends.[160] He preached Jesus Christ as the remedy for sin and embraced the new worship innovations that were sweeping through Iowa Yearly Meeting. In an article in the *Newberg Graphic* reprinted from the *Cincinnati Commercial-Gazette* in 1894, his ministry among Friends was described. First the article told how Friends worship services used to be unprogrammed and what that looked like, then it told how Douglas helped to transform Friends worship, and lastly some of the innovations brought about by Douglas's efforts were described as follows:

> With eloquence and pathos that touched men's hearts he [Douglas] drew great throngs about him, until no building in the town was large enough to hold his followers. And thus was laid the foundation of the new Society of Friends. From here [Wilmington, Ohio] Mr. Douglas traveled over the United States, holding revival meetings among the Friends and creating a sensation wherever he went by the power of his oratory. As a result of this agitation every Yearly Meeting in America, except that at Philadelphia, adopted the so-called emotional style of worship. Now the prayer-meeting, congregational singing, and even instrumental music are either encouraged or allowed in the Friends' service in their meeting-houses; and yesterday the Wilmington Yearly Meeting took another progressive step in opposition

---

158. For a sampling of worship meeting orders see "Diaries," reel 1 of 2, 6/15/1890, 6/29/1890, 7/6/1890, 7/17/1890, 7/20/1890, 7/27/1890, 8/22/1890, 8/28/1890, 9/6/1890, 9/7/1890, 9/21/1890, 9/28/1890, 10/6/1890, 10/12/1890.

159. Jones, *Quakers of Iowa*, 118–19.

160. Jones, *Later Periods of Quakerism, Vol. II*, 898, 923.

to their former tenets by providing for regular pastors for the churches in the limits of the meeting.[161]

We can be quite certain that Douglas brought music and altar calls to Newberg Monthly Meeting, at the very least.

Apparently, John Henry Douglas held his first revival meetings at Chehalem Monthly Meeting in the spring of 1889, though his visit did not make the *Newberg Graphic* until about a year after the fact.[162] There is a gap in Hobson's diary from First Month to Ninth Month 1889, so his reaction to Douglas's original series of revival meetings went unrecorded. Douglas returned to Newberg in Fifth Month 1890, and this time held about a two-week-long revival meeting. Hobson wrote in his journal on Fifth Month 26, 1890, the following report: "Revival Sessions Closed to night, with a full house A large work is done more than 100 confess conversion or renewal." Hobson was plainly pleased with the results of the revival. Also, earlier in the week he noted on the 22nd that "The Lord evidently very near runs this work Himself" and on the 23rd that "Franklin & Oliver Hobson, my Grandsons confess a Return to day to the fold of Christ." Douglas also spoke at Monthly Meeting on Sixth Month 7, 1890, during which about forty people were received into membership as a result of his ministry and according to the *Newberg Graphic* Douglas held yet more revival meetings in Seventh Month 1890. The article describing these revival meetings was quite flattering to

> Rev. J.H. Douglas, the revivalist who has been conducting the meetings, has had good houses every afternoon and evening, and has been most successful in his work. The reverend gentleman has certainly sustained his reputation as an able expounder of the bible. For forty years he has been engaged in his present work and in all his efforts he has been remarkably successful. Combining a pleasing presence, an expressive face, a wonderfully good voice and a kindly, earnest manner he commands attention from start to finish. As the result of his work here a large number have been converted."[163]

Once again, Hobson may have been uncomfortable with the way Douglas was winning souls, but he was delighted with the results, especially as far as his grandsons were concerned.

---

161. "A Prominent Man," *Newberg Graphic* (Newberg, OR) August 31, 1894, https://oregonnews.uoregon.edu/lccn/sn96088233/1894-08-31/ed-1/seq-2/.

162. "Rev. John Henry Douglas," *Newberg Graphic* (Newberg, OR) December 19, 1890, https://oregonnews.uoregon.edu/lccn/sn96088233/1890-12-19/ed-1/seq-3/.

163. "Revival," *Newberg Graphic* (Newberg, OR) August 15, 1890, https://oregonnews.uoregon.edu/lccn/sn96088233/1890-08-15/ed-1/seq-3/.

It was during this time that Douglas first brought up the subject of implementing a pastoral system at Newberg Monthly Meeting. There had probably been some discussion about the pastoral system before among the members of Newberg Monthly Meeting, but the meeting was so geographically distant from Iowa that Hobson was able to stave off adopting it. Newberg certainly was an outlier in Iowa Yearly Meeting both physically and in governance. In 1875 Iowa Yearly Meeting had required every monthly meeting within its purview to create a pastoral care committee. And Newberg Monthly Meeting had complied with this requirement in 1879 about a year after achieving monthly meeting status. However, the committee served mainly as a vehicle for coordinating visitation among the ministers, not a means to calling a pastor. In 1886 Iowa Yearly Meeting officially adopted the pastoral system, strongly recommending that each meeting call and pay a pastor of their own, a move actively promoted and endorsed by Douglas. Douglas in his capacity as General Superintendent likely felt a responsibility to unite Newberg Monthly Meeting with the rest of the congregations in Iowa Yearly Meeting by strongly recommending that they also adopt the pastoral system. It only makes sense that Douglas hoped to hasten implementation of the pastoral system in Newberg while he was visiting because he truly believed it was the direction God wanted evangelical Friends to go. We know that Hobson preferred the traditional way of leading a congregation in which unpaid recorded ministers and volunteers carried out the pastoral care and he made his views known, but he was willing to set aside his preferences and unite with Newberg Monthly Meeting when they decided to follow Douglas's vision.[164] Jesse Edwards sheds some light on Hobson's decision to stand aside by telling how Hobson habitually

> presented his views of truth and gave his interpretation of the truth and left it. I dont [sic] think there ever was a man as sincere in his belief of the work of the Holy Spirit. He believed the declaration "Go and preach the Truth: and let the Spirit do its work." In this latter day we preach the truth and undertake to enforce the Truth. If you don't take it you are not in it. William Hobson was not that kind of man at all. He believed so in the power of the Spirit that he could just deliver his message and trust God that the work of the Spirit would do its part and it would not be lost. This is one of the peculiarities that I wish we could maintain as Friends. The power of the Spirit is just as great as it ever was. Our work is to give the truth as we see it.[165]

---

164. Perisho, "History of the Newberg Monthly Meeting," 53–55.
165. Hobson, "Twentyfifth Anniversary," 4.

In his defense, Douglas was not trying to do away with the fine work ministers and volunteers were doing and believed they should continue serving even after a pastor was released to full time, paid ministry.[166]

Douglas returned to Newberg in Twelfth Month 1890, and held yet another series of revival meetings beginning on the 25th. The *Newberg Graphic* had good things to say about these meetings also. First an informative article was offered on First Month 9, 1891:

> The Gospel meetings being held at Friends church and conducted by Rev. J.H. Douglas of Des Moines, Iowa still continue with increasing interest. Sermons of great power were preached on Sunday, both morning and evening when the capacity of the church was taxed to the utmost. It was expected that the meetings would close Sunday night but the interest manifested was so intense that they were continued for another evening and they have been continued from night to night by vote of the congregation. The teaching has been plain, practical and convincing. As a result many have been converted and a great work has been done. When the meetings will close no one seems to know.[167]

Then an update was offered a week later on the 16th of First Month 1891, explaining how the meetings were still going strong:

> The series of meetings being held at Friends' church under the leadership of Rev. J.H. Douglas reached the three week limit Wednesday night and it was expected that the meetings would close that evening, but the interest was so great that everybody insisted on more services, consequently meetings were held yesterday and last night. Such an awakening Newberg has never had before and the enviable reputation our town has had for morality is being strengthened in a very marked degree. Our people appreciate the labors of brother Douglas and many prayers will follow him to other fields of labor.[168]

Sadly, Hobson's health was failing so he could not attend many of these meetings, but he appreciated the ones he was able to attend, noting on Twelfth Month 31, 1890, "Went to meeting at 10.a.m. Heard J.H.D. Pray & Preach. We ought to be Separate from the world. Be definite. He held meeting long: But I liked his servicece [sic] well," and on the First of First Month 1891,

---

166. Perisho, "History of the Newberg Monthly Meeting," 59.

167. "Douglas Meetings," *Newberg Graphic* (Newberg, OR) January 9, 1891, https://oregonnews.uoregon.edu/lccn/sn96088233/1891-01-09/ed-1/seq-3/ .

168. "Revival Meetings," *Newberg Graphic* (Newberg, OR) January 16, 1891, https://oregonnews.uoregon.edu/lccn/sn96088233/1891-01-16/ed-1/seq-3/.

"We went to the 10 o'clock meeting to day in the twohorse wagon Meeting held nearly 4 hours JH Douglas Preached on holiness A great work seemed to be done The Sum of the work centers in this Scripture Christ in you the hope of Glory. So as to place us in a normal condition Wholly subject to the Lord as in the creation." Hobson was pleased with this latest series of revival meetings as noted on First Month 11, 1891, "Had a great days [sic] of rich meetings at Newberg. A Christian Endeavor Society was formed of over 120. Most of the inhabitants of Newberg Large & Small now seem to enjoy the Religious work going on from the many Testmonies [sic] given And the very large attendance last night." On the 14th twelve new converts were added to a number of others that had made decisions previously and on the 15th Hobson wrote, "I stood it pretty well last night at meeting [he felt well physically] & near the close spake a few words of joy & Praise to the Lord for Salvation to So many at Newberg." Shortly after this Hobson attended meeting for the last time on First Month 25, 1891, noting, "J.H.D. there & preached well." Hobson's failing health kept him home from both revival and regular meetings after this.

About a year after his death in Sixth Month 1891, Newberg Monthly Meeting finally adopted the pastoral system following yet another series of revival meetings held by Douglas. Newberg Monthly Meeting Minutes report that in Fifth Month 1892, the "Pastoral Question Committee" called John Henry Douglas as an interim pastor until they could engage a more permanent pastor.[169] Pastor Thomas C. Brown took over from Douglas in Tenth Month 1892, and served the congregation for just under a year.[170] Hobson probably would have reluctantly endorsed Douglas as the first full-time, paid pastor, since he did admire his evangelical enthusiasm, even if he wasn't fully convinced the pastoral system was the way to go. But as it turns out Hobson was spared from seeing the pastoral system in action.

THE DEATH OF SARAH AND WILLIAM HOBSON

Grief and ill health may have also clouded Hobson's desire or ability to resist the changes that were coming to Newberg Monthly Meeting. After a week of serious illness Sarah Hobson, William's wife of forty-six years died in the fall of 1890. Hobson wrote,

> M[onthly] Meeting-day I sent some Certificates by G. Michel & stayed at Home not expecting my wife would live many more

---

169. "Chehalem Monthly Meeting Minutes," 93, 313.
170. "Chehalem Monthly Meeting Minutes," 107, 137.

hours. She Breathed until about 6 p.m. & ceased with [sic] without any extra struggle breathing weaker & weaker until sometimes there would be a moment or two of cessation between efforts of breathing, then again breathing would resume more faintly with a sooner cessation & so shortly ceased to resume breathing at about 6.pm. on the 1 day of 11 mo. 1890, being a daughter of Wm. & Mary Tulburt & born in N.C. on the 10 of 6 mo. 1818. Therefore was at departure 72 years 4 months & 22 days old deceased was married the 8 of 7 mo. 1844. Was the Mother of 3 sons & 3 daughters. One son & two daughters are gone before her. The other two sons & one daughter are with us in Oregon today.[171]

The next day her funeral was held: "Was a favorable day. A large collection of people met at 3.p.m. at Friends meeting-house because of my wife['s] funeral & from thence to the Grave yard. Several Friends bore Testimony on this Occasion We left the Graveyard only a little before dark."[172]

Hobson's cousins Abel Bond and George Hobson, with his family, were visiting at the time and they helped with chores around the farm for a short while before returning to their homes out of state. Hobson also had help from his youngest daughter Anna Blair with housekeeping. But a few days later he was feeling the loss of Sarah sharply. He put a good face on it writing, "Very well this morning I have comfortably enjoyed the night Alone for supper, night, & breakfast Alone & Yet not alone; because always My chief Companion is my King & Shepherd the Lord Jesus whom I have dilighted [sic] to follow & serve from my infantile days."[173] It was difficult to fully engage with ministry at Newberg Friends during this time of mourning.

Hobson also had illness to contend with. He first mentioned an attack of what he called "La Grippe" (influenza) in the spring of 1890. He was unwell from Third Month 8 to 12, but still able to do some limited work around the farm and go to meeting. He mentioned "La Grippe" again on the 19th of Third Month and then not again for some time. His serious decline began shortly after Sarah's death in the early winter of 1890, coinciding with the series of revival meetings held by John Henry Douglas at that time. He may have been a victim of the Russian Influenza Pandemic of 1889 that began in the winter of that year, but returned in diminishing waves through 1894, as explained by editors D. Ann Herring and Sally Carraher in *Miasma*

---

171. Hobson, "Diaries," reel 1 of 2, 11/1/1890.
172. Hobson, "Diaries," reel 1 of 2, 11/2/1890.
173. Hobson, "Diaries," reel 1 of 2, 11/5/1890.

to *Microscopes*.[174] Hobson suffered greatly from congestion, pain in his chest, coughing up phlegm, diarrhea, and later blood in his urine, indicating that his kidneys were affected and his body what shutting down. He may have been experiencing complications brought on by the flu. In mid–First Month he recorded a communication he received from God indicating that he would soon die. He wrote,

> Very soon after midnight had passed, very early this morning The Lord seemed to a[illegible] unto me by Spirit & say thy life will soon end Thou has but little time to spend otherwise than to finish the mission I require of thee to others Thou cannot cur[e] thyself of the Lagrippe [sic] now having fast hold of thee: Neither can any Dr cure thee. Thou canst not live long, only as I am able and may continue thy life some longer. That thou mayest finish the work which I have designed to be done for the benefit of others through thee. I encourage thee to be faithful and obey me to the end & I will be with thee & strengthen thee. That thou may be an instrument of mine yet to do a great work in the earth.[175]

He was able to attend most of Douglas's revival meetings up until First Month 29, 1891, though unable to participate much. Hobson's health continued to deteriorate until he was no longer able to work or care for himself. On his birthday, Second Month 4, 1891, he noted "This day I am 71 years old And I am so seriously afflicted with the la grippe that my recovery seems doubtful I am in the Lords [sic] care I believe; and my only hope of any long continuance is in his power to lengthen my life. I did not saw any wood to day." Anna and her husband Alpheus who had been helping with chores as Hobson's health failed, nursed him tenderly during his last days on earth.[176] The Lord finally called him to his eternal home on Sixth Month 25, 1891, and William Hobson was laid to rest next to Sarah in the Newberg Monthly Meeting Cemetery.

His lord said unto him, Well done, thou good and faithful servant: thou hast been faithful over a few things, I will make thee ruler over many things: enter thou into the joy of thy lord.

MATT 25:21

---

174. Herring and Carraher, *Miasma to Microscopes*, see especially page 38; see also Daugherty, "Russian Flu of 1899."

175. Hobson, "Diaries," reel 1 of 2, 1/18/1891.

176. Hobson, "Diaries," reel 1 of 2, First through Sixth Month 1891.

Bibliography

Anscombe, Francis Charles. *I Have Called You Friends: The Story of Quakerism in North Carolina*. Boston: Christopher, 1959.

"Bald Peak State Scenic Viewpoint." *Oregon State Parks*. https://oregonstateparks.org/index.cfm?do=parkPage.dsp_parkPage&parkId=77.

Barclay, Robert. *Barclay's Apology in Modern English*. Edited by Dean Freiday. 1967 revised ed. Reprint. Newberg, OR: Barclay, 1991.

Beebe, Ralph. *Garden of the Lord*. Newberg, OR: Barclay, 1968.

Bigalke, Zach. "The Oregon Mascot Part 1: The Webfooter Years." *Unbound* (blog). https://blogs.uoregon.edu/scua/2014/12/30/the-oregon-mascot-part-1-the-webfooter-years/.

Bond, Abel. *Abel Bond's Foot Travels From the Atlantic to the Pacific: A Colporteur or Tract Distributor of the Society of Friends*. Carthage, MO: Book and Job, 1889.

Braithwaite, William C. *Second Period of Quakerism*. 1919 ed. Reprint. York, England: William Sessions Limited in association with the Joseph Rowntree Charitable Trust, 1979.

Burial Records. Notes on William and Sarah Hobson. Newberg Friends Cemetery, 500 S. Everest Rd., Newberg, OR 97132.

Carter, Max. "How Quakers Got Their Name." *Quaker Speak* (YouTube). https://www.youtube.com/watch?v=Z21WDwmaR38.

"Chehalem Monthly Meeting Minutes." Notebook. Book 1, June 1, 1878 to May 4, 1889. George Fox University Archives.

Coffin, Addison. Early Settlement of Friends in North Carolina Traditions and Reminiscences, 1894. 1952 transcript ed. [Greensboro, NC]: Typed for The North Carolina Friends Historical Society, 1952. Pamphlet. Guilford College Archives.

Coffin, Rhoda M. *Rhoda M. Coffin: Her Reminiscences, Addresses, Papers and Ancestry*. Edited by Mary Coffin Johnson. New York: Grafton, 1910.

Convict Records. Oregon State Penitentiary, inmate Numbers 499, 500, and 501, April 27, 1873. Registry book. Oregon State Archives.

Cook, Darius B. *History of Quaker Divide: Struggles and Accomplishments of First Settlers, The Story of Their Achievements Forms Interesting Reminiscences in the History of Early Days Meetings—Schools—Farm and Home Life*. Dexter, Iowa: The Dexter Sentinel, 1914.

CPI Inflation Calculator. http://www.in2013dollars.com/1872-dollars-in-2018?amount=300; http://www.in2013dollars.com/us/inflation/1870?amount=250.

Crosfield, Joseph. "North Carolina Yearly Meeting of 1845." *Bulletin of the Friends Historical Society of Philadelphia*. 3, no. 3 (February 1910) 115–121. https://books.

google.com/books?id=211JAQAAMAAJ&printsec=frontcover&source=gbs_ge_summary_r&cad=0#v=onepage&q=crosfield&f=false

Dandelion, Pink. *Quakers: A Very Short Introduction*. Oxford: Oxford University Press, 2008.

Daugherty, Greg. "Russian Flu of 1899: The Deadly Pandemic Few Americans Took Seriously." *History.com*. https://www.history.com/news/1889-russian-flu-pandemic-in-america.

Davis, Earl H. and Marie Davis Wiles, comps. *Hobson: Descendants of George and Elizabeth Hobson*. 2nd ed. N.p., 1978.

Dicken, Samuel and Emily F. Dicken. *Making of Oregon: A Study in Historical Geography, Two Centuries of Oregon Geography, Vol. I*. Portland, OR: Oregon Historical Society, 1979.

Diment, Veldon J., ed. *First Fifty Years: A Record of the First Fifty Years in the Life of Pacific College*. Newberg, OR: Published by Authority of the Board of Managers, 1941.

Doyle, Barbara. *From Then 'Til Now: 1879/2015 Schooling in Newberg, Oregon*. Newberg, OR: Barbara Doyle c/o Chehalem Cultural Center, 2015.

Edmonds, Connor Fitzgerald. "William Hobson and William Keil: Religion and Polity in Nineteenth Century Oregon." Master's thesis, George Fox Evangelical Seminary, April 2006.

Edmonston Jr., George P. *Newberg: Stories from the Grubby End*. Newberg, OR: Oregon, 2014.

———. "Yamhill County's Most Interesting City." *Newberg Downtown Coalition*. http://newbergdowntown.org/community/history/.

Elliot, Errol T. *Quakers on the American Frontier: A History of the Westward Migrations, Settlements, and Developments of Friends on the American Continent*. Richmond, IN: Friends United, 1969.

"Erysipelas." *Healthline.com*. https://www.healthline.com/health/erysipelas.

Evans, Thomas. *Examples of Youthful Piety: Principally Intended for the Instruction of Young Persons*. Reprint [1851]. Philadelphia: For Sale at Friends' Book Store, No. 304 Arch Street, n.d.

Evans, William. *Journal of the Life and Religious Services of William Evans, A Minister of the Gospel in the Society of Friends*. Philadelphia: Caxton of Sherman/For Sale at Friend's Book Store, No. 304 Arch ST., 1870. https://archive.org/stream/journaloflifereooevan#page/n7.

Fox, George. *Journal of George Fox*. Edited by Rufus M. Jones. Reprint 1983. Richmond, IN: Friends United, 1908.

Friends Pacific Academy. *Catalogue, 1886–7 of Friends' Pacific Academy Established in 1885, at Newberg, Yamhill County, Or*. Portland, OR: Himes the Printer, 1887. George FoxUniversity Archives.

Fuller, Tom and Christy Van Heukelem. *Images of America Newberg*. Charleston, SC: Arcadia, 2010.

Gaston, Joseph. *Portland Oregon Its History and Builders in Connection with the Antecedent Explorations, Discoveries and Movements of the Pioneers That Selected the Site for the Great City of the Pacific, Volume II*. Portland, OR: S. J. Clarke, 1911. https://books.google.com/books/about/Portland_Oregon_Its_History_and_Builders.html?id=XvYUAAAAYAAJ.

Gilbert, Dorothy Lloyd. *Guilford a Quaker College*. Reprint [1967]. Greensboro, NC: Printed for Guilford College by Jos. J. Stone, 1937.
Goldsmith, Myron Dee. "William Hobson and the Founding of Quakerism in the Pacific Northwest." PhD diss., Boston University Graduate School, 1962.
Gurney, Joseph John, *Memoirs of Joseph John Gurney: with Selections from his Journal and Correspondence, In Two Volumes, Vol. II*. Edited by Joseph Bevan Braithwaite. Norwich: Fletcher and Alexander, 1854.
Haines, Marie. *Brave Rebels*. Newberg, OR: Barclay, 1974.
Hamm, Thomas. "History of Quaker Plain Speech." *QuakerSpeak* (YouTube). https://www.youtube.com/watch?v=nBIVNK5Lq58.
———. *Quakers in America*. NY: Columbia University Press, 2003.
———. *Transformation of American Quakerism: Orthodox Friends, 1880-1907*. Bloomington, IN: Indiana University Press, 1988.
Harkness, Ione Juanita Beale, "Certain Community Settlements of Oregon" Master's thesis, Los Angeles: University of Southern California, 1925.
Herring, D. Ann and Sally Carraher, eds. *Miasma to Microscopes: The Russian InfluenzaPandemic in Hamilton*. Hamilton, Ontario, Canada: Department of Anthropology McMaster University, n.d. https://pdfs.semanticscholar.org/3b9f/e54c79a2503b47c13f0ff71ceob81ebbof2b.pdf.
Hinshaw, Seth B. *Carolina Quaker Experience 1665-1985: An Interpretation*. [Greensboro NC]: North Carolina Yearly Meeting North Carolina Friends Historical Society, 1984.
———. *Carolina Quakers: Three Hundred Years 1672-1972*. Greensboro, NC: North Carolina Yearly Meeting Christian Education Committee, 1971.
———. and Mary Edith Hinshaw, eds. *Carolina Quakers: Our Heritage Our Hope, Tercentenary 1672-1972*. Greensboro, NC: North Carolina Yearly Meeting, 1972.
"History." *Iowa Yearly Meeting*. https://www.iaym.org/aboutus/history/.
"History of the Niles Passenger Depot." *Niles Depot Model Railroads and Museum*. https://www.nilesdepot.org/niles/history.html.
Hoag, Joseph. *Journal of the Life of Joseph Hoag: An Eminent Minister of the Gospel, in the Society of Friends*. Auburn, [NY]: Knapp & Peck, Auburn Journal Office, 1861.
"Hoag, Joseph, 1762-1846." *Institute for Advanced Technology in the Humanities*. http://socialarchive.iath.virginia.edu/ark:/99166/w6ng6gxq.
Hobson, O.J. "Twentyfifth Anniversary of the Establishment of the Quarterly Meeting of Friends at Newberg, Oregon on November 10, 1912." Notes. Newberg Friends Church Collection. George Fox University Archives.
Hobson, Samuel. "Memories of Samuel Hobson," n.d. Transcription of a manuscript. Hobson Family Collection. George Fox University Archives.
Hobson, William. "Address to Our School Children on Music and Singing," n.d. Essay. Hobson Family Collection. George Fox University Archives.
———. "Diaries," 1859-1865, 1870-1878, 1885-1891. Microfilmed notebooks, 2 reels. Hobson Family Collection. George Fox University Archives.
———. "Memorandum," [1876]. Notebook. George Fox University Archives.
———. William Hobson to Caleb Hobson, Honey Creek, Hardin County, IA, February 4, 1857. Copy. Hobson Family Collection. George Fox University Archives.
———. William Hobson to William and Mary Tulburt, Hamptonsville, Surry County, NC, October 1847. Copy. Hobson Family Collection. George Fox University Archives.

Iowa Yearly Meeting. *Iowa Yearly Meeting of Friends, Remembering 100 Years of History.* N.p.: Iowa Yearly Meeting of Friends, 1963.

Jay, Allen. *Autobiography of Allen Jay: Born 1831, Died 1910.* Philadelphia: John C. Winston, 1910.

"Jesse Hobson." *findagrave.com.* https://www.findagrave.com/memorial/6178822/jesse-hobson.

Jones, Louis Thomas. *Quakers of Iowa.* Iowa City, IA: State Historical Society of Iowa, 1914.

Jones, Rufus M. *Later Periods of Quakerism, Vols. I and II.* London: Macmillan 1921.

———. with Isaac Sharpless and Amelia M. Gummere. *Quakers in the American Colonies.* New York: Russell & Russell, 1962.

Kelsey, Rayner W. "Quakerism Beyond the Mississippi." *American Friend* 17, no. 27 (July 7, 1910) 423–25; 17, no. 30 (July 28, 1910) 468–471; 17, no. 33 (August 18, 1910) 520–23.

King, Thomas M. *History of San Jose Quakers, West Coast Friends.* San Bernardino, CA: Thomas M. King, 2012.

Lang, William L. "Joel Palmer (1810–1881)." *Oregon Encyclopedia.* https://oregonencyclopedia.org/articles/palmer_joel_1810_1881_/#.XZTOki3MxTY.

Lawrence & Ogilbe and M. Schmidt & Co. Map of Yamhill Co., Oregon, 1879. ¾ inch to 1 mile. 15338102 (Portland, OR: Lawrence & Ogilbe, 1879). *Library of Congress.* http://hdl.loc.gov/loc.gmd/g4293y.la000695.

Lindsey, Robert and Sarah. *Travels of Robert and Sarah Lindsey.* London: Samuel Harris, 1886.

McBride, John R. *Overland to Oregon: Yamhill Country 1846.* Edited by Floyd Bunn. [Lafayette, OR:] [Yamhill County Historical Society], n.d. Originally published in the *Capitol Journal,* Salem, OR (February 4–March 23, 1926).

Miller, Jennie D. "History of Newberg: Complied from facts gathered in 1936, 1937, and 1938" Unpublished typescript. [Newberg, OR: Newberg Public Library, 1938].

Minear, Mark. *Richmond 1887: A Quaker Drama Unfolds.* Richmond, IN: Friends United, 1987.

Moore, J. Floyd. *Friends in the Carolinas.* 2nd printing. Greensboro, NC: Guilford College, [1964].

Nedry, H.S. "Friends Come to Oregon: I, Newberg Meeting." *Oregon Historical Quarterly* 45, no. 3 (1944) 195–217.

"New Garden Boarding School Register: 1837–February 1842." Registry book. Guilford College Archives.

Newberg Downtown Coalition Historical Walking Tour guide. *Newberg Downtown Coalition.* http://newbergdowntown.org/attractions/historical-walking-tour/.

North Carolina Yearly Meeting of Friends. *Minutes of North Carolina Yearly Meeting Held at New Garden Guilford County, NC.* Jamestown, NC: J. Sherwood, 1845.

Oregon Yearly Meeting. *Minutes of Oregon Yearly Meeting of Friends Church.* Newberg, OR: Newberg Graphic Print, 1893.

Pacific College. *Pacific College Oregon [Handbook], 1891–92.* Newberg, OR: Graphic Print, 1891.

"Parrott Mountain." Peakbagger.com. https://www.peakbagger.com/peak.aspx?pid=32879.

Paul, Mercedes J. "Extracts from the Diaries of William Hobson," n.d. Paper. Hobson Family Collection. George Fox University Archives.

Perisho, Stephen Z. "History of the Newberg Monthly Meeting, 1878–1893." An intensified studies senior research paper, Newberg, OR: George Fox College, 1983.

Punshon, John. *Portrait in Grey: A Short History of the Quakers*. London: Quaker Home Service, 1986.

"Rachel Hobson Reece." findagrave.com. https://www.findagrave.com/memorial/7800 8460/rachel-reece.

Rees, John H. "History of Friends Church, June 6, 1906." Paper. Newberg Friends Church Collection. George Fox University Archives.

Robbins, William G. "Willamette Valley." *Oregon Encyclopedia*. https://oregonencyc lopedia.org/articles/willamette_valley/#.XcxWTC3MxTY.

Roser, Max, Hannah Ritchie and Bernadeta Dadonaite. "Child and Infant Mortality." *OurWorldInData*. https://ourworldindata.org/child-mortality.

Russell, Elbert. *History of Quakerism*. Reprint [1941]. Richmond, IN: Friends United, 1979.

Sandler, Martin W. *Iron Rails, Iron Men and the Race to Link the Nation: The Story of the Transcontinental Railroad*. Somerville, MA: Candlewick, 2015.

Scott, Leslie M. "History of the Narrow Gauge Railroad in the Willamette Valley." *Oregon Historical Quarterly* 20, no. 2 (1919) 141–48. https://en.wikisource.org/wiki/Oregon_Historical_Quarterly/Volume_20/History_of_the_narrowgauge_railroad_in_the_Willamette_Valley.

Smith, V. Chapman, comp. "American Anti-Slavery and Civil Rights Timeline." *Independence Hall Association*. http://www.ushistory.org/more/timeline.htm.

Smith, Warren Dupre. "Physical and Economic Geography of Oregon." Eugene, OR: *The Commonwealth Review of the University of Oregon* New Series 7, no. 2 (April 1925) 33, 40; New Series 7, no. 4 (October 1925) 76, 138, 161.

Stanbrough, Amos C. "History of Pacific College." Master's thesis, Eugene, OR: University of Oregon, 1934.

"Stephen G. Hobson." findagrave.com. https://www.findagrave.com/memorial/1270 03030/stephen-g-hobson#view-photo=104781707.

Stoller, Ruth, comp. *Old Yamhill: The Early History of its Towns and Cities*. Lafayette, OR: Yamhill County Historical Society, 1976.

Thomas, Allen C. and Richard M. *History of the Friends in America*. 4th ed. Philadelphia: John C. Winston, 1905.

———. *A History of the Friends in America*. 5th ed. Revised and Enlarged by Allen C. Thomas. Philadelphia: John C. Winston, 1919.

Union Publishing Company, comps. *History of Hardin County Iowa: together with sketches of its towns, villages and townships, educational, civil, military and political history: portraits of prominent persons, and biographies of representative citizens*. Springfield, IL: Union, 1883. https://books.google.com/books?id=Mk4oAQAAM AAJ&printsec=frontcover&source=gbs_ge_summary_r&cad=0#v=onepage&q&f=false.

United States Department of the Interior. "Newberg Quadrangle [map]." (7.5 minute series. 45122–C8–TF–024). United States Geological Survey (Denver, Colorado, 1985). "Digital General Land Office Maps." (Quadrant 1 index. 3s 2w). *University of Oregon Library*. https://library.uoregon.edu/map/GIS/Data/Oregon/GLO.

Weeks, Stephen B. *Southern Quakers and Slavery: A Study in Institutional History*. Baltimore: Johns Hopkins, 1896.

White, Julia S. "History of North Carolina Yearly Meeting." *Bulletin of Friends Historical Society of Philadelphia* 3, no.1 (February 1909) 2–14. https://books.google.com/books?id=211JAQAAMAAJ&printsec=frontcover&source=gbs_ge_summary_r&cad=0#v=onepage&q=Julia%20white&f=false; https://www.jstor.org/stable/41944824?seq=1#metadata_info_tab_contents.

Woodward, Amanda C. "Reminiscences Given at the Fiftieth Anniversary of Newberg Monthly Meeting of Friends," June 1928. Paper. Hobson Family Collection. George Fox University Archives.

Woodward, Walter C. "Quakerism Beyond the Mississippi." *American Friend* 17, no. 38 (September 22, 1910) 600–3.

Woolman, John. *Journal and Major Essays of John Woolman*. Edited by Phillips P. Moulton. Reprint 1989. Richmond, IN: Friends United, 1971.

"Yamhill County, Oregon (1870)." *World Population Review*. http://worldpopulationreview.com/us-counties/or/yamhill-county-population/

www.ingramcontent.com/pod-product-compliance
Lightning Source LLC
Chambersburg PA
CBHW071245230426